# HowExpert to 365 Hobbies

## The Ultimate A to Z Handbook to Discover, Learn, and Explore a New Hobby Every Day of the Year

### HowExpert

Copyright © 2024 Hot Methods, Inc. DBA HowExpert™

www.HowExpert.com

For more tips related to this topic, visit HowExpert.com/365hobbies.

# Recommended Resources

- HowExpert.com – How To Guides on All Topics from A to Z by Everyday Experts.
- HowExpert.com/free – Free HowExpert Email Newsletter.
- HowExpert.com/books – HowExpert Books
- HowExpert.com/courses – HowExpert Courses
- HowExpert.com/clothing – HowExpert Clothing
- HowExpert.com/membership – HowExpert Membership Site
- HowExpert.com/affiliates – HowExpert Affiliate Program
- HowExpert.com/jobs – HowExpert Jobs
- HowExpert.com/writers – Write About Your #1 Passion/Knowledge/Expertise & Become a HowExpert Author.
- HowExpert.com/resources – Additional HowExpert Recommended Resources
- YouTube.com/HowExpert – Subscribe to HowExpert YouTube.
- Instagram.com/HowExpert – Follow HowExpert on Instagram.
- Facebook.com/HowExpert – Follow HowExpert on Facebook.
- TikTok.com/@HowExpert – Follow HowExpert on TikTok.

# Publisher's Foreword

Dear HowExpert Reader,

HowExpert publishes quick 'how to' guides on all topics from A to Z by everyday experts.

At HowExpert, our mission is to discover, empower, and maximize everyday people's talents to ultimately make a positive impact in the world for all topics from A to Z…one everyday expert at a time!

HowExpert guides are written by everyday people just like you and me, who have a passion, knowledge, and expertise for a specific topic.

We take great pride in selecting everyday experts who have a passion, real-life experience in a topic, and excellent writing skills to teach you about the topic you are also passionate about and eager to learn.

We hope you get a lot of value from our HowExpert guides, and it can make a positive impact on your life in some way. All of our readers, including you, help us continue living our mission of positively impacting the world for all spheres of influences from A to Z.

If you enjoyed one of our HowExpert guides, then please take a moment to send us your feedback from wherever you got this book.

Thank you, and I wish you all the best in all aspects of life.

To your success,

Byungjoon "BJ" Min  민병준
Founder & Publisher of HowExpert
HowExpert.com

PS…If you are also interested in becoming a HowExpert author, then please visit our website at HowExpert.com/writers. Thank you & again, all the best!
John 3:16

## COPYRIGHT, LEGAL NOTICE AND DISCLAIMER:

COPYRIGHT © 2024 HOT METHODS, INC. (DBA HOWEXPERT™). ALL RIGHTS RESERVED WORLDWIDE. NO PART OF THIS PUBLICATION MAY BE REPRODUCED IN ANY FORM OR BY ANY MEANS, INCLUDING SCANNING, PHOTOCOPYING, OR OTHERWISE WITHOUT PRIOR WRITTEN PERMISSION OF THE COPYRIGHT HOLDER.

DISCLAIMER AND TERMS OF USE: PLEASE NOTE THAT MUCH OF THIS PUBLICATION IS BASED ON PERSONAL EXPERIENCE AND ANECDOTAL EVIDENCE. ALTHOUGH THE AUTHOR AND PUBLISHER HAVE MADE EVERY REASONABLE ATTEMPT TO ACHIEVE COMPLETE ACCURACY OF THE CONTENT IN THIS GUIDE, THEY ASSUME NO RESPONSIBILITY FOR ERRORS OR OMISSIONS. ALSO, YOU SHOULD USE THIS INFORMATION AS YOU SEE FIT, AND AT YOUR OWN RISK. YOUR PARTICULAR SITUATION MAY NOT BE EXACTLY SUITED TO THE EXAMPLES ILLUSTRATED HERE; IN FACT, IT'S LIKELY THAT THEY WON'T BE THE SAME, AND YOU SHOULD ADJUST YOUR USE OF THE INFORMATION AND RECOMMENDATIONS ACCORDINGLY.

THE AUTHOR AND PUBLISHER DO NOT WARRANT THE PERFORMANCE, EFFECTIVENESS OR APPLICABILITY OF ANY SITES LISTED OR LINKED TO IN THIS BOOK. ALL LINKS ARE FOR INFORMATION PURPOSES ONLY AND ARE NOT WARRANTED FOR CONTENT, ACCURACY OR ANY OTHER IMPLIED OR EXPLICIT PURPOSE.

ANY TRADEMARKS, SERVICE MARKS, PRODUCT NAMES OR NAMED FEATURES ARE ASSUMED TO BE THE PROPERTY OF THEIR RESPECTIVE OWNERS, AND ARE USED ONLY FOR REFERENCE. THERE IS NO IMPLIED ENDORSEMENT IF WE USE ONE OF THESE TERMS.

NO PART OF THIS BOOK MAY BE REPRODUCED, STORED IN A RETRIEVAL SYSTEM, OR TRANSMITTED BY ANY OTHER MEANS: ELECTRONIC, MECHANICAL, PHOTOCOPYING, RECORDING, OR OTHERWISE, WITHOUT THE PRIOR WRITTEN PERMISSION OF THE AUTHOR.

ANY VIOLATION BY STEALING THIS BOOK OR DOWNLOADING OR SHARING IT ILLEGALLY WILL BE PROSECUTED BY LAWYERS TO THE FULLEST EXTENT. THIS PUBLICATION IS PROTECTED UNDER THE US COPYRIGHT ACT OF 1976 AND ALL OTHER APPLICABLE INTERNATIONAL, FEDERAL, STATE AND LOCAL LAWS AND ALL RIGHTS ARE RESERVED, INCLUDING RESALE RIGHTS: YOU ARE NOT ALLOWED TO GIVE OR SELL THIS GUIDE TO ANYONE ELSE.

THIS PUBLICATION IS DESIGNED TO PROVIDE ACCURATE AND AUTHORITATIVE INFORMATION WITH REGARD TO THE SUBJECT MATTER COVERED. IT IS SOLD WITH THE UNDERSTANDING THAT THE AUTHORS AND PUBLISHERS ARE NOT ENGAGED IN RENDERING LEGAL, FINANCIAL, OR OTHER PROFESSIONAL ADVICE. LAWS AND PRACTICES OFTEN VARY FROM STATE TO STATE AND IF LEGAL OR OTHER EXPERT ASSISTANCE IS REQUIRED, THE SERVICES OF A PROFESSIONAL SHOULD BE SOUGHT. THE AUTHORS AND PUBLISHER SPECIFICALLY DISCLAIM ANY LIABILITY THAT IS INCURRED FROM THE USE OR APPLICATION OF THE CONTENTS OF THIS BOOK.

HOT METHODS, INC. DBA HOWEXPERT
EMAIL: SUPPORT@HOWEXPERT.COM
WEBSITE: WWW.HOWEXPERT.COM

COPYRIGHT © 2024 HOT METHODS, INC. (DBA HOWEXPERT™)
ALL RIGHTS RESERVED WORLDWIDE.

# Table of Contents

Recommended Resources ................................................................. 2
Publisher's Foreword ...................................................................... 3
Book Overview .............................................................................. 15
Introduction: The Joy of Hobbies ................................................... 17
January: Arts and Crafts ................................................................. 19
    January 1: Airbrushing ............................................................... 20
    January 2: Animation ................................................................. 21
    January 3: Basket Weaving ........................................................ 22
    January 4: Beadwork .................................................................. 23
    January 5: Calligraphy ............................................................... 24
    January 6: Candle Making ......................................................... 25
    January 7: Collage ..................................................................... 26
    January 8: Crochet ..................................................................... 27
    January 9: Decoupage ................................................................ 28
    January 10: Drawing .................................................................. 29
    January 11: Embroidery ............................................................. 30
    January 12: Engraving ............................................................... 31
    January 13: Felting .................................................................... 32
    January 14: Flower Arranging .................................................... 33
    January 15: Glassblowing .......................................................... 34
    January 16: Hand Lettering ........................................................ 35
    January 17: Illustration .............................................................. 36
    January 18: Jewelry Making ...................................................... 37
    January 19: Knitting .................................................................. 38
    January 20: Latch Hooking ........................................................ 39
    January 21: Macramé ................................................................. 40
    January 22: Needlepoint ............................................................ 41
    January 23: Origami .................................................................. 42
    January 24: Painting .................................................................. 43
    January 25: Quilting .................................................................. 44
    January 26: Repurposing ........................................................... 45
    January 27: Scrapbooking .......................................................... 46
    January 28: Stained Glass .......................................................... 47
    January 29: Tapestry Weaving ................................................... 48
    January 30: Upcycling ............................................................... 49
    January 31: Wood Carving ........................................................ 50
    Conclusion for January .............................................................. 51
February: Building and DIY ........................................................... 52
    February 1: Appliance Repair .................................................... 53
    February 2: Blacksmithing ........................................................ 54

February 3: Bricklaying ................................................................... 55
February 4: Cabinet Making ........................................................... 56
February 5: Carpentry ..................................................................... 57
February 6: Dollhouse Making ....................................................... 58
February 7: Electronics Repair ....................................................... 59
February 8: Furniture Restoration .................................................. 60
February 9: Gardening .................................................................... 61
February 10: Home Brewing ........................................................... 62
February 11: Interior Design ........................................................... 63
February 12: Jewelry Repair ........................................................... 64
February 13: Kite Making ............................................................... 65
February 14: Lamp Making ............................................................. 66
February 15: Metalworking ............................................................. 67
February 16: Needle Felting ........................................................... 68
February 17: Organization .............................................................. 69
February 18: Plumbing .................................................................... 70
February 19: Recycling Projects ..................................................... 71
February 20: Soap Making .............................................................. 72
February 21: Tile Laying ................................................................. 73
February 22: Upholstery .................................................................. 74
February 23: Vegetable Gardening ................................................. 75
February 24: Wallpapering ............................................................. 76
February 25: Woodworking ............................................................ 77
February 26: Xeriscaping ................................................................ 78
February 27: Yard Maintenance ..................................................... 79
February 28: Zoning and Planning ................................................. 80
Conclusion for February ................................................................. 81
March: Collecting ............................................................................... 82
March 1: Antique Clock Collecting ................................................ 83
March 2: Antique Tool Collecting .................................................. 84
March 3: Book Collecting ............................................................... 85
March 4: Bottle Cap Collecting ...................................................... 86
March 5: Coin Collecting (Numismatics) ....................................... 87
March 6: Comic Book Collecting ................................................... 88
March 7: Diecast Car Collecting ..................................................... 89
March 8: Doll Collecting ................................................................. 90
March 9: Ephemera Collecting ....................................................... 91
March 10: Fossil Collecting ............................................................ 92
March 11: Glassware Collecting ..................................................... 93
March 12: Hat Collecting ................................................................ 94
March 13: Insect Collecting ............................................................ 95

 March 14: Jewelry Collecting ........................................................... 96
 March 15: Knife Collecting ............................................................. 97
 March 16: Lantern Collecting .......................................................... 98
 March 17: Matchbox Car Collecting ............................................... 99
 March 18: Numismatics .................................................................. 100
 March 19: Oil Lamp Collecting ....................................................... 101
 March 20: Pen Collecting ................................................................ 102
 March 21: Quilt Collecting .............................................................. 103
 March 22: Rock and Mineral Collecting ......................................... 104
 March 23: Stamp Collecting (Philately) .......................................... 105
 March 24: Toy Collecting ................................................................ 106
 March 25: Umbrella Collecting ....................................................... 107
 March 26: Vintage Poster Collecting ............................................... 108
 March 27: Vinyl Record Collecting ................................................. 109
 March 28: Watch Collecting ............................................................ 110
 March 29: Xylophone Collecting ..................................................... 111
 March 30: Yardstick Collecting ....................................................... 112
 March 31: Zippo Lighter Collecting ................................................ 113
 Conclusion for March ...................................................................... 114
April: Food and Drink ............................................................................ 115
 April 1: Appetizer Making ............................................................... 116
 April 2: Baking ................................................................................. 117
 April 3: Brining ................................................................................ 118
 April 4: Cake Decorating ................................................................. 119
 April 5: Canning ............................................................................... 120
 April 6: Dessert Pairing .................................................................... 121
 April 7: Distilling ............................................................................. 122
 April 8: Edible Flowers .................................................................... 123
 April 9: Ethnic Cooking ................................................................... 124
 April 10: Fermenting ........................................................................ 125
 April 11: Gourmet Cooking .............................................................. 126
 April 12: Herb Gardening ................................................................. 127
 April 13: Ice Cream Making ............................................................. 128
 April 14: Jam Making ....................................................................... 129
 April 15: Knife Skills ....................................................................... 130
 April 16: Latte Art ............................................................................ 131
 April 17: Meal Planning ................................................................... 132
 April 18: Noodle Making .................................................................. 133
 April 19: Organic Cooking ............................................................... 134
 April 20: Pastry Making ................................................................... 135
 April 21: Quick Pickling .................................................................. 136

April 22: Recipe Development ........................................................... 137
April 23: Sourdough Baking .............................................................. 138
April 24: Tea Blending ...................................................................... 139
April 25: Udon Noodles .................................................................... 140
April 26: Vinegar Making .................................................................. 141
April 27: Wine Making ..................................................................... 142
April 28: Xocolatl (Chocolate Making) ............................................. 143
April 29: Yogurt Making ................................................................... 144
April 30: Zest Preservation ............................................................... 145
Conclusion for April ......................................................................... 146
May: Games and Entertainment ............................................................ 147
May 1: Action Figure Collecting ...................................................... 148
May 2: Airsoft ................................................................................... 149
May 3: Board Games ........................................................................ 150
May 4: Board Game Design ............................................................. 151
May 5: Card Games .......................................................................... 152
May 6: Chess ..................................................................................... 153
May 7: Darts ...................................................................................... 154
May 8: Dungeons and Dragons ......................................................... 155
May 9: Electronic Gaming ................................................................ 156
May 10: Escape Rooms .................................................................... 157
May 11: Fantasy Sports .................................................................... 158
May 12: Game Design ...................................................................... 159
May 13: Horse Racing ...................................................................... 160
May 14: Improv Comedy .................................................................. 161
May 15: Jigsaw Puzzles .................................................................... 162
May 16: Karaoke ............................................................................... 163
May 17: Live Streaming ................................................................... 164
May 18: Magic Tricks ....................................................................... 165
May 19: Narrative Games ................................................................. 166
May 20: Online Gaming ................................................................... 167
May 21: Poker ................................................................................... 168
May 22: Quiz Nights ......................................................................... 169
May 23: Role-Playing Games (RPGs) .............................................. 170
May 24: Social Deduction Games .................................................... 171
May 25: Tabletop Games .................................................................. 172
May 26: Urban Exploration Games .................................................. 173
May 27: Virtual Reality Gaming ...................................................... 174
May 28: Word Games ....................................................................... 175
May 29: Xbox Gaming ...................................................................... 176
May 30: Yard Games ........................................................................ 177

    May 31: Zombie Games .................................................................... 178
    Conclusion for May ........................................................................ 179
June: Music and Performing Arts ........................................................180
    June 1: A Cappella.......................................................................... 181
    June 2: Accordion Playing.............................................................. 182
    June 3: Ballet .................................................................................. 183
    June 4: Banjo Playing .................................................................... 184
    June 5: Choir Singing .................................................................... 185
    June 6: Clarinet Playing ................................................................. 186
    June 7: DJing ................................................................................. 187
    June 8: Drumming ......................................................................... 188
    June 9: Electric Guitar ................................................................... 189
    June 10: Flute Playing ................................................................... 190
    June 11: Guitar Playing ................................................................. 191
    June 12: Harmonica ....................................................................... 192
    June 13: Improvisational Theater .................................................. 193
    June 14: Jazz Dance....................................................................... 194
    June 15: Karaoke ........................................................................... 195
    June 16: Lyre Playing .................................................................... 196
    June 17: Music Composition ......................................................... 197
    June 18: Orchestra Participation .................................................... 198
    June 19: Percussion........................................................................ 199
    June 20: Quena (Andean Flute) .....................................................200
    June 21: Rap ..................................................................................201
    June 22: Saxophone Playing ..........................................................202
    June 23: Singing ............................................................................203
    June 24: Theater Acting.................................................................204
    June 25: Ukulele ............................................................................205
    June 26: Violin Playing .................................................................206
    June 27: Whistling .........................................................................207
    June 28: Xylophone .......................................................................208
    June 29: Yodeling ..........................................................................209
    June 30: Zither Playing .................................................................210
    Conclusion for June .......................................................................211
July: Nature and Outdoors ..................................................................212
    July 1: Archery ..............................................................................213
    July 2: Astronomy..........................................................................214
    July 3: Backpacking.......................................................................215
    July 4: Birdwatching......................................................................216
    July 5: Canoeing ............................................................................217
    July 6: Desert Hiking .....................................................................218

July 7: Dog Training .................................................................................. 219
July 8: Environmental Conservation ....................................................... 220
July 9: Falconry ........................................................................................ 221
July 10: Fishing ........................................................................................ 222
July 11: Gardening ................................................................................... 223
July 12: Herb Foraging ............................................................................ 224
July 13: Ice Fishing .................................................................................. 225
July 14: Javelin Throwing ........................................................................ 226
July 15: Kayaking .................................................................................... 227
July 16: Landscaping ............................................................................... 228
July 17: Mountain Biking ........................................................................ 229
July 18: Nature Photography ................................................................... 230
July 19: Orienteering ................................................................................ 231
July 20: Paddleboarding ........................................................................... 232
July 21: Quail Hunting ............................................................................. 233
July 22: Rock Climbing ........................................................................... 234
July 23: Scuba Diving .............................................................................. 235
July 24: Tree Climbing ............................................................................. 236
July 25: Underwater Photography ............................................................ 237
July 26: Volcano Hiking .......................................................................... 238
July 27: Wildlife Tracking ....................................................................... 239
July 28: Xeriscaping ................................................................................. 240
July 29: Yachting ...................................................................................... 241
July 30: Zip Lining ................................................................................... 242
July 31: Zoo Volunteering ....................................................................... 243
Conclusion for July .................................................................................. 244

August: Personal Development ................................................................... 245
August 1: Affirmations ............................................................................ 246
August 2: Anxiety Management .............................................................. 247
August 3: Balance .................................................................................... 248
August 4: Budgeting ................................................................................ 249
August 5: Conflict Resolution .................................................................. 250
August 6: Creativity Exercises ................................................................. 251
August 7: Decision Making ..................................................................... 252
August 8: Decluttering ............................................................................. 253
August 9: Emotional Healing ................................................................... 254
August 10: Emotional Intelligence ........................................................... 255
August 11: Fitness Planning ..................................................................... 256
August 12: Focus Techniques .................................................................. 257
August 13: Goal Setting ........................................................................... 258
August 14: Gratitude Practice .................................................................. 259

- August 15: Habit Building ... 260
- August 16: Journaling ... 261
- August 17: Kindness ... 262
- August 18: Leadership Skills ... 263
- August 19: Meditation ... 264
- August 20: Nutrition ... 265
- August 21: Organization ... 266
- August 22: Public Speaking ... 267
- August 23: Quitting Bad Habits ... 268
- August 24: Resilience Building ... 269
- August 25: Self-Care ... 270
- August 26: Time Management ... 271
- August 27: Understanding Body Language ... 272
- August 28: Visualization ... 273
- August 29: Writing Affirmations ... 274
- August 30: Yoga ... 275
- August 31: Zen Habits ... 276
- Conclusion for August ... 277

September: Science and Technology ... 278
- September 1: Artificial Intelligence ... 279
- September 2: Biology ... 280
- September 3: Blockchain Technology ... 281
- September 4: Chemistry ... 282
- September 5: Cryptography ... 283
- September 6: Data Science ... 284
- September 7: Drone Flying ... 285
- September 8: Electronics ... 286
- September 9: Forensics ... 287
- September 10: Geology ... 288
- September 11: Hacking ... 289
- September 12: Internet of Things (IoT) ... 290
- September 13: Java Programming ... 291
- September 14: Kinematics ... 292
- September 15: Laser Engraving ... 293
- September 16: Microbiology ... 294
- September 17: Nanotechnology ... 295
- September 18: Optics ... 296
- September 19: Physics ... 297
- September 20: Quantum Computing ... 298
- September 21: Robotics ... 299
- September 22: Space Exploration ... 300

- September 23: Tinkering.................................................................301
- September 24: Underwater Robotics .................................................302
- September 25: Virtual Reality ...........................................................303
- September 26: Weather Science .......................................................304
- September 27: X-ray Imaging...........................................................305
- September 28: Y2K Bug History ......................................................306
- September 29: Zoological Illustration................................................307
- September 30: Zoology....................................................................308
- Conclusion for September................................................................309

October: Sports and Fitness ...................................................................310
- October 1: Aerobics ........................................................................311
- October 2: Archery .........................................................................312
- October 3: Badminton.....................................................................313
- October 4: Biking............................................................................314
- October 5: Canoeing .......................................................................315
- October 6: CrossFit.........................................................................316
- October 7: Dance Fitness .................................................................317
- October 8: Disc Golf.......................................................................318
- October 9: Endurance Running.........................................................319
- October 10: Exercise Routines..........................................................320
- October 11: Fencing........................................................................321
- October 12: Gymnastics...................................................................322
- October 13: Handball......................................................................323
- October 14: Ice Hockey...................................................................324
- October 15: Jogging........................................................................325
- October 16: Kickboxing...................................................................326
- October 17: Lacrosse ......................................................................327
- October 18: Marathon Training ........................................................328
- October 19: Netball.........................................................................329
- October 20: Obstacle Course Racing .................................................330
- October 21: Pilates..........................................................................331
- October 22: Quidditch.....................................................................332
- October 23: Rock Climbing .............................................................333
- October 24: Soccer..........................................................................334
- October 25: Tennis..........................................................................335
- October 26: Ultimate Frisbee ...........................................................336
- October 27: Volleyball.....................................................................337
- October 28: Weightlifting ................................................................338
- October 29: Xtreme Sports ..............................................................339
- October 30: Yoga............................................................................340
- October 31: Zumba .........................................................................341

    Conclusion for October .......................................................................... 342
November: Travel and Exploration ............................................................ 343
    November 1: Adventure Travel .............................................................. 344
    November 2: Backpacking ..................................................................... 345
    November 3: Camping ........................................................................... 346
    November 4: Cave Exploring ................................................................ 347
    November 5: Cultural Tours .................................................................. 348
    November 6: Desert Camping ............................................................... 349
    November 7: Eco-Tourism ..................................................................... 350
    November 8: Fishing ............................................................................. 351
    November 9: Glamping ......................................................................... 352
    November 10: Hiking ............................................................................ 353
    November 11: Island Hopping ............................................................... 354
    November 12: Jungle Trekking .............................................................. 355
    November 13: Kayaking ........................................................................ 356
    November 14: Luxury Travel ................................................................. 357
    November 15: Mountain Climbing ........................................................ 358
    November 16: National Park Tours ....................................................... 359
    November 17: Off-Roading ................................................................... 360
    November 18: Photography Tours ......................................................... 361
    November 19: Quadcopter Flying ......................................................... 362
    November 20: Road Tripping ................................................................ 363
    November 21: Sailing ............................................................................ 364
    November 22: Train Travel ................................................................... 365
    November 23: Urban Exploration .......................................................... 366
    November 24: Volcano Hiking .............................................................. 367
    November 25: Wildlife Safaris .............................................................. 368
    November 26: X-Country Skiing ........................................................... 369
    November 27: Yacht Cruising ............................................................... 370
    November 28: Zip Lining ...................................................................... 371
    November 29: Zoo Tours ....................................................................... 372
    November 30: Zorbing .......................................................................... 373
    Conclusion for November ..................................................................... 374
December: Writing and Literature .............................................................. 375
    December 1: Anthology Editing ............................................................ 376
    December 2: Autobiography Writing ..................................................... 377
    December 3: Blogging ........................................................................... 378
    December 4: Book Reviewing ............................................................... 379
    December 5: Copywriting ...................................................................... 380
    December 6: Creative Writing ............................................................... 381
    December 7: Diary Keeping .................................................................. 382

December 8: Digital Publishing ............................................................. 383
December 9: Editing ............................................................................ 384
December 10: Essay Writing ............................................................... 385
December 11: Flash Fiction ................................................................. 386
December 12: Ghostwriting ................................................................. 387
December 13: Historical Fiction Writing ............................................ 388
December 14: Inspirational Writing .................................................... 389
December 15: Journaling ..................................................................... 390
December 16: Kinetic Poetry ............................................................... 391
December 17: Letter Writing ............................................................... 392
December 18: Memoir Writing ............................................................ 393
December 19: Novel Writing ............................................................... 394
December 20: Opinion Pieces ............................................................. 395
December 21: Playwriting ................................................................... 396
December 22: Quoting ......................................................................... 397
December 23: Research Writing .......................................................... 398
December 24: Scriptwriting ................................................................. 399
December 25: Travel Writing .............................................................. 400
December 26: Urban Fantasy Writing ................................................. 401
December 27: Verse Writing ............................................................... 402
December 28: Wordplay ...................................................................... 403
December 29: Xerox Art ...................................................................... 404
December 30: Year-End Reflection Writing ....................................... 405
December 31: Zine Creation ................................................................ 406
Conclusion for December .................................................................... 407
Conclusion: Reflecting on Your Year of Hobbies .................................... 408
Appendices ................................................................................................ 410
    Appendix A: Resources for Hobbies ................................................. 410
    Appendix B: Hobby Journals and Logs ............................................. 412
    Appendix C: Community and Clubs ................................................. 414
About the Author ...................................................................................... 417
About the Publisher .................................................................................. 417
Recommended Resources ........................................................................ 418

# Book Overview

HowExpert Guide to 365 Hobbies: The Ultimate A to Z Handbook to Discover, Learn, and Explore a New Hobby Every Day of the Year

If you're looking to explore a new hobby every day and unlock your creative potential, then HowExpert Guide to 365 Hobbies is your ultimate resource.

Welcome to a year-long adventure filled with creativity, discovery, and growth. This guide is your gateway to mastering a diverse range of hobbies, organized from A to Z and tailored to fit every month. Whether you're seeking to ignite your creativity, improve DIY skills, connect with nature, or find a new passion, this book offers endless inspiration and practical tips to enrich your life daily.

Inside this book, you'll find:
- Introduction: The Joy of Hobbies – Discover how hobbies can enrich your life, reduce stress, and spark joy. Use this guide to explore new passions daily or focus on specific interests.
- January: Arts and Crafts – Start your year with creativity by diving into hobbies like painting, knitting, and wood carving. Each day introduces a new craft to let your artistic side shine.
- February: Building and DIY – Channel your inner handyman or handywoman with projects ranging from carpentry to gardening. Perfect for anyone who loves to build, fix, or create with their hands.
- March: Collecting – Explore the fascinating world of collecting, from antiques to rare books and coins. Learn the ins and outs of starting, maintaining, and expanding your collection.
- April: Food and Drink – Satisfy your culinary curiosity by mastering the art of baking, brewing, and gourmet cooking. This chapter is a feast for your taste buds, with a new food-related hobby daily.
- May: Games and Entertainment – Unleash your inner gamer with a month of board games, video games, and other forms of entertainment. Whether you're into strategy or action, there's something for every gamer.
- June: Music and Performing Arts – Harmonize your love for music and performing arts by exploring instruments, singing, and acting. Each hobby helps you express yourself through sound and movement.
- July: Nature and Outdoors – Embrace the outdoors with hobbies like hiking, birdwatching, and gardening. Perfect for nature lovers and adventurers, these

activities connect you with the natural world.
- August: Personal Development – Focus on self-improvement with hobbies that nurture your mind and soul, from journaling to meditation. This chapter is about building better habits, enhancing well-being, and fostering personal growth.
- September: Science and Technology – Dive into science with hobbies ranging from robotics to astronomy. Ideal for curious minds, this chapter expands your understanding through hands-on experiments and tech projects.
- October: Sports and Fitness – Get moving with a variety of physical activities that promote fitness and fun. Whether you're into yoga, weightlifting, or extreme sports, this chapter keeps you active, energized, and healthy.
- November: Travel and Exploration – Feed your wanderlust with hobbies that encourage exploration, from camping to cultural tours. This chapter is your passport to adventure, offering new ways to discover the world.
- December: Writing and Literature – Cap off the year by indulging in the written word. Whether writing your memoirs or crafting fiction, these literary hobbies inspire you to unleash your creativity and reflect on your experiences.
- Conclusion: Reflecting on Your Year of Hobbies – Reflect on your journey with tips on exploring new activities, embracing lifelong learning, and finding new inspirations.
- Appendices – Delve into resources, journals, and community connections to keep your hobby pursuits thriving and ensure your passion for learning never fades.

Whether you're a seasoned hobbyist or just starting out, HowExpert Guide to 365 Hobbies is your go-to source for daily inspiration and growth. Buy the book today and embark on a year-long adventure of discovery, creativity, and fun!

HowExpert publishes how-to guides on all topics from A to Z. Visit HowExpert.com to learn more.

# Introduction: The Joy of Hobbies

## 1. Welcome to Your Year of Hobbies

Welcome to HowExpert Guide to 365 Hobbies: The Ultimate A to Z Handbook to Discover, Learn, and Explore a New Hobby Every Day of the Year. This book is your passport to a year-long adventure filled with creativity, discovery, and personal growth. Whether you're looking to ignite a new passion, enhance your skills, or simply find a way to relax and unwind, this guide has something for everyone. With 365 hobbies—one for every day of the year—you'll never run out of new experiences to explore.

## 2. Overview of the Book and How to Use It

This book is organized to provide you with a daily dose of inspiration. Each month focuses on a specific category, allowing you to immerse yourself in a diverse range of activities, from arts and crafts in January to writing and literature in December. Each hobby is presented in a way that's easy to understand, with step-by-step instructions, tips, and insights that will help you get started and improve over time.

*You Can Use This Book in Several Ways:*
- **Daily Exploration:** Follow the calendar and try a new hobby each day, making every day of the year a new adventure.
- **Monthly Focus:** Concentrate on one category per month, allowing yourself to dive deeper into a specific area of interest.
- **Personalized Journey:** Pick and choose hobbies that resonate with you, tailoring your experience to your personal interests and goals.

## 3. Benefits of Having a Hobby

Having a hobby is more than just a way to pass the time—it's a vital part of a balanced and fulfilling life. Here are some of the key benefits:
- **Stress Relief:** Engaging in a hobby can provide a much-needed break from the pressures of daily life, allowing you to relax and recharge.
- **Creativity Boost:** Many hobbies stimulate creativity, helping you think outside the box and approach problems in new ways.
- **Skill Development:** Hobbies often involve learning new skills or improving existing ones, which can be both personally rewarding and professionally beneficial.

- **Social Connections:** Many hobbies can be shared with others, offering opportunities to connect with like-minded individuals and build lasting friendships.
- **Personal Growth:** Hobbies encourage self-improvement and personal development, fostering a sense of achievement and boosting your confidence.

## 4. How This Guide Will Help You Explore, Learn, and Master a Variety of Hobbies

This guide is designed to be your trusted companion as you embark on this year-long journey of hobby exploration. Here's how it will support you:
- **Variety and Diversity:** With 365 hobbies, this guide covers a wide range of interests, ensuring that there's something for everyone, no matter your age, background, or experience level.
- **Step-by-Step Guidance:** Each hobby is broken down into manageable steps, making it easy for beginners to get started and for experienced hobbyists to refine their skills.
- **Inspiration and Motivation:** The daily structure of this guide will keep you inspired and motivated to try new things, helping you discover passions you never knew you had.
- **Lifelong Learning:** This guide encourages you to continue exploring beyond the pages of this book. The appendices offer additional resources, hobby journals, and community connections to support your ongoing journey.

**By the end of the year, you'll have not only explored a wide array of hobbies but also enriched your life in countless ways. Let's get started on this exciting adventure—your year of hobbies awaits!**

# January: Arts and Crafts

*January is the perfect month to kickstart your year of hobbies with arts and crafts, a category that celebrates creativity, self-expression, and hands-on learning. Engaging in arts and crafts allows you to explore a wide range of materials, techniques, and styles, all while creating something uniquely your own. From the precision of airbrushing to the intricate beauty of stained glass, each day in January offers a new opportunity to delve into the world of artistic creation.*

# *January 1: Airbrushing*

## 1. The Precision of Airbrushing

Airbrushing is a versatile and precise technique that uses compressed air to spray paint or ink onto a surface. This method is favored in various creative fields, from fine art to automotive painting, due to its ability to produce smooth gradients, intricate details, and flawless finishes. Airbrushing allows artists to create highly realistic images, special effects, and even custom designs on various surfaces, making it a powerful tool in the world of art and design.

## 2. Tools and Materials

- Airbrush Gun: The central tool for this hobby, available in single-action or dual-action models, where dual-action offers more control.
- Compressor: Provides the necessary air pressure, essential for consistent and smooth paint application.
- Airbrush Paints: These are specially formulated to be thin enough for airbrushing, ensuring vibrant colors and smooth application without clogging the airbrush.
- Stencils: Used to create sharp, precise shapes and patterns, stencils are essential for achieving complex designs.
- Cleaning Kit: Regular maintenance of your airbrush gun is crucial to avoid clogs and ensure longevity, making a cleaning kit indispensable.

## 3. Techniques and Tips

- Start with Simple Projects: Begin with basic shapes and lines to become familiar with the airbrush gun's control and behavior.
- Layering and Gradients: Build up colors in thin layers, gradually increasing intensity to avoid oversaturation and achieve smooth transitions.
- Practice on Different Surfaces: Experiment with airbrushing on canvas, metal, plastic, and fabric to understand how the paint interacts with each.
- Consistent Maintenance: Clean your airbrush thoroughly after each use to prevent paint buildup, which can cause clogs and affect performance.

# *January 2: Animation*

## 1. The Magic of Animation

Animation is the art of bringing images, characters, and stories to life through motion. It has evolved from traditional hand-drawn techniques to sophisticated 3D modeling and computer-generated imagery (CGI). Whether you're interested in traditional 2D animation, stop-motion, or digital animation, this field combines creativity, storytelling, and technical skills, offering endless possibilities for artistic expression and entertainment.

## 2. Tools and Materials

- Animation Software: Programs like Adobe Animate, Toon Boom Harmony, or Blender provide a wide range of tools for creating digital animations.
- Graphics Tablet: A must-have for digital animators, a tablet allows for precise drawing and smooth motion capture, simulating traditional drawing methods.
- Camera for Stop-Motion: For stop-motion animation, a high-quality camera is essential to capture each frame clearly and consistently.
- Storyboarding Tools: Whether digital or on paper, storyboards help plan out key scenes, movements, and transitions, ensuring a coherent narrative.

## 3. Techniques and Tips

- Master the Basics: Focus on foundational principles like timing, spacing, and the use of squash and stretch to bring life and personality to your animations.
- Frame Rate Mastery: Understanding and choosing the right frame rate (commonly 24 FPS for film) is key to achieving the desired flow and realism in your animation.
- Short Animations First: Begin with short, simple animations to practice movement and timing before tackling more complex projects.
- Study Classic Animations: Analyze well-known animations to learn how professionals create emotion, fluidity, and compelling narratives through motion.

# *January 3: Basket Weaving*

## 1. The Art of Basket Weaving

Basket weaving is one of the oldest crafts, involving the interlacing of flexible materials such as reed, willow, or rattan to create baskets and other woven items. This craft is both functional and artistic, offering endless possibilities for creating beautiful and durable pieces that can be used in everyday life or as decorative items.

## 2. Tools and Materials

- Weaving Materials: Common choices include reeds, rattan, willow, and seagrass, each offering different textures and finishes.
- Soaking Basin: Essential for soaking materials to make them more pliable and easier to weave without breaking.
- Weaving Tools: Awls, bodkins, and knives are used for manipulating and cutting the materials during the weaving process.
- Finishing Products: Varnishes or oils help protect and preserve the final product, adding durability and a polished look.

## 3. Techniques and Tips

- Learn Basic Patterns: Start with basic weave patterns like the over-and-under weave to understand the foundational techniques of basket weaving.
- Maintain Moisture: Keep your weaving materials wet during the process to prevent them from becoming brittle and breaking.
- Experiment with Textures: Combine different materials and weaving techniques to add complexity and texture to your baskets.
- Finishing Touches: After completing your basket, apply a finish to enhance its durability and appearance, ensuring it lasts for years.

# *January 4: Beadwork*

## 1. The Intricacies of Beadwork

Beadwork is the art of creating decorative designs by stringing or stitching beads together. This craft can range from simple jewelry making to intricate bead embroidery on clothing or accessories. Beadwork allows for endless creativity, offering a vast array of colors, shapes, and materials to work with, resulting in pieces that are both beautiful and meaningful.

## 2. Tools and Materials

- Beads: Choose from a variety of materials like glass, seed, gemstone, or plastic, each offering different textures and appearances.
- Needles and Thread: Use fine beading needles and strong, flexible thread such as nylon or silk to string beads securely and create detailed patterns.
- Beading Mat: A soft mat helps prevent beads from rolling away and keeps your workspace organized.
- Findings: Clasps, jump rings, and other findings are necessary for finishing your beadwork, particularly in jewelry projects.

## 3. Techniques and Tips

- Start with Basic Patterns: Begin with simple designs like single-strand necklaces or bracelets to practice threading and patterning.
- Use a Bead Mat: This will keep your beads in place and make the beading process smoother and more efficient.
- Learn Various Stitches: Master different beadwork stitches, such as peyote, brick, and herringbone, to expand your creative options.
- Design Before Stringing: Lay out your beads in the desired pattern before stringing them to ensure a balanced and aesthetically pleasing design.

# *January 5: Calligraphy*

## 1. The Elegance of Calligraphy

Calligraphy is the art of beautiful handwriting, focusing on the form and style of each letter to create visually appealing text. This ancient art form has been practiced for centuries and remains popular for its aesthetic appeal and the meditative quality of its practice. Calligraphy is used in a variety of applications, from wedding invitations to personal journaling, and can be both a creative outlet and a form of self-expression.

## 2. Tools and Materials

- Calligraphy Pens: Dip pens, fountain pens, and brush pens are all used in different styles of calligraphy, each offering unique line qualities.
- Inks: High-quality inks are essential for achieving smooth, consistent lines. While black ink is traditional, colored inks can add a creative touch.
- Paper: Use smooth, high-quality paper designed for calligraphy to ensure clean, crisp lines and prevent bleeding or feathering.
- Guide Sheets: Lined or grid paper helps maintain consistent letter size, spacing, and angle, particularly when practicing new styles.

## 3. Techniques and Tips

- Practice Basic Strokes: Focus on mastering basic strokes before forming letters to build a solid foundation for your calligraphy.
- Experiment with Styles: Try different calligraphy styles, such as Gothic, Italic, or Copperplate, to discover what resonates with you.
- Mindful Practice: Approach calligraphy as a mindful practice, focusing on each stroke and enjoying the process of creating beautiful lettering.
- Consistency is Key: Regular practice is essential to developing your skills and achieving consistent, elegant lettering.

# *January 6: Candle Making*

## 1. The Craft of Candle Making

Candle making is both a practical and creative hobby that allows you to create custom candles tailored to your preferences in scent, color, and design. Whether you're making candles for relaxation, home decor, or gifts, this hobby offers endless possibilities for personalization. The process of candle making can be as simple or as complex as you want it to be, making it suitable for beginners and experienced crafters alike.

## 2. Tools and Materials

- Wax: Soy, beeswax, and paraffin are the most common types of wax used in candle making, each offering different burning properties and appearances.
- Wicks: Choosing the right wick size for your container and wax type is crucial for ensuring a clean, even burn.
- Fragrance Oils: Add fragrance oils to create scented candles that fill your space with delightful aromas.
- Dyes: Liquid or solid dyes can be added to the wax to create candles in any color you desire.
- Molds and Containers: Use molds to create shaped candles or containers for jar candles.

## 3. Techniques and Tips

- Melt Wax Safely: Use a double boiler to melt wax evenly and safely, avoiding overheating, which can affect the quality of the candle.
- Center Your Wick: Ensure the wick is centered in your mold or container for an even burn and to prevent tunneling.
- Experiment with Additives: Try adding essential oils, herbs, or dried flowers to customize your candles further and add visual interest.
- Allow Proper Cooling: Let candles cool slowly and evenly to prevent cracks or sinkholes, ensuring a smooth, professional finish.

# *January 7: Collage*

## 1. The Creativity of Collage

Collage is an art form that involves assembling different materials—such as paper, fabric, and photographs—onto a surface to create a new, unified piece. This technique allows for endless experimentation and can be as simple or complex as you desire. Collage is a great way to explore texture, color, and composition in a tactile and hands-on way, making it a versatile and engaging art form.

## 2. Tools and Materials

- Base Material: Choose a sturdy surface like canvas, wood, or heavy paper as the base for your collage.
- Adhesives: Use glue sticks, gel mediums, or mod podge to adhere your materials to the base securely and evenly.
- Materials for Collage: Gather a variety of papers, fabric scraps, magazine cutouts, and other found objects to create your collage.
- Cutting Tools: Use sharp scissors or an X-Acto knife for precise cutting and trimming of your materials.

## 3. Techniques and Tips

- Plan Your Layout: Before gluing anything down, arrange your materials on the base to see how they work together and make adjustments as needed.
- Layering for Depth: Experiment with layering different materials to create depth and visual interest in your collage.
- Mix Media: Combine collage with other art forms like painting or drawing to add complexity and richness to your piece.
- Balanced Composition: Pay attention to the composition, ensuring that no one area of the collage dominates or overwhelms the rest.

# *January 8: Crochet*

## 1. The Art of Crochet

Crochet is a needlework technique that uses a single hook to interlock loops of yarn, thread, or other materials to create fabric. Unlike knitting, which uses two needles, crochet's versatility allows you to create intricate patterns, lace, or thick, warm textiles. It's a calming and rewarding hobby that can produce anything from clothing to home decor.

## 2. Tools and Materials

- Crochet Hooks: Available in various sizes, hooks are selected based on the thickness of the yarn and the desired stitch size.
- Yarn: Choose yarns of different weights, textures, and colors depending on your project. Wool, cotton, and acrylic are popular choices.
- Patterns: Patterns provide step-by-step instructions for creating specific crochet projects.
- Stitch Markers: Useful for keeping track of your place in more complex patterns.

## 3. Techniques and Tips

- Learn Basic Stitches: Start with basic stitches like single crochet, double crochet, and slip stitch before moving on to more complex patterns.
- Use a Gauge Swatch: Create a small test swatch to check your tension and ensure your finished project will be the correct size.
- Follow Patterns Carefully: Pay attention to instructions and stitch counts to avoid mistakes, particularly in more intricate designs.
- Experiment with Textures: Try using different yarns or stitch techniques to add texture and interest to your projects.

# *January 9: Decoupage*

## 1. The Versatility of Decoupage

Decoupage is the art of decorating an object by gluing colored paper cutouts onto it, often combining this with special paint effects, gold leaf, or other decorative elements. This technique is incredibly versatile and can be used to decorate furniture, boxes, frames, and more. It's a fantastic way to personalize items and transform ordinary objects into works of art.

## 2. Tools and Materials

- Base Object: Common objects for decoupage include wooden boxes, trays, picture frames, and furniture.
- Paper Cutouts: Use decorative paper, magazine clippings, or even fabric for your cutouts.
- Adhesives: Mod Podge or decoupage glue works well for adhering paper to your base object and sealing it afterward.
- Brushes: Use soft brushes to apply glue smoothly and evenly, and to smooth out any wrinkles in the paper.
- Sealants: Apply a clear sealant or varnish to protect your finished piece and give it a glossy, professional finish.

## 3. Techniques and Tips

- Prepare Your Surface: Sand and clean your base object to ensure a smooth, even surface for the decoupage.
- Precision Cutting: Carefully cut out your paper elements to avoid jagged edges and to fit them perfectly onto your object.
- Smooth as You Go: Use a brayer or a flat tool to smooth out any air bubbles or wrinkles as you apply the paper.
- Layer for Effect: Layering different papers or using different techniques can add depth, texture, and visual interest to your finished piece.

## *January 10: Drawing*

### 1. The Foundation of Visual Arts

Drawing is one of the most fundamental and accessible forms of visual art. Whether you're sketching with a pencil, creating detailed ink illustrations, or experimenting with charcoal, drawing allows you to express ideas, emotions, and stories through lines and shapes. It's a skill that can be continuously refined and applied to countless other artistic endeavors.

### 2. Tools and Materials

- Drawing Pencils: Available in various grades, from soft (B) to hard (H), each pencil provides a different type of line or shading.
- Paper: Use sketch pads, drawing paper, or specialized surfaces like Bristol board, depending on your medium and style.
- Erasers: A good eraser, like a kneaded eraser, allows for corrections without damaging the paper.
- Charcoal and Pastels: For more expressive and bold drawings, charcoal and pastels offer rich, dramatic marks.

### 3. Techniques and Tips

- Practice Basic Shapes: Start by mastering basic shapes like circles, squares, and triangles, which form the foundation of more complex drawings.
- Study Light and Shadow: Understanding how light interacts with objects is crucial for creating realistic drawings. Practice shading techniques to add depth and dimension.
- Use References: Drawing from life or using photo references can improve your accuracy and help you understand proportions.
- Experiment with Styles: Explore different drawing styles, such as realism, abstract, or cartooning, to find what resonates with you.

# *January 11: Embroidery*

## 1. The Timeless Craft of Embroidery

Embroidery is the art of decorating fabric with needle and thread, creating intricate designs and patterns. This craft has been practiced for centuries and remains popular for its versatility and the personal touch it can add to clothing, accessories, and home decor. Whether you're stitching a simple monogram or a detailed scene, embroidery allows you to express your creativity through textile art.

## 2. Tools and Materials

- Embroidery Hoops: Hoops hold your fabric taut, making it easier to work on your design and ensuring even stitching.
- Needles: Embroidery needles have larger eyes to accommodate thicker threads and make stitching easier.
- Embroidery Floss: Available in a wide range of colors, embroidery floss is a type of thread specifically designed for this craft.
- Fabric: Choose fabrics like cotton, linen, or canvas for your embroidery projects.
- Patterns: Use printed or drawn patterns as a guide for your stitches.

## 3. Techniques and Tips

- Start with Basic Stitches: Learn basic stitches like the running stitch, backstitch, and satin stitch before attempting more complex designs.
- Use a Hoop: Keeping your fabric taut with an embroidery hoop will help you achieve more even stitches and a polished look.
- Plan Your Design: Sketch your design on paper or directly on the fabric before starting to ensure everything is in the right place.
- Experiment with Texture: Combine different stitches and thread thicknesses to add texture and depth to your embroidery.

# *January 12: Engraving*

## 1. The Precision of Engraving

Engraving is the process of cutting or carving designs into a hard surface, such as metal, glass, or wood. This art form requires precision and patience but offers the reward of creating intricate and permanent designs. Engraving is commonly used for jewelry, decorative items, and personalized gifts, making it a versatile and highly rewarding hobby.

## 2. Tools and Materials

- Engraving Tools: Depending on the material, you may use gravers, burins, or rotary tools with engraving bits.
- Materials: Common materials for engraving include metal, glass, and wood, each offering unique challenges and results.
- Stencils: Stencils can help guide your design, especially for text or repetitive patterns.
- Safety Gear: Use safety glasses and gloves to protect yourself while engraving, especially when working with glass or metal.

## 3. Techniques and Tips

- Start with Simple Designs: Begin with basic shapes and lines to get a feel for the tools and the material you're working with.
- Use the Right Tool: Different materials require different tools and techniques. Research the best tools for your specific project.
- Practice on Scrap Material: Before engraving on your final piece, practice on scrap material to perfect your technique.
- Steady Your Hand: Use both hands to steady the engraving tool and maintain control over your movements for more precise results.

# *January 13: Felting*

## 1. The Texture of Felting

Felting is a process of matting, condensing, and pressing fibers together to create fabric. There are two main types of felting: wet felting and needle felting. Wet felting uses water and soap to mat the fibers, while needle felting uses barbed needles to interlock the fibers. Felting can be used to create sculptures, accessories, and even garments, offering a unique texture and creative potential.

## 2. Tools and Materials

- Wool Roving: Wool fibers are the primary material used in felting. Choose from a variety of colors and textures to suit your project.
- Felting Needles: Barbed needles are essential for needle felting, as they help to interlock the wool fibers.
- Foam Pad: A foam pad provides a safe surface to needle felt on, protecting both your work surface and the needle.
- Water and Soap: Used in wet felting to help the fibers mat together.

## 3. Techniques and Tips

- Start with Simple Shapes: For beginners, starting with basic shapes like balls or cylinders helps you learn the felting process and build confidence.
- Use Layers: In wet felting, layering different colors of wool can create beautiful effects as they blend together.
- Needle with Care: When needle felting, be mindful of the needle's position to avoid breaking it or injuring yourself.
- Experiment with Texture: Felting allows for unique textures and finishes. Try combining different types of wool or incorporating other fibers to add interest to your projects.

# *January 14: Flower Arranging*

## 1. The Art of Flower Arranging

Flower arranging, or floristry, is the art of creating beautiful compositions using flowers, foliage, and other natural materials. This hobby combines artistic creativity with an appreciation for nature, allowing you to create arrangements that bring beauty and tranquility into your home. Whether for a special occasion or everyday enjoyment, flower arranging is a fulfilling and meditative practice.

## 2. Tools and Materials

- Flowers and Foliage: Choose fresh flowers and greenery in complementary colors and textures to create a harmonious arrangement.
- Floral Foam: Used to anchor flowers in arrangements, helping them stay in place and remain hydrated.
- Vases and Containers: Select vases, baskets, or other containers that complement your arrangement and suit the style you're aiming for.
- Pruning Shears: Essential for trimming stems, shaping foliage, and ensuring your flowers are prepared for arrangement.
- Floral Wire and Tape: Used to secure flowers and create more complex arrangements, especially in larger or more intricate designs.

## 3. Techniques and Tips

- Start with a Focal Point: Choose a central flower or feature to build your arrangement around, giving it focus and structure.
- Consider Color Harmony: Use a color wheel to select flowers that harmonize or contrast pleasingly, enhancing the overall visual impact.
- Play with Height and Depth: Arrange flowers at different heights and depths to create a sense of balance, movement, and natural flow.
- Change Water Regularly: To keep your arrangements fresh, change the water daily, re-cut stems as needed, and remove any wilted flowers.

# *January 15: Glassblowing*

## 1. The Artistry of Glassblowing

Glassblowing is a fascinating and ancient art form where molten glass is shaped and blown into beautiful, intricate forms. This hobby requires specialized equipment and training but offers the reward of creating stunning glass pieces ranging from vases to intricate sculptures. The process of shaping hot glass is both challenging and deeply satisfying, making it a unique and rewarding creative outlet.

## 2. Tools and Materials

- Glass Furnace: A furnace is needed to heat glass to the molten state required for blowing.
- Blowpipe: A long metal tube used to gather molten glass and shape it by blowing air through the pipe.
- Tools for Shaping: Jacks, shears, and paddles are used to shape and manipulate the glass into the desired forms.
- Colorants: Metal oxides and other materials are added to glass to create different colors and effects.
- Safety Gear: Heat-resistant gloves, goggles, and protective clothing are essential to protect yourself from the intense heat and sharp glass edges.

## 3. Techniques and Tips

- Start with Basic Shapes: Begin by creating simple forms like paperweights or small vases to master the basics of gathering and shaping glass.
- Control Your Breath: The amount of air you blow into the pipe affects the size and shape of your glass piece. Practice controlling your breath for consistent results.
- Keep the Glass Moving: Constantly turning the blowpipe ensures the glass remains evenly heated and shaped, preventing it from cooling and becoming unworkable.
- Learn from Experts: Glassblowing is a complex skill that benefits greatly from instruction and observation. Take classes or watch experienced glassblowers to learn advanced techniques and safety practices.

## *January 16: Hand Lettering*

### 1. The Art of Hand Lettering

Hand lettering is the art of drawing letters rather than writing them. This hobby combines elements of typography, calligraphy, and illustration, allowing you to create decorative text for posters, invitations, and other projects. Unlike calligraphy, where each stroke is predetermined, hand lettering is more freeform and artistic, giving you complete creative control over the appearance of each letter.

### 2. Tools and Materials

- Pens and Markers: Brush pens, fine liners, and chisel-tip markers are popular tools for hand lettering, each offering different line qualities and effects.
- Paper: Use smooth, bleed-proof paper to achieve crisp, clean lines and prevent ink from feathering or bleeding.
- Pencils and Erasers: Sketch out your designs in pencil before finalizing them in ink, allowing you to make adjustments and refine your work.
- Rulers and Compasses: Useful for creating guides, maintaining consistent letter size, and ensuring balanced spacing and composition.

### 3. Techniques and Tips

- Practice Basic Letter Shapes: Start by practicing basic letterforms and understanding how different tools create different effects and styles.
- Explore Different Styles: Try out various lettering styles, such as serif, sans-serif, script, or decorative fonts, to find your unique style and voice.
- Use Guidelines: Draw faint guidelines to help maintain consistent letter height, angle, and spacing, especially when creating complex designs.
- Add Flourishes and Embellishments: Once comfortable with basic letters, experiment with adding flourishes, shadows, and other decorative elements to your designs to enhance their visual impact.

# *January 17: Illustration*

## 1. The World of Illustration

Illustration is a form of visual art that combines drawing and storytelling. Whether for books, magazines, posters, or personal projects, illustration allows you to create images that convey ideas, emotions, and narratives. This hobby offers endless possibilities, from realistic depictions to abstract designs, allowing you to develop your unique style and voice as an artist.

## 2. Tools and Materials

- Drawing Tablets: For digital illustration, a drawing tablet and stylus are essential tools, providing precision and control in your artwork.
- Traditional Media: Pencils, inks, watercolors, and markers are commonly used for hand-drawn illustrations, each offering different textures and effects.
- Software: Programs like Adobe Illustrator, Procreate, or Clip Studio Paint are popular choices for digital illustration, offering a wide range of tools and features.
- Reference Materials: Collect references, such as photos or models, to help guide your illustrations and ensure accuracy in your work.

## 3. Techniques and Tips

- Develop Your Style: Explore different illustration styles and techniques to find what best expresses your vision and resonates with your audience.
- Use References: Reference images can help improve the accuracy and detail of your illustrations, particularly in realistic or complex scenes.
- Experiment with Mediums: Don't be afraid to mix digital and traditional mediums or try new tools to discover what works best for your process and style.
- Practice Storytelling: Good illustrations often tell a story or convey a message. Practice incorporating narrative elements into your work to create engaging and meaningful art.

# *January 18: Jewelry Making*

## 1. The Craft of Jewelry Making

Jewelry making is a versatile and rewarding hobby that allows you to create personalized accessories using a wide range of materials and techniques. From simple beaded necklaces to intricate metalwork, jewelry making offers endless possibilities for creativity and self-expression. Whether you're creating pieces for yourself, as gifts, or even to sell, this hobby combines artistic design with hands-on craftsmanship.

## 2. Tools and Materials

- Beads and Gemstones: Choose from a variety of materials, including glass beads, semi-precious stones, and pearls, each offering different colors, textures, and effects.
- Wire and Findings: Jewelry wire, clasps, and other findings are essential for constructing and finishing your pieces, ensuring durability and functionality.
- Pliers and Cutters: Round-nose pliers, flat-nose pliers, and wire cutters are basic tools for shaping wire, attaching components, and ensuring clean cuts.
- Metalworking Tools: For those interested in metal jewelry, tools like hammers, anvils, and soldering kits are necessary for more advanced designs.
- Design Board: A design board helps plan and organize your jewelry layout before assembly, ensuring a balanced and cohesive design.

## 3. Techniques and Tips

- Start with Simple Projects: Begin with basic beading or wire-wrapping techniques before progressing to more complex designs, allowing you to build skills gradually.
- Learn Basic Wirework: Mastering basic wirework, such as making loops, wrapping wire, and connecting components, is crucial for many jewelry projects.
- Pay Attention to Details: Small details, like the choice of findings and the quality of your finishes, can greatly impact the overall appearance and durability of your jewelry.
- Experiment with Materials: Don't limit yourself to traditional materials—experiment with alternative materials like wood, resin, or recycled items to create unique and innovative pieces.

# *January 19: Knitting*

## 1. The Comfort of Knitting

Knitting is a time-honored craft that involves creating fabric by interlocking loops of yarn with knitting needles. This hobby is not only relaxing and meditative but also highly practical, allowing you to make everything from cozy scarves and sweaters to intricate lace patterns. Knitting offers a wonderful balance between creativity and functionality, making it a beloved pastime for many.

## 2. Tools and Materials

- Knitting Needles: Available in various sizes and materials, including bamboo, metal, and plastic. Choose needles based on the yarn weight and project.
- Yarn: Select yarns in different textures, colors, and weights to suit your project. Wool, cotton, and acrylic are popular choices for their different properties and effects.
- Stitch Markers: These small rings help keep track of your place in complex patterns, making it easier to follow intricate designs.
- Patterns: Patterns provide step-by-step instructions for creating specific knitted items, from simple scarves to more complex garments and accessories.

## 3. Techniques and Tips

- Learn Basic Stitches: Start with basic stitches like knit and purl before moving on to more advanced techniques like cabling or lace knitting.
- Gauge Matters: Always check your gauge before starting a project to ensure the finished item will be the correct size, particularly when following a pattern.
- Practice Makes Perfect: Like any skill, knitting improves with practice. Start with small projects to build your confidence and skill level gradually.
- Join a Knitting Group: Knitting groups offer support, inspiration, and camaraderie as you work on your projects, providing a sense of community and shared learning.

# *January 20: Latch Hooking*

## 1. The Craft of Latch Hooking

Latch hooking is a textile art that involves pulling loops of yarn through a canvas to create rugs, wall hangings, or other textured items. This craft is relatively easy to learn and can be a fun, relaxing way to create colorful, durable pieces. Latch hooking is often enjoyed for its tactile nature and the satisfaction of watching a design come to life as you work.

## 2. Tools and Materials

- Latch Hook Tool: A special tool with a hinged hook that helps pull yarn through the canvas, creating the signature latch hook loops.
- Canvas: Pre-cut canvas with a grid pattern serves as the base for your latch hook project, guiding the placement of each yarn piece.
- Yarn: Cut yarn into short, uniform lengths. Pre-cut yarn packs are available, or you can cut your own from skeins to match your desired color scheme.
- Patterns: Use printed patterns as guides for placing yarn in the correct colors and locations, ensuring a cohesive and visually pleasing design.

## 3. Techniques and Tips

- Start with a Kit: For beginners, latch hook kits provide all the necessary materials and a pre-designed pattern, making it easier to get started and learn the basics.
- Keep Yarn Consistent: Cut your yarn to uniform lengths to ensure even loops and a consistent texture across your project.
- Work in Sections: Tackle your project one section at a time to stay organized and make the process more manageable, particularly with larger designs.
- Secure the Edges: Finish your project by binding or hemming the edges of the canvas to prevent fraying and ensure a polished, durable final piece.

# *January 21: Macramé*

## 1. The Art of Macramé

Macramé is a form of textile art that involves knotting cords or strings into decorative patterns. This craft has seen a resurgence in popularity, particularly for home decor items like wall hangings, plant hangers, and even furniture. Macramé's versatility allows for endless creative possibilities, from simple designs using basic knots to complex, layered pieces that can serve as statement art in any space.

## 2. Tools and Materials

- Macramé Cord: Choose cords in various thicknesses and materials, such as cotton, jute, or nylon, depending on your project's needs and desired texture.
- Scissors: Sharp scissors are essential for cutting cords to the desired length and for trimming any excess after knotting.
- Measuring Tape: Use a measuring tape to ensure your cords are the correct length for your design, avoiding waste and ensuring consistency.
- Dowel Rods or Rings: These provide a base or structure for your macramé project, especially for wall hangings or plant hangers.
- Pins or Clips: Helpful for holding cords in place while you work, ensuring your knots stay secure and your design stays aligned.

## 3. Techniques and Tips

- Learn Basic Knots: Start with basic knots like the square knot, half hitch, and lark's head knot. These form the foundation of most macramé designs and are essential for creating more complex patterns.
- Use a Pattern: Following a pattern can help guide your project, especially if you're new to macramé or tackling a more intricate design.
- Practice Tension Control: Consistent tension is key to achieving even, balanced designs. Practice maintaining the same tension across all knots to avoid uneven sections.
- Experiment with Scale: Try using different cord thicknesses and knot sizes to create visual interest and texture in your projects, adding depth and complexity to your macramé pieces.

# *January 22: Needlepoint*

## 1. The Precision of Needlepoint

Needlepoint is a form of embroidery where designs are stitched onto a canvas using a variety of yarns or threads. This craft is known for its detailed and often intricate patterns, making it a rewarding hobby for those who enjoy working with their hands. Needlepoint projects can range from small ornaments to large wall hangings, offering plenty of opportunities for creativity and expression.

## 2. Tools and Materials

- Canvas: Stiff, open-weave fabric serves as the base for needlepoint. Pre-printed canvases are available for those who prefer working with a guide, offering designs directly on the fabric.
- Yarn or Thread: Wool, silk, or cotton threads are commonly used in needlepoint, chosen based on the desired texture, color vibrancy, and durability of the finished piece.
- Needles: Tapestry needles with blunt tips are used to avoid splitting the canvas threads and to easily guide the yarn through the fabric.
- Frames or Hoops: Using a frame or hoop keeps the canvas taut and makes stitching easier and more precise, particularly for detailed work.
- Patterns: Patterns can be printed on the canvas or followed from a chart, guiding the placement of each stitch and ensuring the design's accuracy.

## 3. Techniques and Tips

- Start with Small Projects: Begin with a small project to learn the basic stitches and get a feel for the craft, building confidence and skill before moving on to more complex designs.
- Use a Frame: A frame or hoop keeps your canvas taut and helps maintain even tension in your stitches, ensuring a smooth and professional-looking final piece.
- Follow the Grain: Always stitch in the same direction to maintain consistency and avoid distorting the canvas, which can affect the overall appearance of the design.
- Explore Different Stitches: Needlepoint isn't limited to just one stitch. Learn a variety of stitches, such as the tent stitch, basketweave stitch, and cross stitch, to add texture, depth, and complexity to your work.

# January 23: Origami

## 1. The Elegance of Origami

Origami is the Japanese art of paper folding, where a single sheet of paper is transformed into a detailed sculpture through a series of folds. This ancient art form is both simple and complex, depending on the design, and can range from basic shapes to intricate, life-like models. Origami is a meditative and creative practice that requires patience and precision, making it a rewarding hobby for those who enjoy detailed work.

## 2. Tools and Materials

- Origami Paper: Specially designed origami paper is thin, strong, and comes in various colors and patterns. However, any square sheet of paper can be used for basic models.
- Bone Folder: A tool used to create crisp, precise folds, enhancing the quality and appearance of your origami.
- Tweezers: Useful for making small, delicate folds, particularly in more complex models that require precision.
- Diagrams or Instructions: Follow diagrams or video tutorials to learn new folds and models, ensuring accuracy and helping you understand the sequence of steps.

## 3. Techniques and Tips

- Start with Simple Models: Begin with basic models like cranes, flowers, or boats to learn the foundational folds and build your confidence before attempting more complex designs.
- Focus on Precision: Accurate, precise folds are crucial in origami. Take your time to ensure each fold is sharp and exact, which will improve the overall appearance of your model.
- Practice Patience: Some origami models can be complex and require many steps. Be patient and take breaks if needed to avoid frustration and ensure quality work.
- Explore Modular Origami: Once you've mastered single-sheet models, try modular origami, where multiple pieces are folded and assembled into complex structures, offering a new level of challenge and creativity.

# *January 24: Painting*

## 1. The Freedom of Painting

Painting is one of the most expressive and versatile forms of visual art. Whether you're using oils, acrylics, watercolors, or gouache, painting allows you to explore color, texture, and composition in limitless ways. From abstract works to realistic portraits, this hobby offers endless possibilities for creativity and personal expression.

## 2. Tools and Materials

- Brushes: Different brushes create different effects. Round brushes are versatile, while flat brushes are great for bold strokes. Fan brushes can create textures, and detail brushes are for fine lines and intricate work.
- Paints: Choose from oils, acrylics, watercolors, or gouache, depending on your preferred style and medium. Each type of paint offers unique qualities in terms of texture, drying time, and finish.
- Canvas or Paper: Canvas is popular for oil and acrylic painting, while watercolor paper is necessary for watercolors to achieve the desired effects and durability.
- Palette and Palette Knives: A palette is used to mix paints, and palette knives help in applying thick, textured layers or for mixing colors.
- Easel: An easel provides a stable surface for your canvas, allowing for comfortable painting at various angles and in different environments.

## 3. Techniques and Tips

- Experiment with Techniques: Try different painting techniques such as glazing, impasto, dry brushing, or washes to find what suits your style and preferences.
- Study Color Theory: Understanding color relationships can help you create harmonious and dynamic compositions, enhancing the impact of your artwork.
- Practice Drawing: Strong drawing skills can enhance your painting by improving your understanding of form, perspective, and proportion.
- Work in Layers: Building your painting in layers can add depth, richness, and complexity to your work, allowing you to develop your ideas gradually and make adjustments as needed.

# *January 25: Quilting*

## 1. The Tradition of Quilting

Quilting is the craft of stitching together layers of fabric to create a quilt, which can be used as a blanket, wall hanging, or decorative item. This hobby blends creativity with practicality, allowing you to design intricate patterns and create heirloom-quality pieces. Quilting has a rich history and continues to be a beloved craft for its warmth, comfort, and artistic potential.

## 2. Tools and Materials

- Fabric: Choose fabrics in a variety of colors, patterns, and textures. Cotton is commonly used for quilting due to its durability and ease of use.
- Batting: The middle layer of a quilt, providing warmth, thickness, and the desired texture and weight for the finished piece.
- Needles and Thread: Strong needles and thread are essential for stitching through multiple layers of fabric, ensuring durability and longevity of the quilt.
- Rotary Cutter and Mat: A rotary cutter is used to cut fabric precisely, while a self-healing mat protects your work surface and ensures accurate cutting.
- Quilt Patterns: Patterns provide step-by-step instructions and measurements for cutting and assembling your quilt, guiding you through the design and construction process.

## 3. Techniques and Tips

- Start with a Simple Pattern: Beginner quilters should start with a simple pattern, such as a nine-patch or log cabin, to learn the basic techniques and build confidence.
- Cut Accurately: Precise cutting is crucial for ensuring that your quilt pieces fit together correctly and create a smooth, professional finish.
- Press as You Go: Iron each seam flat as you sew to keep your quilt top smooth and professional-looking, reducing bulk and ensuring accurate seams.
- Practice Patience: Quilting can be time-consuming, but the end result is worth the effort. Take your time to ensure each step is done correctly, and enjoy the process of creating something beautiful and meaningful.

# *January 26: Repurposing*

## 1. The Creativity of Repurposing

Repurposing, or upcycling, is the process of transforming old or discarded items into something new and functional. This eco-friendly hobby encourages creativity and resourcefulness, allowing you to give new life to items that might otherwise be thrown away. Whether it's turning an old ladder into a bookshelf or using wine corks to create a bulletin board, repurposing is both practical and artistic.

## 2. Tools and Materials

- Salvaged Items: Old furniture, jars, fabric scraps, and other discarded items can all be repurposed, offering endless creative possibilities and reducing waste.
- Tools: Depending on your project, you may need basic tools like hammers, screwdrivers, saws, and drills, as well as more specialized tools for certain materials.
- Paint and Finishes: Use paint, stain, or varnish to refresh and protect repurposed items, giving them a new look and extending their life.
- Adhesives: Strong adhesives like wood glue, epoxy, or hot glue are often needed for assembly, ensuring durability and stability.
- Embellishments: Decorate your repurposed items with stencils, decals, fabric, or other materials to add a personal touch and enhance their visual appeal.

## 3. Techniques and Tips

- Start with Simple Projects: If you're new to repurposing, start with small, manageable projects that don't require advanced skills or tools, allowing you to build confidence and learn the basics.
- Think Outside the Box: Look at items for their potential, not just their current use. A little creativity can transform almost anything into something new and useful, offering unique solutions and artistic expression.
- Plan Your Project: Before you start, plan out your project, including the materials and tools you'll need, the steps involved, and any challenges you might encounter.
- Focus on Functionality: While aesthetics are important, ensure your repurposed item is functional, durable, and safe to use, balancing beauty with practicality.

# *January 27: Scrapbooking*

## 1. The Personal Touch of Scrapbooking

Scrapbooking is the art of preserving memories by creatively arranging photos, mementos, and decorative elements in an album. This hobby blends storytelling with visual design, allowing you to create personalized keepsakes that capture special moments. Scrapbooking is a wonderful way to document your journey and express creativity.

## 2. Tools and Materials

- Scrapbook Album: Choose an album with acid-free pages to preserve your memories and keep them vibrant over time.
- Photos and Mementos: Collect photos, ticket stubs, postcards, and other items that hold personal significance and tell your story.
- Decorative Paper: Use patterned or textured paper to create backgrounds, borders, and accents, adding depth and interest to your pages.
- Adhesives: Acid-free adhesives like glue dots or double-sided tape ensure your photos and papers stay in place without damage.
- Embellishments: Stickers, ribbons, buttons, and stamps add decorative touches to personalize your scrapbook.
- Journaling Pens: Use archival-quality pens to add captions, dates, and notes, providing context and narrative to your visual memories.

## 3. Techniques and Tips

- Plan Your Layouts: Before adhering anything, plan your layouts to ensure everything fits and looks balanced, allowing for adjustments before committing to the design.
- Tell a Story: Use your photos and mementos to tell a story, adding captions and notes to provide context and meaning.
- Mix and Match Materials: Combine different papers, textures, and embellishments to create visually interesting pages that reflect your personal style.
- Keep it Personal: Let your scrapbook reflect your style and creativity. Don't hesitate to experiment, making it uniquely yours and creating a meaningful keepsake.

# *January 28: Stained Glass*

## 1. The Beauty of Stained Glass

Stained glass is an art form that involves creating designs with pieces of colored glass held together by lead strips or copper foil. This craft has been used for centuries to create stunning windows, lamps, and decorative panels. The interplay of light and color in stained glass makes it a unique and captivating medium, offering endless possibilities for creativity and artistic expression.

## 2. Tools and Materials

- Glass Cutter: A glass cutter is used to score and cut glass into desired shapes, ensuring precise and clean edges.
- Lead Came or Copper Foil: Lead came or copper foil is used to join the glass pieces together, forming the structure of the stained glass piece.
- Soldering Iron: A soldering iron is used to bond the lead or copper joints, securing the glass pieces in place and creating a sturdy, durable finished product.
- Flux: Flux is applied to the joints before soldering to ensure a strong bond and clean, professional-looking seams.
- Safety Gear: Safety glasses, gloves, and a mask protect you from glass shards, fumes, and other hazards associated with stained glass work.

## 3. Techniques and Tips

- Start with a Simple Design: Begin with a simple pattern to learn the basic techniques of cutting, fitting, and joining glass, building your skills gradually.
- Cut Glass Carefully: Use a steady hand and even pressure when cutting glass to achieve clean, precise cuts that fit together seamlessly.
- Use a Grinder: A glass grinder smooths the edges of your glass pieces, ensuring they fit together perfectly and reducing the risk of sharp edges.
- Solder with Care: Take your time when soldering to ensure strong, clean joints without excess solder, creating a polished, professional finish.

# *January 29: Tapestry Weaving*

## 1. The Craft of Tapestry Weaving

Tapestry weaving is a form of textile art where threads are woven on a loom to create decorative wall hangings or fabric pieces. This craft allows you to explore color, texture, and pattern in a highly tactile way. Tapestry weaving can be simple or complex, making it a versatile hobby that can grow with your skill level, offering endless creative possibilities.

## 2. Tools and Materials

- Loom: A loom holds your warp threads in place while you weave, providing the structure for your tapestry and allowing you to create even, consistent weaves.
- Yarn: Use different types of yarn to create various textures, patterns, and color combinations in your tapestry, enhancing its visual and tactile appeal.
- Weaving Needles: Long needles help guide the yarn through the warp threads, making it easier to create precise, detailed patterns.
- Shuttle: A shuttle is used to carry the weft yarn across the warp threads, speeding up the weaving process and ensuring even, consistent tension.
- Comb or Beater: Used to push down the weft yarn and keep your weaving tight and even, ensuring a smooth, professional-looking finished product.

## 3. Techniques and Tips

- Start with a Small Loom: A small frame loom is perfect for beginners, allowing you to focus on learning the basic techniques before progressing to larger projects.
- Experiment with Texture: Use different yarn thicknesses, materials, and weaving techniques to add texture, depth, and visual interest to your tapestry.
- Learn Basic Weaving Techniques: Start with plain weave and experiment with more advanced techniques like soumak, rya knots, and twill to expand your creative options.
- Plan Your Design: Before starting, sketch out your design or create a color plan to ensure you have the right materials and understand the sequence of your weaving, making the process smoother and more enjoyable.

# *January 30: Upcycling*

## 1. The Creativity of Upcycling

Upcycling is the process of transforming discarded or unused items into something of higher value or quality. This eco-friendly hobby fosters creativity and sustainability, allowing you to reduce waste while creating unique, functional items. Upcycling projects can range from simple tasks like decorating old jars to more complex endeavors like converting pallets into furniture, offering endless opportunities for artistic expression and practical solutions.

## 2. Tools and Materials

- Discarded Items: Repurpose items like furniture, clothing, or containers found around your home for your upcycling projects.
- Tools: Depending on the project, you may need basic tools like saws, hammers, sanders, or sewing machines, and occasionally more specialized tools.
- Paint and Finishes: Refresh upcycled items with paint, stain, or varnish to enhance their appearance and extend their life.
- Adhesives: Use strong adhesives like wood glue, epoxy, or fabric glue to ensure durability and stability in your creations.
- Embellishments: Decorate your upcycled items with stencils, decals, or fabric to add a personal touch and enhance visual appeal.

## 3. Techniques and Tips

- Start with Simple Projects: If you're new to upcycling, begin with small, manageable projects that don't require advanced skills or tools. This will help you build confidence and master the basics.
- Think Creatively: Look at items with a fresh perspective and think about how they can be transformed into something new and useful, offering unique solutions and artistic expression.
- Plan Your Project: Before starting, plan your project carefully, including the materials and tools you'll need, the steps involved, and any potential challenges. This ensures a smooth and successful process.
- Focus on Quality: While creativity is key, make sure your finished product is durable, functional, and safe to use, balancing beauty with practicality and sustainability.

# *January 31: Wood Carving*

## 1. The Skill of Wood Carving

Wood carving is the art of shaping wood into decorative or functional objects using various tools. This craft requires patience, precision, and a keen eye for detail, but the results can be incredibly rewarding. From simple whittling to intricate relief carvings, wood carving allows you to transform a raw piece of wood into a work of art, offering endless possibilities for creativity and craftsmanship.

## 2. Tools and Materials

- Carving Knives: A basic set of carving knives is essential for most wood carving projects, providing the control and precision needed for detailed work.
- Gouges and Chisels: These tools are used for removing larger amounts of wood and shaping your piece, allowing for more complex and varied designs.
- Mallet: Used to strike chisels and gouges, providing the force needed to carve harder woods and achieve deeper cuts.
- Wood: Choose a wood that suits your project. Softwoods like basswood are easier to carve, while hardwoods like oak provide more durability and a different carving experience.
- Sandpaper and Finishes: Smooth your finished piece with sandpaper and protect it with oil, varnish, or wax, enhancing its appearance and longevity.

## 3. Techniques and Tips

- Start with Softwood: Softwoods like basswood or pine are easier to carve and great for beginners, allowing you to learn the basics without excessive difficulty.
- Practice Basic Cuts: Learn basic cuts like the push cut, stop cut, and V-cut to build your skills and confidence, preparing you for more advanced techniques.
- Use Sharp Tools: Keep your carving tools sharp to make cleaner cuts and reduce the risk of injury, ensuring a smooth and enjoyable carving experience.
- Plan Your Design: Sketch your design on the wood before you start carving to guide your work and avoid mistakes, making the process smoother and more efficient.

## *Conclusion for January*

As you reach the end of January, you've explored a diverse array of arts and crafts, each offering its own unique challenges and rewards. From the precision of airbrushing to the meditative practice of wood carving, these hobbies have allowed you to express your creativity, develop new skills, and discover the joy of making. Whether you've found a new passion or simply enjoyed the process, the arts and crafts you've tried this month have laid the foundation for a year filled with creativity and personal growth. Keep experimenting, keep creating, and most importantly, keep enjoying the art of making as you continue your journey through the year.

# February: Building and DIY

*February is all about Building and DIY, focusing on hands-on projects that combine creativity, practicality, and technical skill. Whether you're repairing an appliance, crafting a piece of furniture, or engaging in intricate blacksmithing, this month is dedicated to the satisfaction that comes from building something with your own hands. Each day offers a new opportunity to learn, create, and enhance your living space or skill set.*

# *February 1: Appliance Repair*

## 1. The Practicality of Appliance Repair

Appliance repair is a valuable skill that allows you to fix household appliances like refrigerators, washing machines, and dishwashers, saving money and reducing waste. Understanding the basics of appliance repair can also prevent the need for costly professional services and extend the life of your appliances.

## 2. Tools and Materials

- Screwdrivers: A variety of screwdrivers, including Phillips and flathead, are essential for accessing appliance components.
- Multimeter: Used to test electrical circuits and ensure proper function.
- Wrenches and Pliers: Useful for loosening and tightening bolts and screws.
- Replacement Parts: Keep common replacement parts like belts, hoses, and fuses on hand.
- User Manuals: User manuals often contain troubleshooting tips and diagrams to guide repairs.

## 3. Techniques and Tips

- Diagnose the Problem: Before disassembling, use your senses—sight, sound, and smell—to identify potential issues.
- Safety First: Always unplug appliances and discharge capacitors before beginning any repair.
- Keep Parts Organized: Use small containers or trays to keep screws and parts organized during disassembly.
- Follow the Manual: Refer to the user manual for specific repair instructions and part numbers.

# *February 2: Blacksmithing*

## 1. The Art of Blacksmithing

Blacksmithing is the ancient craft of shaping metal using heat, hammer, and anvil. This skill is both an art and a science, requiring knowledge of metal properties and a steady hand. From simple hooks to intricate wrought iron gates, blacksmithing offers endless opportunities for creativity and craftsmanship.

## 2. Tools and Materials

- Forge: A forge heats metal until it is malleable. Coal, gas, or electric forges are commonly used.
- Anvil: The anvil provides a surface for hammering and shaping the heated metal.
- Hammer: Blacksmithing hammers come in various shapes and weights for different tasks.
- Tongs: Tongs are used to hold and manipulate hot metal.
- Protective Gear: Safety glasses, gloves, and aprons protect against heat, sparks, and sharp metal edges.

## 3. Techniques and Tips

- Start with Simple Projects: Begin with basic items like hooks or simple tools to learn the fundamental techniques.
- Control the Heat: Proper control of the forge's heat is crucial for successful blacksmithing. Too hot, and the metal may burn; too cool, and it won't shape easily.
- Master Basic Techniques: Focus on mastering drawing out (thinning metal), upsetting (thickening metal), and bending.
- Practice Patience: Blacksmithing is a time-consuming craft that requires patience and precision.

# *February 3: Bricklaying*

## 1. The Foundations of Bricklaying

Bricklaying is the craft of constructing walls, pathways, and other structures using bricks and mortar. This skill is fundamental in construction and DIY projects, allowing you to create durable, long-lasting structures. Whether building a garden wall or a barbecue pit, bricklaying combines precision, strength, and aesthetic appeal.

## 2. Tools and Materials

- Trowel: A trowel is used to spread mortar and shape it between bricks.
- Brick Hammer: Used to cut and shape bricks as needed.
- Level: Ensures that each layer of bricks is level and plumb.
- Mortar Mix: The mixture that binds bricks together. It typically consists of cement, sand, and water.
- Brick Jointers: Used to smooth and shape the mortar joints between bricks.

## 3. Techniques and Tips

- Start with a Solid Foundation: Ensure the base of your structure is level and solid to prevent future shifting or cracking.
- Mix Mortar Properly: Follow the manufacturer's instructions for mixing mortar to achieve the correct consistency.
- Use a String Line: A string line helps keep your bricks straight and level as you build.
- Clean as You Go: Wipe away excess mortar from the bricks before it dries to keep your work neat and professional-looking.

# *February 4: Cabinet Making*

## 1. The Precision of Cabinet Making

Cabinet making is a woodworking craft focused on creating cabinets, furniture, and other storage solutions. This skill requires precision, attention to detail, and a good understanding of wood properties. Whether you're building kitchen cabinets or a custom bookshelf, cabinet making combines functionality with aesthetics.

## 2. Tools and Materials

- Table Saw: Essential for cutting large pieces of wood accurately.
- Router: Used for shaping edges, cutting grooves, and adding decorative details.
- Clamps: Keep your pieces securely in place while gluing or assembling.
- Wood: Choose high-quality hardwoods or plywood depending on your project.
- Finishing Supplies: Stain, varnish, and paint are used to protect and enhance the appearance of your cabinets.

## 3. Techniques and Tips

- Measure Twice, Cut Once: Precision is key in cabinet making. Double-check your measurements before cutting.
- Plan Your Design: Sketch your design and make a cut list before starting to ensure all pieces fit together correctly.
- Use Jigs: Jigs help ensure consistent cuts and drilling, especially when making multiple identical pieces.
- Focus on Joinery: Strong joints are crucial for durable cabinets. Learn techniques like dovetail, mortise and tenon, and biscuit joints.

# *February 5: Carpentry*

## 1. The Craft of Carpentry

Carpentry involves constructing and repairing wooden structures, furniture, and other items. This versatile skill is fundamental to many DIY projects and home improvements. Whether building a deck, framing a house, or crafting custom furniture, carpentry combines technical knowledge with creative problem-solving.

## 2. Tools and Materials

- Saw: A handsaw or circular saw is essential for cutting wood to size.
- Hammer: Used for driving nails and assembling structures.
- Measuring Tape: Accurate measurements are critical in carpentry to ensure pieces fit together properly.
- Wood: Choose the right type of wood for your project, considering factors like strength, durability, and appearance.
- Fasteners: Nails, screws, and bolts are used to join pieces of wood together.

## 3. Techniques and Tips

- Master Basic Cuts: Learn to make straight, miter, and bevel cuts accurately with your saw.
- Understand Wood Grain: The direction of the wood grain affects how you cut and assemble pieces. Work with the grain for stronger, cleaner cuts.
- Use a Carpenter's Square: A square ensures your cuts and assemblies are at the correct angles.
- Practice Joinery: Learn different joinery techniques, such as butt joints, lap joints, and dovetail joints, to create strong, durable connections.

# *February 6: Dollhouse Making*

## 1. The Creativity of Dollhouse Making

Dollhouse making involves constructing miniature houses and furniture, often replicating historical styles or creating whimsical designs. This hobby combines carpentry, interior design, and model-making skills, offering endless creative possibilities. Whether building a Victorian mansion or a modern loft, dollhouse making is a rewarding and detailed-oriented craft.

## 2. Tools and Materials

- Miniature Lumber: Small-scale wood pieces are used to construct the dollhouse frame and furniture.
- Glue: Strong adhesives like wood glue or tacky glue are essential for assembling miniature pieces.
- Paint and Finishes: Use paint, wallpaper, and varnish to decorate and protect your dollhouse.
- Furniture Kits: Ready-made kits or plans help you create detailed, realistic miniature furniture.
- Miniature Accessories: Add finishing touches with tiny lamps, rugs, and other accessories.

## 3. Techniques and Tips

- Start with a Kit: Beginner kits provide pre-cut pieces and instructions, making it easier to learn the basics of dollhouse construction.
- Pay Attention to Scale: Ensure all components are scaled correctly for a realistic look.
- Customize Your Design: Once comfortable with the basics, try customizing your dollhouse with unique designs, layouts, and furniture.
- Take Your Time: Dollhouse making requires patience and precision. Take your time to ensure each piece is carefully crafted and assembled.

# *February 7: Electronics Repair*

## 1. The Precision of Electronics Repair

Electronics repair involves troubleshooting and fixing electronic devices like smartphones, computers, and household gadgets. This skill is valuable in a world increasingly reliant on technology, allowing you to save money and reduce electronic waste by repairing rather than replacing devices.

## 2. Tools and Materials

- Screwdrivers: Precision screwdrivers are necessary for opening and repairing small electronic devices.
- Soldering Iron: Used to repair or replace small components on circuit boards.
- Multimeter: Measures electrical voltage, current, and resistance, helping diagnose issues.
- Replacement Parts: Keep common components like resistors, capacitors, and connectors on hand.
- Anti-Static Tools: Wrist straps and mats prevent static electricity from damaging sensitive electronic components.

## 3. Techniques and Tips

- Learn Basic Electronics: Understanding basic electronic principles and components is crucial for effective repairs.
- Diagnose Before Disassembling: Use your multimeter and visual inspection to diagnose problems before opening the device.
- Practice Soldering: Good soldering skills are essential for repairing circuit boards and small components.
- Work in a Clean Environment: Dust and debris can interfere with electronics repair. Keep your workspace clean and organized.

# *February 8: Furniture Restoration*

## 1. The Art of Furniture Restoration

Furniture restoration involves repairing and refinishing old or damaged furniture to restore its original beauty and functionality. This craft requires a mix of woodworking, upholstery, and finishing skills, allowing you to preserve valuable antiques or give new life to worn-out pieces. Furniture restoration is both a sustainable practice and a creative challenge.

## 2. Tools and Materials

- Sandpaper and Scrapers: Used to remove old finishes and prepare the wood for refinishing.
- Wood Glue and Clamps: Essential for repairing loose joints and broken pieces.
- Stain and Varnish: Stains bring out the wood's natural color, while varnish protects the surface.
- Upholstery Tools: If restoring upholstered furniture, you'll need tools like staple guns, fabric, and padding.
- Wood Filler: Used to repair small cracks and holes in the wood.

## 3. Techniques and Tips

- Start with a Thorough Cleaning: Before beginning any repairs, clean the furniture thoroughly to remove dirt and grime.
- Remove Old Finish Carefully: Use sandpaper or chemical strippers to remove old finishes, taking care not to damage the wood.
- Repair Before Refinishing: Fix any structural issues before applying new stain or varnish.
- Match the Original Style: When possible, try to match the original finish and style of the piece to preserve its authenticity.

# *February 9: Gardening*

## 1. The Joy of Gardening

Gardening is the practice of growing and cultivating plants, whether for food, beauty, or enjoyment. This hobby can range from maintaining a small herb garden to cultivating a large vegetable patch or ornamental garden. Gardening provides physical exercise, mental relaxation, and the satisfaction of nurturing life.

## 2. Tools and Materials

- Trowel and Spade: Essential for digging, planting, and transplanting.
- Pruning Shears: Used to trim plants and remove dead or overgrown branches.
- Watering Can or Hose: Watering is crucial for maintaining healthy plants.
- Soil and Fertilizer: Choose the right soil and fertilizers for your plants to ensure they receive the nutrients they need.
- Seeds and Plants: Select plants suited to your climate and gardening goals.

## 3. Techniques and Tips

- Start with Easy Plants: Begin with hardy, low-maintenance plants like herbs or succulents if you're new to gardening.
- Understand Your Soil: Test your soil's pH and nutrient levels to choose the best plants for your garden.
- Water Wisely: Overwatering can be just as harmful as underwatering. Learn the specific needs of your plants.
- Practice Crop Rotation: In vegetable gardening, rotating crops helps prevent soil depletion and reduces the risk of pests and diseases.

# *February 10: Home Brewing*

## 1. The Craft of Home Brewing

Home brewing is the process of making beer, wine, or other alcoholic beverages at home. This hobby combines chemistry, cooking, and creativity, allowing you to experiment with flavors and techniques to create your own unique brews. Whether brewing a simple ale or crafting a complex stout, home brewing is both a science and an art.

## 2. Tools and Materials

- Brewing Kit: A basic kit includes a fermenter, airlock, siphon, and bottles.
- Ingredients: Water, malt, hops, and yeast are the basic ingredients for beer. For wine, you'll need fruit, sugar, and yeast.
- Sanitizers: Keeping your equipment clean and sanitized is crucial to prevent contamination.
- Hydrometer: Measures the alcohol content of your brew by testing its specific gravity.
- Bottles and Caps: Store your finished brew in bottles, using a capper to seal them.

## 3. Techniques and Tips

- Start with a Kit: Beginner kits simplify the brewing process, making it easier to learn the basics.
- Sanitize Everything: Proper sanitation prevents unwanted bacteria and wild yeast from spoiling your brew.
- Control Fermentation Temperature: The temperature during fermentation affects the flavor and quality of your brew. Follow the recommended range for your yeast.
- Experiment with Flavors: Once you've mastered basic brewing, try adding different fruits, spices, or hops to create unique flavors.

# *February 11: Interior Design*

## 1. The Art of Interior Design

Interior design is the practice of enhancing the interior of a space to create a more aesthetically pleasing and functional environment. This hobby combines creativity with practicality, allowing you to design and arrange rooms in ways that reflect your personal style while optimizing space and function.

## 2. Tools and Materials

- Measuring Tape: Accurate measurements are essential for planning furniture layout and ensuring everything fits.
- Mood Board: Use a mood board to collect ideas, colors, and materials that inspire your design.
- Paint and Wallpaper: Choose colors and patterns that reflect your style and enhance the space.
- Furniture and Accessories: Select furniture that complements the space and adds functionality.
- Lighting: Proper lighting can transform a room. Consider ambient, task, and accent lighting in your design.

## 3. Techniques and Tips

- Start with a Plan: Measure your space and create a floor plan before purchasing furniture or making changes.
- Consider Functionality: Ensure your design is not only beautiful but also functional for the room's intended use.
- Use Color Wisely: Color can affect the mood and perception of space. Use lighter colors to make a room feel larger and darker tones for coziness.
- Mix Textures and Patterns: Combining different textures and patterns adds depth and interest to your design.

# *February 12: Jewelry Repair*

## 1. The Precision of Jewelry Repair

Jewelry repair involves fixing broken or damaged jewelry pieces, from restringing beads to soldering broken chains. This skill is valuable for preserving sentimental items or maintaining the beauty and function of your jewelry collection. Jewelry repair requires a steady hand, attention to detail, and knowledge of various materials and techniques.

## 2. Tools and Materials

- Pliers: Round-nose, flat-nose, and chain-nose pliers are essential for most jewelry repairs.
- Soldering Kit: Used for repairing broken metal pieces.
- Jewelry Glue: Strong adhesives for reattaching stones or other components.
- Beading Thread and Needles: For restringing beaded necklaces or bracelets.
- Magnifying Glass: Helps you see small details clearly while working.

## 3. Techniques and Tips

- Start with Simple Repairs: Begin with easy fixes like replacing jump rings or reattaching clasps.
- Use the Right Tools: Invest in quality tools that are specifically designed for jewelry repair.
- Practice Soldering: Soldering is a common repair technique that requires practice to master.
- Be Patient: Jewelry repair is delicate work that requires patience and precision.

# *February 13: Kite Making*

## 1. The Joy of Kite Making

Kite making is a creative and fun craft that involves designing, constructing, and flying your own kites. This hobby combines elements of art, engineering, and outdoor activity, making it enjoyable for people of all ages. Whether creating a simple diamond kite or an elaborate box kite, the process of making and flying a kite is both rewarding and exhilarating.

## 2. Tools and Materials

- Frame Materials: Bamboo, dowels, or lightweight plastic rods are used to create the kite frame.
- Sail Material: Use lightweight materials like paper, plastic, or fabric for the kite's sail.
- String: Strong, lightweight string or kite line is essential for flying your kite.
- Glue and Tape: Used to assemble the kite and attach the sail to the frame.
- Tail: Add a tail made of ribbon or fabric strips to help stabilize the kite.

## 3. Techniques and Tips

- Start with a Simple Design: Begin with a basic kite shape like a diamond or triangle to learn the construction process.
- Balance the Kite: Ensure your kite is balanced by placing the frame and sail correctly. An unbalanced kite won't fly well.
- Choose the Right Day: Wind conditions greatly affect kite flying. Choose a day with steady, moderate wind for the best results.
- Experiment with Designs: Once you're comfortable with the basics, try creating kites with different shapes, sizes, and decorations.

# *February 14: Lamp Making*

## 1. The Craft of Lamp Making

Lamp making involves creating custom lamps by assembling parts, wiring, and adding decorative elements. This hobby combines creativity with practical skills, allowing you to design unique lighting solutions for your home. Whether repurposing an old item into a lamp or building one from scratch, lamp making is both functional and artistic.

## 2. Tools and Materials

- Lamp Kit: Includes the necessary electrical components like the socket, cord, and switch.
- Lamp Base: Choose or create a base for your lamp, such as a vase, piece of wood, or metal object.
- Lampshade: Select or make a lampshade that complements your design.
- Drill and Bits: Used for creating holes in the base to run the wiring.
- Glue and Adhesives: Used to secure parts and add decorative elements.

## 3. Techniques and Tips

- Start with a Kit: Lamp kits simplify the wiring process and provide all the necessary components.
- Safety First: Always follow safety guidelines when working with electrical components.
- Get Creative with the Base: Almost any object can be turned into a lamp base with the right modifications.
- Experiment with Lampshades: Customize your lampshade with paint, fabric, or other decorations to match your style.

# *February 15: Metalworking*

## 1. The Precision of Metalworking

Metalworking involves shaping and joining metals to create functional or decorative objects. This craft encompasses a variety of techniques, including welding, forging, and machining. Metalworking is both a technical and artistic skill, allowing you to create everything from custom tools to intricate sculptures.

## 2. Tools and Materials

- Welder: Used to join metal pieces together by melting the edges and fusing them.
- Anvil and Hammer: Essential for forging and shaping metal.
- Cutting Tools: Angle grinders, saws, and shears are used to cut metal to size.
- Safety Gear: Protect yourself with gloves, goggles, and a welding helmet.
- Metal Stock: Choose metal types and sizes based on your project, such as steel, aluminum, or copper.

## 3. Techniques and Tips

- Start with Simple Projects: Begin with basic metalworking techniques like cutting and joining before moving on to more complex tasks.
- Learn to Weld: Welding is a fundamental metalworking skill that allows you to join metal pieces securely.
- Understand Metal Properties: Different metals have different properties, such as strength and flexibility. Choose the right metal for your project.
- Practice Safety: Metalworking can be dangerous if proper safety precautions aren't followed. Always wear protective gear and work in a well-ventilated area.

# *February 16: Needle Felting*

## 1. The Art of Needle Felting

Needle felting is a craft that involves using a barbed needle to interlock wool fibers, creating solid, sculpted shapes. This hobby is perfect for making small sculptures, toys, or decorative items. Needle felting is easy to learn and offers endless possibilities for creativity.

## 2. Tools and Materials

- Wool Roving: The primary material for needle felting, available in a variety of colors.
- Felting Needles: Barbed needles that catch and interlock wool fibers as you stab them into shape.
- Foam Pad: A soft surface to work on, protecting both your needles and your work surface.
- Armature Wire: Used to create a skeleton for larger or more complex sculptures.

## 3. Techniques and Tips

- Start with Simple Shapes: Begin by felting basic shapes like balls or cylinders to learn the technique.
- Layer Colors: Add different colors of wool in layers to create detailed and colorful sculptures.
- Use a Light Touch: Felting is a gradual process. Use light, repeated stabbing motions to shape your wool.
- Experiment with Details: Once you've mastered the basics, try adding intricate details like facial features or patterns to your projects.

## *February 17: Organization*

### 1. The Power of Organization

Organization is the process of arranging and managing your space and belongings to create a more efficient and stress-free environment. This skill is valuable in both personal and professional settings, helping you to stay on top of tasks, reduce clutter, and improve productivity.

### 2. Tools and Materials

- Storage Bins: Use bins and boxes to group similar items and keep them together.
- Shelving: Shelves help maximize vertical space and keep items off the floor.
- Labels: Labeling boxes, bins, and shelves makes it easy to find and return items to their proper places.
- Drawer Dividers: Dividers keep small items organized and prevent clutter in drawers.
- Decluttering Guides: Books or online resources can provide tips and strategies for decluttering and organizing your space.

### 3. Techniques and Tips

- Start Small: Begin with a single drawer or closet to avoid feeling overwhelmed.
- Declutter First: Remove items you no longer need or use before organizing what remains.
- Group Similar Items: Organize by category, such as office supplies, kitchen tools, or clothing.
- Create a System: Establish a system for maintaining organization, such as regularly scheduled decluttering sessions or assigning a place for everything.

# *February 18: Plumbing*

## 1. The Practicality of Plumbing

Plumbing involves the installation and repair of pipes, fixtures, and other systems that carry water and gas in a building. This skill is essential for maintaining a functional home, allowing you to handle minor repairs and installations yourself. Basic plumbing knowledge can save you time and money by reducing the need for professional services.

## 2. Tools and Materials

- Pipe Wrenches: Essential for gripping and turning pipes during installation or repair.
- Plunger: Used to clear clogs in toilets and drains.
- Pipe Cutter: A tool for cutting pipes to size.
- Teflon Tape: Used to seal threaded pipe joints and prevent leaks.
- Pipe Fittings: Connectors, elbows, and other fittings are used to join pipes together.

## 3. Techniques and Tips

- Learn the Basics: Understand the fundamentals of plumbing, including how water and waste systems work in your home.
- Know When to Shut Off the Water: Always turn off the water supply before starting any plumbing work.
- Use Teflon Tape: Wrap Teflon tape around threaded joints to create a watertight seal.
- Keep a Plunger Handy: A plunger is a simple but effective tool for clearing clogs in toilets and drains.

# *February 19: Recycling Projects*

## 1. The Creativity of Recycling Projects

Recycling projects involve repurposing and transforming waste materials into new, functional items. This eco-friendly hobby encourages creativity and resourcefulness, allowing you to reduce waste while creating unique, handmade products. From turning old magazines into coasters to building furniture from pallets, recycling projects are both sustainable and satisfying.

## 2. Tools and Materials

- Recyclable Materials: Collect items like plastic bottles, glass jars, newspapers, and cardboard for your projects.
- Cutting Tools: Scissors, utility knives, and saws are often needed to reshape materials.
- Glue and Adhesives: Strong adhesives are essential for assembling your projects.
- Paint and Finishes: Use paint, varnish, or other finishes to protect and beautify your recycled creations.
- Embellishments: Add decorative touches like fabric, beads, or buttons to personalize your projects.

## 3. Techniques and Tips

- Start with Simple Projects: Begin with easy projects like making paper beads or upcycling jars into planters.
- Think Creatively: Look at waste materials with a fresh perspective, considering how they can be transformed into something useful.
- Plan Ahead: Gather all the materials and tools you'll need before starting your project.
- Focus on Functionality: Ensure your finished project is both practical and durable.

# *February 20: Soap Making*

## 1. The Craft of Soap Making

Soap making is the process of creating homemade soap using natural ingredients like oils, lye, and fragrances. This hobby allows you to customize your soap with different scents, colors, and textures, creating a product that's both functional and luxurious. Soap making is a rewarding and creative process that results in high-quality, personalized products.

## 2. Tools and Materials

- Soap Base: Choose from melt-and-pour bases or make your own using oils and lye.
- Molds: Use silicone molds to shape your soap into various designs.
- Fragrance Oils: Add scents to your soap using essential oils or fragrance oils.
- Colorants: Use natural or synthetic colorants to add color to your soap.
- Safety Gear: Protect yourself with gloves, goggles, and long sleeves when handling lye.

## 3. Techniques and Tips

- Start with Melt-and-Pour: If you're new to soap making, melt-and-pour bases are a simple way to get started.
- Measure Accurately: Precise measurements are crucial for successful soap making, especially when working with lye.
- Customize Your Soap: Experiment with different oils, fragrances, and additives like oatmeal or dried flowers.
- Allow for Curing Time: Cold process soap requires several weeks of curing time before it's ready to use.

# *February 21: Tile Laying*

## 1. The Precision of Tile Laying

Tile laying involves installing tiles on floors, walls, or countertops to create durable and attractive surfaces. This skill is valuable for home improvement projects, allowing you to enhance your space with materials like ceramic, porcelain, or natural stone. Proper tile laying requires precision, patience, and attention to detail.

## 2. Tools and Materials

- Tile Cutter: A tile cutter is used to cut tiles to the desired size and shape.
- Trowel: Used to spread adhesive evenly across the surface.
- Spacers: Spacers ensure consistent gaps between tiles for grout lines.
- Grout: Grout fills the spaces between tiles, sealing and protecting the installation.
- Level: A level ensures that your tiles are laid evenly and flat.

## 3. Techniques and Tips

- Prepare the Surface: Ensure the surface is clean, level, and dry before laying tiles.
- Plan Your Layout: Dry-fit your tiles to plan the layout and avoid awkward cuts or small pieces at the edges.
- Use Spacers: Consistent spacing between tiles is crucial for a professional-looking finish.
- Apply Grout Evenly: After the adhesive has set, apply grout evenly, filling all gaps between tiles.

# *February 22: Upholstery*

## 1. The Art of Upholstery

Upholstery involves covering furniture with fabric, padding, and springs to create a comfortable and visually appealing finish. This skill is useful for restoring old furniture, creating custom pieces, or simply updating the look of your home. Upholstery requires a mix of sewing, carpentry, and design skills, making it a rewarding and versatile hobby.

## 2. Tools and Materials

- Upholstery Fabric: Choose durable, high-quality fabric for your project.
- Staple Gun: Used to attach fabric to the furniture frame.
- Padding: Foam or batting is used to create a soft, comfortable surface.
- Upholstery Needles: Long, strong needles are needed for sewing through thick fabric and padding.
- Webbing and Springs: Provide support and structure to upholstered furniture.

## 3. Techniques and Tips

- Start with a Simple Project: Begin with a simple chair or ottoman to learn the basics of upholstery.
- Measure Accurately: Take precise measurements to ensure your fabric fits correctly with minimal waste.
- Use the Right Tools: Invest in quality tools, such as a staple gun and upholstery needles, for the best results.
- Pay Attention to Detail: Neat corners, smooth seams, and even padding are key to professional-looking upholstery.

# *February 23: Vegetable Gardening*

## 1. The Satisfaction of Vegetable Gardening

Vegetable gardening is the practice of growing your own vegetables, herbs, and fruits at home. This hobby is both practical and rewarding, providing fresh, healthy produce right from your backyard. Vegetable gardening also promotes sustainability, reduces grocery costs, and offers a deeper connection to nature.

## 2. Tools and Materials

- Garden Fork: Used for loosening soil and preparing planting beds.
- Trowel: Essential for planting seeds, seedlings, and transplants.
- Watering Can or Hose: Regular watering is crucial for healthy vegetable plants.
- Fertilizer: Organic or synthetic fertilizers provide the nutrients your plants need to thrive.
- Seeds and Plants: Choose vegetable varieties that suit your climate and gardening goals.

## 3. Techniques and Tips

- Start with Easy Crops: Begin with beginner-friendly vegetables like lettuce, tomatoes, or radishes.
- Prepare the Soil: Healthy soil is the foundation of a successful garden. Add compost or organic matter to improve fertility and drainage.
- Water Consistently: Vegetables need regular watering, especially during dry spells. Water deeply to encourage strong root growth.
- Practice Companion Planting: Some plants grow better together. Learn about companion planting to maximize space and improve yields.

# *February 24: Wallpapering*

## 1. The Craft of Wallpapering

Wallpapering involves applying decorative paper to walls to enhance a room's aesthetic. This skill is a popular choice for home improvement projects, allowing you to transform a space with patterns, textures, and colors. Proper wallpapering requires careful preparation and attention to detail for a smooth, professional finish.

## 2. Tools and Materials

- Wallpaper Paste: Adhesive used to attach the wallpaper to the wall.
- Wallpaper Brush: Used to apply paste and smooth the wallpaper.
- Utility Knife: A sharp knife is essential for trimming wallpaper to fit.
- Measuring Tape: Accurate measurements ensure your wallpaper fits correctly without wasting material.
- Smoothing Tool: Helps remove air bubbles and ensure the wallpaper adheres evenly.

## 3. Techniques and Tips

- Prepare the Walls: Clean and smooth your walls before applying wallpaper to ensure a secure bond.
- Measure Twice, Cut Once: Accurate measurements are crucial for matching patterns and avoiding gaps or overlaps.
- Start from the Center: Begin applying wallpaper from the center of the wall and work outward to ensure an even application.
- Smooth as You Go: Use a smoothing tool to remove air bubbles and creases as you apply each strip of wallpaper.

# *February 25: Woodworking*

## 1. The Craft of Woodworking

Woodworking is the art of shaping and assembling wood to create furniture, decor, or functional items. This hobby ranges from simple projects like birdhouses to complex furniture making, combining creativity with practical skills. Woodworking allows you to work with your hands, create personalized items, and develop a deeper understanding of materials and techniques.

## 2. Tools and Materials

- Saw: Essential for cutting wood to the desired size and shape.
- Chisels: Used for carving and shaping wood.
- Hammer: A basic tool for driving nails and assembling projects.
- Wood: Choose the right type of wood for your project, considering factors like strength, durability, and appearance.
- Finishing Supplies: Sandpaper, stain, and varnish are used to smooth and protect your finished piece.

## 3. Techniques and Tips

- Start with Basic Projects: Begin with simple projects like a shelf or small box to build your skills.
- Understand Wood Properties: Different woods have different characteristics, such as hardness and grain. Choose wood that suits your project and skill level.
- Practice Joinery: Learn different types of joinery, such as dovetails, mortise and tenon, and biscuit joints, for stronger, more durable projects.
- Take Your Time: Precision is key in woodworking. Take your time to measure, cut, and assemble each piece carefully.

# *February 26: Xeriscaping*

## 1. The Sustainability of Xeriscaping

Xeriscaping is a landscaping method that uses drought-resistant plants and water-efficient designs to create beautiful, sustainable gardens. This approach is ideal for areas with limited water resources or those looking to reduce their environmental impact. Xeriscaping emphasizes the use of native plants, efficient irrigation, and thoughtful design.

## 2. Tools and Materials

- Drought-Resistant Plants: Choose native or adapted plants that require minimal water.
- Mulch: Mulch helps retain moisture and reduce weeds in your garden.
- Drip Irrigation System: Efficient irrigation systems like drip lines deliver water directly to the roots of plants.
- Rocks and Gravel: Used to create pathways, borders, and ground cover in xeriscaped gardens.
- Soil Amendments: Improve soil structure and water retention with compost or organic matter.

## 3. Techniques and Tips

- Plan Your Design: Create a plan that groups plants with similar water needs together and considers sun exposure, soil type, and drainage.
- Choose Native Plants: Native plants are well adapted to local conditions and require less water and maintenance.
- Use Mulch: Mulching around plants helps retain moisture, reduce evaporation, and prevent weeds.
- Install Efficient Irrigation: Drip irrigation systems are ideal for xeriscaping, delivering water directly to the roots and minimizing waste.

# *February 27: Yard Maintenance*

## 1. The Essentials of Yard Maintenance

Yard maintenance involves regular care and upkeep of your outdoor spaces, including lawns, gardens, and landscaping features. This ongoing task ensures that your yard remains healthy, attractive, and safe. Yard maintenance includes mowing, trimming, watering, and seasonal tasks like leaf removal or winterizing plants.

## 2. Tools and Materials

- Lawn Mower: Essential for keeping your grass at a healthy length.
- Pruning Shears: Used to trim trees, shrubs, and plants.
- Rake: Helps collect leaves, grass clippings, and other debris.
- Hose and Sprinkler: Regular watering is crucial for maintaining a healthy lawn and garden.
- Fertilizer and Weed Control: Use these products to promote healthy growth and prevent weeds.

## 3. Techniques and Tips

- Mow Regularly: Regular mowing keeps your lawn healthy and prevents overgrowth.
- Water Wisely: Water your lawn and plants in the early morning or late evening to reduce evaporation and maximize absorption.
- Trim and Prune: Regular pruning promotes healthy growth and improves the appearance of trees and shrubs.
- Seasonal Maintenance: Adapt your yard care routine to the season, such as raking leaves in the fall or preparing plants for winter.

# *February 28: Zoning and Planning*

## 1. The Importance of Zoning and Planning

Zoning and planning involve understanding and following local regulations and guidelines for land use, construction, and development. This knowledge is essential for anyone involved in building, renovating, or landscaping projects, ensuring that your work complies with legal requirements and community standards.

## 2. Tools and Materials

- Zoning Maps: Provide information on the designated uses for different areas of land.
- Permits: Required for certain types of construction, renovations, or land use changes.
- Surveying Equipment: Used to measure and map out property boundaries.
- Building Codes: Regulations that dictate the standards for construction and renovation projects.
- Planning Guides: Resources that provide information on local zoning laws and planning processes.

## 3. Techniques and Tips

- Research Local Regulations: Before starting any project, research local zoning laws and building codes to ensure compliance.
- Obtain Necessary Permits: Some projects require permits or approval from local authorities. Obtain these before beginning work.
- Work with Professionals: For large or complex projects, consider consulting with a planner, surveyor, or architect to ensure everything is done correctly.
- Keep Records: Maintain records of permits, plans, and communications with local authorities for future reference.

## *Conclusion for February*

February's Building and DIY projects have equipped you with a diverse set of skills, from the precision of appliance repair to the artistry of metalworking. As you've delved into these hands-on activities, you've likely discovered the satisfaction that comes from creating, repairing, and enhancing your surroundings with your own hands. Each project has offered not only practical benefits but also a deeper connection to the art of making and building. As you continue through the year, carry forward the confidence and creativity you've cultivated this month, applying these skills to new challenges and opportunities in the months to come.

# March: Collecting

*March is dedicated to the fascinating and diverse world of collecting. Collecting is more than just gathering objects; it is a journey through history, culture, and personal passions. Each day this month, you'll explore a different type of collectible, ranging from antique tools to vintage posters. This chapter will provide insights into how to start, build, and enjoy your own collection, whether you are a seasoned collector or just beginning.*

# *March 1: Antique Clock Collecting*

## 1. The Art of Antique Clock Collecting

Antique clock collecting involves acquiring clocks from various periods and cultures. Clocks are both functional items and pieces of art, reflecting the technological and aesthetic values of their time. Collecting antique clocks allows you to explore the history of timekeeping and appreciate the craftsmanship and design of these instruments.

## 2. Tools and Materials

- Display Solutions: Use shelves or cabinets to display your clocks. Choose display methods that provide adequate support and prevent damage to delicate components.
- Cleaning Supplies: Use soft cloths and gentle cleaners to maintain the condition of your clocks. Regular cleaning prevents dust buildup and preserves the wood and metal components.
- Restoration Tools: Restore or preserve clocks with appropriate Tools and Materials. Learn how to safely restore antique clocks, including repairing movements, polishing metal, and refinishing wood.

## 3. Techniques and Tips

- Historical Clocks: Focus on clocks from specific periods, such as the 19th century or the mid-20th century. Research the history and evolution of clock design to identify valuable and historically significant pieces.
- Cultural Clocks: Collect clocks from different cultures, each with unique designs. Explore the symbolic meanings and cultural significance of clocks in various societies.
- Mechanism Collecting: Focus on specific clock mechanisms, such as pendulum or spring-driven clocks. Understanding the different mechanisms used in clocks can enhance your appreciation of their design and function.

# *March 2: Antique Tool Collecting*

## 1. The Appeal of Antique Tool Collecting

Antique tool collecting is about preserving and appreciating the craftsmanship of bygone eras. These tools are tangible pieces of history, each with its own story. Whether it's a carpenter's plane from the 19th century or a blacksmith's hammer, antique tools offer a glimpse into the working lives of people in the past. Collecting these tools not only connects you to the history of craftsmanship but also allows you to appreciate the evolution of technology and design.

## 2. Tools and Materials

- Display Cases: Protect and showcase your tools with appropriate display cases that highlight their craftsmanship while keeping them safe from dust and damage.
- Condition Assessment: Tools in good condition with identifiable maker's marks are more valuable. Learn to evaluate the wear, patina, and functionality of tools to determine their historical and monetary value.
- Research Materials: Books, online resources, and membership in collector's clubs are essential for identifying, dating, and learning about the history of the tools in your collection.

## 3. Techniques and Tips

- Identify Maker's Marks: These marks can significantly increase a tool's value and help date the piece. Familiarize yourself with common makers and their marks to become proficient in identifying valuable tools.
- Restoration vs. Preservation: Decide whether to restore tools or keep them in their original condition. Restoration can enhance the tool's appearance and function, but preservation maintains its historical integrity.
- Specialization: Focus on a specific trade (e.g., woodworking, blacksmithing) or era (e.g., Victorian, Colonial) to create a cohesive and meaningful collection. Specializing can deepen your knowledge and appreciation of the tools you collect.

# *March 3: Book Collecting*

## 1. The World of Book Collecting

Book collecting allows you to explore the world of literature, history, and art through the written word. Collecting rare or first-edition books is both intellectually rewarding and potentially profitable. Each book in your collection can represent a unique piece of history, an important cultural moment, or a personal favorite author. Whether you focus on a specific genre, author, or era, book collecting offers a lifelong pursuit of knowledge and beauty.

## 2. Tools and Materials

- Bookshelves: Proper storage is essential to protect books from damage. Invest in sturdy, adjustable bookshelves that allow for different book sizes and provide good air circulation.
- Bookends and Covers: Use bookends to prevent warping and dust covers to protect from light and dust exposure. Acid-free covers are ideal to prevent damage over time.
- Cataloging System: Keeping track of your collection with a cataloging system, whether digital or physical, can be very helpful. Include details such as edition, condition, and provenance to maintain a comprehensive record.

## 3. Techniques and Tips

- Edition and Condition: First editions and books in pristine condition are the most valuable. Learn to distinguish between various editions and assess a book's condition based on industry standards.
- Provenance: A book's history of ownership can add significant value, especially if it has been owned by notable individuals or contains unique inscriptions. Research the provenance of your books to enhance their historical context.
- Specialization: Focus on a particular genre (e.g., science fiction, poetry), author (e.g., Hemingway, Austen), or time period (e.g., Renaissance, 20th century) to build a specialized and meaningful collection.

# *March 4: Bottle Cap Collecting*

## 1. The Appeal of Bottle Cap Collecting

Bottle cap collecting, or crown cap collecting, is a hobby that captures the history and evolution of beverage branding. Each cap is a small work of art, representing the beverage it sealed. The hobby is accessible, easy to start, and offers endless possibilities for expanding your collection. Collecting bottle caps also allows you to explore the rich diversity of beverages from around the world, from craft beers to soft drinks, and appreciate the design and marketing trends of different eras.

## 2. Tools and Materials

- Storage Solutions: Use binders with plastic sleeves, shadow boxes, or display cases to organize and showcase your caps. Ensure that your storage method protects the caps from moisture and environmental damage.
- Cleaning Supplies: Mild soap and water can clean used caps without damaging them. For delicate caps, use a soft brush and gentle cleaning techniques to avoid scratching or fading.
- Cataloging: Digital tools or simple spreadsheets help keep track of your collection. Include details such as brand, country of origin, and year of production to build a detailed and organized collection.

## 3. Techniques and Tips

- Brand and Design Focus: Collect caps from specific brands, regions, or with particular designs. This can help you create themed collections that tell a story or highlight certain aspects of beverage history.
- Condition and Rarity: Pristine caps, especially rare or limited editions, are the most sought after. Learn to assess the condition of caps and understand the factors that contribute to their rarity.
- Geographical Diversity: Expand your collection by including caps from different countries. This adds cultural diversity to your collection and allows you to explore international beverage markets and design trends.

# *March 5: Coin Collecting (Numismatics)*

## 1. The World of Coin Collecting (Numismatics)

Coin collecting, or numismatics, is one of the oldest and most respected hobbies. Coins hold historical, cultural, and economic significance. Whether you collect ancient coins, currency from a specific country, or commemorative issues, each coin tells a unique story. This hobby allows you to delve into history, economics, politics, and art, all through the lens of small metal objects that have traveled through time and across the globe.

## 2. Tools and Materials

- Coin Albums and Holders: Use acid-free albums and holders to store and display coins. Proper storage prevents tarnishing and physical damage, ensuring the long-term preservation of your collection.
- Magnifying Glass: Necessary for examining the fine details of coins, such as mint marks, inscriptions, and any imperfections that might affect value.
- Soft Gloves: Wear gloves to avoid tarnishing the coins with oils from your hands. This is especially important for high-value or rare coins where maintaining pristine condition is crucial.

## 3. Techniques and Tips

- Grading and Condition: Learn how to grade coins based on their condition, as this greatly affects value. Familiarize yourself with the grading scales used by professional numismatists to accurately assess your coins.
- Collecting by Era or Region: Focus on coins from a specific historical period (e.g., Roman Empire, 19th century) or region (e.g., Europe, Asia) to build a cohesive and historically significant collection.
- Rarity and Historical Significance: Seek out coins with limited mintage or those with errors, as these often hold greater value and intrigue among collectors. Research the historical context of each coin to fully appreciate its significance.

# *March 6: Comic Book Collecting*

## 1. The Popularity of Comic Book Collecting

Comic book collecting combines a love of storytelling, art, and pop culture. From superheroes to indie comics, the world of comics is vast and varied. Many comics appreciate in value over time, making this hobby not only enjoyable but also potentially lucrative. Comic books are windows into different cultural eras, reflecting societal values, trends, and the evolution of visual storytelling. Collecting comics allows you to preserve these pieces of popular culture and explore the creative talents behind them.

## 2. Tools and Materials

- Comic Book Sleeves and Backing Boards: Use archival-quality sleeves and boards to prevent damage from light, moisture, and handling. Proper storage is essential to maintaining the condition and value of your comics.
- Storage Boxes: Keep your comics organized and protected from environmental factors such as light, humidity, and dust. Invest in sturdy, acid-free storage boxes designed specifically for comics.
- Cataloging Software: Helps you track the details of your collection, including condition, value, and publication history. A well-organized catalog can also help you identify gaps in your collection and manage your inventory.

## 3. Techniques and Tips

- Condition and Grading: Even slight imperfections can significantly affect a comic's value. Learn to grade comics accurately and understand the factors that impact their condition, such as creases, discoloration, and spine wear.
- First Appearances: Issues featuring the debut of a major character are particularly valuable. Keep an eye out for key issues that mark the first appearance of iconic superheroes or villains, as these are often highly sought after.
- Publisher and Print Runs: Comics from major publishers with limited print runs are often more sought after. Research the history of publishers and the significance of certain print runs to identify valuable editions for your collection.

# *March 7: Diecast Car Collecting*

## 1. The Fascination with Diecast Car Collecting

Diecast car collecting appeals to those who appreciate the craftsmanship and detail in miniature replicas of real vehicles. These models often represent classic cars, race cars, and iconic vehicles from film and television. Collecting diecast cars allows you to explore the intersection of automotive history, design, and popular culture, all in a highly detailed and tangible form.

## 2. Tools and Materials

- Display Cases: Protect your cars from dust and damage while showcasing them. Consider display cases with lighting to highlight the intricate details of your models.
- Cleaning Supplies: Soft brushes

and cloths maintain the condition of your cars without scratching the paint. Regular cleaning ensures that your models remain in pristine condition.
- Cataloging Software: Track your collection with details like make, model, scale, and year. An organized catalog helps you manage your collection and identify areas for expansion.

## 3. Techniques and Tips

- Scale Collecting: Focus on cars of a specific scale, such as 1:18 or 1:64. Collecting within a specific scale can help you create a cohesive and visually harmonious display.
- Era Collecting: Collect cars from a particular time period, such as classic 1950s vehicles or modern supercars. This approach allows you to explore the evolution of automotive design and technology.
- Brand Collecting: Focus on models from specific manufacturers, like Hot Wheels, Matchbox, or Dinky Toys. Brand loyalty can lead to a deep and specialized collection that reflects the history and legacy of certain manufacturers.

# *March 8: Doll Collecting*

## 1. The Art of Doll Collecting

Doll collecting spans cultures and centuries, representing both playthings and artistic creations. From antique porcelain dolls to modern fashion dolls, this hobby allows you to explore history, craftsmanship, and cultural significance. Dolls can reflect societal norms, fashion trends, and the artistry of different periods, making them fascinating subjects for collectors who appreciate both their aesthetic and historical value.

## 2. Tools and Materials

- Display Cabinets: Glass-front cabinets protect dolls from dust while displaying them beautifully. Ensure your display provides adequate support to prevent damage to delicate materials.
- Doll Stands: Maintain the posture of your dolls and prevent them from tipping over. Adjustable stands are ideal for supporting dolls of various sizes and shapes.
- Cleaning Supplies: Soft brushes and cloths are essential for maintaining delicate materials like porcelain and fabric. Use appropriate cleaning products to avoid damaging sensitive surfaces.

## 3. Techniques and Tips

- Antique Dolls: Focus on dolls from specific historical periods, such as the Victorian or Edwardian eras. Research the makers and materials of these dolls to understand their place in history.
- Fashion Dolls: Collect dolls that represent changing fashions and styles, such as Barbie, Blythe, or Madame Alexander dolls. Fashion dolls can serve as cultural icons, reflecting the trends and ideals of their time.
- Cultural Dolls: Explore dolls that reflect different cultures and traditions, such as Japanese Kokeshi dolls or Russian Matryoshka dolls. Cultural dolls can offer insights into the customs, beliefs, and artistry of various societies.

# *March 9: Ephemera Collecting*

## 1. The World of Ephemera Collecting

Ephemera refers to printed materials that were originally intended for short-term use, such as postcards, tickets, brochures, and advertisements. Collecting ephemera allows you to preserve pieces of history that capture cultural trends and societal changes. This hobby offers a unique glimpse into the everyday life of the past, showcasing the transient yet meaningful aspects of culture and communication.

## 2. Tools and Materials

- Archival Storage Boxes: Protect delicate paper items from light and deterioration. Choose acid-free, archival-quality materials to ensure the longevity of your collection.
- Mylar Sleeves: Provide protection while allowing items to be viewed without handling. Mylar is ideal for preserving fragile items like old posters, letters, or photographs.
- Flat Files: Store larger pieces like posters or maps to prevent creasing. Flat files offer ample space for organizing and protecting large, flat items in your collection.

## 3. Techniques and Tips

- Postcards: Collect postcards from different eras, regions, or with specific themes. Postcards can be fascinating cultural artifacts, offering insights into historical tourism, communication, and art.
- Advertisements: Vintage ads provide insight into past consumer trends and marketing strategies. They also reflect the design aesthetics and societal values of their time.
- Event Memorabilia: Items like concert tickets, playbills, and event programs capture cultural moments and can be highly collectible. Focus on significant events or iconic performances to build a collection that tells a compelling story.

# *March 10: Fossil Collecting*

## 1. The Science and Joy of Fossil Collecting

Fossil collecting connects you directly with the history of life on Earth. By collecting fossils, you explore the ancient past, discovering the remains of plants and animals that lived millions of years ago. This hobby offers a unique combination of scientific inquiry and outdoor adventure, making it appealing to both amateur paleontologists and nature enthusiasts.

## 2. Tools and Materials

- Rock Hammer: For splitting rocks and extracting fossils. A good hammer is essential for accessing fossils embedded in stone.
- Chisels and Brushes: For carefully removing fossils from rock. Precision tools help you extract fossils without damaging them.
- Field Guide: Essential for identifying fossils. Use a field guide to learn about different types of fossils and how to locate them.
- Storage Solutions: Padded containers protect fossils during transport and storage, preventing damage to these delicate specimens.

## 3. Techniques and Tips

- Field Research: Identify potential fossil sites and consider obtaining necessary permits. Researching locations known for fossil finds can significantly increase your chances of success.
- Excavation: Carefully extract fossils using appropriate tools to avoid damaging them. Take your time during excavation to preserve the integrity of the fossils.
- Identification: Use a field guide or consult with experts to identify your finds. Cataloging your fossils with detailed notes on their location and type adds value to your collection.

# *March 11: Glassware Collecting*

## 1. The Art of Glassware Collecting

Glassware collecting involves acquiring decorative or functional glass items, such as antique bottles, vases, and drinking glasses. This hobby celebrates the craftsmanship of glassmaking, from utilitarian objects to exquisite works of art. Collecting glassware allows you to appreciate the diversity of styles, techniques, and historical periods represented in glassmaking.

## 2. Tools and Materials

- Display Shelves: Protect glassware while displaying it. Choose shelves that provide sturdy support and adequate lighting to showcase the brilliance and detail of your glassware.

- Cleaning Supplies: Soft cloths and gentle cleaners maintain the clarity and luster of your glassware. Avoid abrasive materials that can scratch or dull the surface.

- Lighting: Proper lighting enhances the display of glassware, highlighting its color, texture, and craftsmanship. Consider using LED lights that do not emit heat, which can damage delicate glass.

## 3. Techniques and Tips

- Antique Glass: Focus on items from specific historical periods, such as Victorian or Art Deco. Research the different styles and techniques used in each era to identify valuable pieces.

- Pressed Glass: Mass-produced glassware with molded patterns, popular in the 19th and early 20th centuries. Pressed glass offers an affordable entry point into glassware collecting while still offering historical interest.

- Hand-Blown Glass: Collect artisanal glass items valued for their craftsmanship. Hand-blown glass pieces are often unique, with variations in color and form that add to their charm and collectibility.

# *March 12: Hat Collecting*

## 1. The Charm of Hat Collecting

Hat collecting involves acquiring hats from various periods, cultures, and designers. Whether you're interested in vintage fedoras, military headgear, or contemporary fashion pieces, hat collecting allows you to explore fashion history and personal expression. Each hat in your collection can tell a story about the time and place it was worn, as well as the social status, occupation, or personality of its owner.

## 2. Tools and Materials

- Hat Stands or Mannequins: Maintain the shape of hats and make them easier to display. Proper support is essential to prevent hats from becoming misshapen over time.
- Storage Boxes: Protect hats from dust and damage by storing them in boxes. Use acid-free tissue paper to stuff and support the inside of hats, maintaining their shape.
- Cleaning Supplies: Brushes and gentle cleaners maintain the condition of hats, especially those made from delicate materials like straw or felt. Use specific cleaners for different types of materials to avoid damage.

## 3. Techniques and Tips

- Vintage Hats: Focus on hats from specific eras, such as the 1920s or 1960s. Vintage hats often reflect the fashion trends and cultural norms of their time, making them interesting and valuable collectibles.
- Designer Hats: Collect hats from famous designers known for their craftsmanship, such as Philip Treacy or Coco Chanel. Designer hats can be both fashion statements and works of art.
- Cultural and Military Headgear: Explore hats that represent different cultures or military histories, such as berets, turbans, or military helmets. These hats offer a glimpse into the customs, traditions, and values of various societies.

# *March 13: Insect Collecting*

## 1. The Science of Insect Collecting

Insect collecting combines natural science with exploration. By collecting and studying insects, you can learn about biodiversity, ecosystems, and the role these creatures play in the environment. Insect collecting can also lead to discoveries about species behavior, adaptation, and evolution, making it a rewarding hobby for both amateur entomologists and nature enthusiasts.

## 2. Tools and Materials

- Insect Net: Capture flying insects without harming them. A fine mesh net is ideal for catching small and delicate insects.
- Collecting Jars: Ventilated containers for holding insects until they can be preserved. Ensure the jars are secure and provide enough ventilation to keep the insects alive temporarily.
- Pins and Mounts: For mounting and displaying insects. Use appropriate pins and mounting boards to preserve the insects' natural posture and prevent damage.
- Field Guide: Helps identify different species. A field guide specific to your region or area of interest can greatly enhance your ability to identify and learn about the insects you collect.

## 3. Techniques and Tips

- Field Collection: Capture insects in their natural habitat using nets and jars. Early morning or late afternoon is often the best time for insect activity.
- Preservation: Pin insects to a mounting board or store them in alcohol to preserve them. Learn proper techniques for preserving different types of insects to ensure they remain intact and identifiable.
- Identification: Use a field guide to identify species and document your collection. Keeping detailed records of where and when you collected each insect can add scientific value to your collection.

# March 14: Jewelry Collecting

## 1. The Glamour of Jewelry Collecting

Jewelry collecting involves acquiring pieces that range from antique heirlooms to contemporary designs. This hobby celebrates the artistry, craftsmanship, and materials that go into creating wearable art. Collecting jewelry allows you to appreciate the beauty and significance of different designs, materials, and cultural influences across history.

## 2. Tools and Materials

- Jewelry Boxes: Protect and organize your collection. Look for boxes with soft linings and compartments to prevent scratching and tangling.
- Cleaning Supplies: Use soft cloths, mild cleaners, and jewelry polish to maintain the condition of your pieces. Be sure to use the appropriate cleaner for each type of material, such as gold, silver, or gemstones.
- Magnifying Glass: Examine hallmarks and craftsmanship. A magnifying glass can help you identify maker's marks, metal purity stamps, and other details that indicate the authenticity and value of a piece.

## 3. Techniques and Tips

- Fine Jewelry: Collect pieces made from precious metals and gemstones. Focus on items with verified hallmarks and certificates of authenticity to ensure you are acquiring genuine pieces.
- Vintage and Antique Jewelry: Focus on items from specific historical periods, such as the Victorian, Edwardian, or Art Deco eras. Understanding the characteristics of jewelry from these periods can help you identify valuable pieces.
- Ethnographic Jewelry: Explore jewelry from different cultures, such as Native American silver and turquoise pieces or African beadwork. Ethnographic jewelry reflects the traditions, beliefs, and artistic styles of the cultures that created it.

# March 15: Knife Collecting

## 1. The Art and Utility of Knife Collecting

Knife collecting combines an appreciation for craftsmanship with an interest in history and utility. Knives have been used for thousands of years, and collecting them allows you to explore the evolution of design and materials. Whether you collect historical knives, utility knives, or art knives, this hobby offers a rich blend of practicality and aesthetics.

## 2. Tools and Materials

- Display Cases: Protect and showcase your knives. Choose cases that offer secure storage while allowing for easy viewing of the knives' details.
- Cleaning and Sharpening Tools: Maintain the condition of your knives with appropriate cleaning and sharpening tools. Regular maintenance ensures that your knives remain in top condition, whether they are functional or purely decorative.
- Protective Gloves: Use gloves when handling sharp blades to avoid injury. Proper handling is essential, especially when dealing with antique or finely crafted knives.

## 3. Techniques and Tips

- Historical Knives: Focus on knives from specific historical periods, such as medieval or 19th-century knives. Research the history and usage of these knives to understand their significance and value.
- Utility and Tactical Knives: Collect knives designed for specific purposes, such as hunting, fishing, or military use. Utility knives offer insights into the practical applications of knife design across different fields.
- Art Knives: Focus on custom-made knives that are also works of art. These knives often feature intricate designs, exotic materials, and exceptional craftsmanship, making them highly collectible.

# March 16: Lantern Collecting

## 1. The Charm of Lantern Collecting

Lantern collecting involves acquiring lanterns from various periods and cultures. These items, once essential for light, are now collectible artifacts that reflect the technological and aesthetic values of their time. Lanterns can range from simple, functional designs to elaborate, decorative pieces, offering a wide variety of styles and materials to collect.

## 2. Tools and Materials

- Display Shelves: Protect your lanterns from dust while displaying them. Choose shelves that are sturdy enough to support the weight of the lanterns and positioned to prevent accidental knocks.
- Cleaning Supplies: Use soft cloths and gentle cleaners to maintain their condition. Regular cleaning prevents the buildup of dust and tarnish, preserving the lanterns' appearance.
- Restoration Tools: Restore or preserve lanterns with appropriate Tools and Materials. Learn how to safely restore antique lanterns, including replacing glass panes, polishing metal, and repairing mechanisms.

## 3. Techniques and Tips

- Historical Lanterns: Focus on lanterns from specific periods, such as the Victorian era. Research the different types of lanterns used during these periods to identify valuable and historically significant pieces.
- Cultural Lanterns: Collect lanterns from different cultures, each with its unique design. Explore the symbolic meanings and cultural significance of lanterns in various societies.
- Fuel Types: Collect lanterns based on their fuel type, such as oil, kerosene, or gas. Understanding the different fuel types used in lanterns can enhance your appreciation of their design and function.

# *March 17: Matchbox Car Collecting*

## 1. The Fascination with Matchbox Car Collecting

Matchbox car collecting appeals to enthusiasts who appreciate the detail and craftsmanship in miniature vehicles. These cars represent a wide range of vehicles, from classic models to modern supercars. Collecting Matchbox cars allows you to explore the history of automotive design and marketing, all in a highly accessible and collectible form.

## 2. Tools and Materials

- Display Cases: Protect your cars from dust and damage while showcasing them. Consider using cases with adjustable shelves to accommodate different sizes of cars.
- Cleaning Supplies: Soft brushes maintain the condition of your cars. Regular cleaning helps prevent dust buildup and keeps your cars looking their best.
- Cataloging Software: Track your collection with details like make, model, and year. An organized catalog helps you manage your collection and identify areas for expansion.

## 3. Techniques and Tips

- Era Collecting: Focus on cars from specific time periods, such as the 1950s or 1980s. This approach allows you to explore the evolution of automotive design and technology over time.
- Brand Collecting: Collect models from specific manufacturers like Matchbox. Focusing on a particular brand can help you create a cohesive and specialized collection.
- Series Collecting: Collect cars from specific series or sets. Series collecting can be particularly satisfying as it allows you to complete a set and appreciate the thematic design of the collection.

# *March 18: Numismatics*

## 1. The World of Numismatics

Numismatics, or coin collecting, is a hobby that spans history and geography. Each coin tells a story of its time and place, offering insights into economics, politics, and culture. Whether you focus on ancient coins, modern currency, or commemorative issues, numismatics allows you to explore a rich tapestry of history through small, tangible artifacts.

## 2. Tools and Materials

- Coin Albums and Holders: Use acid-free materials to store coins. Proper storage prevents tarnishing and physical damage, ensuring the long-term preservation of your collection.

- Magnifying Glass: Examine details like mint marks and inscriptions. A magnifying glass is essential for accurately assessing the condition and value of coins.

- Soft Gloves: Prevent tarnishing by handling coins with gloves. Wearing gloves protects coins from oils and dirt that can damage their surfaces.

## 3. Techniques and Tips

- Grading and Condition: Learn to grade coins to assess their value. Familiarize yourself with the grading scales used by professional numismatists to accurately assess your coins.

- Era or Region Collecting: Focus on coins from specific periods or regions, such as ancient Rome or modern Europe. Specializing in a particular era or region can deepen your knowledge and appreciation of your collection.

- Rarity and Errors: Seek out rare coins or those with minting errors. Coins with unique characteristics or historical significance are often more valuable and sought after by collectors.

# *March 19: Oil Lamp Collecting*

## 1. The Appeal of Oil Lamp Collecting

Oil lamp collecting involves acquiring lamps from various periods and cultures. These lamps, once essential for lighting, are now collectible artifacts that reflect technological and aesthetic values. Oil lamps can range from simple, utilitarian designs to ornate, decorative pieces, offering a wide variety of styles and materials to collect.

## 2. Tools and Materials

- Display Shelves: Protect lamps from dust while displaying them. Choose shelves that are sturdy enough to support the weight of the lamps and positioned to prevent accidental knocks.
- Cleaning Supplies: Use soft cloths and gentle cleaners to maintain their condition. Regular cleaning prevents the buildup of dust and tarnish, preserving the lamps' appearance.
- Restoration Tools: Restore or preserve oil lamps with appropriate Tools and Materials. Learn how to safely restore antique lamps, including replacing glass chimneys, polishing metal, and repairing mechanisms.

## 3. Techniques and Tips

- Historical Lamps: Focus on lamps from specific periods, such as the 19th century. Research the different types of lamps used during these periods to identify valuable and historically significant pieces.
- Cultural Lamps: Collect lamps from different cultures, each with unique designs. Explore the symbolic meanings and cultural significance of lamps in various societies.
- Fuel Types: Collect lamps based on their fuel type, such as oil or kerosene. Understanding the different fuel types used in lamps can enhance your appreciation of their design and function.

# *March 20: Pen Collecting*

## 1. The Art of Pen Collecting

Pen collecting involves acquiring writing instruments from various periods and manufacturers. Pens are both functional tools and pieces of art, reflecting the technological and cultural values of their time. Collecting pens allows you to appreciate the craftsmanship, design, and history of these writing instruments, from simple ballpoints to luxurious fountain pens.

## 2. Tools and Materials

- Display Cases: Protect and showcase your pens. Choose cases with individual slots or compartments to keep pens secure and prevent them from touching each other.
- Cleaning Supplies: Use soft cloths and gentle cleaners to maintain the condition of your pens. Regular cleaning prevents ink buildup and keeps your pens in working order.
- Cataloging Software: Track your collection with details like make, model, and year. An organized catalog helps you manage your collection and identify areas for expansion.

## 3. Techniques and Tips

- Vintage Pens: Focus on pens from specific periods, such as the early 20th century. Research the history and evolution of pen design to identify valuable and historically significant pieces.
- Brand Collecting: Collect pens from specific manufacturers, such as Montblanc or Parker. Focusing on a particular brand can help you create a cohesive and specialized collection.
- Limited Editions: Seek out rare or limited-edition pens for your collection. Limited editions often feature unique designs and materials, making them highly collectible and valuable.

# *March 21: Quilt Collecting*

## 1. The Art and Craft of Quilt Collecting

Quilt collecting involves acquiring quilts from various periods and cultures. Quilts are both functional items and pieces of art, reflecting the cultural and aesthetic values of their makers. Collecting quilts allows you to appreciate the craftsmanship, design, and history of these textile creations, from simple patchwork quilts to elaborate applique designs.

## 2. Tools and Materials

- Storage Solutions: Store quilts in a cool, dry place to prevent damage. Use acid-free tissue paper to wrap and support the quilts, avoiding direct sunlight and moisture that can cause fading and mildew.
- Display Solutions: Use quilt racks or frames to display your quilts. Choose display methods that provide adequate support and prevent creases or stretching.
- Cleaning Supplies: Use gentle cleaners to maintain the condition of your quilts. Hand washing or professional cleaning is recommended for delicate or antique quilts to avoid damage.

## 3. Techniques and Tips

- Historical Quilts: Focus on quilts from specific periods, such as the 19th century. Research the history and techniques used in these quilts to identify valuable and historically significant pieces.
- Cultural Quilts: Collect quilts from different cultures, each with unique designs. Explore the symbolic meanings and cultural significance of quilts in various societies.
- Pattern Collecting: Focus on specific quilt patterns, such as Log Cabin or Double Wedding Ring. Specializing in particular patterns can deepen your knowledge and appreciation of quilt design and history.

# *March 22: Rock and Mineral Collecting*

## 1. The Science and Beauty of Rock and Mineral Collecting

Rock and mineral collecting involves acquiring specimens from various geological formations. These specimens are both scientifically significant and aesthetically beautiful, reflecting the natural history of our planet. Collecting rocks and minerals allows you to explore the diversity of Earth's materials, from common minerals to rare gemstones.

## 2. Tools and Materials

- Rock Hammer: For splitting rocks and extracting specimens. A good hammer is essential for accessing specimens embedded in stone.
- Chisels and Brushes: For carefully removing specimens from rock. Precision tools help you extract specimens without damaging them.
- Field Guide: Essential for identifying rocks and minerals. Use a field guide to learn about different types of specimens and how to locate them.
- Storage Solutions: Use padded containers to protect your specimens during transport and storage, preventing damage to these delicate pieces.

## 3. Techniques and Tips

- Field Research: Identify potential collecting sites and obtain necessary permits. Researching locations known for specific types of specimens can significantly increase your chances of success.
- Excavation: Carefully extract specimens using appropriate tools to avoid damaging them. Take your time during excavation to preserve the integrity of the specimens.
- Identification: Use a field guide or consult with experts to identify your finds. Cataloging your specimens with detailed notes on their location and type adds value to your collection.

# *March 23: Stamp Collecting (Philately)*

## 1. The World of Stamp Collecting (Philately)

Stamp collecting, or philately, is a hobby that spans history and geography. Each stamp tells a story of its time and place, offering insights into politics, culture, and technology. Whether you focus on thematic stamps, country-specific issues, or rare errors, stamp collecting allows you to explore a rich tapestry of history through small, colorful pieces of paper.

## 2. Tools and Materials

- Stamp Albums: Use acid-free albums to store stamps. Proper storage prevents fading and physical damage, ensuring the long-term preservation of your collection.
- Magnifying Glass: Examine details like watermarks and perforations. A magnifying glass is essential for accurately assessing the condition and value of stamps.
- Tongs: Handle stamps with tongs to avoid damaging them. Using tongs prevents oils and dirt from transferring to the stamps, which can cause deterioration.

## 3. Techniques and Tips

- Thematic Collecting: Focus on stamps with specific themes, such as animals, famous people, or historical events. Thematic collecting allows you to create a cohesive and visually appealing collection.
- Country Collecting: Collect stamps from specific countries or regions. Specializing in a particular country can deepen your knowledge and appreciation of its history and culture.
- Era Collecting: Focus on stamps from specific periods, such as the 19th century or World War II. Collecting by era allows you to explore the historical context and significance of different stamps.

# March 24: Toy Collecting

## 1. The Joy of Toy Collecting

Toy collecting involves acquiring toys from various periods and manufacturers. Toys are both playthings and pieces of history, reflecting the cultural and technological values of their time. Collecting toys allows you to explore the evolution of design, materials, and marketing, from simple wooden toys to complex electronic games.

## 2. Tools and Materials

- Display Cases: Protect and showcase your toys. Choose cases with adjustable shelves and secure doors to keep toys safe from dust and damage.
- Cleaning Supplies: Use soft cloths and gentle cleaners to maintain the condition of your toys. Regular cleaning prevents dust buildup and keeps your toys looking their best.
- Cataloging Software: Track your collection with details like make, model, and year. An organized catalog helps you manage your collection and identify areas for expansion.

## 3. Techniques and Tips

- Vintage Toys: Focus on toys from specific periods, such as the early 20th century or the 1980s. Vintage toys often reflect the cultural and technological trends of their time, making them valuable collectibles.
- Brand Collecting: Collect toys from specific manufacturers, such as Mattel or Hasbro. Focusing on a particular brand can help you create a cohesive and specialized collection.
- Limited Editions: Seek out rare or limited-edition toys for your collection. Limited editions often feature unique designs and materials, making them highly collectible and valuable.

# *March 25: Umbrella Collecting*

## 1. The Uniqueness of Umbrella Collecting

Umbrella collecting involves acquiring umbrellas from various periods and cultures. Umbrellas are both functional items and pieces of art, reflecting the cultural and aesthetic values of their time. Collecting umbrellas allows you to explore the evolution of design and materials, from simple, utilitarian models to ornate, decorative pieces.

## 2. Tools and Materials

- Display Solutions: Use stands or racks to display your umbrellas. Choose display methods that provide adequate support and prevent damage to delicate materials.
- Cleaning Supplies: Use soft cloths and gentle cleaners to maintain the condition of your umbrellas. Regular cleaning prevents dust buildup and preserves the fabric and frame.
- Storage Solutions: Store umbrellas in a cool, dry place to prevent damage. Avoid direct sunlight and moisture, which can cause fading and mildew.

## 3. Techniques and Tips

- Historical Umbrellas: Focus on umbrellas from specific periods, such as the 19th century or the Art Deco era. Research the history and evolution of umbrella design to identify valuable and historically significant pieces.
- Cultural Umbrellas: Collect umbrellas from different cultures, each with unique designs. Explore the symbolic meanings and cultural significance of umbrellas in various societies.
- Designer Umbrellas: Collect umbrellas from famous designers or brands, such as Burberry or Pasotti. Designer umbrellas often feature luxurious materials and craftsmanship, making them highly collectible.

# March 26: Vintage Poster Collecting

## 1. The Art of Vintage Poster Collecting

Vintage poster collecting involves acquiring posters from various periods and cultures. Posters are both functional items and pieces of art, reflecting the cultural and aesthetic values of their time. Collecting vintage posters allows you to explore the history of advertising, cinema, and art, and appreciate the unique visual language of poster design.

## 2. Tools and Materials

- Display Frames: Protect and showcase your posters in frames. Choose frames with UV-protective glass to prevent fading and damage from light exposure.
- Cleaning Supplies: Use soft cloths and gentle cleaners to maintain the condition of your posters. Regular cleaning prevents dust buildup and preserves the paper and ink.
- Storage Solutions: Store posters flat in a cool, dry place to prevent damage. Avoid rolling or folding posters, as this can cause creases and tears.

## 3. Techniques and Tips

- Historical Posters: Focus on posters from specific periods, such as the early 20th century or the 1960s. Research the history and evolution of poster design to identify valuable and historically significant pieces.
- Cultural Posters: Collect posters from different cultures, each with unique designs. Explore the symbolic meanings and cultural significance of posters in various societies.
- Advertising Posters: Focus on posters used as promotional items. Advertising posters often feature unique designs and logos, making them highly collectible and valuable.

# *March 27: Vinyl Record Collecting*

## 1. The Art of Vinyl Record Collecting

Vinyl record collecting involves acquiring records from various genres and periods. Vinyl records are both functional music items and pieces of history, reflecting the cultural and technological values of their time. Collecting vinyl records allows you to explore the evolution of music, from early jazz recordings to modern rock albums, and appreciate the unique sound quality and artwork of vinyl.

## 2. Tools and Materials

- Record Cleaning Kit: Maintain the condition of your records with a cleaning kit. Regular cleaning prevents dust buildup and reduces the risk of scratches.
- Record Sleeves: Protect your records from dust and scratches by storing them in sleeves. Use both inner and outer sleeves for maximum protection.
- Storage Solutions: Store records upright in a cool, dry place to prevent warping. Avoid stacking records, as this can cause damage over time.

## 3. Techniques and Tips

- Genre Collecting: Focus on records from specific genres, such as jazz, rock, or classical. Specializing in a particular genre can help you build a cohesive and meaningful collection.
- Era Collecting: Collect records from specific periods, such as the 1960s or 1980s. Era collecting allows you to explore the history and evolution of music across different decades.
- Artist Collecting: Focus on records from specific artists or bands, such as The Beatles or David Bowie. Artist collecting allows you to explore the discography and career of your favorite musicians.

# *March 28: Watch Collecting*

## 1. The Elegance of Watch Collecting

Watch collecting involves acquiring timepieces from various periods and manufacturers. Watches are both functional items and pieces of art, reflecting the technological and aesthetic values of their time. Collecting watches allows you to explore the history of timekeeping, from simple pocket watches to complex mechanical timepieces, and appreciate the craftsmanship and design of these instruments.

## 2. Tools and Materials

- Watch Box: Protect and showcase your watches in a watch box. Choose a box with individual compartments to keep watches secure and prevent them from touching each other.

- Cleaning Supplies: Use soft cloths and gentle cleaners to maintain the condition of your watches. Regular cleaning prevents dust buildup and keeps your watches in working order.

- Watch Winder: Keep automatic watches running smoothly with a watch winder. A winder ensures that your watches are always ready to wear and helps maintain their accuracy.

## 3. Techniques and Tips

- Vintage Watches: Focus on watches from specific periods, such as the early 20th century or the 1970s. Vintage watches often reflect the technological and design trends of their time, making them valuable collectibles.

- Brand Collecting: Collect watches from specific manufacturers, such as Rolex or Omega. Focusing on a particular brand can help you create a cohesive and specialized collection.

- Limited Editions: Seek out rare or limited-edition watches for your collection. Limited editions often feature unique designs and materials, making them highly collectible and valuable.

# *March 29: Xylophone Collecting*

## 1. The Musicality of Xylophone Collecting

Xylophone collecting involves acquiring xylophones from various periods and cultures. Xylophones are both musical instruments and pieces of history, reflecting the cultural and technological values of their time. Collecting xylophones allows you to explore the evolution of percussion instruments and appreciate the craftsmanship and design of these instruments.

## 2. Tools and Materials

- Display Solutions: Use stands or racks to display your xylophones. Choose display methods that provide adequate support and prevent damage to delicate materials.
- Cleaning Supplies: Use soft cloths and gentle cleaners to maintain the condition of your xylophones. Regular cleaning prevents dust buildup and preserves the wood and metal components.
- Storage Solutions: Store xylophones in a cool, dry place to prevent damage. Avoid direct sunlight and moisture, which can cause fading and warping.

## 3. Techniques and Tips

- Historical Xylophones: Focus on xylophones from specific periods, such as the 19th century or the mid-20th century. Research the history and evolution of xylophone design to identify valuable and historically significant pieces.
- Cultural Xylophones: Collect xylophones from different cultures, each with unique designs. Explore the symbolic meanings and cultural significance of xylophones in various societies.
- Brand Collecting: Collect xylophones from specific manufacturers, such as Deagan or Musser. Brand collecting allows you to explore the legacy and craftsmanship of well-known xylophone makers.

# March 30: Yardstick Collecting

## 1. The Practicality of Yardstick Collecting

Yardstick collecting involves acquiring yardsticks from various periods and manufacturers. Yardsticks are both functional tools and pieces of history, reflecting the cultural and technological values of their time. Collecting yardsticks allows you to explore the evolution of measurement tools and appreciate the craftsmanship and design of these simple yet essential objects.

## 2. Tools and Materials

- Display Solutions: Use racks or frames to display your yardsticks. Choose display methods that provide adequate support and prevent damage to delicate materials.
- Cleaning Supplies: Use soft cloths and gentle cleaners to maintain the condition of your yardsticks. Regular cleaning prevents dust buildup and preserves the wood and metal components.
- Storage Solutions: Store yardsticks in a cool, dry place to prevent damage. Avoid direct sunlight and moisture, which can cause fading and warping.

## 3. Techniques and Tips

- Vintage Yardsticks: Focus on yardsticks from specific periods, such as the early 20th century or the mid-20th century. Research the history and evolution of yardstick design to identify valuable and historically significant pieces.
- Brand Collecting: Collect yardsticks from specific manufacturers, such as Stanley or Lufkin. Brand collecting allows you to explore the legacy and craftsmanship of well-known yardstick makers.
- Advertising Yardsticks: Focus on yardsticks used as promotional items. Advertising yardsticks often feature unique designs and logos, making them highly collectible and valuable.

# *March 31: Zippo Lighter Collecting*

## 1. The Utility of Zippo Lighter Collecting

Zippo lighter collecting involves acquiring lighters from various periods and manufacturers. Zippo lighters are both functional tools and pieces of history, reflecting the cultural and technological values of their time. Collecting Zippo lighters allows you to explore the evolution of lighter design and appreciate the craftsmanship and durability of these iconic tools.

## 2. Tools and Materials

- Display Cases: Protect and showcase your lighters. Choose cases with individual compartments to keep lighters secure and prevent them from touching each other.
- Cleaning Supplies: Use soft cloths and gentle cleaners to maintain the condition of your lighters. Regular cleaning prevents dust buildup and preserves the metal components.
- Fuel Supplies: Keep your lighters in working condition with proper fuel. Regularly check and refill the fuel to ensure your lighters remain functional.

## 3. Techniques and Tips

- Vintage Lighters: Focus on lighters from specific periods, such as the mid-20th century or the 1970s. Vintage lighters often reflect the technological and design trends of their time, making them valuable collectibles.
- Brand Collecting: Collect lighters from specific manufacturers, such as Zippo or Ronson. Focusing on a particular brand can help you create a cohesive and specialized collection.
- Limited Editions: Seek out rare or limited-edition lighters for your collection. Limited editions often feature unique designs and materials, making them highly collectible and valuable.

## *Conclusion for March*

As March comes to an end, you've journeyed through the diverse and fascinating world of collecting. Each day introduced you to a different type of collectible, from antique tools to vintage posters, offering insights into the history, culture, and personal passions that drive collectors. Collecting is more than just a hobby; it's a way to preserve and appreciate the stories behind each item. Whether you're drawn to the elegance of vintage jewelry, the practicality of Zippo lighters, or the nostalgia of vinyl records, the world of collecting offers endless opportunities for discovery and enjoyment. As you continue to build your collections, remember that the value of each item is not just in its rarity or condition, but in the personal meaning it holds for you.

# April: Food and Drink

*April is a month dedicated to the culinary arts and the craft of beverage making. Food and drink are integral parts of our daily lives, and this chapter will take you on a journey through a variety of techniques, traditions, and innovations. From the art of baking and fermenting to the delicate craft of tea blending and wine making, each day in April presents an opportunity to explore new flavors and develop your culinary skills.*

# *April 1: Appetizer Making*

## 1. The Art of Appetizer Making

Appetizers introduce a meal, tantalizing the taste buds and setting the stage for what's to come. Crafting appetizers involves creativity and a keen understanding of flavors. From simple bites to elaborate small plates, the goal is to create dishes that are both visually appealing and delicious. A well-made appetizer not only satisfies hunger but also excites the palate, offering a preview of the meal.

## 2. Tools and Materials

- Cutting Boards and Knives: Essential for precision in preparing ingredients. A variety of knives, including chef's, paring, and utility knives, cover all your slicing and chopping needs.
- Small Plates and Platters: Presentation matters, so having the right serving ware enhances the appeal. Choose plates that match your appetizer's style.
- Cooking Gadgets: Tools like mandolins, piping bags, and skewers are useful. Microplanes for zesting and immersion blenders for dips can elevate your appetizers.
- Ingredients: Fresh herbs, spices, and high-quality ingredients are key. Invest in artisanal cheeses, premium olive oils, and exotic spices to add depth.

## 3. Techniques and Tips

- Flavor Balancing: Master balancing sweet, salty, sour, bitter, and umami flavors. For example, pair salty prosciutto with sweet melon or spicy jalapeño with cool cream cheese.
- Presentation: Visual appeal is crucial; use garnishes and plating techniques to elevate dishes. Consider height, color contrast, and texture.
- Portion Control: Appetizers should be small but satisfying, offering two to three bites that leave guests wanting more.
- Experimentation: Try new flavors or presentation styles to keep your appetizers fresh. Incorporate global ingredients like wasabi or tahini.
- Seasonal Ingredients: Use seasonal produce to enhance flavors and support sustainability.

# *April 2: Baking*

## 1. The Science and Joy of Baking

Baking is both an art and a science, requiring precise measurements and timing. Whether making bread, pastries, or cakes, baking transforms simple ingredients into delicious treats. The joy of baking comes from creating something from scratch and the comforting aroma that fills your home. Baking allows creativity within a framework, making it challenging and rewarding.

## 2. Tools and Materials

- Mixing Bowls and Whisks: Essential for combining ingredients. Stainless steel bowls are durable, and various whisk sizes suit different tasks.
- Baking Pans and Sheets: Quality non-stick pans ensure even baking and easy release. Consider shapes like loaf pans, cake pans, and muffin tins.
- Measuring Cups and Spoons: Precision is key, so accurate measurements are crucial. Invest in dry and liquid measuring tools.
- Oven Thermometer: Ensures your oven maintains the correct temperature.
- Pastry Brush and Rolling Pin: Useful for glazes and rolling dough. A marble rolling pin keeps dough cool, and a silicone brush ensures even application.

## 3. Techniques and Tips

- Understanding Ingredients: Know how yeast, baking powder, and baking soda work to achieve the desired texture and rise.
- Temperature Control: Baking at the right temperature ensures even cooking. Preheat your oven and avoid opening the door too often.
- Experiment with Flavors: Once you master the basics, try adding spices, extracts, or zest. Incorporate unique ingredients like matcha or lavender.
- Timing is Everything: Pay attention to baking times to avoid undercooking or overbaking. Use a timer and check for doneness by appearance and feel.
- Decorating: Enhance your baked goods with icing, glazes, and toppings. Consider piping designs or dusting with powdered sugar for an elegant finish.

# *April 3: Brining*

## 1. The Technique of Brining

Brining enhances the flavor and juiciness of meats by soaking them in a salt, water, and sometimes sugar or spice solution. Commonly used for poultry and pork, it also works for fish and vegetables. Brining retains moisture during cooking and infuses subtle flavors, making it ideal for lean cuts that tend to dry out.

## 2. Tools and Materials

- Large Containers: Use non-reactive containers like glass or plastic, large enough to fully submerge the food in the brine.
- Kosher Salt: Preferred for brining due to its purity and larger grains. Avoid iodized salt, which can add a metallic taste.
- Herbs and Spices: Customize your brine with thyme, rosemary, bay leaves, peppercorns, or cloves. Add depth with citrus peels, garlic, or juniper berries.
- Meat Thermometer: Ensures the brined meat is cooked to the proper internal temperature, crucial for food safety, especially with poultry.
- Brining Bags: Heavy-duty, leak-proof bags for brining large cuts. They save space and are ideal for refrigerator storage.

## 3. Techniques and Tips

- Time Management: Brining times vary by food size and type. Brine for the appropriate amount of time to avoid over-salting; smaller cuts need less time, while whole birds or large roasts need more.
- Rinsing and Drying: Rinse food after brining to remove excess salt and pat dry before cooking to prevent over-salting and achieve a crisp exterior.
- Flavor Enhancements: Experiment with herbs, spices, or fruit juices for unique flavors. Apple cider brine adds sweetness to pork, while citrus brine complements poultry.
- Temperature Control: Keep the brine and food cool to prevent bacterial growth, storing in the refrigerator or a cooler with ice packs.
- Resting Time: Allow brined meats to rest before cooking to ensure even flavor distribution.

# *April 4: Cake Decorating*

## 1. The Artistry of Cake Decorating

Cake decorating merges culinary skills with artistic expression. Whether it's a birthday, wedding, or special dessert, the decoration makes a cake memorable. From simple buttercream swirls to intricate fondant designs, cake decorating lets you unleash creativity. It's an art form combining technique, color theory, and a steady hand to create edible masterpieces.

## 2. Tools and Materials

- Piping Bags and Tips: Essential for detailed decorations like borders, flowers, and lettering. Various tip shapes and sizes create different textures and patterns.
- Spatulas and Scrapers: Smooth and even out frosting with precision. Offset spatulas are ideal for spreading icing evenly.
- Fondant Tools: Use rolling pins, cutters, and molds to shape fondant decorations. Fondant smoothers achieve a flawless finish, while cutters offer custom designs.
- Turntable: A turntable allows smooth cake rotation for even decoration, crucial for symmetrical designs.
- Edible Decorations: Add flair with edible glitter, sprinkles, or elegant touches like gold leaf, sugar pearls, or fresh flowers.

## 3. Techniques and Tips

- Crumb Coating: Apply a thin frosting layer to catch crumbs before the final coat, ensuring a smooth finish.
- Color Mixing: Mix food coloring to achieve perfect shades. Gel-based colors offer vibrant hues without altering frosting consistency.
- Practice Piping: Practice on parchment paper before decorating the cake to get comfortable with different tip shapes and pressures.
- Layering and Stacking: Ensure cake layers are even and secure. Use dowels or cake boards for support in multi-tiered cakes.
- Creative Designs: Experiment with marbling, ombre, textured finishes, airbrushing, stenciling, or sugar work to make your cakes unique.

# *April 5: Canning*

## 1. The Tradition of Canning

Canning preserves food by sealing it in airtight containers, extending the shelf life of fruits, vegetables, and meats while locking in flavors and nutrients. This traditional skill lets you enjoy seasonal produce year-round, reduce food waste, and stock your pantry with home-preserved foods.

## 2. Tools and Materials

- Canning Jars and Lids: Use high-quality jars with lids that form a proper seal to prevent spoilage. Mason jars are the most common and come in various sizes.
- Water Bath Canner or Pressure Canner: Choose the method based on the food type—water bath for high-acid foods like fruits, and pressure canning for low-acid foods like meats.
- Jar Lifter: A tool for safely removing hot jars from boiling water, essential for avoiding burns and ensuring a secure grip.
- Canning Funnel: Helps fill jars neatly without spills. A wide-mouth funnel makes it easier to transfer liquids and solids.
- Lid Wands: Magnetic tools that lift sterilized lids from hot water without contaminating them.

## 3. Techniques and Tips

- Sterilization: Always sterilize jars and lids before use to prevent contamination. Boil for 10 minutes or use a dishwasher's sterilize setting.
- Headspace Management: Leave the recommended space between the food and lid to allow for expansion, ensuring a proper seal.
- Labeling: Clearly label jars with contents and date to track your preserves and use older ones first.
- Processing Times: Follow recommended times based on altitude, food type, and method to ensure safety.
- Storage: Store canned goods in a cool, dark place to maintain quality and prevent seal degradation.

# *April 6: Dessert Pairing*

## 1. The Art of Dessert Pairing

Pairing desserts with the right drinks or accompaniments can elevate the dining experience. Whether it's matching rich chocolate cake with bold red wine or pairing light sorbet with sparkling wine, dessert pairing requires an understanding of flavors and textures. The right pairing enhances both dessert and drink, creating a harmonious balance that pleases the palate.

## 2. Tools and Materials

- Tasting Glasses: Use appropriate glassware to enhance the flavor and aroma of different beverages.
- Serving Utensils: Ensure you have the right tools, like a cake knife or parfait spoon, to serve desserts properly.
- Flavor Reference Guide: Use a guide to understand complementary flavors, whether from books, apps, or charts.
- Presentation Dishes: Elegant dishes and platters showcase the pairing, adding to the overall experience.
- Pairing Notes: Keep a journal of successful pairings to refine your palate and develop a deeper understanding.

## 3. Techniques and Tips

- Flavor Balance: Match dessert intensity with the drink. A rich dessert pairs well with a robust drink, while lighter desserts go with more delicate beverages. For example, pair dense chocolate cake with full-bodied port wine.
- Consider Texture: Pair creamy desserts with crisp beverages for delightful contrast, like panna cotta with dry Champagne.
- Experiment: Try unconventional pairings to discover exciting combinations. Consider cheese with fruit-based desserts or herbal infusions with chocolate.
- Temperature Matters: Serve drinks and desserts at optimal temperatures to enhance flavors. Warm desserts pair well with cold beverages, and vice versa.
- Timing: Serve pairings at the right moment to ensure maximum enjoyment, considering meal flow and transitions.

# *April 7: Distilling*

## 1. The Craft of Distilling

Distilling is the process of separating liquid components through boiling and condensation, often to produce spirits like whiskey, vodka, or gin. It requires precision, patience, and a deep understanding of ingredients and the process. Home distilling can be rewarding, but it's crucial to follow legal guidelines and safety precautions. The process involves careful temperature and timing control to create high-quality, flavorful spirits.

## 2. Tools and Materials

- Still: The primary equipment for distilling, available in various sizes and designs. Pot stills are common for whiskey, while column stills are often used for vodka.
- Fermentation Vessels: Airtight containers used to ferment base ingredients before distillation, often equipped with airlocks.
- Hydrometer: Measures alcohol content to ensure desired strength, helping adjust the fermentation process and final proofing.
- Aging Barrels: Used to age spirits and develop complex flavors. Oak barrels are common, imparting vanilla, caramel, and spice notes.
- Bottling Equipment: Includes bottles, corks, and labels for storing and presenting your finished product, ensuring it's preserved for aging or immediate consumption.

## 3. Techniques and Tips

- Temperature Control: Maintain precise temperatures during distillation to achieve correct alcohol separation, crucial for quality.
- Aging: Spirits benefit from aging in barrels, which add flavors and complexity. Experiment with different barrel types, like charred oak or cherry wood, to influence flavor.
- Safety Precautions: Distill in a well-ventilated area and follow regional laws. Distilling can be dangerous if not done correctly, so prioritize safety.
- Flavor Infusion: Add botanicals, herbs, or spices during distillation for unique flavors, as commonly done in gin-making.
- Blending: Combine different distillations to achieve a balanced flavor profile, creating complex, layered spirits.

# *April 8: Edible Flowers*

## 1. The Beauty and Flavor of Edible Flowers

Edible flowers add both beauty and unique flavors to dishes. From the peppery notes of nasturtiums to the sweet scent of lavender, they can enhance salads, desserts, beverages, and more. Knowing which flowers are safe to eat and how to use them can elevate your culinary creations. Edible flowers have been used for centuries in various cultural cuisines, from Asian dishes to European desserts.

## 2. Tools and Materials

- Flower Snips: Small, sharp scissors for harvesting flowers without damage, keeping them fresh for dishes.
- Flower Press: Preserve flowers by pressing them for later decoration, useful in baking or as garnishes.
- Reference Guide: Essential for ensuring flowers are safe to eat, as some can be toxic, so proper identification is crucial.
- Herb Drying Rack: Useful for drying flowers for teas, baking, or decoration. Dried flowers retain flavor and can be stored long-term.
- Storage Containers: Airtight containers preserve dried or pressed flowers' freshness and flavor. Use glass jars or tins to keep them away from moisture and light.

## 3. Techniques and Tips

- Harvesting: Pick flowers early in the morning when they are most hydrated and flavorful. Avoid flowers treated with pesticides or growing near pollutants.
- Usage: Use flowers fresh or preserve them in sugar, syrups, or oils for various dishes. Flowers can be candied, infused into drinks, or mixed into batters.
- Pairing: Match flower flavors with other ingredients for harmony. For example, pair violet sweetness with dark chocolate or nasturtium's peppery taste with goat cheese.
- Presentation: Add color and elegance using whole flowers, petals, or finely chopped, depending on your desired effect.
- Seasonality: Use seasonal flowers for peak flavor, abundance, and affordability, as different flowers bloom at different times.

# *April 9: Ethnic Cooking*

## 1. Exploring the World Through Ethnic Cooking
Ethnic cooking explores the diverse culinary traditions of different cultures. Each cuisine reflects its region's history, climate, and practices. By learning ethnic cooking techniques, you can bring global flavors into your kitchen and gain a deeper appreciation for cultural diversity. It's a chance to expand your culinary skills while honoring the traditions behind each dish.

## 2. Tools and Materials
- Specialized Cookware: Tools like a wok, tagine, or comal are essential for achieving authentic textures and flavors specific to each cuisine.
- Spice Grinder: Freshly ground spices enhance the flavor of ethnic dishes. A quality grinder helps bring out the full aroma and taste of spices.
- Ingredient Sourcing: Authentic ingredients are key; shop at specialty stores or online for items like Thai fish sauce, Indian ghee, or Japanese miso.
- Cookbooks and Online Resources: Reference materials guide you on traditional methods and ingredient substitutions. Look for cookbooks by native chefs or reputable online sources.
- Mortar and Pestle: Essential in many ethnic cuisines for grinding spices, herbs, and pastes, enhancing control over texture and flavor.

## 3. Techniques and Tips
- Learn the Basics: Start with foundational dishes like Italian pasta, Indian curry, or Japanese sushi to build confidence before exploring complex recipes.
- Understand Flavor Profiles: Cuisines like Thai balance sweet, salty, sour, and spicy. Knowing these profiles helps create authentic dishes.
- Cultural Respect: Understand and respect the cultural significance behind the food. Learn about the history and customs associated with the dishes you prepare.
- Experimentation: Once comfortable with basics, experiment with fusion cooking or adapt recipes to your taste while preserving the integrity of the original dish.
- Cooking Techniques: Ethnic cuisines often involve specific techniques like stir-frying, slow-cooking, or fermentation. Mastering these enhances authenticity and flavor.

# *April 10: Fermenting*

## 1. The Tradition of Fermenting

Fermentation is an ancient method of preserving food while enhancing flavor and nutrition. From sauerkraut and kimchi to yogurt and kombucha, fermentation uses beneficial bacteria to transform ingredients. Fermented foods offer complex flavors and health benefits, with each culture having its own unique techniques and traditions.

## 2. Tools and Materials

- Fermentation Vessels: Use glass jars or crocks, as they don't react with acids produced during fermentation. Keep them clean and contaminant-free.
- Airlocks and Weights: Airlocks let gases escape while preventing air entry; weights keep food submerged, ensuring proper fermentation.
- pH Strips: Monitor acidity to ensure safety and prevent harmful bacteria growth.
- Fermentation Crock: A ceramic crock with a water-sealed lid is ideal for large batches, allowing gases to escape while keeping out air.
- Glass Weights: Keep food submerged in brine to ensure proper fermentation and prevent mold.

## 3. Techniques and Tips

- Cleanliness: Sterilize all equipment before starting to avoid contamination. Use boiling water or sterilizing solutions.
- Temperature Control: Maintain a consistent temperature for your type of fermentation; cooler slows the process, while warmer speeds it up.
- Patience: Fermentation takes time, so let it unfold naturally for the best results. Longer fermentation develops more complex flavors.
- Taste Testing: Regularly taste your ferment to monitor progress and stop when it reaches your desired flavor. Flavors continue to develop after refrigeration.
- Experiment: Add different herbs, spices, or vegetables for unique flavors. Try garlic, dill, or mustard seeds in vegetable ferments or fruit in kombucha.

# *April 11: Gourmet Cooking*

## 1. The Excellence of Gourmet Cooking

Gourmet cooking transforms everyday dining into an art form by focusing on high-quality ingredients, sophisticated techniques, and meticulous presentation. Whether crafting a multi-course meal or a refined dish, gourmet cooking emphasizes detail, flavor balance, and visual appeal, setting it apart from everyday meals.

## 2. Tools and Materials

- Chef's Knife: A high-quality, sharp knife is essential for precise cuts and efficient preparation, offering better control and reducing fatigue.
- Sauté Pans and Sauciers: Ideal for delicate sauces and perfectly cooked proteins. Stainless steel or copper pans provide even heat distribution.
- Plating Tools: Tweezers, squeeze bottles, and molds assist in precise, artistic plating, allowing for beautiful food arrangement.
- Sous-Vide Equipment: This precise cooking method uses low-temperature water baths for even cooking and moisture retention. A sous-vide machine and vacuum sealer are essential.
- Microplane: Perfect for zesting citrus, grating spices, or adding delicate garnishes like chocolate or cheese.

## 3. Techniques and Tips

- Mastering Techniques: Learn techniques like sous-vide, reduction, and emulsification to create gourmet dishes and elevate your cooking.
- Ingredient Quality: Use the freshest, highest-quality ingredients to enhance flavors. Organic produce, grass-fed meats, and artisan cheeses make a significant difference.
- Plating: Presentation is key; focus on color, texture, and symmetry. Use negative space, height, and garnishes for visually appealing plates.
- Flavor Pairing: Experiment with unusual flavor combinations, such as pairing sweet with savory or adding acidity to balance richness.
- Timing: Coordinate the cooking of each component to ensure everything is served at its peak, especially in multi-course meals.

# *April 12: Herb Gardening*

## 1. The Benefits of Herb Gardening

Herb gardening is a rewarding hobby that provides fresh, aromatic herbs for cooking, teas, and home remedies. Growing your own herbs ensures the freshest flavors and allows you to try varieties not always available in stores. Herb gardening also enhances your garden with beautiful foliage and pleasant fragrances, creating a delightful sensory experience.

## 2. Tools and Materials

- Pots and Planters: Choose containers with good drainage suited to the herb plants' size. Terra cotta pots are popular for their airflow to roots.
- Quality Soil: Use well-draining, nutrient-rich soil to support healthy herb growth. Add compost or organic matter to enrich the soil.
- Pruning Shears: Regular pruning keeps herbs healthy and encourages new growth. Sharp shears ensure clean cuts, reducing the risk of disease.
- Watering Can: A watering can with a fine rose head is ideal for gently watering delicate seedlings and mature plants.
- Grow Lights: Use grow lights indoors or in low-light areas to ensure your herbs receive enough light to thrive.

## 3. Techniques and Tips

- Sunlight and Watering: Most herbs need plenty of sunlight and regular watering, but avoid overwatering. Herbs like rosemary and thyme prefer drier conditions, while basil and mint thrive with more moisture.
- Harvesting: Regularly harvest your herbs by cutting just above a set of leaves to encourage further growth. Morning harvesting, when oils are most concentrated, yields the best flavor.
- Preservation: Preserve excess herbs by drying, freezing, or infusing them in oils or vinegars. Dried herbs store for months, while frozen herbs retain fresh flavor when thawed.
- Companion Planting: Plant herbs that benefit each other, like basil with tomatoes or mint with cabbage. Companion planting can improve growth and deter pests.
- Seasonal Care: Move tender herbs indoors during colder months or protect them with cloches. Hardy herbs like sage and thyme can withstand cooler temperatures but may benefit from mulching.

# *April 13: Ice Cream Making*

## 1. The Delight of Ice Cream Making

Making ice cream at home lets you customize flavors, control ingredients, and enjoy a fresh treat. Whether you prefer classic vanilla or adventurous combinations like lavender honey, homemade ice cream is a fun way to indulge your sweet tooth. Creating ice cream from scratch offers endless possibilities for flavor and texture.

## 2. Tools and Materials

- Ice Cream Maker: A quality machine is essential for churning smooth, creamy ice cream. Whether hand-cranked or electric, the right maker ensures consistent texture.
- Mixing Bowls: Use stainless steel or glass bowls to combine ingredients and chill the mixture before freezing.
- Storage Containers: Airtight containers maintain texture and prevent freezer burn. Shallow containers aid quicker freezing and easier scooping.
- Whisk and Spatula: Essential for mixing ingredients and folding in add-ins like chocolate chips or fruit. A silicone spatula is ideal for scraping bowls.
- Candy Thermometer: Crucial for custard-based ice creams, where precise temperature control ensures the right consistency.

## 3. Techniques and Tips

- Base Preparation: Master your ice cream base, whether custard-based or simple cream and sugar. A well-made base is key to smooth, flavorful ice cream.
- Flavor Infusion: Experiment with adding vanilla beans, fruit purees, or spices during base preparation. Steeping ingredients like coffee beans or mint leaves infuses rich flavors.
- Proper Churning: Follow your ice cream maker's instructions to churn to the right consistency. Avoid over-churning, which can make the ice cream icy.
- Add-Ins and Swirls: Fold in nuts, chocolate chips, or fruit near the end of churning. Layer swirls of caramel or fudge when transferring to the storage container.
- Serving: Let ice cream soften slightly at room temperature before serving for the best texture. A warm scoop helps create perfect, round scoops.

# *April 14: Jam Making*

## 1. The Tradition of Jam Making

Jam making is a time-honored tradition that preserves seasonal fruits' flavors. Whether using strawberries, blueberries, or apricots, homemade jam captures summer's sweetness in a jar. It's a simple process resulting in a delicious spread for toast, pastries, and more. Making jam at home allows you to control ingredients, ensuring a healthier, more flavorful product than store-bought versions.

## 2. Tools and Materials

- Canning Jars and Lids: Use sterilized jars to safely preserve your jam. Mason jars with two-part lids are ideal for creating an airtight seal that keeps jam fresh for months.
- Maslin Pan: A wide, shallow pan ideal for making jam as it allows quick evaporation of liquid. The large surface area helps achieve the right consistency and prevents overcooking.
- Thermometer: Monitor your jam's temperature to ensure it reaches the setting point. A candy or jam thermometer is essential for accuracy.
- Ladle and Funnel: Use these to transfer hot jam into jars without spills or burns. A wide-mouthed funnel ensures neat, efficient filling.
- Pectin: A natural thickening agent found in fruit that helps jam set properly. Use liquid or powdered pectin, depending on the recipe.

## 3. Techniques and Tips

- Pectin Use: Understand how pectin affects jam texture. Some fruits, like apples and citrus, are naturally high in pectin, while others may require added pectin.
- Sugar Ratios: Balance sugar and fruit for desired sweetness and preservation. Too little sugar can prevent setting, while too much can overpower the fruit's flavor.
- Setting Test: Use the wrinkle test on a cold plate to check consistency. If a drop wrinkles when pushed, it's ready to jar.
- Boiling Time: Ensure your jam boils rapidly to activate pectin and evaporate excess moisture. A rolling boil is crucial for proper setting.
- Storage: Store jam in a cool, dark place to preserve its color and flavor. Once opened, refrigerate and use within a few weeks.

# *April 15: Knife Skills*

## 1. The Importance of Knife Skills

Mastering knife skills is fundamental to cooking. Good technique ensures efficiency, safety, and precision in the kitchen. Whether slicing, dicing, or julienning, proper knife skills elevate your cooking and make the process more enjoyable. Confident knife handling transforms your cooking experience, making it faster, more efficient, and improving your dishes' appearance.

## 2. Tools and Materials

- Chef's Knife: A sharp, well-balanced chef's knife is essential for most tasks, used for chopping, slicing, and dicing various ingredients.
- Paring Knife: Useful for delicate tasks like peeling and trimming, its small size allows precision work such as deveining shrimp or coring apples.
- Cutting Board: A sturdy, non-slip board protects your knives and provides a safe surface for cutting. Wooden or plastic boards are preferred for durability and easy cleaning.
- Sharpening Stone: Keeps knives in peak condition by sharpening regularly. A sharp knife is safer and more efficient than a dull one.
- Knife Guard: A protective cover keeps blades sharp and prevents accidents during storage.

## 3. Techniques and Tips

- Grip and Posture: Learn to grip a knife properly and maintain safe posture while cutting. Use a pinch grip on the blade and keep fingers curled under on the hand holding the food.
- Cutting Techniques: Practice chopping, slicing, and dicing to improve speed and precision, each serving a specific purpose from creating uniform pieces to enhancing presentation.
- Knife Maintenance: Keep knives sharp for safety and efficiency. Regularly hone with a steel rod to keep the edge aligned, and sharpen occasionally to restore the blade.
- Chopping Speed: Increase speed by practicing regularly, focusing on consistency. Over time, you'll develop muscle memory for quicker, more accurate cuts.
- Safety Precautions: Always cut away from your body and avoid leaving knives in the sink or unattended on the counter to prevent accidents.

# *April 16: Latte Art*

## 1. The Creativity of Latte Art

Latte art involves creating designs on a latte by carefully pouring steamed milk into espresso, adding an artistic touch to your coffee. With practice, you can create hearts, rosettas, tulips, and more, turning your morning coffee into a work of art. Latte art enhances the coffee experience by showcasing skill and attention to detail.

## 2. Tools and Materials

- Espresso Machine: A machine with a steam wand is essential for the microfoam needed for latte art. The quality of the espresso also impacts the final look.
- Milk Pitcher: A stainless steel pitcher with a pointed spout helps control the milk flow for detailed designs.
- Espresso Beans: High-quality beans ensure a strong, rich base. Freshness and roast level influence crema and flavor.
- Thermometer: A thermometer helps steam milk to the perfect temperature, crucial for smooth, velvety microfoam.
- Latte Art Pen: A fine-tipped tool for etching intricate designs. Useful for detailed artwork but not essential for basic patterns.

## 3. Techniques and Tips

- Microfoam Creation: Practice steaming milk to create velvety microfoam. Aerate just enough to create tiny bubbles, then fold the milk for a smooth texture.
- Pouring Technique: Control the flow and speed of the milk pour to shape your design. Start from a higher angle, then lower the pitcher to form the design.
- Practice Designs: Begin with simple designs like hearts and progress to more complex patterns. Consistency in espresso shots and milk steaming is key.
- Temperature Control: Steam milk to 150°F-160°F for the best texture. Overheated milk can scald, while underheated milk may not froth properly.
- Experimentation: Experiment with different milks or coffee to see how they affect the design. Non-dairy milks like almond or oat can also create beautiful art with the right technique.

# *April 17: Meal Planning*

## 1. The Benefits of Meal Planning

Meal planning organizes your weekly meals, ensuring balanced nutrition while saving time and money. By planning ahead, you make healthier choices, reduce food waste, and streamline grocery shopping. Meal planning adds variety to your diet, preventing repetitive meals and encouraging new recipes.

## 2. Tools and Materials

- Planner or App: Use a meal planning app or calendar to organize your meals. Digital apps can offer features like recipe storage, grocery lists, and nutritional info.
- Shopping List: Create a list based on your meal plan to ensure you have all necessary ingredients. Organize by store sections for efficient shopping.
- Storage Containers: Prepare meals in advance and store them in airtight containers. Glass containers are ideal as they are microwave and oven-safe.
- Cookbooks and Online Resources: Gather recipes to keep your meal plan diverse. Choose recipes that fit your dietary preferences and goals.
- Freezer Bags: Store prepped ingredients or meals in labeled freezer bags for easy reheating later.

## 3. Techniques and Tips

- Balanced Meals: Ensure each meal includes protein, carbs, and vegetables for optimal nutrition. Use the plate method—half vegetables, a quarter protein, a quarter whole grains.
- Batch Cooking: Prepare large quantities of food to portion out and use throughout the week, saving time and ensuring you always have a healthy meal ready.
- Flexibility: Be flexible to accommodate schedule changes or cravings. Keep backup meals or pantry staples on hand for easy adaptation.
- Prep Ahead: Chop vegetables, marinate proteins, or cook grains in advance to simplify weeknight meals. Prepping on the weekend makes weekday cooking easier.
- Incorporate Leftovers: Plan meals that use leftovers to reduce waste. For example, roast chicken one night can become chicken salad or soup the next day.

# *April 18: Noodle Making*

## 1. The Craft of Noodle Making

Making noodles from scratch is a rewarding process that lets you customize the texture and flavor of your pasta. Whether you're making Italian pasta, Asian noodles, or something in between, homemade noodles elevate any dish with their freshness. Noodle making connects you to culinary traditions and allows experimentation with shapes, flavors, and techniques.

## 2. Tools and Materials

- Pasta Machine/Rolling Pin: A pasta machine rolls out even sheets of dough, while a rolling pin offers a more hands-on approach.
- Cutting Tools: Use a sharp knife or specialized cutters for various noodle shapes, from fettuccine to ravioli.
- Flour: High-quality flour is key for achieving the right texture. Use all-purpose for versatility, or semolina for a firmer bite.
- Dough Scraper: Helps mix and knead the dough, as well as lift and transfer it without tearing. Also useful for cleaning the work surface.
- Drying Rack: Ideal for hanging noodles to dry if not cooking immediately, preventing them from sticking together.

## 3. Techniques and Tips

- Dough Preparation: Knead until smooth and elastic for a good texture. Resting the dough for at least 30 minutes relaxes the gluten, making it easier to roll out.
- Shaping: Experiment with shapes, from spaghetti to lasagna sheets. Ensure filled pasta is well-sealed to prevent leaks during cooking.
- Cooking: Fresh noodles cook quickly. Test for al dente by tasting; they should be tender with a slight bite.
- Flour Dusting: Lightly dust noodles with flour to prevent sticking during rolling or cutting, especially for longer noodles like linguine.
- Storage: Freeze uncooked noodles in small portions on a baking sheet, then transfer to a sealed bag for longer storage.

# *April 19: Organic Cooking*

## 1. The Principles of Organic Cooking

Organic cooking emphasizes using ingredients grown without synthetic pesticides, herbicides, or fertilizers. It's about cooking with natural ingredients that benefit your health and the environment. This approach focuses on sustainability and seasonal produce, helping you create meals that are delicious and nourishing for both body and planet.

## 2. Tools and Materials

- Organic Ingredients: Source from local farmers' markets or organic grocery sections, ensuring they meet strict agricultural standards.
- Reusable Shopping Bags: Use reusable, biodegradable bags made from natural fibers like cotton or jute to reduce waste.
- Composting Bin: Turn kitchen scraps into compost to enrich garden soil and reduce waste.
- Glass Storage Containers: Store produce and leftovers in glass containers to avoid chemicals from plastic and keep food fresher longer.
- Herb Garden: Grow your own organic herbs like basil, mint, and parsley for fresh flavors, even in small spaces.

## 3. Techniques and Tips

- Seasonal Eating: Use seasonal ingredients for the freshest, most flavorful dishes, often more affordable and supporting local farmers.
- Minimal Processing: Keep cooking simple to let natural flavors shine by focusing on fresh, whole ingredients.
- Sustainability: Reduce waste by using every part of the ingredient, like making broth from vegetable scraps or zesting citrus peels.
- Preservation: Learn canning, drying, and freezing to preserve produce at its peak, enjoying summer flavors year-round.
- Supporting Local Farmers: Buy directly from farmers or join a CSA to support sustainable practices and ensure the freshest produce.

# *April 20: Pastry Making*

## 1. The Precision of Pastry Making

Pastry making is a delicate craft requiring precise measurements and technique. From flaky croissants to delicate éclairs, mastering pastry opens up delicious possibilities. Understanding the science behind pastry-making is key to perfecting texture and flavor. Each step, from mixing to baking, contributes to the success of the final product.

## 2. Tools and Materials

- Pastry Blender or Food Processor: These tools cut butter into flour for perfect pastry dough. A blender is ideal for hand-mixing, while a processor speeds up the process.
- Rolling Pin: Essential for rolling dough evenly. A heavy, smooth rolling pin ensures consistent thickness.
- Pastry Brush: Apply glazes, egg washes, or seal edges with a silicone brush for even application.
- Pastry Cutter: Cuts dough into shapes for cookies, pies, or pastries, offering various decorative effects.
- Baking Weights: Used to keep pastry from puffing during blind baking, these reusable weights ensure even heat distribution.

## 3. Techniques and Tips

- Cold Ingredients: Keep ingredients cold to prevent butter from melting, creating steam pockets for a light, flaky texture.
- Resting Dough: Rest dough in the fridge to relax gluten, making it easier to work with and preventing shrinkage during baking.
- Baking Time: Monitor pastries closely to achieve a golden-brown color. Avoid overbaking, which dries out pastries, and underbaking, which leaves them doughy.
- Lamination: For layered pastries, folding and rolling butter into dough is crucial for creating more layers and a flakier texture.
- Filling Techniques: Ensure the filling is evenly distributed and not too wet to avoid sogginess, using thickening agents like cornstarch or flour as needed.

# *April 21: Quick Pickling*

## 1. The Simplicity of Quick Pickling

Quick pickling is an easy way to preserve vegetables while adding flavor. Unlike traditional pickling, which takes weeks, quick pickling can be done in just a few hours or overnight. It's a versatile technique for vegetables and even fruits, ideal for adding a tangy crunch to dishes like sandwiches, salads, and charcuterie boards.

## 2. Tools and Materials

- Glass Jars: Sterilized glass jars, like Mason jars with tight-fitting lids, maintain freshness and prevent spills.
- Vinegar: Use white, apple cider, or rice vinegar as the base for your pickling solution, each offering a unique flavor profile.
- Spices: Customize your pickles with spices like dill, mustard seeds, garlic, or peppercorns. Fresh herbs, chili flakes, and bay leaves add depth of flavor.
- Mandoline: A mandoline slicer ensures uniform vegetable slices, leading to even pickling and better presentation.
- Pickling Salt: Use pure, additive-free salt for pickling, as regular salt may cloud the brine.

## 3. Techniques and Tips

- Slice Uniformly: Cut vegetables into uniform pieces for even pickling. Thicker slices retain crunch, while thinner slices absorb more flavor.
- Boiling the Brine: Boil vinegar, water, and spices before pouring over vegetables. This dissolves salt and infuses the brine with spice flavors.
- Storage: Store pickles in the refrigerator for several weeks. For best flavor, let them marinate for at least 24 hours before eating.
- Flavor Combinations: Experiment with different vegetables and spices to create unique flavors, like red onions with thyme or cucumbers with dill.
- Serving Ideas: Use quick pickles as a garnish or part of an appetizer platter. Their bright acidity balances rich or fatty dishes.

# *April 22: Recipe Development*

## 1. The Creativity of Recipe Development

Recipe development involves creating new dishes by experimenting with ingredients, techniques, and flavors. Whether tweaking an existing recipe or inventing something new, it's a way to express creativity in the kitchen. The process blends science and art, requiring knowledge of cooking principles and a willingness to explore new combinations through testing, tasting, and refining.

## 2. Tools and Materials

- Notebook or App: Track ideas, measurements, and cooking times. Documenting the process helps refine recipes and allows for easy adjustments later.
- Scale: Use a kitchen scale for precise measurements, especially in baking, to ensure consistency and reproducibility.
- Taste Testers: Feedback from others can provide insights into flavor balance, texture, and appeal, helping refine your recipes.
- Reference Books: Cookbooks and guides offer inspiration and foundational knowledge on flavor pairing, techniques, and cuisines.
- Ingredient Substitutes: Experiment with substitutes to accommodate dietary restrictions or create dish variations, expanding creative possibilities.

## 3. Techniques and Tips

- Start Simple: Begin with a basic concept and build by adding new ingredients or techniques. Simple recipes are easier to tweak and provide a clear starting point.
- Balance Flavors: Aim for a balance of sweet, salty, sour, bitter, and umami in your dishes, considering each ingredient's role in the overall taste.
- Test and Refine: Test your recipe multiple times, making necessary adjustments. Take notes on what works and what doesn't.
- Presentation: Consider color, texture, and plating, as presentation affects both perception and enjoyment of food.
- Seasonal Ingredients: Use seasonal produce to enhance flavor and appeal. Fresher ingredients inspire new recipe ideas and improve overall dish quality.

# *April 23: Sourdough Baking*

## 1. The Craft of Sourdough Baking

Sourdough baking is an ancient art that uses wild yeast and bacteria to leaven bread. The process begins with fermenting flour and water to create a starter, which is then used to make the dough. Sourdough's tangy flavor and chewy texture develop through a long fermentation process, requiring both patience and practice. This method not only enhances flavor but also improves digestibility.

## 2. Tools and Materials

- Sourdough Starter: A healthy starter is key for good sourdough. You can make your own or get one from a reliable source. Regular feeding keeps it active.
- Dutch Oven: Traps steam, creating a crusty exterior and tender interior.
- Lame: A sharp blade for scoring dough, allowing it to expand and creating decorative crust patterns.
- Bench Scraper: Useful for handling sticky dough, dividing loaves, and cleaning surfaces.
- Banneton: A proofing basket that shapes the dough as it rises, with ridges that leave a pattern and a linen liner to prevent sticking.

## 3. Techniques and Tips

- Feeding the Starter: Keep your starter healthy by feeding it regularly with flour and water. A well-fed starter bubbles and doubles in size, showing it's ready.
- Bulk Fermentation: Let the dough ferment slowly at a cool temperature for better flavor and texture. Longer fermentation develops tanginess and complexity.
- Scoring: Master scoring to control expansion and create decorative crust patterns. Deep cuts allow for proper expansion, while shallow cuts offer subtle designs.
- Steam in Baking: Ensure enough steam for a good rise and crispy crust, using a Dutch oven or a pan of water in the oven.
- Patience is Key: Patience is essential, from developing the starter to proofing the dough. Rushing can lead to dense or uneven bread.

# *April 24: Tea Blending*

## 1. The Art of Tea Blending

Tea blending involves combining various tea leaves, herbs, spices, and botanicals to create unique flavors. Whether you prefer a soothing herbal mix or a bold black tea, blending your own allows you to customize the flavor profile. The key is understanding how different teas and ingredients interact to form a balanced, harmonious blend.

## 2. Tools and Materials

- Loose Leaf Tea: Start with high-quality loose leaf teas for better flavor and aroma compared to bagged tea.
- Herbs and Spices: Experiment with ingredients like mint, ginger, and dried fruits to add complexity and achieve desired effects—whether calming or invigorating.
- Storage Containers: Use airtight containers, such as glass jars or tins, to keep your blends fresh and aromatic.
- Tea Strainer: A fine mesh strainer or infuser is essential for brewing loose leaf tea efficiently.
- Measuring Spoon: Ensure consistent portions of tea and ingredients with a measuring spoon, helping you recreate blends accurately.

## 3. Techniques and Tips

- Balancing Flavors: Adjust ratios of tea leaves, herbs, and spices to achieve a balanced flavor. Start with small batches and tweak to your taste.
- Themed Blends: Create blends based on themes like seasonal flavors, mood enhancement, or health benefits—e.g., a winter blend with cinnamon and cloves, or a calming mix of chamomile and lavender.
- Steeping Time: Monitor steeping times to avoid bitterness, especially with herbs that can become over-steeped. Begin with a shorter time and adjust according to taste.
- Custom Blends: Add unique ingredients like rare teas or special herbs to personalize your blends, making them one-of-a-kind.
- Labeling: Clearly label your blends with ingredients and proportions to track experiments and refine your recipes.

# *April 25: Udon Noodles*

## 1. The Tradition of Udon Noodles

Udon noodles are thick, chewy Japanese noodles made from wheat flour, water, and salt. A staple of Japanese cuisine, they are often served in broth or stir-fried with vegetables and meat. Making udon from scratch involves kneading, rolling, and cutting the dough for the perfect texture. The result is a versatile noodle used in various dishes, from soups to cold salads.

## 2. Tools and Materials

- Mixing Bowl: Use a large, stable bowl for combining ingredients and kneading the dough.
- Rolling Pin: A sturdy rolling pin, traditionally wooden, flattens the dough to the desired thickness.
- Sharp Knife: A sharp knife ensures uniform noodles, leading to even cooking and better texture.
- Boiling Pot: A large pot is necessary for boiling the noodles freely without sticking.
- Flour for Dusting: Extra flour prevents sticking and aids in rolling and cutting.

## 3. Techniques and Tips

- Dough Preparation: Knead until smooth and elastic, about 10-15 minutes. Resting the dough develops gluten, resulting in chewier noodles.
- Rolling and Cutting: Roll dough evenly to your preferred thickness. Thicker noodles are heartier, while thinner noodles cook faster.
- Boiling: Cook in boiling water until noodles float, then rinse under cold water to remove excess starch.
- Serving: Serve hot in broth or cold with dipping sauces. Experiment with different broths and toppings like tempura, green onions, and sesame seeds.
- Storage: Fresh udon can be refrigerated for a few days or frozen for longer storage. Dust with flour before freezing and store in an airtight container.

# *April 26: Vinegar Making*

## 1. The Craft of Vinegar Making

Vinegar making is a fermentation process that turns alcohol into acetic acid, creating a tangy condiment. Whether making apple cider, balsamic, or flavored vinegars, the process requires patience and careful monitoring. Homemade vinegar has a depth of flavor surpassing store-bought varieties and can be customized with herbs, fruits, or spices. It's a rewarding way to use excess fruit or wine and add creativity to your pantry.

## 2. Tools and Materials

- Glass Jar or Crock: Use a non-reactive container like glass or ceramic for fermenting. Avoid metal, which can affect flavor.
- Cheesecloth: Cover the container with cheesecloth for airflow while keeping out dust and pests.
- Mother of Vinegar: A gelatinous substance with acetic acid bacteria, essential for fermentation. Purchase a mother or use raw, unfiltered vinegar to create your own.
- Wooden Spoon: Stir with a wooden spoon during fermentation to avoid metal reactions.
- Storage Bottles: Store vinegar in sterilized glass bottles with tight lids. Dark bottles protect from light, preserving flavor.

## 3. Techniques and Tips

- Starting the Fermentation: Combine alcohol (wine, cider, or beer) with the mother of vinegar. Alcohol content should be around 5-7% for optimal fermentation.
- Fermentation Time: Let the mixture ferment in a warm, dark place for weeks to months, depending on desired flavor. Taste periodically to check progress.
- Straining: Once vinegar reaches desired acidity, strain out the mother and solids using cheesecloth or a fine mesh strainer for clear, smooth vinegar.
- Flavoring: Experiment with herbs, spices, or fruits to infuse additional flavors. For example, add garlic and rosemary for savory vinegar or berries for a fruity twist.
- Aging: Aging vinegar for a few months deepens flavor and smooths out harsh notes. Store in a cool, dark place to mature.

# *April 27: Wine Making*

## 1. The Craft of Wine Making

Wine making involves fermenting grapes or other fruits to produce wine, a tradition spanning thousands of years. Making wine at home allows experimentation with grape varieties, blends, and aging methods. While the process can be complex, it's a rewarding hobby resulting in a product that can be enjoyed for years. Home winemakers can customize their wine to their taste, from dry to sweet, creating something unique.

## 2. Tools and Materials

- Fermentation Vessel: A glass carboy or stainless steel fermenter is ideal, allowing some headspace for fermentation.
- Hydrometer: Measures specific gravity to determine alcohol content and track fermentation.
- Airlock: Allows carbon dioxide to escape while preventing air entry, crucial for avoiding oxidation and contamination.
- Wine Yeast: Specialized yeast ferments sugars into alcohol, affecting flavor, aroma, and alcohol content.
- Bottling Equipment: Includes bottles, corks, and a corker. Dark bottles protect wine from light degradation.

## 3. Techniques and Tips

- Grape Selection: Choose high-quality grapes or fruit for the best wine, considering ripeness, sugar content, and acidity.
- Crushing and Pressing: Crush grapes to release juice; press to extract as much liquid as possible. Skins can be left in must for color and tannins in red wines.
- Fermentation: Monitor temperature as it affects fermentation speed and flavor complexity. Cooler temperatures preserve delicate aromas, while warmer ones speed up the process.
- Racking: Siphon wine off sediment to clarify and prevent off-flavors, doing it gently to avoid oxygen exposure.
- Aging: Age in bottles or barrels to develop flavor. The length depends on the wine type and personal preference.

# *April 28: Xocolatl (Chocolate Making)*

## 1. The Art of Xocolatl (Chocolate Making)

Xocolatl, the Aztec word for chocolate, represents the rich tradition of making chocolate from cacao beans. This delicate process involves roasting, grinding, and tempering cacao to create smooth, flavorful chocolate. Whether making dark, milk, or flavored chocolate, mastering the craft allows you to create custom confections that are as enjoyable to make as they are to eat.

## 2. Tools and Materials

- Cacao Beans: Start with high-quality beans for the best flavor. Different varieties offer unique profiles, from fruity to deep and earthy.
- Roasting Pan: Use a roasting pan or oven to roast the beans, developing their flavor. Roasting is crucial for bringing out chocolate's rich, complex notes.
- Grinder or Melanger: Grind roasted beans into a smooth paste (cocoa mass). A stone grinder or melanger ensures even grinding and a fine texture.
- Tempering Machine: A tempering machine controls the crystallization of cocoa butter, giving chocolate its smooth texture and glossy finish, along with its characteristic snap.
- Chocolate Molds: Shape the chocolate into bars, truffles, or other confections using silicone or polycarbonate molds for easy release.

## 3. Techniques and Tips

- Roasting: Roast cacao beans at a low temperature to develop flavor without burning. Stir frequently for even roasting.
- Grinding: Grind beans slowly to prevent overheating, which can cause the chocolate to lose temper. Grinding should take several hours for a smooth texture.
- Tempering: Carefully control the chocolate's temperature as it cools to achieve the right texture and shine. Improper tempering can lead to a dull appearance and grainy texture.
- Flavoring: Add flavors like vanilla, chili, or sea salt, balancing to avoid overpowering the natural cacao taste.
- Molding and Setting: Pour tempered chocolate into molds and set at a cool, consistent temperature. Once set, the chocolate should release easily with a smooth, glossy finish.

# *April 29: Yogurt Making*

## 1. The Simplicity of Yogurt Making

Yogurt making involves fermenting milk with live cultures to produce a creamy, tangy product. Homemade yogurt is often richer and more flavorful than store-bought and can be customized with various types of milk, flavors, and textures. Making yogurt at home allows you to control the ingredients, ensuring a natural, healthy product without additives or preservatives.

## 2. Tools and Materials

- Yogurt Maker or Thermos: A yogurt maker maintains the ideal temperature for fermentation, but a thermos can also work well. Consistent warmth is key to encouraging beneficial bacteria growth.
- Milk: Use fresh whole, low-fat, or non-dairy milk. The type of milk affects the yogurt's thickness and flavor.
- Starter Culture: A small amount of live-culture yogurt or powdered starter begins the fermentation process. The culture contains the bacteria that convert milk into yogurt.
- Thermometer: Monitor the milk temperature to ensure it stays within the optimal fermentation range, typically between 110°F and 115°F.
- Cheesecloth: For thicker, Greek-style yogurt, use cheesecloth to strain and remove excess whey.

## 3. Techniques and Tips

- Heating the Milk: Heat the milk to around 180°F, then cool to 110°F before adding the starter culture. This step helps denature proteins, resulting in thicker yogurt.
- Inoculation: Stir in the starter culture gently to distribute the bacteria evenly. Avoid overmixing, as this can disrupt fermentation.
- Incubation: Keep the mixture at a steady temperature for 6-12 hours, depending on your desired tartness. Longer incubation results in a tangier flavor.
- Flavoring: Add flavorings like honey, vanilla, or fruit after the yogurt has set. Stir gently to maintain the yogurt's texture.
- Storing and Serving: Store yogurt in the refrigerator to stop fermentation and enjoy within a week. Serve plain, with fresh fruit, or as a base for smoothies and desserts.

# *April 30: Zest Preservation*

## 1. The Art of Zest Preservation

Zest preservation involves saving the flavorful outer peel of citrus fruits for future use. Packed with essential oils, zest adds bright, aromatic flavor to both sweet and savory dishes. Preserving zest captures the fresh taste of citrus even when the fruit is out of season. It's a versatile ingredient used in baking, cooking, cocktails, and more.

## 2. Tools and Materials

- Microplane: The ideal tool for zesting citrus, finely grating the peel without removing the bitter pith. It's easy to use and creates light, fluffy zest.
- Citrus Fruits: Choose fresh, organic lemons, limes, oranges, or grapefruits. Organic fruits are free from pesticides that can linger on the peel.
- Dehydrator or Oven: Use a dehydrator or low-temperature oven to dry zest, preserving it for long-term storage. Drying intensifies flavor and extends shelf life.
- Airtight Containers: Store dried zest in airtight containers to protect from moisture and light. Glass jars or vacuum-sealed bags work well.
- Labeling Materials: Label containers with the type of zest and the preservation date to track freshness and variety.

## 3. Techniques and Tips

- Zesting Technique: Apply light pressure when zesting to avoid the bitter white pith. Rotate the fruit to remove only the outermost layer.
- Drying the Zest: Spread zest in a single layer on a baking sheet and dry in the oven at the lowest setting, or use a dehydrator. Ensure the zest is completely dry before storing.
- Freezing: For quick preservation, zest the fruit and freeze in small portions. Freeze flat before transferring to a container for easy use.
- Infusion: Infuse zest in sugar, salt, or oils to create flavored ingredients for various recipes. Citrus-infused sugar can be used in baking or as a sweetener for tea.
- Storage: Store dried zest in a cool, dark place, and use within six months for the best flavor. Zest may lose potency over time, so use it while still fragrant.

## *Conclusion for April*

April has been a culinary journey, exploring a wide range of food and drink techniques from appetizer making to zest preservation. This month has offered insights into both traditional and modern practices in the culinary world, emphasizing the importance of flavor, technique, and creativity. Whether you've discovered a new passion for baking, developed a skill for distilling, or simply enjoyed making homemade yogurt, the skills and knowledge gained this month will enhance your culinary repertoire. As you continue your journey in the kitchen, remember that the joy of food and drink lies in experimentation, learning, and sharing your creations with others.

# May: Games and Entertainment

*May is all about games and entertainment, a month dedicated to the joy of play, creativity, and strategy. From collecting action figures and designing board games to engaging in live-action role-playing and online gaming, this chapter covers a wide array of activities that challenge the mind, foster social connections, and offer endless entertainment. Whether you're interested in the history of games or the latest in virtual reality, May's activities provide a diverse exploration of what it means to play.*

# *May 1: Action Figure Collecting*

## 1. The Fascination with Action Figure Collecting

Action figure collecting is more than just amassing toys; it's about preserving pieces of pop culture and reliving the nostalgia of childhood. Collectors often focus on specific franchises, eras, or characters, making this hobby a unique way to connect with favorite stories and heroes. Whether it's superheroes, movie icons, or animated characters, each figure represents a piece of history and culture.

## 2. Tools and Materials

- Display Cases: Protect and showcase your figures in clear, dust-free cases. Proper display not only enhances the visual appeal but also preserves the condition of the figures.

- Condition and Packaging: Original packaging can significantly increase the value of action figures, so consider storing figures in their boxes if possible. Mint condition and intact packaging are crucial for collectors looking to maintain or increase the value of their collection.

- Cataloging Tools: Use software or apps to track your collection, including details like condition, rarity, and value. Organizing your collection helps in managing it efficiently and understanding its worth.

## 3. Techniques and Tips

- Specialization: Focus your collection on a particular theme, such as superheroes, vintage figures, or a specific franchise like Star Wars. Specializing allows you to build a more cohesive and valuable collection.

- Condition Awareness: Learn to assess the condition of figures, as mint-condition items with intact packaging are often the most valuable. Understanding the grading systems used by collectors can help you make informed purchasing decisions.

- Networking: Join collector communities online or at conventions to exchange tips, buy, sell, and trade figures. Engaging with other collectors can provide valuable insights and opportunities to expand your collection.

# *May 2: Airsoft*

## 1. The Thrill of Airsoft

Airsoft is a competitive team sport that simulates military combat using replica firearms that shoot plastic pellets. It's a physically demanding and strategic game that requires teamwork, quick thinking, and an understanding of tactics. Airsoft enthusiasts enjoy the adrenaline rush and the camaraderie that comes with playing in organized skirmishes. The sport is not just about shooting but involves strategy, communication, and discipline.

## 2. Tools and Materials

- Airsoft Guns: Choose from a variety of replicas, including rifles, pistols, and shotguns, each with different specifications. Your choice of weapon should match your play style and the role you prefer in team scenarios.
- Protective Gear: Safety is paramount in airsoft; always wear eye protection, and consider additional gear like helmets, vests, and gloves. Protecting your body ensures you can play safely and confidently.
- Tactical Gear: Use tactical vests, pouches, and holsters to carry extra ammunition and equipment. Being well-equipped allows you to stay in the game longer and perform better under pressure.

## 3. Techniques and Tips

- Tactics and Strategy: Work with your team to develop strategies that maximize your strengths and exploit the opponent's weaknesses. Whether it's defending a position or launching an attack, strategy is key to success.
- Communication: Use radios or hand signals to communicate with teammates during gameplay. Clear communication can be the difference between victory and defeat in a fast-paced environment.
- Weapon Maintenance: Regularly clean and maintain your airsoft guns to ensure reliability and accuracy. Proper maintenance prevents malfunctions and keeps your equipment in top condition.

# *May 3: Board Games*

## 1. The Joy of Playing Board Games

Board games are a timeless form of entertainment that bring people together to compete, strategize, and have fun. From classic games like Monopoly and Chess to modern strategy games like Settlers of Catan, board games cater to all ages and interests, offering a way to unplug and engage in face-to-face interaction. They are a great way to bond with family and friends, exercise your mind, and enjoy a shared experience.

## 2. Tools and Materials

- Game Collection: Start building a collection of games that cover various genres, such as strategy, party, cooperative, and abstract games. A diverse collection ensures that there's always a game to match the mood and group size.
- Game Accessories: Consider adding accessories like card sleeves, dice trays, and storage solutions to enhance the gaming experience. Proper storage and protection keep your games in good condition and ready for play.
- Game Table: A dedicated table with a smooth surface and ample space for game components can improve gameplay comfort and organization. Having a designated space for gaming can make setup and play more enjoyable.

## 3. Techniques and Tips

- Learn the Rules: Take the time to thoroughly understand the rules of each game, as this enhances the experience and reduces confusion during play. Being familiar with the rules also helps in teaching the game to others.
- Strategy Development: Work on developing strategies based on the mechanics of the game, whether it's resource management, bluffing, or area control. Understanding different strategies can increase your chances of winning and make the game more engaging.
- Social Interaction: Emphasize the social aspect of board gaming, encouraging friendly competition and cooperation. Board games are a great way to build connections and create lasting memories.

# *May 4: Board Game Design*

## 1. The Creativity of Board Game Design

Designing board games is a creative process that involves inventing new rules, mechanics, and themes to create a fun and engaging experience. Whether you're inspired by classic games or looking to innovate, board game design challenges you to think critically about gameplay, balance, and player interaction. This hobby allows you to explore your creativity while developing problem-solving skills and understanding human behavior.

## 2. Tools and Materials

- Prototyping Materials: Use cardboard, markers, and other craft supplies to create initial prototypes of your game. Early prototypes help you visualize your ideas and identify potential issues.
- Playtesting: Gather a group of players to test your game, providing feedback on gameplay, rules, and enjoyment. Playtesting is an essential part of refining your game and ensuring it's fun and balanced.
- Game Design Software: Consider using software tools to create more polished versions of your game components. Digital tools can help you design, print, and share your game more efficiently.

## 3. Techniques and Tips

- Theme and Mechanics: Start by deciding on a theme and the core mechanics that will drive your game. The theme should be engaging, and the mechanics should be easy to learn but offer depth in strategy.
- Iteration: Be prepared to revise your game multiple times based on feedback and testing. Continuous improvement is key to developing a successful game.
- Market Research: Study existing games to understand what makes them successful and identify gaps in the market. Knowing your audience and what they enjoy can guide your design process.

# *May 5: Card Games*

## 1. The Versatility of Card Games

Card games are a versatile and portable form of entertainment that can be enjoyed almost anywhere. Whether you're playing a fast-paced game of Poker, a strategic round of Bridge, or a casual game of Uno, card games offer endless variety and challenge. Their compact nature makes them ideal for travel, social gatherings, and quick play sessions.

## 2. Tools and Materials

- Decks of Cards: Build a collection of standard playing cards as well as specialized decks for games like Magic: The Gathering or Cards Against Humanity. Having a variety of decks allows you to play a wide range of games.
- Card Protectors: Use card sleeves to protect valuable or frequently used cards from wear and tear. Preserving your cards extends their lifespan and keeps them looking new.
- Shuffling Tools: Card shufflers can help ensure a fair and thorough shuffle, especially for large decks. Proper shuffling keeps the game fair and more unpredictable.

## 3. Techniques and Tips

- Master the Rules: Whether you're playing a traditional card game or a modern collectible card game, understanding the rules is crucial. Familiarize yourself with the variations and house rules that may apply to different games.
- Strategy and Bluffing: Develop strategies that incorporate elements of bluffing, probability, and risk management. In games like Poker, the ability to read opponents and control your own tells can be as important as the cards you hold.
- Learning New Games: Be open to learning new card games to keep your game nights fresh and exciting. Exploring different genres, from trick-taking to deck-building games, broadens your gaming repertoire and keeps things interesting.

# *May 6: Chess*

## 1. The Strategy of Chess

Chess is one of the oldest and most respected strategy games in the world. It's a game of deep thinking, foresight, and tactical planning. Whether you're a beginner or an experienced player, chess offers endless opportunities for intellectual growth and competition. The game's complexity and depth have made it a subject of study for centuries, and mastering it requires a blend of creativity, discipline, and mental endurance.

## 2. Tools and Materials

- Chess Set: Invest in a quality chess set with pieces that are comfortable to handle and a board that is easy to read. Whether you prefer classic wooden pieces or modern designs, the right set enhances the playing experience.
- Chess Clock: For timed games, a chess clock adds an element of pressure and keeps the game moving. Learning to manage your time effectively is a crucial skill in competitive chess.
- Chess Books and Resources: Study guides and books on chess strategy can help improve your understanding of the game. Reading about famous games and openings can inspire new strategies and deepen your knowledge.

## 3. Techniques and Tips

- Opening Principles: Learn common openings and the principles that guide them, such as controlling the center and developing your pieces. A strong opening can set the tone for the rest of the game.
- Tactics and Strategy: Practice common tactics like forks, pins, and skewers, and develop long-term strategies to control the board. Combining tactical awareness with strategic planning increases your chances of outmaneuvering your opponent.
- Endgame Mastery: Focus on mastering the endgame, where precise calculation and knowledge of key positions are crucial. The endgame often decides the outcome of a match, so honing these skills is essential for success.

# *May 7: Darts*

## 1. The Skill of Darts

Darts is a game of precision, hand-eye coordination, and focus. It's a popular pub game that can also be enjoyed at home, offering a fun way to compete and improve your aim. Whether you're playing casually or in a league, darts is a skillful game that rewards practice and concentration. The game's simplicity makes it accessible to beginners, while its depth provides a challenge for seasoned players.

## 2. Tools and Materials

- Dartboard: A standard bristle dartboard is essential for consistent play, with the bullseye and segments clearly marked. Proper installation and lighting enhance visibility and accuracy.
- Darts: Choose darts that match your grip and throwing style, with options for different weights, flights, and shafts. Experimenting with different setups can help you find the perfect dart for your technique.
- Scoreboard: Keep track of scores with a chalkboard, dry-erase board, or electronic scorer. Having a clear and accessible scoreboard ensures fair play and helps maintain focus on the game.

## 3. Techniques and Tips

- Grip and Stance: Develop a consistent grip and stance to improve your accuracy. A stable and balanced stance provides the foundation for a smooth and controlled throw.
- Throwing Technique: Focus on smooth, controlled throws with follow-through for the best results. Consistency in your throwing motion is key to achieving accurate and repeatable results.
- Practice Drills: Use drills to improve specific skills, such as aiming for the triple 20 or practicing doubles for finishing. Regular practice helps to refine your technique and build confidence in your abilities.

# *May 8: Dungeons and Dragons*

## 1. The Immersive World of Dungeons and Dragons

Dungeons and Dragons (D&D) is a tabletop role-playing game (RPG) that allows players to create characters and embark on adventures in a fantasy world. With a mix of storytelling, strategy, and improvisation, D&D offers a unique and immersive gaming experience where the only limit is your imagination. The game's collaborative nature fosters creativity, teamwork, and problem-solving skills.

## 2. Tools and Materials

- Core Rulebooks: The Player's Handbook, Dungeon Master's Guide, and Monster Manual are essential for playing and running a game. These books provide the rules, lore, and guidelines needed to create and navigate the game's world.

- Dice Sets: A full set of polyhedral dice (D4, D6, D8, D10, D12, D20) is necessary for rolling attacks, skill checks, and other game mechanics. Each type of dice serves a different purpose in the game, adding an element of chance and excitement.

- Character Sheets: Use character sheets to keep track of your character's stats, abilities, and inventory. Detailed record-keeping ensures that your character's progress and development are accurately reflected in the game.

## 3. Techniques and Tips

- Character Creation: Take time to create a character with a rich backstory and motivations, which adds depth to the game. A well-developed character enhances your role-playing experience and provides opportunities for growth and storytelling.

- Collaboration: Work with your fellow players and the Dungeon Master to create an engaging and cooperative story. Teamwork and communication are essential for overcoming challenges and achieving your goals.

- Improvisation: Be prepared to think on your feet, as D&D often involves unexpected challenges and opportunities. Embracing the unpredictable nature of the game adds to its excitement and keeps the adventure dynamic.

# *May 9: Electronic Gaming*

## 1. The Evolution of Electronic Gaming

Electronic gaming encompasses a wide range of video games played on consoles, PCs, and mobile devices. From retro classics to cutting-edge virtual reality experiences, electronic gaming offers diverse genres, innovative gameplay, and global communities. It's a hobby that has evolved from simple arcade games to complex, immersive worlds. Gamers can explore new narratives, compete in high-stakes tournaments, and connect with others across the globe.

## 2. Tools and Materials

- Gaming Console or PC: Choose a platform that suits your gaming preferences, whether it's a console like PlayStation or Xbox, or a gaming PC. Each platform offers unique advantages and game libraries, so selecting the right one depends on your interests and play style.
- Controllers and Peripherals: Invest in quality controllers, headsets, and other peripherals for an enhanced gaming experience. High-quality equipment can improve your performance and comfort during extended play sessions.
- Game Library: Build a collection of games that cover various genres, such as action, RPGs, strategy, and sports. A diverse library ensures that you always have something new and exciting to play.

## 3. Techniques and Tips

- Skill Development: Practice regularly to improve your skills, whether it's hand-eye coordination, strategy, or teamwork. Many games require a combination of quick reflexes, tactical thinking, and effective communication to succeed.
- Community Engagement: Join online communities or local gaming groups to share tips, participate in tournaments, and make friends. Engaging with other gamers can enhance your experience and provide opportunities for collaboration and competition.
- Balance: Maintain a healthy balance between gaming and other activities to avoid burnout or negative impacts on health. Setting boundaries and taking breaks ensures that gaming remains an enjoyable and positive part of your life.

# *May 10: Escape Rooms*

## 1. The Challenge of Escape Rooms

Escape rooms are immersive, real-life games where players work together to solve puzzles and complete objectives to "escape" a themed room within a set time limit. These games test problem-solving skills, teamwork, and creativity, offering a thrilling experience that combines fun and mental challenge. Whether you're unlocking secret passages, solving riddles, or deciphering codes, escape rooms provide a unique and engaging adventure.

## 2. Tools and Materials

- Booking and Planning: Research and book an escape room that matches your group's interests and skill level. Many escape rooms offer themes and difficulty levels to suit different preferences.
- Team Communication: Effective communication is key to solving puzzles and managing time. Ensure that everyone in the group is on the same page and working towards the common goal.
- Puzzle-Solving Tools: While escape rooms usually provide all necessary tools, brushing up on common puzzle-solving techniques (like pattern recognition or codebreaking) can give you an edge. Understanding the types of puzzles commonly used in escape rooms can help you approach challenges more effectively.

## 3. Techniques and Tips

- Divide and Conquer: Assign tasks to different team members based on their strengths to solve puzzles efficiently. Specializing allows your team to tackle multiple challenges simultaneously.
- Stay Calm: Keep a cool head under pressure, as panic can hinder clear thinking. Remaining composed helps you see connections and solutions that might be missed in a rushed state.
- Explore Everything: Thoroughly search the room for clues and items that may help you progress. Attention to detail is crucial, as even the smallest hint can lead to a breakthrough.
- Time Management: Keep an eye on the clock and pace yourselves accordingly. Knowing when to ask for a hint or when to move on from a puzzle is important to maximize your chances of success.

# *May 11: Fantasy Sports*

## 1. The Strategy of Fantasy Sports

Fantasy sports allow you to build and manage a virtual team of real-life athletes, competing against others based on the players' actual performance in games. It's a game of strategy, research, and decision-making, where knowledge of the sport and its players can lead to victory. The competitive nature of fantasy sports adds an extra layer of excitement to watching your favorite sports, as your success is directly tied to the performance of your selected players.

## 2. Tools and Materials

- Fantasy Sports Platform: Choose a platform or app that supports the sport you're interested in, such as football, basketball, or baseball. Each platform offers different features, so select one that fits your needs, whether it's live scoring, player news, or trade options.

- Research Tools: Stay updated with player stats, injury reports, and game schedules to make informed decisions. Keeping abreast of the latest news helps you anticipate changes and adjust your strategy accordingly.

- Draft Strategy: Develop a strategy for drafting players, balancing high-performing stars with potential breakout players. A well-planned draft sets the foundation for a successful season.

## 3. Techniques and Tips

- In-Depth Research: The more you know about the players and teams, the better your chances of building a winning fantasy team. Regularly analyze player performance, trends, and matchups to stay ahead of the competition.

- Adaptability: Be ready to make quick decisions when unexpected events (like injuries) occur. Flexibility is key to managing your roster effectively throughout the season.

- Trade Savvy: Engage in trades to improve your team's prospects, but be cautious not to overpay for players. Evaluating the long-term impact of trades helps you maintain a strong and balanced team.

# *May 12: Game Design*

## 1. The Innovation of Game Design

Game design is the process of creating the rules, mechanics, and overall experience of a game. Whether designing a video game, board game, or card game, this hobby involves creativity, technical skill, and a deep understanding of what makes a game enjoyable and engaging. Game designers must consider the player experience, balancing challenge with reward, and ensuring the game is both fun and accessible.

## 2. Tools and Materials

- Design Software: Use game design software to create prototypes, build game levels, and test mechanics. Software like Unity, Unreal Engine, or Tabletop Simulator can be invaluable in bringing your ideas to life.
- Prototyping Materials: For board or card games, use paper, cardboard, and markers to create initial prototypes. Physical prototypes allow you to test and refine your game mechanics before moving to more polished versions.
- Playtesting Groups: Gather a group of testers to provide feedback on your game's balance, fun factor, and clarity of rules. Regular playtesting is crucial to identifying and addressing any issues in your design.

## 3. Techniques and Tips

- Understand Player Experience: Focus on how players will interact with and experience your game, aiming to create a satisfying and engaging experience. Consider what emotions you want to evoke and how your game mechanics support that goal.
- Iterative Design: Be prepared to revise and refine your game multiple times based on playtesting feedback. Each iteration brings you closer to a polished, balanced, and enjoyable game.
- Balance and Fairness: Ensure that your game is balanced, with no one strategy or character being overwhelmingly powerful. Fairness is key to keeping players engaged and ensuring the longevity of your game.

# *May 13: Horse Racing*

## 1. The Excitement of Horse Racing

Horse racing is one of the oldest and most thrilling sports, combining speed, strategy, and the bond between horse and rider. Whether you're a spectator, a bettor, or involved in the sport, horse racing offers a unique blend of tradition, competition, and excitement. The spectacle of race day, with its vibrant atmosphere and the adrenaline rush of watching horses thundering down the track, is an experience like no other.

## 2. Tools and Materials

- Racing Program: Study the racing program to understand the horses, jockeys, and conditions for each race. Familiarizing yourself with the details helps you make informed predictions and enhances your enjoyment of the races.
- Binoculars: If attending a race, binoculars help you follow the action on the track. Being able to see the details of the race adds to the excitement and allows you to spot potential winners.
- Betting Strategy: Develop a betting strategy based on form, odds, and track conditions if you choose to wager. Responsible betting adds an extra layer of engagement, but it's important to approach it with caution and discipline.

## 3. Techniques and Tips

- Learn the Terminology: Understanding racing terms like "furlong," "handicap," and "photo finish" enhances your enjoyment and understanding of the sport. The more you know, the more you can appreciate the nuances of each race.
- Track Conditions: Pay attention to track conditions, as they can significantly impact a horse's performance. Different horses perform better on different surfaces, so this knowledge can inform your betting or predictions.
- Responsible Betting: If betting, do so responsibly, setting a budget and sticking to it. Betting should enhance your enjoyment of the sport, not lead to financial stress.

# *May 14: Improv Comedy*

## 1. The Creativity of Improv Comedy

Improv comedy is a spontaneous form of theater where actors create scenes and dialogue on the spot, often based on audience suggestions. It's a fun and challenging art form that enhances creativity, quick thinking, and teamwork. Improv comedy is not only entertaining to watch but also a great skill to learn for anyone interested in performing arts, public speaking, or simply boosting their confidence.

## 2. Tools and Materials

- Warm-Up Exercises: Start with exercises that loosen up the mind and body, such as word association or physical warm-ups. These exercises help get your creative juices flowing and prepare you for the unpredictability of improv.
- Stage Space: Practice in a space that allows for free movement and interaction between performers. Having a comfortable and flexible environment is key to effective improvisation.
- Improv Prompts: Use prompts or scenarios to kickstart scenes and inspire creativity. These can be simple phrases, situations, or character ideas that challenge you to think on your feet.

## 3. Techniques and Tips

- Yes, And: The fundamental rule of improv is to accept what your scene partner offers ("Yes") and build on it ("And"). This approach keeps the scene moving forward and fosters collaboration.
- Listening: Pay close attention to your scene partners to react authentically and keep the scene flowing. Improv is as much about listening as it is about speaking, and being present in the moment is crucial.
- Character Development: Focus on creating strong, memorable characters that drive the narrative of the scene. Whether it's a quirky voice or a distinctive physical trait, memorable characters make improv scenes more engaging and entertaining.

# *May 15: Jigsaw Puzzles*

## 1. The Satisfaction of Jigsaw Puzzles

Jigsaw puzzles offer a relaxing and satisfying challenge, as you work to assemble a complete picture from hundreds or thousands of pieces. Puzzling is a great way to unwind, sharpen your focus, and enjoy quiet time alone or with others. From simple puzzles to intricate designs, there's a puzzle for everyone, and the sense of accomplishment when the final piece is placed is unmatched.

## 2. Tools and Materials

- Puzzle Mat or Board: Use a dedicated mat or board to assemble your puzzle, which can be easily rolled up or moved if needed. A stable surface ensures that pieces stay in place and makes it easier to work on large puzzles.
- Sorting Trays: Organize pieces by color, edge, or pattern to streamline the assembly process. Sorting helps you identify the right pieces more quickly and can make the puzzle-solving process more efficient.
- Puzzle Glue: If you wish to preserve your completed puzzle, use puzzle glue to keep the pieces in place. Gluing and framing a completed puzzle allows you to display your hard work as art.

## 3. Techniques and Tips

- Edge Pieces First: Start by assembling the border of the puzzle to create a framework for the rest of the pieces. This gives you a clear starting point and makes it easier to work inward.
- Color and Pattern Grouping: Sort and group pieces by color or pattern to make finding the right pieces easier. Working on distinct sections of the puzzle helps you make progress more quickly.
- Patience: Take your time and enjoy the process; puzzling is as much about the journey as it is about the finished product. The gradual discovery and assembly can be meditative and rewarding.

# *May 16: Karaoke*

## 1. The Fun of Karaoke

Karaoke is a popular form of entertainment where individuals sing along to recorded music using a microphone. It's a fun activity for parties, gatherings, or even solo practice at home. Karaoke allows you to express yourself, enjoy music, and connect with others through shared performances. Whether you're a seasoned singer or just having fun, karaoke brings people together through the universal language of music.

## 2. Tools and Materials

- Karaoke Machine or App: Use a karaoke machine or app to access a wide range of songs and lyrics. Modern apps often include features like scoring and recording, adding extra layers of fun.
- Microphone: A good-quality microphone enhances your singing experience and ensures clear sound. Investing in a microphone with good sound quality can make a big difference in your performances.
- Speakers: Invest in quality speakers to ensure your performance is heard loud and clear. Good speakers can bring your karaoke sessions to life, making them more enjoyable for everyone involved.

## 3. Techniques and Tips

- Song Choice: Choose songs that match your vocal range and style for the best performance. Singing songs you're comfortable with will help you feel more confident and deliver a better performance.
- Confidence: Don't worry about being perfect; karaoke is about having fun and enjoying the moment. Confidence and enthusiasm often matter more than technical skill in karaoke.
- Group Participation: Encourage others to join in for duets or group songs, making the experience more interactive and enjoyable. Karaoke is often more fun when shared, so invite friends to sing along.

# *May 17: Live Streaming*

## 1. The Appeal of Live Streaming

Live streaming is the act of broadcasting real-time video content to an online audience. Whether you're streaming video games, hosting a talk show, or sharing a live event, live streaming offers a way to connect with viewers in a dynamic and interactive format. It's a powerful tool for content creators, gamers, and anyone looking to share their experiences with the world. The immediacy and interactivity of live streaming make it a unique way to engage with an audience.

## 2. Tools and Materials

- Streaming Software: Use software like OBS or Streamlabs to broadcast your content with overlays, alerts, and other enhancements. These tools help you create a professional-looking stream with minimal effort.
- Camera and Microphone: Invest in a good-quality camera and microphone for clear video and audio. High-quality equipment helps ensure that your stream is visually appealing and easy to listen to.
- Stable Internet Connection: A fast, reliable internet connection is essential to avoid lag and maintain stream quality. Consistent streaming quality is key to keeping your audience engaged.

## 3. Techniques and Tips

- Engagement: Interact with your audience through chat, shout-outs, and Q&A sessions to build a loyal community. Responding to viewers' comments and questions in real-time makes your stream more interactive and engaging.
- Consistency: Stream regularly and at consistent times to build an audience and keep viewers coming back. Regular streaming helps you build a dedicated following and improve your content over time.
- Content Variety: Mix up your content with different themes, games, or formats to keep your streams fresh and exciting. Variety helps keep your audience interested and attracts new viewers.

# *May 18: Magic Tricks*

## 1. The Mystery of Magic Tricks

Performing magic tricks is an art that captivates audiences by creating illusions that defy logic and challenge perceptions. From simple sleight of hand to elaborate stage illusions, magic tricks are about skill, showmanship, and the ability to amaze and entertain. Magic has a long history of mystifying audiences, and learning magic tricks can be both a fun hobby and a way to entertain others.

## 2. Tools and Materials

- Magic Props: Start with basic props like cards, coins, and ropes, which are used in many classic tricks. These simple tools can create a wide variety of illusions when used skillfully.
- Practice Mirror: Use a mirror to practice your tricks and perfect your sleight of hand from the audience's perspective. Watching yourself perform helps you refine your technique and presentation.
- Magic Books or Tutorials: Learn new tricks and techniques from books, videos, or online courses. Studying the work of other magicians can inspire you and help you develop your own style.

## 3. Techniques and Tips

- Practice: Mastering a magic trick requires repetition and practice to ensure smooth execution. The more you practice, the more confident you'll be when performing in front of an audience.
- Presentation: Magic is as much about how you present the trick as it is about the trick itself; work on your storytelling and patter. Engaging presentation can turn a simple trick into a memorable experience.
- Audience Interaction: Engage with your audience, drawing them into the mystery and making them a part of the performance. Interaction makes the magic feel more personal and can enhance the overall impact of your performance.

# *May 19: Narrative Games*

## 1. The Immersion of Narrative Games

Narrative games are a genre of games where storytelling plays a central role. These games often feature rich plots, complex characters, and decision-making that impacts the outcome of the story. Whether in video games, tabletop RPGs, or interactive fiction, narrative games offer deep, immersive experiences that engage the player's imagination. These games are perfect for those who enjoy a strong narrative and the ability to influence the direction of the story.

## 2. Tools and Materials

- Game Platforms: Choose a platform that supports narrative games, such as a console, PC, or tabletop setting. Each platform offers different experiences, so select one that aligns with your preferences.

- Story Guides: Use guides or online resources to explore different story paths and endings. Exploring multiple outcomes enhances your appreciation of the game's narrative complexity.

- Character Sheets: For tabletop RPGs, character sheets help track decisions, stats, and the progression of your character's story. Keeping detailed records allows you to stay immersed in your character's journey.

## 3. Techniques and Tips

- Engage with the Story: Immerse yourself in the game's narrative by paying attention to dialogue, lore, and character development. The more invested you are in the story, the more rewarding the experience will be.

- Decision-Making: Consider the consequences of your choices, as they often have lasting effects on the story. Thoughtful decision-making can lead to different outcomes and create a more personalized experience.

- Replayability: Many narrative games offer multiple endings or paths, so consider replaying to experience different outcomes. Replaying the game allows you to explore alternative storylines and gain a deeper understanding of the narrative.

# *May 20: Online Gaming*

## 1. The Community of Online Gaming

Online gaming connects players from around the world in competitive or cooperative gameplay. Whether you're battling in a first-person shooter, strategizing in a multiplayer online battle arena (MOBA), or exploring worlds in a massively multiplayer online role-playing game (MMORPG), online gaming offers a dynamic and social experience. The global reach of online gaming creates opportunities for friendships, rivalries, and collaborative gameplay.

## 2. Tools and Materials

- Gaming Platform: Choose a platform that supports your preferred type of online game, whether it's a console, PC, or mobile device. Each platform offers different advantages, so select one that suits your gaming style.

- Headset and Microphone: Communicate with teammates and other players using a quality headset with a built-in microphone. Clear communication is key to effective teamwork and coordination in online games.

- Stable Internet Connection: A fast and reliable connection is crucial for lag-free gaming. Consistent performance is essential to stay competitive in the fast-paced world of online gaming.

## 3. Techniques and Tips

- Teamwork: In many online games, teamwork and communication are key to success, so work closely with your team. Coordinated strategies often lead to victory, and building rapport with teammates enhances the overall experience.

- Skill Development: Regular practice and learning from more experienced players can help you improve your skills. Watching tutorials, studying game mechanics, and participating in training sessions can accelerate your progress.

- Positive Community Engagement: Be respectful and sportsmanlike in your interactions with other players, contributing to a positive gaming environment. A positive attitude fosters a welcoming community and can make gaming more enjoyable for everyone.

# *May 21: Poker*

## 1. The Strategy of Poker

Poker is a popular card game that combines skill, strategy, and psychology. Whether playing for fun or in competitive settings, poker challenges players to read their opponents, manage risk, and make calculated decisions. The thrill of poker lies in its blend of chance and strategy, making each hand unpredictable. Mastering poker requires a deep understanding of probability, human behavior, and strategic thinking.

## 2. Tools and Materials

- Poker Chips: Use a set of poker chips to keep track of bets and enhance the experience. Chips add a tactile element to the game, making it feel more authentic and engaging.
- Card Deck: A quality deck of cards is essential for a smooth and professional game. Invest in durable, well-made cards to ensure consistent shuffling and dealing.
- Poker Table: A dedicated poker table with a felt surface and chip holders can elevate the game's ambiance. The right table enhances the experience, providing a comfortable and organized playing environment.

## 3. Techniques and Tips

- Learn the Hands: Familiarize yourself with the different poker hands, from high card to royal flush, and their rankings. Knowing the hierarchy of hands is fundamental to making informed betting decisions.
- Bluffing: Master the art of bluffing to deceive your opponents and control the game. Successful bluffing requires a deep understanding of your opponents' tendencies and the ability to maintain a convincing poker face.
- Bankroll Management: Manage your chips wisely, knowing when to bet, fold, or raise based on your hand and the game's dynamics. Effective bankroll management is key to long-term success in poker, helping you stay in the game even during losing streaks.

# *May 22: Quiz Nights*

## 1. The Fun of Quiz Nights

Quiz nights are social events where participants answer trivia questions across various categories, competing for points and prizes. Whether held at a pub, community center, or online, quiz nights are a fun way to test your knowledge, bond with friends, and enjoy a bit of friendly competition. Quiz nights combine entertainment with education, making them a popular choice for social gatherings.

## 2. Tools and Materials

- Quiz Questions: Prepare a variety of questions across different categories, such as history, sports, music, and pop culture. A diverse set of questions keeps the quiz engaging and challenges participants' knowledge.
- Answer Sheets: Provide answer sheets for participants to record their responses. Simple, organized sheets make it easy to track answers and tally scores.
- Scoring System: Use a clear scoring system to track team or individual scores throughout the quiz. Consistent and transparent scoring ensures fairness and adds to the competitive atmosphere.

## 3. Techniques and Tips

- Team Strategy: Assemble a diverse team with different strengths to cover a wide range of topics. A well-rounded team increases your chances of success by leveraging everyone's unique knowledge.
- Timing: Set time limits for answering questions to keep the quiz moving and maintain energy. Time management is crucial for keeping the event lively and ensuring that all rounds are completed on time.
- Engagement: Keep the atmosphere lively with a charismatic host, fun banter, and interactive rounds. A great host can make or break a quiz night, so choose someone who can entertain and keep the participants engaged.

# *May 23: Role-Playing Games (RPGs)*

## 1. The Imagination of Role-Playing Games

Role-playing games (RPGs) allow players to create characters and embark on adventures in a fictional world, guided by a set of rules and the imagination of the players and game master. RPGs can be tabletop games like Dungeons & Dragons, or digital games with immersive storylines. These games offer endless possibilities for creativity, storytelling, and character development. RPGs are unique in that they combine elements of gaming, storytelling, and performance art.

## 2. Tools and Materials

- Rulebooks: Essential for understanding the mechanics, character creation, and world-building aspects of the game. Rulebooks provide the framework for the game, guiding both the players and the game master through the adventure.
- Character Sheets: Track your character's stats, abilities, and inventory. Detailed character sheets help players stay organized and focused on their character's development.
- Dice Sets: Use polyhedral dice to determine the outcomes of actions and events in the game. Dice add an element of chance to the game, making each decision and action more exciting and unpredictable.

## 3. Techniques and Tips

- Character Development: Create a character with a backstory, goals, and personality traits that make them unique and interesting. A well-developed character enhances the storytelling aspect of RPGs and makes the game more engaging.
- Collaborative Storytelling: Work with other players and the game master to build a cohesive and engaging story. Collaboration is key to creating a dynamic and immersive RPG experience.
- Role-Playing: Fully immerse yourself in your character's role, making decisions and reacting to events as they would. Embracing your character's personality and motivations adds depth to the game and makes it more enjoyable for everyone involved.

# *May 24: Social Deduction Games*

## 1. The Intrigue of Social Deduction Games

Social deduction games are a genre of party games where players try to uncover hidden roles or identities within the group, often involving deception, logic, and persuasion. Popular examples include games like Werewolf, Mafia, and The Resistance. These games are highly interactive, requiring players to use their wits and social skills to achieve their objectives. Social deduction games are a great way to test your ability to read people, strategize, and influence others.

## 2. Tools and Materials

- Role Cards: Use cards to assign secret roles to each player. The secrecy of roles adds to the tension and excitement of the game, as players try to figure out who is who.
- Game Tokens: These may represent votes, resources, or other in-game items that influence the outcome. Tokens can help keep track of players' actions and decisions throughout the game.
- Timer: Some games use a timer to add pressure and keep the pace of the game lively. Timers ensure that decisions are made quickly, adding to the intensity and urgency of the gameplay.

## 3. Techniques and Tips

- Observation: Pay close attention to other players' behavior and speech to detect lies or hidden motives. Sharp observation skills are crucial in social deduction games, as subtle cues can reveal much about a player's intentions.
- Deception: If your role requires it, practice lying convincingly without giving away your true intentions. Successful deception can turn the tide of the game in your favor, but it requires careful planning and execution.
- Persuasion: Use logic and charisma to influence other players and steer the game in your favor. Persuasive arguments can sway opinions and help you achieve your objectives, whether you're trying to uncover the truth or conceal your role.

# *May 25: Tabletop Games*

## 1. The Variety of Tabletop Games

Tabletop games encompass a wide range of games played on a flat surface, including board games, card games, miniatures games, and more. These games often involve strategy, chance, and social interaction, providing hours of entertainment for players of all ages and interests. Tabletop games are perfect for bringing people together, whether for a casual game night or a competitive tournament.

## 2. Tools and Materials

- Game Components: Depending on the game, you may need boards, cards, dice, miniatures, tokens, and other pieces. Well-crafted components enhance the tactile experience of playing and can add to the game's thematic immersion.
- Storage Solutions: Organize your game components with storage boxes or inserts to keep everything neat and accessible. Proper storage ensures that your games stay in good condition and are easy to set up and put away.
- Play Area: Ensure you have a dedicated space with enough room for all players and components. A comfortable and organized play area enhances the gaming experience and makes it easier to focus on the game.

## 3. Techniques and Tips

- Game Rules: Familiarize yourself with the rules before playing, and keep them handy for reference during the game. Understanding the rules is key to enjoying the game and playing it correctly.
- Strategy Development: Study the game's mechanics and develop strategies to improve your chances of winning. Strategic thinking and planning can make the difference between victory and defeat in tabletop games.
- Player Interaction: Engage with other players, whether it's through trading, negotiation, or competition, to enhance the experience. Tabletop games often rely on social interaction, so building rapport with other players can make the game more enjoyable for everyone.

# *May 26: Urban Exploration Games*

## 1. The Adventure of Urban Exploration Games

Urban exploration games, often referred to as "urban ex," involve exploring and interacting with real-world environments in a game-like fashion. These games may involve scavenger hunts, augmented reality experiences, or geocaching, where players use GPS to find hidden treasures. Urban exploration games blend the thrill of discovery with physical activity and problem-solving. They offer a unique way to explore your surroundings while engaging in a fun and challenging activity.

## 2. Tools and Materials

- Smartphone or GPS Device: Essential for navigation and accessing game clues or locations. Technology plays a central role in many urban exploration games, helping players find and interact with game elements.

- Map and Compass: For traditional exploration games, a map and compass can enhance the experience. Navigating without digital aids adds an extra layer of challenge and authenticity to the game.

- Notebook: Keep track of clues, puzzles, or discoveries during your exploration. Taking notes helps you remember important details and can be crucial to solving complex challenges.

## 3. Techniques and Tips

- Safety First: Always prioritize safety by exploring in groups, staying aware of your surroundings, and respecting private property. Urban exploration can involve risks, so it's important to take precautions and avoid dangerous situations.

- Navigation Skills: Brush up on your map reading and navigation skills to efficiently find locations and complete challenges. Being able to navigate accurately is key to success in many urban exploration games.

- Observation: Pay attention to details in your environment, as they may hold clues or keys to progressing in the game. Sharp observational skills can help you spot hidden elements and solve puzzles more effectively.

# May 27: Virtual Reality Gaming

## 1. The Immersion of Virtual Reality Gaming

Virtual reality (VR) gaming offers an immersive experience that transports players into a fully interactive 3D environment. With the use of VR headsets and controllers, players can engage in a wide range of activities, from exploring fantastical worlds to simulating real-life experiences. VR gaming is at the forefront of gaming technology, offering a glimpse into the future of entertainment. The immersive nature of VR gaming makes it a unique and exciting way to experience games.

## 2. Tools and Materials

- VR Headset: Invest in a quality VR headset that offers a comfortable fit and high-resolution display. A good headset is essential for a smooth and immersive VR experience, reducing motion sickness and enhancing visual fidelity.
- Controllers: Use motion controllers to interact with the virtual environment, whether it's picking up objects or wielding weapons. Controllers are your hands in the virtual world, so choose ones that are responsive and comfortable.
- Play Area: Ensure you have enough space to move around safely while wearing the VR headset. Clearing your play area of obstacles is crucial to avoid accidents and ensure a safe gaming experience.

## 3. Techniques and Tips

- Motion Comfort: Take breaks and adjust settings to minimize motion sickness, especially if you're new to VR gaming. Gradually acclimating to VR can help you enjoy longer gaming sessions without discomfort.
- Game Selection: Explore different genres of VR games, from action and adventure to puzzle and fitness, to find what you enjoy most. The variety of experiences available in VR is vast, so take the time to discover what suits your tastes.
- Safety: Clear your play area of obstacles and ensure you have enough room to move freely while immersed in the game. Safety should always be a priority in VR gaming to prevent injuries.

# *May 28: Word Games*

## 1. The Challenge of Word Games

Word games are a genre of games that test players' vocabulary, spelling, and linguistic creativity. From classic games like Scrabble and Boggle to modern mobile apps like Words with Friends, word games offer a fun and educational way to challenge your mind and expand your language skills. Word games are perfect for those who love language and enjoy a good mental workout.

## 2. Tools and Materials

- Game Board or App: Depending on the game, you may need a physical board and tiles or a digital version on your smartphone or tablet. Each format offers a different experience, so choose the one that best suits your preferences.
- Dictionary: Keep a dictionary handy to verify words and settle disputes. A dictionary is an essential tool for ensuring fair play and resolving any disagreements during the game.
- Letter Tiles or Cards: For games like Scrabble, letter tiles are essential for forming words on the board. Organizing and using your tiles strategically is key to success in these games.

## 3. Techniques and Tips

- Vocabulary Expansion: Regularly learn new words to increase your vocabulary and improve your performance in word games. Expanding your vocabulary gives you more options when playing and can help you score higher.
- Strategic Placement: In games like Scrabble, placement of your words is as important as the words themselves; aim for double or triple word scores. Strategic placement can significantly boost your score and give you an edge over your opponents.
- Practice: The more you play, the better you'll get at spotting word opportunities and making the most of your letters. Regular practice helps you develop the skills needed to excel in word games.

# *May 29: Xbox Gaming*

## 1. The Community of Xbox Gaming

Xbox gaming offers a vast array of video games across multiple genres, with a strong online community and access to exclusive titles. Whether you're playing solo campaigns, competing in multiplayer matches, or exploring indie games, Xbox gaming provides a rich and diverse experience for players. The community aspect of Xbox gaming adds a social dimension, making it easy to connect with other gamers.

## 2. Tools and Materials

- Xbox Console: Choose the right Xbox console for your gaming needs, whether it's the latest Series X or the more affordable Series S. Each console offers different features and capabilities, so select the one that fits your gaming style.
- Controller: Invest in a comfortable, responsive controller for the best gaming experience. A good controller is essential for precise inputs and comfortable gameplay.
- Xbox Game Pass: Consider subscribing to Xbox Game Pass for access to a large library of games to download and play. Game Pass offers great value for gamers who want to explore a wide variety of titles without purchasing each one individually.

## 3. Techniques and Tips

- Explore Game Pass: Take advantage of Xbox Game Pass to try new games and discover hidden gems. Game Pass gives you the opportunity to explore different genres and find games you might not have considered otherwise.
- Achieve Milestones: Work towards unlocking achievements and milestones in games to enhance your gaming experience. Achievements add extra challenges and goals, giving you more reasons to keep playing.
- Community Engagement: Join Xbox communities, participate in online forums, and attend gaming events to connect with other players. Engaging with the Xbox community can enhance your gaming experience and help you make new friends.

# *May 30: Yard Games*

## 1. The Fun of Yard Games

Yard games are outdoor activities that can be enjoyed by people of all ages, often during gatherings like barbecues, picnics, or parties. Popular yard games include cornhole, horseshoes, bocce ball, and ladder toss. These games are simple to set up and play, making them perfect for casual, fun-filled afternoons. Yard games bring people together in a relaxed, outdoor setting, making them ideal for socializing and enjoying the fresh air.

## 2. Tools and Materials

- Game Sets: Invest in durable game sets that can withstand outdoor conditions, such as wooden or plastic cornhole boards and bags. Quality game sets ensure that your games will last for many seasons of outdoor fun.
- Playing Area: Designate a flat, open space in your yard or park for setting up your games. A well-prepared playing area helps ensure that everyone can participate comfortably and safely.
- Scoreboard: Keep track of scores with a simple scoreboard, adding a competitive element to your games. A scoreboard helps maintain the competitive spirit and adds to the fun.

## 3. Techniques and Tips

- Game Rules: Familiarize yourself with the rules of each yard game to ensure fair play and maximum enjoyment. Understanding the rules helps everyone enjoy the games and prevents any disputes or confusion.
- Team Play: Yard games are often more fun with teams, so organize players into pairs or groups for friendly competition. Team play adds a social element to the games and can make the experience more engaging.
- Adaptability: Be ready to adapt the games to suit your space, weather, and group size, ensuring everyone can participate. Flexibility in game setup and rules helps ensure that everyone has a good time, regardless of the circumstances.

# *May 31: Zombie Games*

## 1. The Thrill of Zombie Games

Zombie games are a popular genre in both video games and tabletop games, where players face off against hordes of undead in a fight for survival. These games often combine elements of horror, strategy, and action, providing an adrenaline-pumping experience that challenges players to think quickly and act decisively. The appeal of zombie games lies in their intense atmosphere and the challenge of surviving against overwhelming odds.

## 2. Tools and Materials

- Game Platform: Choose a platform that supports your preferred type of zombie game, whether it's a console, PC, or board game. Each platform offers a different experience, so select the one that best suits your gaming style.

- Weapons and Equipment: In video games, equip your character with the best weapons and gear to fend off zombies. In tabletop games, manage your resources wisely to survive. Proper equipment is crucial to surviving the challenges posed by zombie games.

- Strategy Guides: Use strategy guides or online resources to learn the best tactics for surviving zombie encounters. Understanding the game's mechanics and strategies can greatly improve your chances of success.

## 3. Techniques and Tips

- Resource Management: In many zombie games, managing limited resources like ammunition, health packs, and food is crucial to survival. Efficient resource management can make the difference between life and death in these games.

- Cooperative Play: Team up with other players in cooperative zombie games to increase your chances of surviving. Working together enhances the experience and can make even the most challenging encounters more manageable.

- Adaptability: Be ready to adapt your strategies as the game progresses, whether it's facing stronger enemies or navigating changing environments. Flexibility is key to overcoming the unpredictable challenges that zombie games present.

## *Conclusion for May*

May has taken you on a journey through the world of games and entertainment, exploring activities that challenge the mind, foster creativity, and bring people together. From the strategic depths of chess and poker to the immersive experiences of virtual reality and role-playing games, this month has highlighted the diversity and excitement that games can offer. Whether you've discovered a new favorite hobby in collecting action figures, designing board games, or mastering the art of karaoke, the skills and enjoyment you've gained will enhance your appreciation for the many forms of entertainment available. As you continue to explore the world of games, remember that the ultimate goal is to have fun, connect with others, and enjoy the process of play.

# June: Music and Performing Arts

*June is dedicated to the exploration of music and performing arts, where creativity takes on a life of its own through sound, movement, and performance. This month invites you to discover or deepen your connection with the arts, offering a range of activities that span from playing musical instruments to engaging in theatrical performance. Each day in June introduces a new way to express your emotions, tell stories, and connect with others through the universal languages of music and the performing arts. Whether you're strumming a guitar, dancing to a rhythm, or composing your own music, this chapter encourages you to explore the full spectrum of creative expression.*

# *June 1: A Cappella*

## 1. The Harmony of A Cappella Singing

A cappella singing is the art of creating music using only the human voice for melody, harmony, rhythm, and vocal percussion. Groups often perform intricate arrangements that blend multiple voices into a rich, full sound. Popular across genres from choral to pop, a cappella requires strong vocal skills like pitch accuracy, breath control, and the ability to blend with other singers. It's a fulfilling way to explore vocal abilities and make music as part of a group.

## 2. Tools and Materials

- Pitch Pipe or Tuner: Ensures your voice starts on the correct pitch and stays in tune with the group, crucial for maintaining harmony.
- Recording Device: Recording rehearsals and performances helps you review and improve your singing, identifying areas needing work on pitch, blend, or timing.
- Sheet Music: Keep arrangements handy to learn your part thoroughly, ensuring you contribute confidently to the group's sound.
- Vocal Warm-Ups: Essential exercises prepare your voice before rehearsals and performances, improving pitch accuracy, vocal strength, and blend.

## 3. Techniques and Tips

- Pitch Accuracy: Focus on matching pitches accurately and staying in tune with others for harmonious music.
- Blend and Balance: Work on blending with other singers, matching tone, volume, and vowel shapes for a smooth, unified sound.
- Breath Control: Develop breath control to sustain phrases and maintain vocal power, crucial for even singing, especially in complex arrangements.
- Vocal Percussion: If your group includes vocal percussion, practice creating beats and rhythms with your voice to add depth and drive to the music.
- Performance Dynamics: Vary volume and intensity to create contrast and emotion, making your performance more engaging and expressive.

# *June 2: Accordion Playing*

## 1. The Versatility of Accordion Playing

Accordion playing blends melody, harmony, and rhythm into a cohesive performance. The accordion is versatile, producing sounds from soulful folk melodies to intricate classical compositions. Whether solo or in an ensemble, accordionists can explore various genres and traditions, making it a rewarding instrument for all types of music. The instrument's unique sound, driven by bellows, keys, and buttons, allows for deep musical expression and technical mastery.

## 2. Tools and Materials

- Accordion: Choose between a piano accordion with a keyboard or a button accordion with buttons. Each offers different playing experiences and suits various musical styles. A well-crafted accordion ensures better sound quality and ease of play.
- Music Stand: A reliable stand holds sheet music at eye level, ensuring proper posture. Adjustable stands are recommended for different environments.
- Sheet Music: Start with beginner-friendly tunes and progress to more complex compositions as your skills improve. A variety of genres broadens your repertoire.
- Cleaning Kit: Regular maintenance preserves the accordion's longevity and ensures it produces the best sound. Kits typically include brushes and cloths for the instrument's delicate components.

## 3. Techniques and Tips

- Bellows Control: The bellows control airflow, volume, and expression. Practice smooth, even movements for consistent sound quality and explore dynamic variations. Mastering bellows control adds emotional depth and range to performances.
- Finger Dexterity: Regularly practice scales and arpeggios to develop the finger strength and agility needed for complex pieces. Finger exercises improve precision and speed, essential for advanced playing.
- Musical Expression: Use the bellows to manipulate volume and tone, exploring different styles to fully appreciate the accordion's versatility. Experiment with dynamics and phrasing to convey emotions, from lively polkas to slow, haunting ballads.

## *June 3: Ballet*

### 1. The Discipline of Ballet

Ballet is a refined art form emphasizing grace, precision, and storytelling through movement. It serves as the foundation for many dance styles, known for its strict technique, including positions, turns, leaps, and gestures. Ballet demands physical strength, flexibility, musicality, and the ability to convey emotions through dance. The discipline instills focus, dedication, and perseverance, qualities that extend beyond the studio.

### 2. Tools and Materials

- Ballet Slippers: Lightweight shoes that provide flexibility and grip, crucial for precise movements. Leather or canvas slippers with elastic bands ensure a secure fit.
- Leotard and Tights: Form-fitting attire lets instructors see your alignment and posture, ensuring correct technique. This clothing also facilitates ease of movement, essential for complex ballet steps.
- Barre: A stationary handrail used for warm-up exercises that develop balance, strength, and flexibility, laying the foundation for advanced movements. The barre supports dancers during exercises focused on posture and alignment.
- Music: Classical music typically accompanies ballet practice, providing rhythm and emotional context. It helps dancers develop timing, rhythm, and an understanding of musical phrasing.

### 3. Techniques and Tips

- Posture and Alignment: Proper posture is critical in ballet. Keep your back straight, shoulders down, and core engaged throughout movements for graceful execution. Good posture enhances movement aesthetics and prevents injury.
- Flexibility and Strength: Regular stretching and strengthening exercises, especially for the legs and core, are essential for the range of motion required in ballet. Pilates or yoga can further improve flexibility and core strength, vital in ballet.
- Musicality: Pay close attention to the music, ensuring your movements sync with the rhythm and express the emotions of the score. Understanding the music adds depth, transforming technical steps into a moving performance.

# *June 4: Banjo Playing*

## 1. The Liveliness of Banjo Playing

The banjo is a rhythmic instrument that brings a distinctive sound to bluegrass, folk, and country genres. Its bright, percussive tone can drive a band's rhythm or shine in solo performances. Whether strumming chords or picking melodies, the banjo offers an energetic way to engage with music. Banjo players can explore various styles, from traditional clawhammer to modern fingerpicking, each with its own flavor and challenges. The banjo's versatility and distinct sound make it a favorite among musicians and audiences.

## 2. Tools and Materials

- Banjo: Choose from 4-string, 5-string, or 6-string banjos based on your music style. The 5-string is popular in bluegrass, while the 4-string tenor suits jazz.
- Picks: Thumb and finger picks are essential for the crisp, bright sound of banjo playing, offering precision and speed. Metal picks are favored for their durability and clear tone.
- Tuner: A reliable tuner is crucial for keeping your banjo in tune, especially given its sensitivity to tension and temperature. A clip-on tuner is convenient for quick adjustments.
- Capo: A capo allows you to change the key of a song without altering chord shapes, making it easier to play with other musicians or accommodate different vocal ranges.

## 3. Techniques and Tips

- Roll Patterns: Master basic roll patterns like forward, backward, and alternating rolls, foundational for bluegrass banjo playing. These enhance fingerpicking speed and precision, driving the music forward.
- Chording Techniques: Learn common chord shapes, especially in the key of G, standard for banjo tuning. Familiarity with these chords lets you play a wide range of songs. Practice smooth chord transitions to maintain a steady rhythm.
- Syncopation and Rhythm: Practice with a metronome or backing track to improve timing and rhythm, crucial in banjo music. Syncopation, emphasizing the off-beat, adds energy and excitement to your performance.

# *June 5: Choir Singing*

## 1. The Harmony of Choir Singing

Choir singing is a collective musical experience that unites voices in harmony, creating a rich, powerful sound. Whether in a church, school, or community choir, members learn to blend their voices, follow a conductor, and perform as a cohesive unit. Choir singing develops vocal skills and fosters a sense of community. Harmonizing with others and contributing to a unified sound is deeply rewarding and spiritually uplifting, promoting a sense of belonging as singers work together towards a common goal.

## 2. Tools and Materials

- Sheet Music: Familiarize yourself with the music for rehearsals and performances. Reading music is helpful but not always necessary; many choirs provide recordings to learn by ear.
- Pitch Pipe or Tuner: These tools help you find your starting note and stay in tune, especially in a cappella pieces where no instrument provides the starting note.
- Recording Device: Recording rehearsals helps you review and improve your part before the final performance. Listening back lets you hear how your voice blends and identify areas for improvement.
- Choir Folder: A sturdy folder organizes your sheet music and keeps it in good condition, often designed for comfort during long rehearsals.

## 3. Techniques and Tips

- Breath Control: Proper breath support is essential for maintaining pitch and sustaining long phrases. Practice diaphragmatic breathing to strengthen your support system, allowing you to sing with more power and endurance during rehearsals and performances.
- Blending: Choir singing requires blending your voice with others. Listen carefully and adjust your volume and tone to match the group, ensuring a harmonious sound where no individual voice stands out unless directed by the conductor.
- Diction and Articulation: Clear diction is crucial in choir singing, especially in large groups. Focus on enunciating words clearly without disrupting the musical flow. Follow the conductor's instructions on emphasizing consonants and shaping vowels for a unified choir sound.

# *June 6: Clarinet Playing*

## 1. The Versatility of Clarinet Playing

The clarinet is a versatile woodwind instrument prominent in genres from classical to jazz. Its rich tone and wide range make it a favorite among musicians. Whether as a soloist or in an ensemble, clarinetists can explore a broad repertoire that highlights the instrument's expressive capabilities. The clarinet's agility allows it to produce everything from soft melodies to fast, intricate passages, making it essential in orchestras, bands, and chamber groups.

## 2. Tools and Materials

- Clarinet: A quality instrument is crucial for good sound. Beginners usually start with a Bb clarinet, the most common type. Advanced players might explore other types like the A clarinet or bass clarinet for different tonal qualities.
- Reeds: Reeds are vital for sound production and need regular replacement. The reed's strength affects playability and tone, so experimenting with different strengths helps find your ideal sound.
- Music Stand: A stable, adjustable stand is essential for holding sheet music at a comfortable height, whether sitting or standing.
- Ligature and Mouthpiece: The ligature secures the reed on the mouthpiece, impacting tone and response. A quality mouthpiece and ligature can significantly enhance your playing.

## 3. Techniques and Tips

- Embouchure: The way you shape your mouth on the mouthpiece is key to a clear, focused tone. Consistent embouchure practice improves sound quality and is crucial for a rich tone across all registers.
- Breath Support: Strong breath support ensures steady airflow, necessary for smooth phrases and a full, resonant sound.
- Fingering Techniques: Regular scale and arpeggio practice develops fast, accurate finger movements, essential for complex music. Fingering exercises also improve technical agility and note transitions.
- Articulation: Master tonguing techniques for clean, crisp articulation. Clarinetists need to excel in both staccato (short, detached notes) and legato (smooth, connected notes) to play expressively across a wide range of music.

# *June 7: DJing*

## 1. The Art of DJing

DJing is a creative musical art that involves curating, mixing, and manipulating music to create a unique experience. DJs set the mood at events by blending tracks, controlling crowd energy, and introducing new music. DJing requires a good ear, rhythm, and crowd-reading skills. The art lies in track selection and executing smooth transitions, effects, and techniques to keep the mix engaging.

## 2. Tools and Materials

- DJ Controller or Turntables: Choose between digital controllers or traditional turntables. Controllers are beginner-friendly, while turntables offer a hands-on approach. High-quality gear ensures better control and sound.
- Mixer: Essential for blending tracks, adjusting levels, and applying effects. Some controllers include mixers; others require a separate unit.
- DJ Software: Programs like Serato, Traktor, or Rekordbox organize music, set cues, and manage mixes, offering tools for beatmatching, looping, and effects.
- Headphones: Key for cueing tracks and making precise adjustments. Look for headphones with good isolation and clarity.
- Speakers: High-quality speakers are crucial for practice and performance. Monitor speakers suit studios; PA systems are needed for live events.

## 3. Techniques and Tips

- Beatmatching: Sync the tempo of two tracks for smooth transitions. Practice pitch adjustments and cueing with headphones to ensure seamless mixes and consistent energy.
- EQ and Effects: Balance bass, mids, and highs, and use effects like reverb or echo to add depth. These tools create dynamic soundscapes and keep your set interesting.
- Track Selection: Know your music library and understand your audience. A well-curated playlist and good crowd reading ensure your set resonates and engages.
- Practice Transitions: Smooth transitions maintain flow. Practice crossfading, cutting, and scratching to enhance mixes and add personal style.

# *June 8: Drumming*

## 1. The Foundation of Drumming

Drumming is the heartbeat of music, providing rhythm, structure, and energy to any ensemble. It's physically demanding and mentally engaging, requiring coordination, timing, and creativity. As a drummer, you drive the music in rock bands, jazz trios, or orchestras. Drumming also offers a unique outlet for expression, allowing you to communicate emotions through rhythm and dynamics. From simple grooves to complex solos, drumming is a fundamental and versatile musical skill.

## 2. Tools and Materials

- Drum Kit: A standard kit includes a bass drum, snare drum, toms, hi-hat, and cymbals. Beginners can start with a basic setup and expand as they advance.
- Drumsticks: Choose sticks that feel comfortable and suit your music style. Different sticks offer varying weights and balance, affecting your playing.
- Practice Pad: Essential for developing stick control, speed, and accuracy, and useful for quiet practice.
- Metronome: Crucial for developing timing, helping you stay in time and play consistently with others.
- Drum Throne: A comfortable, adjustable throne is important for maintaining good posture and stamina during practice.

## 3. Techniques and Tips

- Grip and Posture: Proper grip and posture are essential for control and endurance. Learn the correct way to hold sticks and sit at your kit to avoid injury and play efficiently.
- Rudiments: Mastering rudiments like single strokes, double strokes, and paradiddles builds technique and forms the foundation for complex drumming.
- Groove and Timing: Focus on consistent groove and timing. Practice with a metronome or recordings to develop your internal sense of time, crucial for playing with others.
- Dynamic Control: Work on varying dynamics, from soft ghost notes to powerful accents. This adds expression and texture, making your drumming more engaging.

# *June 9: Electric Guitar*

## 1. The Power of Electric Guitar

The electric guitar is central to modern music, defining genres like rock, blues, jazz, and metal. Its versatility allows players to create a wide range of sounds, from clean tones to distorted riffs. Combined with effects pedals and amplifiers, the guitar offers endless creative possibilities. Whether shredding solos, riffing, or crafting ambient soundscapes, the electric guitar is a powerful tool for musical expression.

## 2. Tools and Materials

- Electric Guitar: Choose a guitar that suits your genre and feels comfortable. Popular models include the Fender Stratocaster, Gibson Les Paul, and Ibanez RG, each offering unique tonal qualities.
- Amplifier: An amp projects your sound, ranging from small practice models to powerful tube amps for live performances. Your choice of amp greatly impacts your tone.
- Effects Pedals: Pedals like overdrive, distortion, delay, and reverb shape your sound. Experimenting with pedals helps develop a signature tone.
- Guitar Picks: Picks vary in thickness and material, affecting playing style and tone. Thicker picks offer control, while thinner picks are better for strumming.
- Tuner: Keeping your guitar in tune is crucial. A clip-on or pedal tuner allows quick adjustments.

## 3. Techniques and Tips

- Power Chords: Power chords are a rock staple, offering a simple yet powerful way to create a driving sound. Practice clean transitions, as they are the backbone of many songs.
- Finger Exercises: Regular exercises build strength, flexibility, and speed, essential for solos and riffs. Practice scales, arpeggios, and hammer-ons/pull-offs to enhance dexterity.
- Improvisation: Develop improvisation by playing with backing tracks. Focus on scales, phrasing, and bending to create expressive solos.
- Tone Control: Experiment with tone and volume knobs, pickup settings, and amp controls to discover different sounds. Mastering tone manipulation is key to achieving the desired sound for any style.

# *June 10: Flute Playing*

## 1. The Elegance of Flute Playing

The flute is a graceful woodwind instrument, known for its clear, bright sound that can soar in an orchestra or blend in an ensemble. It's used across various genres, from classical to jazz. The flute's light tone is ideal for both lyrical melodies and rapid passages. Playing the flute requires strong breath control, precise finger movements, and a keen sense of phrasing. Whether performing a solo or in an ensemble, the flute adds a unique voice to the music.

## 2. Tools and Materials

- Flute: A well-maintained flute is essential for producing a clear tone. Beginners typically start with a standard C flute, while advanced players may explore alto or bass flutes for different tonal ranges.
- Cleaning Rod and Cloth: Regular cleaning prevents moisture buildup and maintains sound quality and longevity.
- Music Stand: A stable stand keeps sheet music at eye level, ensuring proper posture and ease of reading while playing.
- Tuner: A tuner ensures your flute is in tune, essential for harmonious playing. Flutes are sensitive to temperature, so tuning adjustments may be necessary.

## 3. Techniques and Tips

- Embouchure: Your embouchure, or how you shape your mouth on the mouthpiece, is critical for producing a clear tone. Practice a relaxed, consistent embouchure to achieve a pure sound across all registers.
- Breath Control: Strong breath support is necessary for steady airflow, essential for long phrases and dynamic contrast. Practice breathing exercises to improve lung capacity and control.
- Fingering Techniques: Regularly practice scales and arpeggios to develop quick, accurate finger movements. This is crucial for playing fast passages and complex runs with clarity.
- Articulation: Work on tonguing to achieve clean, precise articulation. Flutists use different articulations, like staccato and legato, to add expression and clarity to the music.

# *June 11: Guitar Playing*

## 1. The Universality of Guitar Playing

Guitar playing is a popular and accessible form of musical expression, embraced across cultures and genres. Whether strumming chords, fingerpicking, or shredding in a band, the guitar offers endless creative possibilities. Its versatility allows it to adapt to almost any musical style, making it essential in both solo and ensemble settings. Learning guitar can be a personal journey of exploration and a communal activity, connecting you with other musicians and audiences.

## 2. Tools and Materials

- Guitar: Choose between an acoustic guitar with a resonant sound or an electric guitar, which can be amplified and modified with effects, each suited to different genres.
- Guitar Picks: Picks vary in thickness and material, affecting playing style and tone. Thicker picks offer control for lead playing, while thinner picks are better for strumming.
- Tuner: Keeping your guitar in tune is essential. Clip-on tuners or tuning apps make it easy to check tuning regularly.
- Capo: A capo changes the key of a song without new chord shapes, useful for playing with others.
- Music Stand: A stable stand holds your sheet music or tablature, helping you read while playing and maintain proper posture.

## 3. Techniques and Tips

- Chord Transitions: Practice smooth chord transitions to improve rhythm and flow. Start with basic chords, then progress to complex barre chords and voicings.
- Fingerpicking: Develop fingerpicking to add texture to your playing. Start simple and gradually incorporate more intricate patterns.
- Strumming Patterns: Experiment with strumming patterns to create varied rhythms. Consistent strumming is key to driving the music, especially in accompaniment.
- Improvisation: Explore improvisation by playing with backing tracks or jamming with others. Focus on scales, phrasing, and dynamics to develop your unique style.

# *June 12: Harmonica*

## 1. The Portability of Harmonica

The harmonica is a compact, versatile instrument widely used in genres like blues, folk, and rock. Its small size makes it highly portable, allowing you to play anytime, anywhere. Despite its simplicity, the harmonica offers a rich variety of sounds, from soulful bends to rhythmic chugs. Learning to play can be a deeply satisfying hobby, offering a unique way to express emotion and connect with American music roots. Its expressive range and accessibility make it popular with both beginners and seasoned musicians.

## 2. Tools and Materials

- Harmonica: Beginners usually start with a diatonic harmonica in C, standard for most instructional material. As you advance, you may explore different keys or chromatic harmonicas for more versatility.
- Harmonica Holder: If you play another instrument like guitar, a holder allows hands-free playing, useful for solo performances or accompaniment.
- Cleaning Cloth: Regular cleaning keeps your harmonica in good condition. Use a soft cloth to wipe down the instrument after playing to remove moisture and prevent corrosion.
- Case: A sturdy case protects your harmonica from damage and is especially useful if you carry multiple harmonicas in different keys.

## 3. Techniques and Tips

- Breathing Techniques: Proper breathing is essential for playing harmonica. Practice controlled breathing to maintain steady airflow and achieve clear, sustained notes, particularly for long phrases and bending notes.
- Bending Notes: Bending is a key technique that adds expressiveness, especially in blues. Practice bending notes by controlling your airflow and mouth shape to achieve the desired pitch variations.
- Cross Harp Playing: Cross harp, or second position playing, involves playing in a different key than the harmonica's tuning, common in blues. This technique creates a more expressive, bluesy sound and allows for more dynamic playing.
- Rhythm and Timing: Develop a strong sense of rhythm, crucial for playing harmonica in a band or with other musicians. Practice with recordings or a metronome to improve timing and groove.

# *June 13: Improvisational Theater*

## 1. The Spontaneity of Improvisational Theater

Improvisational theater, or improv, is a form of live performance where the content is created spontaneously by the performers. Improv fosters creativity, quick thinking, and collaboration, making it valuable for actors and non-actors alike. It's about embracing the unexpected and building scenes in the moment, often leading to humorous or touching outcomes. Improv is used in theater, corporate training, education, and therapy due to its focus on communication and adaptability.

## 2. Tools and Materials

- Comfortable Clothing: Wear clothes that allow free movement during improv exercises. Flexibility and comfort are key, as improv often involves physical activity.
- Improv Games and Exercises: Use various games to practice skills like quick thinking, character development, and scene work. Resources like improv handbooks or online videos can provide inspiration.
- Notebook: Keep a journal to reflect on performances, note successful techniques, and brainstorm ideas for future scenes. Writing down experiences helps track progress and develop skills.

## 3. Techniques and Tips

- Yes, And: The golden rule of improv, where you accept what your partner offers ("yes") and add to it ("and"). This builds scenes collaboratively and keeps momentum.
- Listening Skills: Improv is about listening as much as speaking. Pay attention to your partners and build on their ideas for cohesive scenes.
- Character Commitment: Fully commit to your character, no matter how unexpected it may be. Strong character choices drive the scene and engage the audience.
- Practice Spontaneity: Regularly practice exercises that challenge quick thinking. This builds confidence and helps you react swiftly in unexpected situations.
- Group Dynamics: Improv is a team effort, so focus on collaborating. Support fellow performers by being open to their ideas and contributing positively to the scene.

# June 14: Jazz Dance

## 1. The Energy of Jazz Dance

Jazz dance is an energetic style that blends ballet, modern dance, and African dance traditions. It features syncopated rhythms, fast-paced movements, and expressive style. Jazz dance is versatile, appearing in theater, film, TV, and competitions. It celebrates individuality, allowing dancers to bring their own flair to the movements. Whether dancing to classic jazz or contemporary music, jazz dance offers a dynamic way to express yourself.

## 2. Tools and Materials

- Jazz Shoes: Flexible shoes with support and a full range of movement are essential. Jazz shoes, typically with a split sole, are made from leather or canvas for better flexibility.
- Comfortable Clothing: Wear clothing like leggings and a fitted top that allows free movement. Jazz dance requires comfortable, non-restrictive attire.
- Mirror: A full-length mirror helps you see and adjust your movements, technique, and posture as you dance.
- Music: Jazz music with strong rhythms is key for practice. Create a playlist of classic and contemporary jazz tracks for your sessions.

## 3. Techniques and Tips

- Isolations: Practice isolating body parts like shoulders, hips, and head to create sharp movements. Isolations add texture and contrast to your performance.
- Musicality: Let the music guide your movements. Jazz dance is deeply connected to rhythm and emotion, so interpreting the music is crucial.
- Jazz Walks and Leaps: Master the basics of jazz walks and leaps, foundational movements often used in combinations and across-the-floor exercises.
- Expression: Jazz dance is about performance as much as technique. Work on expressing emotion and energy through your movements to make your performance engaging.
- Choreography Practice: Regularly practice choreography to improve memory, timing, and performing complex routines, combining jazz dance elements into a cohesive performance.

# *June 15: Karaoke*

## 1. The Fun of Karaoke

Karaoke is a social activity where people sing along with recorded music, often in front of an audience. It's a fun way to enjoy music, practice singing, and entertain others. Karaoke lets you express yourself, whether belting out a ballad or rapping a hit. It's a way to connect with friends, share your love of music, and discover hidden talent. Whether at a venue or at home, karaoke is all about having fun and letting loose.

## 2. Tools and Materials

- Karaoke Machine or App: Provides instrumental versions of songs and displays lyrics. Many apps offer pitch correction and background tracks to enhance performance.
- Microphone: A quality microphone is essential for capturing your voice clearly. Wireless microphones allow for easy movement and audience engagement.
- Speakers: Good speakers amplify the music and your voice, ensuring everyone hears your performance. External speakers often provide better sound quality.
- Songbook or Playlist: Keep a list of favorite songs ready to sing, ensuring you're always prepared to perform.

## 3. Techniques and Tips

- Song Selection: Choose songs that suit your vocal range and style. Start with familiar songs to build confidence and gradually take on more challenging ones.
- Breath Control: Practice breathing techniques to sing long phrases without running out of breath. Good breath control is key to sustaining notes and vocal power.
- Stage Presence: Engage with the audience, move to the music, and convey emotion. Karaoke is about entertainment, so put on a show.
- Confidence Building: Regular practice builds confidence and comfort in performing.
- Vocal Warm-Ups: Warm up before singing to prepare your voice and prevent strain. Simple exercises like humming and scales help you hit the right notes.

# June 16: Lyre Playing

## 1. The Ancient Art of Lyre Playing

The lyre is an ancient stringed instrument used in various cultures for thousands of years. It produces a soft, melodic sound that is soothing and evocative. Historically associated with poetry and song, it often accompanied the voice in ancient Greek and Roman performances. Today, it's enjoyed for its simple yet beautiful sound, making it ideal for beginners and those interested in historical music. Lyre playing connects with the past and creates peaceful, reflective music.

## 2. Tools and Materials

- Lyre: Choose one with nylon or gut strings, typically tuned to a pentatonic or diatonic scale. Common models have 7 to 10 strings.
- Tuning Device: A tuning fork or electronic tuner is essential for keeping your lyre in tune. With fewer strings, tuning is quick and easy.
- Sheet Music or Tabs: Start with simple melodies and traditional songs, progressing to more complex compositions or creating your own music.
- Music Stand: Useful for holding sheet music or tabs at eye level, ensuring proper posture while playing.

## 3. Techniques and Tips

- Finger Plucking: Practice plucking the strings with even pressure and clean articulation. The lyre's soft sound is best with gentle, controlled plucking.
- Tuning: Regularly check your lyre's tuning, as it can go out of tune quickly, especially with new strings.
- Melodic Exploration: Experiment with different plucking techniques and scales to explore the lyre's melodic potential.
- Historical Context: Learn the lyre's cultural significance in ancient music to deepen your appreciation and playing experience.
- Relaxation and Meditation: Use lyre playing for relaxation or meditation, creating a calm, reflective atmosphere for personal or group enjoyment.

# *June 17: Music Composition*

## 1. The Creativity of Music Composition

Music composition is the art of creating original music, from simple melodies to complex pieces. It combines creativity with technical knowledge, allowing you to express ideas and emotions through sound. Whether composing for an instrument, band, or orchestra, music composition offers endless possibilities. It involves understanding theory, experimenting with forms, and developing your unique voice as a composer. It's a fulfilling hobby that can lead to lasting works of art.

## 2. Tools and Materials

- Instrument: Use a piano, guitar, or any instrument you're comfortable with to compose. Many prefer the piano for its versatility.
- Sheet Music or Software: Write your compositions using sheet music or digital notation software like Finale, Sibelius, or MuseScore.
- Recording Device: Record your compositions for analysis and refinement. DAWs like Logic Pro, Ableton Live, or GarageBand are excellent for this.
- Reference Materials: Keep music theory books, harmony guides, and orchestration manuals on hand to assist your work.

## 3. Techniques and Tips

- Melodic Development: Start with a simple melody and develop it by adding harmonies and variations. Experiment with ways to transform your themes.
- Harmonic Progressions: Use different chord progressions to create tension and emotion. Understanding harmony is key to resonant music.
- Form and Structure: Ensure your composition has a clear beginning, development, and ending. While common forms are useful, don't hesitate to try unconventional structures.
- Orchestration and Arranging: Learn orchestration to understand how instruments interact, helping you create dynamic compositions.
- Inspiration and Practice: Draw inspiration from various music styles and regularly practice composing to refine your skills and voice as a composer.

# *June 18: Orchestra Participation*

## 1. The Collaboration of Orchestra Participation

Playing in an orchestra is a collaborative experience that involves working with other musicians to create a cohesive performance. Orchestra participation requires discipline, teamwork, and musical skill. As an orchestral musician, you play a specific role within the ensemble, contributing to the overall sound and interpretation of the music. Whether in a community orchestra, school ensemble, or professional symphony, being part of an orchestra allows you to engage with complex music and share in the achievement of a performance.

## 2. Tools and Materials

- Instrument: Keep your instrument well-maintained. Whether you play strings, woodwinds, brass, or percussion, a reliable instrument is crucial for your performance.
- Sheet Music: Study your part thoroughly and mark difficult passages or conductor's instructions. Being well-prepared ensures effective contributions during rehearsals and performances.
- Metronome: Practice with a metronome to maintain consistent timing, essential for ensemble cohesion.
- Tuner: Regular tuning ensures your instrument harmonizes with the orchestra, which is crucial in large ensembles.
- Music Stand: A sturdy, adjustable stand is necessary for holding sheet music during rehearsals and performances.

## 3. Techniques and Tips

- Listening and Blending: Adjust your playing to blend seamlessly with the ensemble, which is key to achieving a unified sound.
- Following the Conductor: Follow the conductor's cues closely to maintain synchronization and guide tempo, dynamics, and phrasing.
- Dynamic Control: Master the ability to play both loudly and softly as required, contributing to the orchestra's expression.
- Sectional Rehearsals: Participate in sectional rehearsals to refine your part and address challenges with your section.
- Emotional Interpretation: Focus on interpreting the emotional content of the music to bring the performance to life and connect with the audience.

# *June 19: Percussion*

## 1. The Rhythmic Foundation of Percussion

Percussion instruments are the backbone of many musical styles, providing rhythm, texture, and energy. From the steady bass drum beat to intricate snare patterns, percussionists play a vital role in both orchestral and contemporary music. The percussion world is vast, with each instrument offering unique sounds and techniques. As a percussionist, developing a strong sense of timing, coordination, and dynamic control is essential. Percussion playing is both physically and mentally engaging, offering endless creative possibilities.

## 2. Tools and Materials

- Drum Kit: A standard kit includes a bass drum, snare, toms, hi-hat, and cymbals, versatile for genres like rock and jazz. Orchestral percussion may require instruments like timpani or marimbas.
- Drumsticks and Mallets: Choose sticks or mallets suited to your instruments, as different options impact your playing style.
- Practice Pad: Useful for honing stick control and rhythm quietly, practice pads are essential for building technique.
- Metronome: Crucial for developing timing, a metronome helps you maintain consistent rhythm.
- Ear Protection: Use earplugs or over-ear protection during long practice sessions or performances to prevent hearing damage.

## 3. Techniques and Tips

- Grip and Stance: Proper grip and stance are crucial for control, endurance, and injury prevention across different percussion instruments.
- Rudiments: Master drum rudiments like single strokes and paradiddles to build technique and improve speed and accuracy.
- Dynamic Control: Practice playing with varied dynamics, from soft to loud, to enhance expression in your drumming.
- Reading Notation: Learn percussion notation, essential for performing in ensembles and orchestras.
- Improvisation and Creativity: Experiment with rhythms, patterns, and sounds. Percussion offers limitless creative possibilities, whether in a band, composing, or jamming.

# *June 20: Quena (Andean Flute)*

## 1. The Mystique of Quena Playing

The quena, a traditional Andean flute, produces a haunting, ethereal sound. Made from bamboo or wood, it has six finger holes and a thumb hole. Rooted in the musical traditions of South America's Andean regions, the quena is used for both folk and contemporary pieces. Its unique tone expresses the Andes' natural beauty and cultural heritage. Playing the quena requires breath control, finger dexterity, and an understanding of its cultural context.

## 2. Tools and Materials

- Quena Flute: Choose a well-crafted quena made from bamboo or wood for optimal sound quality. The material and construction greatly impact tone and playability.
- Tuning Device: A tuner ensures your quena is in tune, especially when playing with other instruments.
- Sheet Music or Tabs: Start with traditional Andean melodies to gain insight into the instrument's cultural significance.
- Music Stand: A stable stand helps hold sheet music at a comfortable height, useful for complex pieces or group playing.

## 3. Techniques and Tips

- Breath Control: Steady airflow is essential for a clear tone. Practice breathing exercises to improve lung capacity and control for long phrases.
- Finger Placement: Precise finger positioning is crucial, as slight misalignment affects pitch and clarity.
- Cultural Context: Learn about the quena's role in Andean music to enrich your playing experience.
- Improvisation: While traditional quena music is structured, improvisation is key in contemporary playing. Experiment with scales and rhythms to develop your style.
- Performance Practice: Regular performances, even informal ones, build confidence and refine technique.

# *June 21: Rap*

## 1. The Art of Rap

Rap is a vocal art form blending rhythm, poetry, and storytelling. A core of hip-hop culture, it has shaped global music. Characterized by rhythmic, rhymed lyrics often addressing social issues or personal experiences, rap involves not just writing compelling lyrics but mastering flow, timing, and impactful delivery. Whether freestyling or recording, rap is a dynamic way to convey messages and connect with audiences.

## 2. Tools and Materials

- Microphone: Essential for recording and practicing rap vocals. Condenser mics suit studios, while dynamic mics are ideal for live performances.
- Notebook: Keep a notebook or digital device to write and refine lyrics, building a library of material.
- Beat Tracks: Practice with instrumental tracks, focusing on timing and flow. Many producers offer beats online to match your style.
- Recording Software: DAWs like Logic Pro, Ableton Live, or GarageBand help with recording, editing, and mixing raps. Recording sessions can aid in refining performance.
- Headphones: Quality headphones with sound isolation are crucial for clearly hearing the beat and vocals during practice or recording.

## 3. Techniques and Tips

- Lyric Writing: Craft lyrics that tell a story, express emotion, or make a statement. Focus on rhyme schemes, wordplay, and your message.
- Flow and Rhythm: Practice rapping with the beat, working on timing and staying in the pocket. Mastering flow is key to an engaging performance.
- Breath Control: Essential for long phrases and vocal power. Practice breathing exercises to boost lung capacity and stamina, vital for live shows.
- Freestyle Practice: Regular freestyling enhances creativity and adaptability, helping you think quickly and flow naturally.
- Performance Skills: Work on stage presence, mic technique, and audience engagement. Confidence and energy are vital for a compelling performance.

# *June 22: Saxophone Playing*

## 1. The Expressiveness of Saxophone Playing

The saxophone is a versatile woodwind instrument used in jazz, classical, and contemporary music. Known for its rich tone, it can produce both smooth melodies and powerful phrases. Whether in a jazz ensemble, concert band, or as a soloist, the saxophone offers vast expressive possibilities. Its ability to convey emotion makes it a favorite for musicians aiming to connect deeply with audiences. Mastering the saxophone involves breath control, finger technique, and nuanced phrasing.

## 2. Tools and Materials

- Saxophone: Choose between alto, tenor, or soprano saxophones, each offering different tonal qualities suited to various styles.
- Reeds: Keep a supply, as they wear out quickly. Experiment with strengths to find what suits your style.
- Mouthpiece: Plays a key role in shaping tone. Beginners use standard mouthpieces, while advanced players may opt for custom options.
- Cleaning Kit: Essential for maintenance, including a swab, brush, and cork grease to ensure longevity.
- Music Stand: A stable stand at a comfortable height is crucial for posture and ease of reading.

## 3. Techniques and Tips

- Breath Support: Practice controlled breathing for steady airflow, crucial for smooth phrases. Diaphragmatic exercises help develop the control needed for expressive playing.
- Fingering Techniques: Regularly practice scales and arpeggios for fast, accurate movements, essential for clarity in complex runs.
- Tone Production: Focus on embouchure and breath control for a clear, rich tone. Experiment with mouthpiece and reed combinations for desired sound.
- Articulation: Practice staccato, legato, and vibrato to add expression and enhance emotional impact.
- Improvisation: Especially in jazz, practice improvising over chord progressions to develop your style, with a strong understanding of harmony and scales.

# *June 23: Singing*

## 1. The Joy of Singing

Singing is a universal form of expression that connects people across cultures and generations. Whether solo, in a choir, or with a band, singing lets you convey emotions and stories through melody. It's an accessible art that doesn't need special equipment, making it a natural way to express yourself. Singing offers physical and emotional benefits, like improving breath control and reducing stress. Whether on stage or in the shower, the joy of singing lies in its power to uplift and connect.

## 2. Tools and Materials

- Microphone: Helps amplify your voice during practice and useful for recording to analyze and improve your performance.
- Piano or Keyboard: Aids in practicing scales, intervals, and pitch accuracy, deepening your understanding of music theory.
- Recording Device: Recording your singing helps review progress and identify areas for improvement.
- Music Stand: Holds sheet music at a comfortable height, aiding in maintaining good posture.
- Vocal Warm-Ups: Exercises like lip trills and scales prepare your voice, preventing strain and ensuring peak performance.

## 3. Techniques and Tips

- Breath Control: Practice diaphragmatic breathing for voice support and long phrases without strain.
- Pitch Accuracy: Improve intonation by matching pitches with a piano or tuning app.
- Vocal Range: Explore your range with scales and arpeggios to choose suitable songs and avoid strain.
- Articulation and Diction: Ensure clear articulation for lyrics to be understood, especially in classical and theater genres.
- Expressiveness: Use dynamics, phrasing, and vocal color to convey emotion and tell a story.
- Regular Practice: Dedicate time daily to technique, repertoire, and performance to improve your singing.

# *June 24: Theater Acting*

## 1. The Art of Theater Acting

Theater acting is a demanding form of performance that brings characters and stories to life on stage, requiring live, unedited performances. This demands skill, preparation, and adaptability. Actors must create believable characters, understand dialogue nuances, and engage with both actors and the audience. Theater is a collaborative art that relies on synergy between actors, directors, and the production team to deliver a compelling performance.

## 2. Tools and Materials

- Scripts: Study your lines, focusing on character motivation and development. Annotate with notes on delivery, movement, and emotions.
- Costumes and Props: Use these during rehearsals to enhance your character and make your portrayal more believable.
- Mirror: Practice in front of a mirror to refine facial expressions and body language, ensuring they align with your character.
- Voice Recorder: Record your lines to practice timing, delivery, and projection, and identify areas for improvement.
- Vocal Exercises: Warm up your voice with exercises to achieve better projection, clarity, and range essential for theater acting.

## 3. Techniques and Tips

- Character Study: Analyze your character's background and motivations to create a nuanced portrayal.
- Vocal Projection: Project your voice to reach the entire theater without straining, ensuring strong vocal delivery.
- Body Language: Focus on posture, gestures, and facial expressions to convey your character's emotions and intentions.
- Improvisation Skills: Practice improv to develop quick thinking and adaptability for unexpected situations on stage.
- Engagement with Other Actors: Build strong connections with fellow actors to create authentic interactions and enhance the performance.
- Emotional Authenticity: Strive for genuine emotions in your performances to connect with the audience.

## *June 25: Ukulele*

### 1. The Simplicity of Ukulele Playing

The ukulele is a small, four-stringed instrument with a bright, cheerful sound, perfect for beginners. Its simplicity and versatility make it ideal for playing various genres, from Hawaiian music to pop songs. The ukulele's lightweight, portable design allows you to play it anywhere, making it a popular choice for musicians of all ages.

### 2. Tools and Materials

- Ukulele: Choose between soprano, concert, tenor, or baritone based on your size and sound preference. Soprano is the smallest, while baritone offers a deeper tone.
- Tuner: A clip-on tuner or tuning app ensures your ukulele stays in tune, essential for harmonizing with other instruments.
- Capo: A capo helps change the song's key without learning new chords, useful for playing with others or adjusting to your vocal range.
- Music Stand: Use a stable stand for sheet music or chord charts, especially helpful for beginners still learning chords.
- Ukulele Case: A case protects your ukulele and makes it easy to transport, with a padded gig bag offering extra protection for travel.

### 3. Techniques and Tips

- Basic Chords: Learn chords like C, G, Am, and F, common in many songs. Practice transitions to play more smoothly.
- Strumming Patterns: Experiment with strumming to create different rhythms, as a consistent technique is key to good playing.
- Fingerpicking: Explore fingerpicking to add complexity and texture, allowing you to play melodies and harmonies together.
- Singing and Playing: Practice singing while playing to improve coordination and timing, enhancing your performances.
- Song Selection: Start with simple songs to build confidence, and progress to more challenging tunes to improve your skills.

# *June 26: Violin Playing*

## 1. The Elegance of Violin Playing

The violin is celebrated for its expressive tone and versatility across genres like classical, jazz, folk, and pop. Mastering the violin requires dedication, but it offers a powerful means of emotional expression. Key techniques include bowing, finger placement, and vibrato, which help produce varied tones and dynamics. Whether in an orchestra, quartet, or as a soloist, the violin allows exploration of complex music and deep emotional expression.

## 2. Tools and Materials

- Violin: Choose a properly sized violin that suits your skill level, ensuring it fits comfortably under your chin.
- Bow: A good bow is vital for tone quality; select one that feels comfortable in your hand.
- Rosin: Apply rosin to your bow regularly to maintain good tone by ensuring proper string grip.
- Shoulder Rest: A shoulder rest provides comfort and supports proper posture, preventing strain.
- Tuner: Use a clip-on tuner or app to keep your violin in tune, essential for harmonizing with others.

## 3. Techniques and Tips

- Bowing Technique: Practice smooth, even bow strokes, keeping the bow parallel to the bridge with controlled pressure.
- Finger Placement: Accurate finger placement is key to playing in tune; practice scales to improve intonation.
- Vibrato: Develop vibrato for warmth and expression by practicing slow, controlled motions.
- Practice Regularly: Daily practice of scales, etudes, and repertoire is crucial for mastering both technique and musicality.
- Playing in Ensembles: Ensemble playing enhances skills like listening, blending, and maintaining rhythm, essential for developing overall musicianship.

# June 27: Whistling

## 1. The Simplicity of Whistling

Whistling is a simple yet expressive way to make music using just your breath and lips. It's a skill that can be picked up by almost anyone and can be used to create melodies, imitate bird songs, or simply pass the time. Whistling has been a part of many cultures for centuries and can be heard in various contexts, from casual whistling while walking to being incorporated into music performances. Despite its simplicity, whistling requires control of breath and pitch, making it a rewarding hobby for those who enjoy making music with minimal tools.

## 2. Tools and Materials

- Moisturize Your Lips: Keeping your lips moisturized prevents them from drying out, which can affect your ability to whistle clearly. Use a lip balm or simply keep your lips hydrated.
- Breathing Exercises: Practice deep breathing exercises to improve your lung capacity and control. Better breath control leads to more sustained and consistent whistling.
- Pitch Practice: Use a piano or tuning app to practice matching pitches. This helps you improve your pitch accuracy and ability to whistle melodies in tune.

## 3. Techniques and Tips

- Lip Positioning: Experiment with different lip shapes and tensions to find the most comfortable and effective position for whistling. The positioning of your tongue also plays a role in shaping the sound.
- Breath Control: Work on controlling your breath to produce steady, even tones. Short, sharp breaths create higher pitches, while long, controlled breaths are better for sustaining notes.
- Pitch Variation: Practice changing the pitch by adjusting the shape of your mouth and the force of your breath. With practice, you can whistle a wide range of notes and even play simple melodies.
- Whistling Along to Music: Practice whistling along to your favorite songs to improve your pitch accuracy and timing. This is a fun way to incorporate whistling into your everyday life.
- Whistling Techniques: Explore different techniques, such as finger whistling for louder sounds or vibrato for adding expression. These variations can expand your whistling repertoire and enhance your musicality.

# *June 28: Xylophone*

## 1. The Brightness of Xylophone Playing

The xylophone, a percussion instrument with wooden bars struck by mallets, produces bright, resonant tones. It's versatile, used across genres from classical to jazz. Known for its clear, bell-like sound, the xylophone can stand out in an ensemble or shine as a solo instrument. Learning to play involves mastering rhythm, coordination, and mallet technique, making it a rewarding instrument for exploring melody and harmony in a percussive form.

## 2. Tools and Materials

- Xylophone: Choose between wooden or synthetic bars based on your preferred sound. Wooden bars offer a warmer tone, while synthetic ones are more durable.
- Mallets: Available in various materials like rubber or plastic, mallets impact the sound and articulation. Experiment to find your preferred style.
- Practice Pad: Useful for silent practice, helping beginners focus on mallet control and rhythm without noise.
- Music Stand: A stable stand is essential for easy reading and maintaining good posture while playing.
- Metronome: Vital for developing timing, a metronome helps maintain steady rhythms, crucial for percussion instruments.

## 3. Techniques and Tips

- Mallet Grip: Practice a relaxed yet controlled grip for precision and clear tones.
- Mallet Control: Regularly practice scales and arpeggios to build coordination and dexterity.
- Rhythm and Timing: Develop a strong sense of rhythm, essential for xylophone playing, using a metronome to stay in sync with others.
- Dynamic Control: Vary dynamics from soft taps to loud strikes to add expression and contrast.
- Sight-Reading: Improve your ability to quickly read new music, a crucial skill for ensemble performances.

# *June 29: Yodeling*

## 1. The Unique Art of Yodeling

Yodeling is a singing style that involves rapid shifts between chest and head voice, creating a distinctive, echoing sound. Originating in the Alpine regions of Europe for communication across mountains, it has become a popular musical style in folk and country music. Yodeling requires precise control of vocal registers and breath support to achieve the characteristic "breaks" between notes. This challenging technique offers a fun and expressive way to explore your voice. Whether yodeling traditional Swiss melodies or incorporating it into modern music, yodeling is a versatile and joyful form of singing.

## 2. Tools and Materials

- Recording Device: Recording your practice sessions helps analyze technique and make improvements. Listening back lets you refine your yodels.
- Pitch Pipe or Tuner: Use a pitch pipe or tuner to practice matching pitches and maintaining accuracy, especially during register transitions.
- Notebook: Keep a notebook for jotting down patterns, lyrics, and tips. This helps track progress and develop your style.
- Vocal Warm-Ups: Essential for preparing your voice, warming up prevents strain and ensures readiness for rapid register shifts in yodeling.

## 3. Techniques and Tips

- Register Shifts: Practice smooth transitions between chest and head voice, focusing on clarity and gradually increasing speed as you gain confidence.
- Breath Control: Strong breath support is crucial for consistent volume and control during shifts. Practice deep breathing to sustain long yodels.
- Pitch Accuracy: Focus on matching pitches accurately, especially during rapid transitions. Use a pitch pipe or tuner for consistent practice.
- Vocal Flexibility: Develop flexibility in your vocal cords with scales, arpeggios, and wide-range exercises, crucial for smooth yodeling shifts.
- Cultural Exploration: Explore yodeling's origins and styles, like Swiss or country yodeling. Understanding its history enhances your performance.

# *June 30: Zither Playing*

## 1. The Delicate Art of Zither Playing

The zither is a stringed instrument known for its delicate, resonant sound in folk and classical music. Played by plucking or strumming with fingers or a plectrum, it produces gentle melodies and harmonies. The zither comes in forms like the concert and alpine zithers, each offering different techniques and musical possibilities. Learning the zither requires finger dexterity, coordination, and an understanding of its unique tuning system. It's a soothing instrument perfect for solo and ensemble performances.

## 2. Tools and Materials

- Zither: Select a zither that matches your musical style, whether classical or traditional folk tunes. Ensure it's well-made and tuned.
- Finger Picks: Use finger picks to enhance plucking efficiency. Experiment with different sizes and materials to find the best fit.
- Music Stand: A stable stand to hold sheet music is essential, especially for the complex notation in zither music.
- Tuning Device: A tuning fork or electronic tuner is necessary to keep your zither in tune, requiring regular adjustments.
- Music Books: Start with beginner-friendly books, advancing to more complex pieces as your skills grow.

## 3. Techniques and Tips

- Finger Dexterity: Practice exercises to develop quick, accurate plucking, crucial for fast passages and complex chords.
- Plucking Technique: Focus on producing a clean sound. Experiment with finger picks or use bare fingers to find your ideal tone.
- Tuning and Maintenance: Regularly tune and maintain your zither to preserve sound quality.
- Learning Tablature: Understand zither tablature, which indicates which strings to pluck. This is key to accurate music reading.
- Cultural Exploration: Explore zither music traditions, from classical to folk, to deepen your appreciation and inspire your performances.

## *Conclusion for June*

As you close out June, reflect on the diverse range of musical and performing arts experiences you've explored. From mastering instruments to developing your vocal talents, this month has been an enriching journey through the world of sound and performance. Continue to nurture your creativity and expression through these activities, as they not only bring joy but also connect you to a broader artistic community.

# July: Nature and Outdoors

*July is dedicated to the wonders of nature and the thrill of outdoor activities. This month encourages you to step outside, breathe in the fresh air, and connect with the natural world. Whether you're seeking adventure, solitude, or a deeper understanding of the environment, these activities offer something for everyone. From archery to zoo volunteering, July's hobbies are about exploration, conservation, and the joy of being in nature.*

# *July 1: Archery*

## 1. The Precision of Archery

Archery is a sport practiced for thousands of years, originally for hunting and warfare, and now enjoyed recreationally and competitively. It demands a combination of mental focus, physical strength, and precise technique. The goal is to hit the center of a target from a set distance, making the sport both meditative and exhilarating as you refine your skills.

## 2. Tools and Materials

- Bow: Choose based on your interests and experience level. Recurve bows are traditional, compound bows offer mechanical advantages, and longbows provide a more historical experience.
- Arrows: Select arrows according to your bow type and draw length. Materials like wood, aluminum, or carbon offer different benefits in terms of weight, durability, and performance.
- Target: A sturdy target is essential. Foam block targets are popular for their durability, while straw bales are a traditional option. Use a target face with scoring rings to track progress.
- Armguard and Finger Tab: These protective items help prevent injury. An armguard shields your forearm, while a finger tab or glove protects your fingers during the draw and release.

## 3. Techniques and Tips

- Stance: Stand with your feet shoulder-width apart, perpendicular to the target, with your weight evenly distributed.
- Draw and Anchor Point: Draw the bowstring smoothly to the same anchor point on your face each time, such as the corner of your mouth or the side of your chin. This helps with accuracy and consistency.
- Aiming and Release: Focus on your target, using a sight or instinctive aiming. Release the string smoothly, relaxing your fingers while maintaining focus on the target after the arrow is released.
- Follow-Through: Hold your position after release to ensure the arrow flies straight. This is crucial for accuracy and helps develop muscle memory.

# *July 2: Astronomy*

## 1. The Wonder of Astronomy

Astronomy is the study of the universe beyond Earth's atmosphere, from our solar system to distant galaxies. It can be as simple as stargazing with the naked eye or as complex as astrophotography with advanced telescopes. Astronomy connects you to the cosmos, offering both scientific understanding and a profound sense of wonder.

## 2. Tools and Materials

- Telescope: The primary tool for observing celestial objects. Refractor telescopes use lenses, while reflectors use mirrors. Choose based on what you want to observe, like planets or deep-sky objects.
- Star Charts and Apps: Essential for navigating the night sky, showing the positions of stars and planets. Smartphone apps can provide real-time guidance.
- Red Light Flashlight: Preserves night vision while reading charts or adjusting equipment, unlike white light, which can interfere with seeing faint objects.
- Notebook and Pen: Keep a log of your observations, noting details like date, time, and conditions. Sketching can also enhance your skills.

## 3. Techniques and Tips

- Dark Sky Sites: For the best experience, find a location far from city lights where the sky is darkest, such as designated dark sky parks.
- Seasonal Viewing: Different constellations and celestial events are visible at different times. Familiarize yourself with these changes to plan observations.
- Planetary Observation: Planets are rewarding to observe; with a decent telescope, you can see details like Saturn's rings, Jupiter's moons, and Venus's phases.
- Astrophotography: Consider capturing images of the night sky. Start with simple setups, like a camera on a tripod, and progress to using telescopes and tracking mounts.

# *July 3: Backpacking*

## 1. The Adventure of Backpacking

Backpacking combines hiking with camping, allowing you to explore remote wilderness areas over multiple days. It's an immersive experience that offers a deep connection with nature, solitude, and the satisfaction of self-sufficiency. Whether navigating rugged mountains, dense forests, or deserts, backpacking challenges your physical endurance and wilderness survival skills.

## 2. Tools and Materials

- Backpack: A good backpack is crucial for carrying all your gear. Choose one that fits well and has enough capacity for your trip's duration, with padded straps, a hip belt, and multiple compartments.
- Shelter: A lightweight tent, tarp, or bivy sack protects you from the elements. Ensure it's durable and appropriate for the climate and terrain.
- Sleeping Bag and Pad: A sleeping bag rated for the expected temperatures and a sleeping pad for insulation and comfort are essential.
- Cooking Gear: A portable stove, lightweight cookware, and a fire starter are necessary for backcountry meals. Pack lightweight, nutritious, and easy-to-prepare food.
- Navigation Tools: A map and compass are vital for wilderness navigation. A GPS device is helpful, but always carry a traditional map and compass as backups.

## 3. Techniques and Tips

- Pack Light: Carry only essentials. Choose lightweight gear, plan meals carefully, and avoid unnecessary items.
- Leave No Trace: Follow Leave No Trace principles to minimize environmental impact. Pack out all trash, avoid disturbing wildlife, and camp 200 feet from water sources.
- Water Management: Plan your route with water sources in mind. Carry a water filter or purification tablets and know where the next water source is.
- Physical Preparation: Backpacking requires good physical fitness. Regular hiking, strength training, and cardio can prepare you for carrying a loaded pack over rough terrain.

# *July 4: Birdwatching*

## 1. The Peace of Birdwatching

Birdwatching, or birding, is the practice of observing birds in their natural habitats. It's a peaceful and educational hobby that connects you with nature and allows you to enjoy the beauty and diversity of bird species. Birdwatching can be done anywhere, from your backyard to remote wilderness areas, and it offers endless opportunities to learn about avian behavior, migration patterns, and ecology.

## 2. Tools and Materials

- Binoculars: A good pair of binoculars is essential for getting a close-up view of birds without disturbing them. Choose binoculars with a magnification of 8x or 10x for birdwatching.
- Field Guide: A field guide will help you identify different bird species. Look for a guide specific to your region, or use a birding app that includes photos, descriptions, and bird calls.
- Notebook and Pen: Keep a birdwatching journal to record the species you observe, their behaviors, and the locations where you find them. Sketching birds can also help you remember their key identifying features.
- Bird Feeder: Attract birds to your yard with a bird feeder. Different types of feeders and seeds will attract different species, providing you with opportunities to observe birds up close.

## 3. Techniques and Tips

- Learn Bird Calls: Familiarize yourself with the calls and songs of local bird species. This will help you identify birds by sound, even if they are hidden from view.
- Timing and Location: Birds are most active during the early morning and late afternoon. Visit different habitats, such as forests, wetlands, and grasslands, to see a variety of species.
- Stay Quiet and Still: Birds are sensitive to noise and movement. Approach slowly, avoid sudden movements, and keep quiet to avoid startling them.
- Join a Birdwatching Group: Consider joining a local birdwatching group or participating in bird counts and conservation projects. This can enhance your knowledge and provide opportunities to observe rare or elusive species.

# *July 5: Canoeing*

## 1. The Serenity of Canoeing

Canoeing is a water-based activity that allows you to explore lakes, rivers, and streams at a leisurely pace. It's a peaceful way to connect with nature, offering a unique perspective from the water. Whether you're paddling through calm waters or navigating gentle rapids, canoeing provides both relaxation and a sense of adventure. It's a versatile activity that can be enjoyed solo or with others, making it ideal for families, friends, or solo adventurers.

## 2. Tools and Materials

- Canoe: Choose a canoe that suits your needs, whether it's for flatwater paddling on lakes or whitewater canoeing on rivers. Canoes come in various sizes and materials, such as aluminum, fiberglass, and plastic.
- Paddles: Use lightweight paddles that are comfortable to grip and appropriately sized for your height and the type of canoeing you'll be doing. Consider carrying a spare paddle in case of emergencies.
- Life Jacket (PFD): Always wear a life jacket or personal flotation device (PFD) while canoeing. It's essential for safety, especially in deeper or faster-moving water.
- Dry Bags: Store your gear in waterproof dry bags to keep it safe from water. This is particularly important for items like clothing, food, and electronics.

## 3. Techniques and Tips

- Basic Paddle Strokes: Learn and practice the basic paddle strokes, such as the forward stroke, draw stroke, and J-stroke. These will help you steer, move forward, and maneuver your canoe effectively.
- Entry and Exit: Practice getting in and out of your canoe in shallow water before heading out on deeper waters. This helps you maintain balance and prevents capsizing.
- Stay Balanced: Distribute weight evenly in the canoe, and keep your movements smooth and controlled to maintain stability. Avoid sudden shifts in weight that could cause the canoe to tip.
- River Safety: If canoeing on rivers, be aware of currents, obstacles, and changes in water levels. Always scout rapids or unfamiliar sections of the river before attempting to navigate them.

# *July 6: Desert Hiking*

## 1. The Challenge of Desert Hiking

Desert hiking is an adventurous activity that involves trekking through arid landscapes characterized by extreme temperatures, rugged terrain, and scarce water sources. Despite these challenges, desert hiking offers stunning scenery, including sand dunes, rocky outcrops, and unique plant and animal life. It requires careful planning, preparation, and respect for the harsh environment.

## 2. Tools and Materials

- Hydration Pack: Carry a hydration pack or water bottles to ensure you have enough water for the hike. In the desert, it's recommended to drink small amounts frequently to stay hydrated.
- Sun Protection: Wear a wide-brimmed hat, sunglasses, and high SPF sunscreen to protect yourself from the intense desert sun. Light-colored, loose-fitting clothing can help keep you cool.
- Map and Compass: Navigation tools are essential in the desert, where trails may be poorly marked or nonexistent. A GPS device can be useful, but always carry a map and compass as a backup.
- First Aid Kit: Include bandages, antiseptic, and tweezers for blisters, cuts, and other minor injuries that can occur during desert hikes.

## 3. Techniques and Tips

- Hike Early or Late: Avoid the heat of the day by hiking in the early morning or late afternoon when temperatures are cooler. This also increases your chances of seeing wildlife, which is more active during these times.
- Pacing and Rest: Take frequent breaks in shaded areas, if available, to avoid overheating. Move at a steady pace and listen to your body, resting whenever necessary.
- Know the Signs of Heat-Related Illness: Be aware of symptoms like dehydration, heat exhaustion, and heatstroke, such as dizziness, nausea, and confusion. If these symptoms occur, stop hiking, find shade, and hydrate.
- Respect the Environment: The desert is a fragile ecosystem. Stay on established trails, avoid disturbing plants and animals, and pack out all trash. Be mindful of your impact, as desert environments recover slowly from human activity.

# *July 7: Dog Training*

## 1. The Bond of Dog Training

Dog training is a rewarding activity that strengthens the bond between you and your dog. It involves teaching obedience, tricks, and good behavior, making your dog a well-behaved and happy companion. Training requires patience, consistency, and positive reinforcement, tailored to your dog's personality and needs. Whether training a puppy or an older dog, the process is both fun and beneficial for you and your pet.

## 2. Tools and Materials

- Leash and Collar: Use a sturdy leash and collar for control during training. A harness may be better for dogs that pull.
- Treats: Small, tasty treats are essential for rewarding your dog during training. Choose high-value treats that your dog loves to motivate them.
- Clicker: A clicker is a popular tool in positive reinforcement training, marking the exact moment your dog performs a desired behavior.
- Training Mat or Crate: A mat or crate can teach your dog to settle in a specific place, useful for house training and calming exercises.

## 3. Techniques and Tips

- Start with Basic Commands: Begin with basic commands like sit, stay, come, and down. These form the foundation for more advanced training and establish communication.
- Positive Reinforcement: Reward your dog immediately after they perform a desired behavior to encourage repetition and build trust.
- Consistency is Key: Be consistent with commands, rewards, and expectations. Use the same words and gestures for each command to avoid confusion.
- Short, Frequent Sessions: Keep sessions short (10-15 minutes) to maintain your dog's interest. Frequent, brief sessions are more effective than long ones.
- Patience and Understanding: Every dog learns at their own pace. Be patient and avoid punishment, focusing on building a positive, trusting relationship.

# *July 8: Environmental Conservation*

## 1. The Responsibility of Environmental Conservation

Environmental conservation involves protecting natural resources and ecosystems to ensure their sustainability for future generations. It includes activities like recycling, habitat restoration, wildlife protection, and advocacy for environmental policies. As a hobby, conservation allows you to make a positive impact on the planet, whether through small daily actions or larger community projects. It's a meaningful way to contribute to the health of the Earth and its inhabitants.

## 2. Tools and Materials

- Reusable Bags and Containers: Reduce your environmental footprint by using reusable bags, water bottles, and food containers instead of single-use plastics.
- Composting Bin: Composting organic waste at home creates nutrient-rich soil for gardening and reduces waste sent to landfills.
- Energy-Efficient Appliances: Investing in energy-efficient appliances like LED light bulbs and low-flow showerheads can significantly reduce your energy and water consumption.
- Gardening Tools: Tools like trowels, pruners, and watering cans are essential for maintaining a garden that supports local wildlife and pollinators.

## 3. Techniques and Tips

- Reduce, Reuse, Recycle: Follow the three Rs to minimize waste. Reduce single-use items, reuse products, and recycle materials to keep them out of landfills.
- Support Local and Sustainable Products: Choose products that are locally sourced, sustainably produced, and environmentally friendly. This supports local economies and reduces the carbon footprint from transportation.
- Volunteer for Conservation Projects: Get involved in local conservation efforts, such as tree planting, habitat restoration, or beach clean-ups. Volunteering is a great way to make a tangible impact and meet like-minded individuals.
- Educate and Advocate: Share your passion for conservation with others. Advocate for environmental policies in your community and support organizations that protect the environment.

# *July 9: Falconry*

## 1. The Tradition of Falconry

Falconry is the ancient art of training birds of prey to hunt in partnership with humans. It's a highly specialized hobby requiring dedication, patience, and deep respect for these majestic birds. Practiced for thousands of years across various cultures, falconry is more than just a hunting method—it's a way to bond with birds of prey and understand their natural behaviors. Falconry is regulated and typically requires an apprenticeship under an experienced falconer, along with obtaining the necessary permits and licenses.

## 2. Tools and Materials

- Falconry Glove: A thick, durable glove is essential for handling birds of prey. The glove protects your arm from the bird's sharp talons and provides a perch.
- Lure: Used during training to simulate prey, typically a piece of leather or fabric, encouraging the bird to chase and catch it.
- Hood: Placed over the bird's head to calm it and prevent distractions when not in flight. It's essential for managing the bird during transport and training.
- Aviary: A secure, well-ventilated aviary, or mews, is necessary for housing your bird when it's not hunting. It should be spacious, clean, and equipped with perches and water.

## 3. Techniques and Tips

- Apprenticeship: Falconry is not a hobby that can be learned overnight. Start with an apprenticeship under an experienced falconer who can teach you the skills and responsibilities of caring for and training a bird of prey.
- Building Trust: Trust between you and your bird is crucial for successful falconry. Spend time handling and feeding your bird to develop a strong bond.
- Flight Training: Training a bird of prey to return to you during free flight requires patience and consistency. Use the lure to reinforce the bird's natural hunting instincts while ensuring it remains under your control.
- Legal and Ethical Considerations: Falconry is heavily regulated to protect both the birds and the environment. Ensure you comply with all local and national regulations, including obtaining necessary permits and adhering to ethical hunting practices.

# *July 10: Fishing*

## 1. The Relaxation of Fishing

Fishing is a time-honored outdoor activity that combines patience, skill, and a love for nature. Whether in a river, lake, or ocean, this hobby offers a peaceful escape from daily life. Fishing can be as simple or complex as you like, from casual shore fishing to deep-sea angling. The goal is to catch fish, but for many, the true joy lies in being outdoors, enjoying the tranquility of the water, and the thrill of a successful catch.

## 2. Tools and Materials

- Fishing Rod and Reel: Choose a rod and reel suited to the type of fishing you plan to do. Fly fishing rods differ from those used for saltwater fishing, so select gear based on your environment and the species you're targeting.
- Bait and Lures: Bait can be live, like worms or minnows, or artificial, like plastic worms or crankbaits. Lures mimic prey movements and can be selected based on the type of fish you're targeting.
- Tackle Box: A tackle box is essential for organizing your fishing gear, including hooks, sinkers, lines, and other accessories. Choose one with compartments to keep everything in place.
- Fishing License: Most places require a fishing license, so ensure you're properly licensed before heading out. Regulations vary, so check the rules in your area.

## 3. Techniques and Tips

- Casting Techniques: Practice your casting technique to improve accuracy and distance. Proper casting is key to placing your bait or lure in the right spot to attract fish.
- Patience and Observation: Fishing often requires long periods of waiting. Use this time to observe your surroundings, watch for fish activity, and enjoy the peaceful environment.
- Catch and Release: If you're not keeping your catch, practice catch and release. Use barbless hooks and handle fish gently to minimize stress and injury before releasing them back into the water.
- Fishing Etiquette: Respect other anglers by giving them space and not encroaching on their fishing spots. Clean up after yourself, and never leave fishing line or trash behind, as these can harm wildlife.

# *July 11: Gardening*

## 1. The Satisfaction of Gardening

Gardening is the practice of growing and cultivating plants, whether for food, flowers, or simply the joy of nurturing life. It's a hobby that connects you with the earth, teaches patience, and rewards you with beauty or a bountiful harvest. Gardening can be done in a backyard, on a balcony, or even indoors with the right setup.

## 2. Tools and Materials

- Garden Tools: Invest in quality tools like a trowel, pruners, and a watering can for maintaining your garden.
- Soil and Fertilizer: Use nutrient-rich soil and appropriate fertilizers to support healthy plant growth.
- Seeds and Plants: Choose plants suited to your climate and space, whether vegetables, herbs, or ornamental flowers.

## 3. Techniques and Tips

- Soil Preparation: Prepare your soil by adding compost or other organic matter to improve fertility and drainage.
- Watering: Water your plants regularly, but avoid overwatering, which can lead to root rot.
- Pest Control: Use natural pest control methods, such as companion planting or insecticidal soap, to protect your garden without harming the environment.

# *July 12: Herb Foraging*

## 1. The Tradition of Herb Foraging

Herb foraging is the practice of searching for and harvesting wild herbs for culinary, medicinal, or aromatic purposes. It's a sustainable way to connect with nature and learn about the plants that grow in your local environment. Foraging requires knowledge of plant identification and a respect for nature's offerings.

## 2. Tools and Materials

- Foraging Basket: Use a lightweight basket to carry your harvested herbs without crushing them.
- Field Guide: Carry a field guide to help identify edible and medicinal herbs in your area.
- Scissors or Knife: Use scissors or a small knife to carefully harvest herbs without damaging the plants.

## 3. Techniques and Tips

- Identification: Learn to identify herbs accurately to avoid harvesting poisonous or harmful plants.
- Sustainable Harvesting: Only take what you need and leave enough for the plants to regenerate and for wildlife to thrive.
- Preservation: Dry or freeze your harvested herbs to preserve them for future use in cooking or remedies.

# *July 13: Ice Fishing*

## 1. The Challenge of Ice Fishing

Ice fishing is a wintertime activity that involves fishing through a hole in the ice on a frozen lake or river. It's a unique and challenging way to fish, requiring specialized equipment and knowledge of ice conditions. Ice fishing combines the thrill of the catch with the quiet beauty of winter landscapes.

## 2. Tools and Materials

- Ice Auger: Use an ice auger to drill holes in the ice for fishing.
- Ice Fishing Rod: Choose a short, sturdy rod designed for ice fishing, along with appropriate bait or lures.
- Shelter: Set up an ice fishing shelter or tent to protect yourself from the wind and cold while you fish.

## 3. Techniques and Tips

- Ice Safety: Always check the thickness and condition of the ice before venturing out, ensuring it's at least 4 inches thick for safe fishing.
- Patience: Ice fishing requires patience, as fish may be less active in the cold, but the reward is often worth the wait.
- Layering: Dress in multiple layers to stay warm, as you'll be sitting still for long periods in freezing temperatures.

# *July 14: Javelin Throwing*

## 1. The Athleticism of Javelin Throwing
Javelin throwing is a track and field event that involves throwing a long, spear-like object as far as possible. It's a sport that requires strength, speed, and precise technique. Javelin throwing is both a competitive and recreational activity, offering a way to develop athletic skills and test your limits.

## 2. Tools and Materials
- Javelin: Choose a javelin that meets the specifications for your competition level or practice needs.
- Track or Field: Practice in a safe, open area, such as a track or field, where you have plenty of space to throw.
- Measuring Tape: Use a measuring tape to track your throws and monitor your progress.

## 3. Techniques and Tips
- Grip and Stance: Learn the proper grip and stance to ensure a strong, controlled throw.
- Run-Up: Focus on your run-up, building speed and momentum before releasing the javelin.
- Follow-Through: Practice a smooth follow-through to maximize distance and accuracy.

# *July 15: Kayaking*

## 1. The Adventure of Kayaking

Kayaking is a water sport that involves paddling a small, narrow boat called a kayak through various water bodies, from calm lakes to rushing rivers. It's a versatile activity that offers both relaxation and adventure, depending on the type of water and kayaking style you choose.

## 2. Tools and Materials

- Kayak: Choose a kayak suited to your activity, whether it's for calm lakes, whitewater, or sea kayaking.
- Paddle: Use a lightweight paddle that is the correct length for your height and kayaking style.
- Life Jacket: Always wear a life jacket while kayaking for safety.

## 3. Techniques and Tips

- Paddling Technique: Practice proper paddling techniques, including forward strokes, sweep strokes, and bracing, to control your kayak effectively.
- Balance: Maintain balance by sitting low and centered in the kayak, keeping your movements smooth and steady.
- Water Safety: Be aware of weather conditions and water currents, and plan your route accordingly to ensure a safe kayaking trip.

# *July 16: Landscaping*

## 1. The Art of Landscaping

Landscaping is the practice of designing and maintaining outdoor spaces to create aesthetically pleasing environments. It involves the selection and placement of plants, the construction of hardscapes, and the integration of natural elements. Landscaping is both a creative and practical hobby that enhances your home and provides a connection to the outdoors.

## 2. Tools and Materials

- Garden Tools: Use tools like shovels, rakes, and pruners to shape and maintain your landscape.
- Plants and Trees: Choose plants, shrubs, and trees that suit your climate and design goals.
- Mulch and Soil: Use mulch and soil amendments to improve plant health and control weeds.

## 3. Techniques and Tips

- Design Planning: Start with a landscape design plan that includes plant placement, hardscapes, and focal points.
- Seasonal Maintenance: Keep your landscape looking its best by performing seasonal maintenance, such as pruning, mulching, and fertilizing.
- Sustainability: Incorporate sustainable practices like xeriscaping, rainwater harvesting, and native plantings to reduce water usage and support local wildlife.

# *July 17: Mountain Biking*

## 1. The Thrill of Mountain Biking

Mountain biking is an exhilarating sport that involves riding bikes over rough terrain, such as trails, hills, and mountains. It's a challenging and rewarding activity that combines physical endurance with technical skill. Mountain biking offers an adrenaline rush and a chance to explore nature from a different perspective.

## 2. Tools and Materials

- Mountain Bike: Choose a mountain bike that suits your riding style, whether it's cross-country, downhill, or trail riding.
- Helmet and Pads: Wear a helmet and protective pads to stay safe while riding.
- Repair Kit: Carry a repair kit with essentials like a tire pump, patch kit, and multi-tool for on-the-go fixes.

## 3. Techniques and Tips

- Trail Awareness: Stay alert on the trail, watching for obstacles, changes in terrain, and other riders.
- Body Position: Practice proper body positioning, keeping your weight centered and adjusting based on the terrain.
- Pacing: Manage your energy by pacing yourself, especially on long or challenging trails, to avoid fatigue.

# *July 18: Nature Photography*

## 1. The Beauty of Nature Photography

Nature photography involves capturing images of the natural world, including landscapes, wildlife, and plants. It's a hobby that requires patience, observation, and an eye for composition. Nature photography allows you to explore the beauty of the outdoors and share it with others through your images.

## 2. Tools and Materials

- Camera: Use a DSLR, mirrorless, or even a smartphone camera with a good lens for nature photography.
- Tripod: A tripod is essential for stable shots, especially in low light or for long exposures.
- Lens Filters: Use lens filters, such as polarizers or ND filters, to enhance your images and manage challenging lighting conditions.

## 3. Techniques and Tips

- Composition: Focus on composition, using techniques like the rule of thirds, leading lines, and framing to create visually appealing images.
- Lighting: Pay attention to natural light, with the golden hour (just after sunrise and before sunset) often providing the best lighting conditions.
- Patience: Be patient, especially when photographing wildlife, as capturing the perfect shot may take time and persistence.

# *July 19: Orienteering*

## 1. The Challenge of Orienteering

Orienteering is an outdoor adventure sport that involves navigating through unfamiliar terrain using a map and compass. It's a mental and physical challenge that requires quick thinking, map-reading skills, and endurance. Orienteering can be done competitively or as a recreational activity, offering a unique way to explore the outdoors.

## 2. Tools and Materials

- Compass: A reliable compass is essential for navigating and orienting your map.
- Topographic Map: Use a topographic map of the area you're navigating to identify landmarks and terrain features.
- Running Gear: Wear comfortable clothing and shoes suitable for running or hiking over various terrains.

## 3. Techniques and Tips

- Map Reading: Practice reading topographic maps to understand contours, symbols, and scales.
- Pacing: Learn to pace yourself and estimate distances based on your stride length to stay on track.
- Stay Calm: Stay calm and focused, even if you get off course, and use your map and compass to reorient and find your way.

# *July 20: Paddleboarding*

## 1. The Calm of Paddleboarding

Paddleboarding, or stand-up paddleboarding (SUP), is a water activity where you stand on a large board and use a paddle to move through the water. It's a relaxing and low-impact way to explore lakes, rivers, and coastal areas. Paddleboarding can be a solo activity or enjoyed with friends, offering both physical exercise and a peaceful connection to nature.

## 2. Tools and Materials

- Paddleboard: Choose a paddleboard that suits your activity, whether it's for calm waters, surfing, or yoga.
- Paddle: Use a lightweight paddle that is the correct length for your height and paddling style.
- Leash: Wear a leash that attaches to your ankle and the board to keep the board close if you fall off.

## 3. Techniques and Tips

- Balance: Practice balancing on the board by standing with your feet shoulder-width apart and your knees slightly bent.
- Paddling Technique: Use your core muscles to paddle, keeping your strokes smooth and consistent.
- Safety: Always wear a life jacket and be aware of weather and water conditions before heading out.

# *July 21: Quail Hunting*

## 1. The Tradition of Quail Hunting

Quail hunting is a challenging and traditional form of upland game hunting that requires skill, patience, and knowledge of the bird's behavior. It's a social and rewarding activity often enjoyed with hunting dogs, who help locate and flush out the birds. Quail hunting offers a connection to nature and the thrill of the hunt in a respectful and sustainable manner.

## 2. Tools and Materials

- Shotgun: Use a shotgun that is suitable for bird hunting, typically a 20-gauge or 12-gauge.
- Hunting Dog: Consider training or hunting with a dog, as they can greatly assist in locating and retrieving quail.
- Hunting Vest: Wear a hunting vest with pockets for shells and other gear, and make sure to wear blaze orange for safety.

## 3. Techniques and Tips

- Scouting: Scout your hunting area beforehand to understand where quail are likely to be found.
- Patience: Be patient and quiet, as sudden movements or noise can easily scare away quail.
- Ethical Hunting: Practice ethical hunting by following regulations, respecting bag limits, and ensuring a quick and humane harvest.

# *July 22: Rock Climbing*

## 1. The Thrill of Rock Climbing

Rock climbing is a physically demanding and mentally challenging sport that involves scaling natural rock formations or artificial climbing walls. It requires strength, endurance, and problem-solving skills. Rock climbing can be done indoors or outdoors, offering a sense of accomplishment and a unique perspective on the landscape.

## 2. Tools and Materials

- Climbing Shoes: Wear climbing shoes with a snug fit and good grip for better control on the rock.
- Harness and Rope: Use a climbing harness and rope for safety, especially when climbing higher or more challenging routes.
- Chalk Bag: Carry a chalk bag to keep your hands dry and improve your grip on the rock.

## 3. Techniques and Tips

- Body Positioning: Focus on body positioning and balance, using your legs to push up rather than relying solely on your arms.
- Route Planning: Study the climbing route before you start, identifying key holds and sequences.
- Safety First: Always check your gear and climbing partner's setup before starting, and never climb without proper safety measures in place.

# *July 23: Scuba Diving*

## 1. The Exploration of Scuba Diving

Scuba diving is an underwater activity that allows you to explore the ocean's depths, discovering marine life and underwater landscapes. It's a thrilling and immersive experience that requires training and certification. Scuba diving offers a unique opportunity to connect with the ocean and observe its wonders up close.

## 2. Tools and Materials

- Scuba Gear: Use a mask, snorkel, fins, wetsuit, regulator, and oxygen tank as part of your diving gear.
- Dive Computer: A dive computer helps you monitor your depth, time underwater, and oxygen levels.
- Underwater Camera: Consider using an underwater camera to capture your diving experiences and the marine life you encounter.

## 3. Techniques and Tips

- Buoyancy Control: Practice controlling your buoyancy to move smoothly through the water and avoid disturbing marine life.
- Equalization: Remember to equalize the pressure in your ears frequently as you descend to avoid discomfort.
- Buddy System: Always dive with a buddy and communicate clearly underwater using hand signals.

# *July 24: Tree Climbing*

## 1. The Joy of Tree Climbing

Tree climbing is a fun and adventurous activity that involves scaling trees using ropes and harnesses. It's a great way to connect with nature, explore forested areas, and enjoy a different perspective from high up in the trees. Tree climbing can be both recreational and competitive, offering physical and mental challenges.

## 2. Tools and Materials

- Climbing Harness: Use a harness designed for tree climbing, ensuring it fits securely and comfortably.
- Ropes and Carabiners: Use sturdy ropes and locking carabiners for safety while climbing and securing your position.
- Helmet: Wear a helmet to protect your head from falling branches or accidental bumps against the tree.

## 3. Techniques and Tips

- Knot Tying: Learn essential knots for tree climbing, such as the figure-eight knot and the clove hitch, to secure yourself safely.
- Foot Placement: Practice placing your feet securely on branches or footholds to maintain balance and stability.
- Respect the Trees: Climb with care, avoiding damage to the tree and leaving no trace of your presence.

# *July 25: Underwater Photography*

## 1. The Art of Underwater Photography

Underwater photography involves capturing images of marine life, underwater landscapes, and the beauty of the ocean's depths. It's a challenging and rewarding hobby that requires special equipment and techniques. Underwater photography allows you to document and share the wonders of the underwater world.

## 2. Tools and Materials

- Underwater Camera: Use a camera designed for underwater use, or invest in a waterproof housing for your existing camera.
- Strobe Lights: Consider using strobe lights to enhance the lighting and color in your underwater photos.
- Fins and Mask: Wear fins and a mask to improve mobility and visibility while taking photos underwater.

## 3. Techniques and Tips

- Buoyancy Control: Master your buoyancy to stay steady while taking photos and avoid disturbing the water.
- Close-Up Shots: Get close to your subject to reduce the amount of water between the lens and the subject, resulting in clearer images.
- Patience: Be patient and wait for the perfect moment, as underwater photography often requires precise timing and calmness.

# *July 26: Volcano Hiking*

## 1. The Adventure of Volcano Hiking

Volcano hiking is an adventurous activity that involves trekking to the summit or around the base of a volcano. It's a unique experience that offers stunning views, geological wonders, and the thrill of exploring active or dormant volcanoes. Volcano hiking requires preparation and respect for the potentially hazardous environment.

## 2. Tools and Materials

- Hiking Boots: Wear sturdy hiking boots with good traction for navigating rocky and uneven terrain.
- Protective Gear: Carry protective gear, such as a face mask and goggles, in case of ash or gas emissions.
- Navigation Tools: Use a map, compass, or GPS device to stay on the designated trails and avoid dangerous areas.

## 3. Techniques and Tips

- Research the Volcano: Learn about the specific volcano you're hiking, including its activity level and any safety warnings.
- Pacing: Pace yourself, as the elevation gain and rugged terrain can make volcano hiking physically demanding.
- Respect the Environment: Stay on marked trails, avoid disturbing geological formations, and follow all safety guidelines.

# *July 27: Wildlife Tracking*

## 1. The Skill of Wildlife Tracking

Wildlife tracking is the practice of identifying and following the signs left by animals in their natural habitat. It's a skill that requires keen observation, knowledge of animal behavior, and patience. Wildlife tracking offers a deeper connection to nature and an understanding of the animals that inhabit it.

## 2. Tools and Materials

- Field Guide: Use a field guide to help identify tracks, scat, and other signs of wildlife.
- Binoculars: Carry binoculars to observe animals from a distance without disturbing them.
- Notebook: Keep a notebook to record your observations, sketches, and findings during your tracking sessions.

## 3. Techniques and Tips

- Observation Skills: Sharpen your observation skills by looking for subtle signs, such as bent grass, disturbed soil, or faint tracks.
- Patience: Tracking requires patience, as animals may move slowly or leave only minimal signs.
- Respect Wildlife: Always respect wildlife by keeping a safe distance and avoiding any actions that could harm or stress the animals.

# *July 28: Xeriscaping*

## 1. The Sustainability of Xeriscaping

Xeriscaping is a landscaping method that focuses on water conservation by using drought-tolerant plants and efficient irrigation techniques. It's an eco-friendly approach to gardening that reduces water usage and maintenance while creating a beautiful and sustainable outdoor space.

## 2. Tools and Materials

- Drought-Tolerant Plants: Choose plants that are well-suited to dry climates, such as succulents, cacti, and native grasses.
- Mulch: Use mulch to retain moisture in the soil and reduce the need for frequent watering.
- Drip Irrigation: Install a drip irrigation system to deliver water directly to the plant roots, minimizing waste.

## 3. Techniques and Tips

- Soil Preparation: Improve soil drainage and fertility by adding organic matter and ensuring proper aeration.
- Plant Grouping: Group plants with similar water needs together to create zones that can be watered efficiently.
- Minimal Watering: Water your xeriscape garden only when necessary, and consider using rainwater harvesting techniques to further conserve resources.

# *July 29: Yachting*

## 1. The Luxury of Yachting

Yachting is the practice of sailing or cruising on a yacht, often for recreation, leisure, or racing. It's a hobby that combines navigation skills with the enjoyment of the open water. Yachting offers a luxurious and adventurous way to explore coastlines, islands, and distant horizons.

## 2. Tools and Materials

- Yacht: Choose a yacht that suits your needs, whether it's for day sailing, cruising, or racing.
- Navigation Equipment: Use GPS, charts, and a compass for navigation, ensuring you stay on course during your journey.
- Safety Gear: Equip your yacht with life jackets, flares, and other safety gear to ensure a safe voyage.

## 3. Techniques and Tips

- Seamanship: Develop your seamanship skills, including knot tying, sail handling, and docking techniques.
- Weather Awareness: Monitor weather conditions closely to avoid storms and rough seas.
- Maintenance: Regularly maintain your yacht to keep it in top condition, ensuring it's seaworthy for all your adventures.

# *July 30: Zip Lining*

## 1. The Excitement of Zip Lining

Zip lining is an exhilarating outdoor activity that involves gliding down a cable from one platform to another, often high above the ground. It's a thrilling way to experience the landscape from a bird's-eye view, combining speed, height, and adventure. Zip lining is suitable for all ages and is often done in scenic locations, such as forests, mountains, or canyons.

## 2. Tools and Materials

- Harness and Helmet: Wear a secure harness and helmet to ensure safety while zip lining.
- Gloves: Use gloves to protect your hands and help control your speed on the line.
- Comfortable Clothing: Dress in comfortable, weather-appropriate clothing that allows for easy movement.

## 3. Techniques and Tips

- Safety Briefing: Always pay attention to the safety briefing provided by the zip line operators before starting.
- Relax and Enjoy: Relax and enjoy the ride, keeping your body aligned and your movements smooth to maximize the experience.
- Braking: Learn how to use the braking system, whether it's hand-operated or automatic, to control your speed and ensure a safe landing.

# *July 31: Zoo Volunteering*

## 1. The Fulfillment of Zoo Volunteering

Zoo volunteering is a rewarding way to contribute to wildlife conservation and education while gaining hands-on experience with animals. Volunteers at zoos assist with a variety of tasks, from animal care and habitat maintenance to educational programs and guest services. It's a meaningful hobby that allows you to support the mission of zoos and connect with animals and people.

## 2. Tools and Materials

- Volunteer Uniform: Wear the appropriate uniform provided by the zoo, which typically includes a shirt, name badge, and sturdy footwear.
- Animal Care Supplies: Depending on your role, you may need to use feeding tools, cleaning supplies, or enrichment items for the animals.
- Educational Materials: Familiarize yourself with educational materials and zoo maps to assist visitors and answer their questions.

## 3. Techniques and Tips

- Training: Complete any required training sessions to learn about zoo protocols, animal behavior, and safety procedures.
- Communication: Communicate effectively with zoo staff, visitors, and fellow volunteers to ensure a positive experience for everyone.
- Passion for Conservation: Bring your passion for wildlife and conservation to your volunteer work, helping to inspire others to care about the natural world.

## *Conclusion for July*

July has been a month of discovery and connection with the great outdoors. From the precision of archery and the thrill of rock climbing to the serenity of gardening and the adventure of volcano hiking, this chapter has offered a diverse range of activities that celebrate nature and the environment. Whether you've honed your skills in wildlife tracking, explored the cosmos through astronomy, or contributed to conservation efforts, the experiences gained this month will deepen your appreciation for the natural world. As you continue to engage with these outdoor hobbies, remember that nature offers endless opportunities for learning, exploration, and personal growth. Embrace the challenges, respect the environment, and enjoy the beauty that surrounds you.

# August: Personal Development

*August is all about personal development—an opportunity to focus on improving yourself in various aspects of life. This month is designed to help you build better habits, enhance your emotional and mental well-being, and develop skills that will lead to a more fulfilling and balanced life. From affirmations to zen habits, the activities in August will guide you on a journey of self-discovery and growth.*

# *August 1: Affirmations*

## 1. The Power of Affirmations

Affirmations are positive statements that you repeat to yourself to challenge and overcome negative thoughts and self-doubt. They help reprogram your subconscious mind, encouraging a more optimistic and self-assured mindset. The consistent practice of affirmations can lead to significant changes in your thought patterns, enhancing your confidence, motivation, and overall mental well-being. By focusing on positive outcomes and reinforcing your self-worth, affirmations can serve as a powerful tool for personal development. Whether you're aiming to boost your self-esteem, achieve specific goals, or simply cultivate a more positive outlook, affirmations can be tailored to suit your needs.

## 2. Tools and Materials

- Journal: Use a dedicated journal to write down your daily affirmations. This practice not only helps reinforce your intentions but also provides a space for reflection and growth.
- Sticky Notes: Place sticky notes with affirmations in visible areas like your mirror, desk, or refrigerator. These visual reminders can keep you focused on your positive intentions throughout the day.
- Mindfulness App: Consider using a mindfulness app that offers daily affirmations and reminders. These apps can provide structure and consistency, helping you maintain your practice even on busy days.

## 3. Techniques and Tips

- Consistency: Repeat your affirmations daily, ideally in the morning or before bed, to reinforce positive beliefs. Consistency is key to reprogramming your subconscious mind and making lasting changes.
- Personalization: Create affirmations that resonate with you personally and address specific areas of your life you want to improve. The more relevant your affirmations are to your goals and desires, the more powerful they will be.
- Visualization: As you say your affirmations, visualize the positive outcomes you desire. This mental imagery can strengthen the impact of your affirmations and help you stay motivated and focused on your goals.

# *August 2: Anxiety Management*

## 1. The Importance of Managing Anxiety

Anxiety management involves using various techniques and strategies to cope with and reduce anxiety. In a fast-paced world, anxiety is common and can affect your mental health, productivity, and overall quality of life. By learning to manage anxiety effectively, you can regain control over your emotions, reduce stress, and improve your overall well-being. Anxiety management isn't just about reducing symptoms; it's about understanding the underlying causes of your anxiety and addressing them in a healthy, proactive way. This process can involve a combination of mental, physical, and emotional strategies designed to help you navigate life's challenges with greater ease and resilience.

## 2. Tools and Materials

- Breathing Exercises: Use deep breathing exercises to calm your nervous system during anxious moments. Techniques such as the 4-7-8 breathing method or diaphragmatic breathing can be particularly effective.
- Meditation Apps: Download meditation apps that offer guided sessions specifically designed to reduce anxiety. These apps provide structure and support, making it easier to incorporate mindfulness into your daily routine.
- Stress Journal: Keep a stress journal to identify triggers and track your progress in managing anxiety. Documenting your experiences can help you recognize patterns and develop more effective coping strategies.

## 3. Techniques and Tips

- Mindful Breathing: Practice mindful breathing, focusing on each breath to bring yourself back to the present moment. This technique can be particularly helpful during moments of acute anxiety, helping you ground yourself and regain control.
- Progressive Muscle Relaxation: Use progressive muscle relaxation to release tension in your body, one muscle group at a time. This technique can help you become more aware of physical tension associated with anxiety and develop better relaxation skills.
- Seek Support: Don't hesitate to talk to a therapist or join a support group if your anxiety feels overwhelming. Professional guidance can provide you with personalized strategies and the reassurance that you're not alone in your struggles.

# *August 3: Balance*

## 1. The Pursuit of Balance

Achieving balance in life means managing various aspects of your personal, professional, and social life. Balance is about prioritizing your time and energy to ensure no single area dominates, leading to a more harmonious existence. In a world focused on productivity and achievement, finding balance can be challenging but is essential for long-term well-being. True balance involves recognizing your needs in areas like work, relationships, health, and personal growth, and making conscious choices to honor those needs. It's about learning to say no to demands that drain your energy and yes to activities that nourish your soul.

## 2. Tools and Materials

- Planner: Use a planner or calendar to schedule activities and allocate time for all important areas. Visually mapping out commitments helps manage time and avoid overextending yourself.
- Daily Routine Checklist: Create a checklist to maintain balance in your daily routine, including work, leisure, and self-care. This tool serves as a reminder to prioritize your well-being alongside responsibilities.
- Mindfulness Practices: Incorporate mindfulness practices to stay grounded and focused. Mindfulness helps you become aware of how you're spending time and energy, allowing necessary adjustments.

## 3. Techniques and Tips

- Prioritization: Prioritize tasks and activities based on importance and urgency to avoid burnout. Focusing on what truly matters helps you achieve more with less effort and maintain a healthier work-life balance.
- Set Boundaries: Establish clear boundaries between work and personal life to maintain balance and prevent overcommitting. This might involve setting specific work hours, creating a dedicated workspace, or disconnecting from technology after hours.
- Regular Reflection: Reflect regularly on your life's balance, making adjustments as needed to stay aligned with your goals and values. Regular self-assessment helps you stay on track and ensures you're living in a way that supports your overall well-being.

# *August 4: Budgeting*

## 1. The Necessity of Budgeting

Budgeting is the process of creating a plan to manage your finances by tracking income and expenses. It helps you make informed financial decisions, save for the future, and avoid debt. A well-crafted budget empowers you to live within your means and achieve your financial goals. Beyond simply tracking money, budgeting allows you to align your spending with your values, ensuring that your financial habits support the life you want to live. Whether you're saving for a big purchase, paying off debt, or planning for retirement, a budget is an essential tool for financial health.

## 2. Tools and Materials

- Budgeting Apps: Use budgeting apps like Mint or YNAB (You Need A Budget) to track your spending and savings. These apps can automate much of the budgeting process, providing insights and alerts that help you stay on track.
- Spreadsheets: Create or download budgeting spreadsheets to organize your income, expenses, and financial goals. Spreadsheets offer a flexible and customizable way to manage your finances, allowing you to tailor your budget to your specific needs.
- Expense Tracker: Keep an expense tracker to monitor your daily spending habits and adjust your budget accordingly. By regularly reviewing your expenses, you can identify areas where you can cut back and save more effectively.

## 3. Techniques and Tips

- Set Financial Goals: Define short-term and long-term financial goals to guide your budgeting process. Clear goals provide motivation and direction, helping you make financial decisions that support your overall objectives.
- Track Every Expense: Record every expense, no matter how small, to get a clear picture of where your money is going. This level of detail can reveal spending patterns and help you make more informed choices about where to allocate your resources.
- Review and Adjust: Regularly review your budget and adjust it as needed to stay on track with your financial goals. Life circumstances change, and your budget should be flexible enough to adapt to new priorities or unexpected expenses.

# *August 5: Conflict Resolution*

## 1. The Art of Conflict Resolution

Conflict resolution involves addressing disagreements in a constructive way that leads to a positive outcome for all parties. It's a crucial skill in both personal and professional settings, helping to maintain healthy relationships and prevent misunderstandings from escalating. Effective conflict resolution requires empathy, communication skills, and a willingness to find common ground. By approaching conflicts with an open mind and focusing on solutions, you can transform potentially negative situations into opportunities for growth and understanding.

## 2. Tools and Materials

- Communication Tools: Use active listening, empathy, and assertiveness to facilitate open and honest communication. These skills are essential for understanding others' perspectives and expressing your own needs clearly and respectfully.
- Conflict Resolution Models: Familiarize yourself with models like the Thomas-Kilmann model to understand different approaches. These frameworks help analyze conflicts and choose the best strategy for resolution.
- Mediation Resources: Consider using mediation resources if conflicts are particularly complex. A neutral third party can help facilitate discussions and guide the parties toward a mutually acceptable solution.

## 3. Techniques and Tips

- Stay Calm: Approach conflicts with a calm and open mind, focusing on the issue rather than personal attacks. Maintaining composure allows you to think clearly and respond thoughtfully.
- Seek Understanding: Make an effort to understand the other person's perspective and find common ground. Showing empathy and validating their feelings creates a more collaborative atmosphere.
- Collaborative Solutions: Work together to find a solution that satisfies both parties, promoting cooperation and mutual respect. A win-win outcome strengthens relationships and fosters positive future interactions.

# *August 6: Creativity Exercises*

## 1. The Power of Creativity Exercises

Creativity exercises are activities designed to stimulate your imagination, encourage innovative thinking, and break free from routine patterns of thought. These exercises can help you generate new ideas, solve problems creatively, and enhance your overall creativity in various aspects of life. Whether you're an artist, a writer, or simply looking to infuse more creativity into your daily life, these exercises can help you tap into your creative potential. By regularly engaging in creativity exercises, you can develop a more flexible and open-minded approach to challenges, allowing you to see possibilities where others might see obstacles.

## 2. Tools and Materials

- Sketchbook: Use a sketchbook to doodle, draw, or brainstorm ideas without constraints. A sketchbook offers a judgment-free space to explore your thoughts visually and experiment with new concepts.
- Creative Prompts: Find or create prompts that challenge you to think creatively, such as "What if?" scenarios or unusual combinations. Prompts can serve as a starting point for creative exploration, pushing you to think outside the box.
- Mind Mapping Tools: Use mind mapping tools to visually organize your thoughts and explore connections between ideas. Mind maps are a powerful way to brainstorm and see the relationships between different concepts, helping you generate new ideas more easily.

## 3. Techniques and Tips

- Free Writing: Set a timer for 10 minutes and write continuously without stopping or editing, allowing your thoughts to flow freely. Free writing can help you bypass your inner critic and access deeper layers of creativity.
- Break Routine: Change your environment or routine to spark new ideas and perspectives. Sometimes, simply stepping away from your usual surroundings can inspire fresh insights and creative solutions.
- Collaborate: Work with others to share ideas and inspire creativity through collaboration. Collaborative projects can introduce you to new ways of thinking and expand your creative horizons, as you learn from the perspectives and experiences of others.

# *August 7: Decision Making*

## 1. The Importance of Effective Decision Making

Decision making is the process of choosing between different options to achieve a desired outcome. Good decision-making skills are essential in both personal and professional life, helping you navigate challenges, seize opportunities, and move forward with confidence. Effective decision making involves analyzing available options, considering potential consequences, and aligning your choices with your values and long-term goals. By honing your decision-making skills, you can become more proactive in shaping your future and more resilient in the face of uncertainty.

## 2. Tools and Materials

- Decision-Making Models: Familiarize yourself with models like pros and cons lists, SWOT analysis, or decision trees. These provide structured approaches to evaluating options and making informed choices.
- Journaling: Use journaling to reflect on past decisions, what you've learned, and how to improve your decision-making process. Reviewing past choices helps identify patterns and develop better strategies for future decisions.
- Mindfulness Practices: Incorporate mindfulness to stay present and focused when making decisions. Mindfulness helps you avoid impulsive choices driven by stress, allowing for more thoughtful and deliberate decisions.

## 3. Techniques and Tips

- Gather Information: Make informed decisions by gathering all relevant information before choosing a course of action. The more you know about your options, the better equipped you'll be to make a decision that aligns with your goals.
- Weigh Options: Consider the potential outcomes of each option, including risks, benefits, and long-term effects. Weighing your options carefully allows you to choose the path that offers the greatest potential for positive impact.
- Trust Your Intuition: Balance logical analysis with intuition, listening to your inner voice when making decisions. While it's important to be rational, your intuition can provide valuable insights that complement your logical thinking.

# *August 8: Decluttering*

## 1. The Benefits of Decluttering

Decluttering involves organizing and simplifying your living or working space by removing unnecessary items. It's about creating a clean, functional environment that reduces stress, increases productivity, and enhances your overall well-being. Decluttering can also lead to mental clarity, as a tidy space often reflects a more focused and peaceful mind. By letting go of excess possessions and organizing your surroundings, you can create a space that supports your lifestyle and allows you to focus on what truly matters. Whether you're tackling a cluttered closet, a messy desk, or an entire home, decluttering can be a transformative process that brings a sense of order and calm to your life.

## 2. Tools and Materials

- Storage Bins: Use storage bins or baskets to categorize and organize items. These containers can help you keep similar items together, making it easier to find what you need and maintain an organized space.
- Donation Boxes: Set up donation boxes for items you no longer need or use. Donating unwanted items not only helps you declutter but also supports those in need, adding a sense of purpose to the process.
- Labeling Tools: Label storage containers to keep everything organized and easy to find. Clear labels can save you time and frustration by ensuring that you always know where your belongings are stored.

## 3. Techniques and Tips

- Start Small: Begin with a small area, like a drawer or closet, to avoid feeling overwhelmed. Tackling one small project at a time can build momentum and give you a sense of accomplishment as you make progress.
- One-In, One-Out Rule: For every new item you bring into your space, remove an old one to maintain balance. This rule helps prevent clutter from accumulating and encourages you to be more mindful about your purchases.
- Regular Maintenance: Schedule regular decluttering sessions to keep your space tidy and prevent clutter from accumulating. By making decluttering a regular habit, you can maintain an organized environment without the need for major cleanouts.

## *August 9: Emotional Healing*

### 1. The Process of Emotional Healing

Emotional healing involves acknowledging, understanding, and releasing past hurts or traumas to move forward with peace and well-being. It can include therapy, self-reflection, and self-compassion. By healing emotionally, you free yourself from the weight of the past and open yourself to a more fulfilling future. Emotional healing isn't linear; it involves revisiting old wounds, confronting difficult emotions, and gradually building resilience. Though challenging, this journey can lead to profound personal growth and deeper self-awareness.

### 2. Tools and Materials

- Therapy or Counseling: Seek support from a therapist or counselor to guide you through the healing process. Professional guidance provides tools and insights to navigate complex emotions and unresolved issues.
- Journaling: Use journaling to explore and process your emotions in a safe, private space. Writing about your experiences can help you gain clarity, express your feelings, and track progress over time.
- Meditation Practices: Incorporate meditation and mindfulness to calm your mind and connect with your emotions. These practices help you become more present and observe your emotions without judgment.

### 3. Techniques and Tips

- Acknowledge Your Emotions: Allow yourself to feel and acknowledge your emotions without judgment. Recognizing and accepting your feelings is the first step toward healing, enabling you to confront and process them in a healthy way.
- Seek Support: Surround yourself with supportive people who offer understanding and encouragement. Whether through friends, family, or a support group, a strong network provides comfort and perspective during the healing process.
- Practice Forgiveness: Work on forgiving yourself and others, releasing lingering resentment or guilt. Forgiveness is a powerful tool for emotional healing, allowing you to let go of the past and move forward with peace and closure.

# *August 10: Emotional Intelligence*

## 1. The Value of Emotional Intelligence

Emotional intelligence (EQ) is the ability to recognize, understand, and manage your own emotions and those of others. It's essential for building strong relationships, navigating social situations, and achieving success. High EQ enhances communication, empathy, and decision-making, making you more effective in interactions. Developing your emotional intelligence can improve relationships, manage stress, and create a more positive environment.

## 2. Tools and Materials

- Emotional Intelligence Assessments: Take assessments to gauge your EQ and identify areas for improvement. These tools offer insights into your emotional strengths and weaknesses, helping you focus on areas that need development.
- Books on EQ: Read books or articles on emotional intelligence to deepen your understanding. Learning from others' experiences provides valuable strategies for enhancing your EQ.
- Mindfulness Practices: Use mindfulness practices to enhance emotional awareness and regulation, helping you respond thoughtfully to emotions rather than reacting impulsively.

## 3. Techniques and Tips

- Self-Awareness: Practice self-awareness by regularly reflecting on your emotions, triggers, and reactions. Understanding your emotional patterns helps you identify areas for growth and develop better emotional management strategies.
- Empathy: Cultivate empathy by actively listening and considering others' perspectives. Empathy is key to connecting with others and responding with compassion.
- Emotional Regulation: Develop strategies for managing difficult emotions, such as deep breathing, taking a break, or reframing thoughts. Effective emotional regulation helps you stay calm in challenging situations.

# *August 11: Fitness Planning*

## 1. The Importance of Fitness Planning

Fitness planning involves creating a structured exercise routine that aligns with your health goals, fitness level, and lifestyle. It's about setting achievable targets and staying motivated to improve your physical well-being. A well-designed fitness plan helps you build strength, increase endurance, and enhance overall health. Fitness planning isn't just about exercise; it's also about creating a balanced approach that includes proper nutrition, rest, and recovery. By planning your routine thoughtfully, you can maximize the benefits of your workouts and make steady progress toward your goals.

## 2. Tools and Materials

- Fitness Tracker: Use a fitness tracker or app to monitor your workouts, steps, and progress. These tools provide valuable data and insights, helping you stay motivated and on track.
- Workout Planner: Create a workout planner that includes your exercise schedule, goals, and progress notes. A detailed plan helps you stay organized and focused, ensuring you make the most of your workouts.
- Exercise Equipment: Gather necessary equipment, such as weights, resistance bands, or yoga mats, to support your routine. Having the right tools can make your workouts more effective and enjoyable.

## 3. Techniques and Tips

- Set Realistic Goals: Set specific, measurable, and achievable fitness goals to keep yourself motivated and on track. Clear goals provide direction and purpose, whether you're aiming to lose weight, build muscle, or improve cardiovascular health.
- Mix It Up: Incorporate a variety of exercises, including strength training, cardio, and flexibility, to prevent boredom and improve overall fitness. Variety ensures you're working all areas of your body and keeps workouts interesting.
- Rest and Recovery: Schedule rest days to allow your body to recover and prevent burnout or injury. Rest is crucial, giving your muscles time to repair and grow stronger, leading to better performance and results.

# *August 12: Focus Techniques*

## 1. The Power of Focus Techniques

Focus techniques are strategies designed to improve your concentration and minimize distractions. Enhancing your focus can lead to greater productivity, better decision-making, and a stronger sense of accomplishment. In a world full of distractions, developing the ability to focus is more important than ever. Whether you're working on a complex project or staying on top of daily tasks, effective focus techniques help you stay on track and achieve your goals more efficiently. By managing your attention and directing it where it's needed most, you can make the most of your time and energy.

## 2. Tools and Materials

- Pomodoro Timer: Use a Pomodoro timer to work in focused intervals with short breaks in between. This technique, which involves working for 25 minutes followed by a 5-minute break, helps maintain focus and prevent burnout.
- Noise-Canceling Headphones: Invest in noise-canceling headphones to block out distractions and create a quiet workspace. A peaceful environment makes it easier to concentrate and stay in the zone, especially in noisy or busy settings.
- Task Manager: Use a task manager or to-do list app to prioritize and organize tasks. By breaking down your work into manageable steps, you can stay focused on one task at a time, reducing the temptation to multitask.

## 3. Techniques and Tips

- Single-Tasking: Focus on one task at a time, avoiding multitasking, which can reduce overall productivity and concentration. By dedicating your full attention to one task, you can complete it more efficiently and to a higher standard.
- Set Clear Goals: Define clear, specific goals for each work session to stay focused and motivated. Knowing exactly what you want to achieve helps you stay on track and avoid distractions.
- Mindfulness Practice: Incorporate mindfulness practices to train your mind to stay present and attentive during tasks. Mindfulness can help you develop greater awareness of your thoughts and distractions, allowing you to refocus more quickly when your mind starts to wander.

# *August 13: Goal Setting*

## 1. The Strategy of Goal Setting

Goal setting involves defining clear, specific objectives to achieve. It's a powerful tool for personal and professional growth, helping you stay focused, motivated, and aligned with your values. Effective goal setting includes breaking down larger goals into manageable steps and creating a plan to achieve them. By setting goals, you create a roadmap that guides your actions and decisions. It's not just about achieving outcomes; it's also about developing the habits and mindset needed to pursue goals with persistence and resilience. Whether advancing in your career, improving health, or developing a new skill, clear goals provide the direction and motivation needed.

## 2. Tools and Materials

- Goal Planner: Use a planner or journal to outline goals, track progress, and reflect on achievements. A dedicated space for goal setting helps you stay organized and focused, making it easier to see your progress and what steps remain.
- Vision Board: Create a vision board that visually represents your goals and serves as a daily reminder of what you're working towards. Surrounding yourself with inspiring images and words keeps your goals top of mind and motivates you.
- SMART Goals Framework: Use the SMART goals framework (Specific, Measurable, Achievable, Relevant, Time-bound) to structure your goals. This framework helps you set clear, actionable goals aligned with your long-term vision and values.

## 3. Techniques and Tips

- Break It Down: Break down large goals into smaller, manageable tasks to make progress feel more achievable. Focusing on one step at a time prevents overwhelm and maintains momentum as you work toward your goals.
- Regular Review: Regularly review your goals and adjust them as needed to stay on track and adapt to changes. Life is dynamic, and your goals may need to evolve as circumstances change or as you gain new insights.
- Celebrate Success: Celebrate successes along the way, no matter how small, to maintain motivation and momentum. Recognizing and rewarding your progress builds confidence in your ability to achieve your goals.

## *August 14: Gratitude Practice*

### 1. The Joy of Gratitude Practice

Gratitude practice involves reflecting on and appreciating the positive aspects of your life. It's a powerful way to enhance well-being, shift focus from negativity, and foster a positive mindset. Practicing gratitude can improve mental health, relationships, and overall happiness. By making it a daily habit, you can cultivate a more joyful life. Gratitude is not just about acknowledging the good; it's also about developing a mindset that seeks and appreciates the positive, even in challenges. This shift in perspective leads to greater resilience, optimism, and deeper contentment.

### 2. Tools and Materials

- Gratitude Journal: Use a journal to write down things you're grateful for each day. Regular journaling helps focus on life's positives, even on difficult days, reinforcing a habit of gratitude.
- Thank You Notes: Write thank you notes to express gratitude to those who've positively impacted your life. Expressing appreciation strengthens relationships and spreads positivity, creating a ripple effect.
- Mindfulness Practice: Incorporate mindfulness practices that focus on appreciating the present moment. Mindfulness helps you notice small blessings, leading to greater daily joy and satisfaction.

### 3. Techniques and Tips

- Daily Reflection: Take a few minutes daily to reflect on what you're grateful for, no matter how big or small. Regular reflection helps develop a positive outlook and increases your overall well-being.
- Express Gratitude: Share your gratitude with others through words or actions. Whether a thank you, note, or gesture, expressing gratitude strengthens relationships and spreads positivity.
- Focus on Positives: Shift your focus from what's lacking to what's abundant, reinforcing a positive mindset. Focusing on the good trains your mind to see opportunities and blessings over obstacles.

# *August 15: Habit Building*

## 1. The Science of Habit Building

Habit building is the process of developing new behaviors that become automatic over time. Good habits can lead to positive changes in your health, productivity, and overall quality of life. Building habits requires consistency, patience, and clear goals. By creating habits that align with your values, you can make lasting changes that enhance your daily life. Habit building is not just about willpower; it's also about crafting an environment and routine that support your desired behaviors. Whether you're aiming to exercise more, eat healthier, or improve time management, the right habits can help you achieve your goals more easily and sustainably.

## 2. Tools and Materials

- Habit Tracker: Use a habit tracker to monitor progress and stay motivated. A visual representation of your progress can provide a sense of accomplishment and encourage you to maintain your new behaviors.
- Cue-Action-Reward Framework: Apply this framework to understand the triggers, behaviors, and rewards of your habits. By identifying and modifying these elements, you can create more effective and sustainable habits.
- Reminders: Set up reminders to prompt you to perform your new habit at the same time each day. Consistent reminders help build a routine and ensure that your habits become a natural part of your daily life.

## 3. Techniques and Tips

- Start Small: Begin with small, manageable habits that are easy to incorporate into your routine. Starting with achievable goals helps build momentum toward more challenging behaviors.
- Consistency: Perform your new habit consistently, ideally at the same time and place each day, to reinforce the behavior. Consistency is key to making habits stick, as it helps your brain automate the behavior more quickly.
- Reward Yourself: Reward yourself after completing your habit to reinforce the positive behavior and maintain motivation. Whether it's a treat, relaxation, or acknowledging your progress, rewards help you stay committed to your new habits.

# *August 16: Journaling*

## 1. The Reflective Practice of Journaling

Journaling involves writing down your thoughts, experiences, and reflections. It's a powerful tool for self-expression, emotional processing, and personal growth. Whether you journal daily or as needed, this practice helps clarify thoughts, reduce stress, and deepen self-understanding. Journaling offers a safe space to explore your innermost thoughts and document your life journey. It also serves as a creative outlet, allowing free expression without judgment. Over time, journaling becomes a valuable resource for tracking growth, identifying patterns, and setting future goals.

## 2. Tools and Materials

- Journal: Choose a journal you enjoy writing in, whether it's a simple notebook or one with guided prompts. The right journal can inspire regular writing and enhance the experience.
- Pens and Markers: Use pens or markers that inspire you, and consider adding color or illustrations to your entries. Creative tools can make journaling feel more like an artistic endeavor, encouraging deeper exploration of your thoughts.
- Prompts: Journaling prompts can inspire your writing, especially when unsure what to write about. Prompts help explore different life aspects and provide structure for reflections.

## 3. Techniques and Tips

- Daily Practice: Make journaling a daily practice, even if just for a few minutes, to build consistency. Regular journaling fosters deeper self-understanding and supports personal growth.
- Free Writing: Write freely without concern for grammar, spelling, or structure—just let your thoughts flow. Free writing helps bypass your inner critic and access your subconscious mind, leading to more authentic reflections.
- Reflective Questions: Ask yourself reflective questions like "What did I learn today?" or "How did I feel about this experience?" to deepen your journaling practice. Reflective questions guide your writing and help you explore thoughts and emotions in greater depth.

# *August 17: Kindness*

## 1. The Impact of Kindness

Kindness is the practice of showing compassion, generosity, and consideration toward others. It's a simple yet powerful way to make a positive impact on the world. Acts of kindness benefit others and enhance your well-being, creating a ripple effect of positivity. Kindness can take many forms, from small gestures to larger acts of generosity. Whether helping a friend, offering a kind word to a stranger, or being patient and understanding, kindness can transform your life and those around you. By cultivating kindness, you contribute to a more compassionate world where everyone feels valued and respected.

## 2. Tools and Materials

- Kindness Journal: Keep a journal to record acts of kindness you've performed or received, and reflect on their impact. Writing about your experiences with kindness can deepen your understanding of its significance and inspire continued positivity.
- Random Acts of Kindness Ideas: Create a list of ideas for random acts of kindness you can perform daily. Having ideas ready makes it easier to incorporate kindness into your routine and encourages seeking opportunities to help others.
- Gratitude Cards: Use gratitude cards or notes to express appreciation and kindness. A handwritten note or card can brighten someone's day and serve as a lasting reminder of your kindness.

## 3. Techniques and Tips

- Small Gestures: Remember that small gestures, like a smile or kind word, can make a big difference in someone's day. Even the simplest acts of kindness can profoundly impact, lifting spirits and creating connection.
- Pay It Forward: Practice paying it forward by doing something kind for someone else, especially if someone has shown you kindness. The pay-it-forward concept encourages a chain reaction of kindness, where each person who benefits from kindness passes it on to another.
- Be Mindful: Be mindful of opportunities to show kindness to a stranger, a friend, or yourself. By staying attuned to the needs of others, you can make kindness a natural and spontaneous part of your daily life, spreading positivity wherever you go.

# *August 18: Leadership Skills*

## 1. The Development of Leadership Skills

Leadership skills involve inspiring, motivating, and guiding others toward a common goal. Whether in a professional setting or personal life, strong leadership skills help navigate challenges, build effective teams, and make a positive impact. Leadership is not just about authority—it's about influence, empathy, and vision. Great leaders see the bigger picture, communicate their vision clearly, and inspire others to work together toward a shared goal. By developing your leadership skills, you can become more confident, effective, and respected in any role, whether leading a project, organizing a community event, or guiding your family through tough times.

## 2. Tools and Materials

- Leadership Books: Read books or articles on leadership to learn from successful leaders' experiences. Studying the strategies and philosophies of others can provide valuable lessons and inspire your leadership style.
- Mentorship: Seek out a mentor who can offer guidance and support as you develop your leadership skills. A mentor provides personalized advice, shares experiences, and helps you navigate leadership challenges with confidence.
- Leadership Assessments: Take leadership assessments to understand your strengths and areas for improvement. These tools provide a baseline for development and help you focus on the skills that will have the greatest impact on your effectiveness.

## 3. Techniques and Tips

- Lead by Example: Set a positive example through your actions, demonstrating the values and behaviors you want to inspire in others. Leading by example shows you hold yourself to the same standards you expect from others.
- Effective Communication: Practice clear, concise, and empathetic communication to build trust and foster collaboration. Great leaders are also great communicators, able to convey ideas clearly and listen to others' needs and concerns.
- Continuous Learning: Commit to continuous learning and self-improvement, staying open to feedback and new ideas. The best leaders are always growing, learning from experiences, and adapting to new challenges and opportunities.

# *August 19: Meditation*

## 1. The Practice of Meditation

Meditation is a mindfulness practice that involves focusing your attention and quieting the stream of thoughts that may crowd your mind. It's a powerful tool for reducing stress, enhancing concentration, and fostering inner peace. Meditation can take various forms, from sitting quietly to guided visualizations. Incorporating meditation into your daily routine can develop greater self-awareness, improve mental clarity, and cultivate a sense of calm and balance in all aspects of your life. Meditation is not just about relaxation; it's also about training your mind to stay present, observe thoughts without judgment, and respond to life's challenges with greater equanimity.

## 2. Tools and Materials

- Meditation Cushion: Use a cushion or chair to sit comfortably during your practice. A supportive cushion helps maintain a stable and relaxed posture, allowing you to focus on your meditation without discomfort.
- Guided Meditation Apps: Download apps offering guided sessions to make it easier to start and maintain a practice. Guided meditations provide structure and support, especially for beginners, helping you stay focused and engaged.
- Relaxing Music: Consider using relaxing music or nature sounds to enhance your meditation experience. Background sounds can create a calming atmosphere, making it easier to let go of distractions and settle into a meditative state.

## 3. Techniques and Tips

- Start Small: Begin with just a few minutes of meditation each day, gradually increasing the duration as you become more comfortable. Starting small builds the habit gradually, making it more sustainable over time.
- Focus on Breath: Use your breath as an anchor, bringing your attention back to it whenever your mind starts to wander. Focusing on your breath helps you stay present and grounded, even when distractions arise.
- Consistency: Practice meditation consistently, ideally at the same time each day, to build a routine and deepen your practice. Consistency is key to reaping meditation's full benefits, helping you develop greater mindfulness and self-awareness over time.

# *August 20: Nutrition*

## 1. The Importance of Nutrition

Nutrition is the cornerstone of good health, influencing your energy, mood, and overall well-being. Understanding nutrition basics and making informed dietary choices can help you maintain a healthy weight, prevent chronic diseases, and improve your quality of life. Nutrition isn't just about eating the right foods; it's about understanding how nutrients affect your body, balancing meals, and making choices that support long-term health. By taking a mindful approach to nutrition, you can create a diet that fuels your body, supports your goals, and enhances your well-being. Whether you're looking to boost energy, manage weight, or eat more healthily, understanding nutrition empowers you to make better choices and achieve your health goals.

## 2. Tools and Materials

- Meal Planner: Use a meal planner to organize meals and ensure a balanced diet. Planning in advance helps you make healthier choices, avoid last-minute takeout, and save time and money.
- Nutrition Apps: Download apps that track your food intake and provide nutritional information to help you make healthier choices. These tools monitor nutrient intake, set dietary goals, and keep you accountable.
- Cookbooks: Invest in cookbooks focused on healthy eating, offering nutritious and delicious recipes. Having a variety of healthy recipes on hand makes it easier to stick to your goals and enjoy cooking.

## 3. Techniques and Tips

- Balanced Diet: Focus on a balanced diet with fruits, vegetables, whole grains, lean proteins, and healthy fats. A balanced diet provides the nutrients your body needs to function optimally, supporting energy, immunity, and overall health.
- Portion Control: Practice portion control to avoid overeating and maintain a healthy weight. Understanding portion sizes and listening to your body's hunger cues help you eat the right amount without feeling deprived.
- Hydration: Stay hydrated by drinking plenty of water, essential for overall health. Proper hydration supports metabolism, aids digestion, and keeps your skin, joints, and organs functioning well.

# *August 21: Organization*

## 1. The Efficiency of Organization

Organization involves creating systems that help you manage time, tasks, and your environment more effectively. Being organized reduces stress, increases productivity, and gives you more control. Whether it's your home, workspace, or schedule, good organization skills lead to a more efficient and enjoyable life. Organization isn't just about tidiness; it's about creating spaces and systems that support your goals and simplify daily responsibilities. By being proactive, you can reduce clutter, streamline processes, and create a peaceful, productive environment. Whether organizing your physical space, digital files, or time, effective organization helps you stay focused, reduce stress, and achieve more with less effort.

## 2. Tools and Materials

- Organizers and Bins: Use organizers, bins, and trays to keep items sorted and accessible. Designated spaces reduce clutter and make it easier to find what you need.
- Calendars and Planners: Maintain a calendar or planner to track appointments, deadlines, and important events. A well-organized schedule helps you stay on top of commitments, avoid stress, and make time for what matters most.
- Labeling Tools: Label your storage containers, shelves, and files to easily find what you need. Clear labels save time and frustration, ensuring everything has a place and is easily found.

## 3. Techniques and Tips

- Declutter Regularly: Regularly declutter your space to keep it organized and prevent unnecessary items from accumulating. Making decluttering a habit helps maintain an organized environment and avoids stress from clutter.
- Create a System: Develop systems for managing different areas of your life, like work, home, and personal projects. Effective systems streamline processes, reduce decision fatigue, and keep you organized and focused on your goals.
- Stay Consistent: Consistently apply your organizational methods to maintain order and avoid falling back into disorganization. Consistency is key to keeping space, schedules, and tasks under control, allowing you to maintain order and efficiency in daily life.

# *August 22: Public Speaking*

## 1. The Skill of Public Speaking

Public speaking is the act of delivering a speech or presentation to an audience. It's a valuable skill that can enhance your career, boost confidence, and improve communication. Whether speaking to a small group or a large audience, mastering public speaking requires preparation, practice, and a clear message. Public speaking isn't just about speaking clearly and confidently; it's also about connecting with your audience, conveying your message effectively, and handling challenges during your presentation. Developing public speaking skills makes you a more persuasive and influential communicator, capable of inspiring, educating, and motivating others.

## 2. Tools and Materials

- Speech Outline: Use an outline to organize thoughts and structure your speech or presentation. A clear outline helps you stay on track, ensuring you cover key points and maintain a logical flow.
- Presentation Tools: Utilize slides, props, or visual aids to enhance your presentation and engage your audience. Visual aids help clarify points, make your presentation memorable, and keep your audience's attention.
- Recording Device: Record practice sessions to analyze your performance and identify areas for improvement. Reviewing recordings refines delivery, body language, and awareness of nervous habits or filler words.

## 3. Techniques and Tips

- Practice: Practice your speech multiple times to become familiar with the content and improve your delivery. The more you practice, the more confident you'll feel during your presentation, allowing you to focus on connecting with your audience rather than worrying about what to say next.
- Body Language: Pay attention to body language, using gestures, eye contact, and posture to convey confidence and engage your audience. Positive body language helps establish a connection with your audience, making you appear more credible and approachable.
- Handle Nerves: Manage nerves by taking deep breaths, visualizing success, and focusing on your message rather than the audience's reaction. Nervousness is natural, but with the right techniques, you can channel that energy into a powerful presentation.

# *August 23: Quitting Bad Habits*

## 1. The Challenge of Quitting Bad Habits

Quitting bad habits involves breaking free from behaviors that negatively impact your health, well-being, or productivity. It's a challenging process requiring self-discipline, determination, and an understanding of your triggers. By quitting bad habits, you create space for positive behaviors that contribute to growth. Bad habits are often deeply ingrained, serving as coping mechanisms, which makes them hard to break. However, with the right strategies and support, you can overcome bad habits and replace them with healthier behaviors. Whether you're quitting smoking, reducing screen time, or curbing unhealthy eating, breaking a bad habit can significantly improve your quality of life.

## 2. Tools and Materials

- Habit Tracker: Use a habit tracker to monitor your progress in quitting bad habits and adopting positive ones. A visual representation of your progress can motivate you and help you stay accountable to your goals.
- Support System: Build a support system of friends, family, or a therapist to encourage and hold you accountable. Having others aware of your goals can make quitting a bad habit more manageable and less isolating.
- Replacement Strategies: Develop strategies to replace bad habits with healthier alternatives like exercise or meditation. Finding a positive activity to replace a bad habit can help you manage cravings, reduce stress, and transition to a healthier lifestyle.

## 3. Techniques and Tips

- Identify Triggers: Identify the triggers that lead to your bad habit and develop strategies to avoid or cope with them. Understanding what prompts your habit can help you avoid those situations or find healthier ways to manage them.
- Take It One Day at a Time: Focus on quitting your habit one day at a time, celebrating small victories. Breaking a bad habit is a marathon, not a sprint, and taking it step by step helps you stay focused and motivated.
- Stay Positive: Stay positive and patient with yourself, recognizing that setbacks are natural and not a reason to give up. Quitting a bad habit is challenging, but with persistence and self-compassion, you can overcome obstacles and achieve lasting change.

# *August 24: Resilience Building*

## 1. The Strength of Resilience Building

Resilience is the ability to bounce back from adversity, challenges, and setbacks. Building resilience involves developing mental toughness, emotional stability, and a positive outlook. Resilience helps you navigate difficult times with grace and emerge stronger, more adaptable, and confident. It's not about avoiding difficulties but facing them head-on and thriving in adversity. By cultivating resilience, you can better cope with stress, recover from setbacks, and maintain a positive attitude even in tough times. Resilience is a skill developed through intentional practice and commitment to personal growth.

## 2. Tools and Materials

- Resilience Training Programs: Participate in training programs or workshops that teach coping strategies and mental toughness. These programs provide tools and techniques for building resilience and developing an adaptable mindset.
- Support Network: Cultivate a strong support network of friends, family, or mentors who offer encouragement and guidance during tough times. A supportive community provides comfort, perspective, and practical advice, making it easier to stay resilient.
- Journaling: Use journaling to reflect on challenges, process emotions, and track your growth in resilience. Writing about your experiences helps you gain clarity, express feelings, and see your progress toward greater resilience.

## 3. Techniques and Tips

- Positive Thinking: Practice positive thinking by reframing negative situations and focusing on solutions rather than problems. A positive mindset helps you see challenges as opportunities for growth rather than obstacles.
- Stress Management: Develop stress management techniques, such as meditation, exercise, or creative outlets, to maintain emotional balance. Effective stress management is key to resilience, helping you stay calm, focused, and capable of handling life's challenges.
- Learn from Challenges: View challenges as opportunities for growth, learning valuable lessons from each experience. Embracing challenges as learning experiences builds resilience, making you more adaptable and resourceful in adversity.

# *August 25: Self-Care*

## 1. The Necessity of Self-Care

Self-care is the practice of nurturing your physical, emotional, and mental well-being. It's about recognizing your needs and making them a priority, ensuring you're equipped to handle life's demands. Self-care can take many forms, from relaxation and leisure activities to healthy lifestyle choices. By making self-care a regular part of your routine, you can reduce stress, prevent burnout, and improve your overall quality of life. Self-care is not a luxury; it's necessary for maintaining your health, happiness, and ability to care for others. Whether you're taking a long bath, going for a walk, or simply taking a few moments to breathe, self-care is essential for living a balanced and fulfilling life.

## 2. Tools and Materials

- Self-Care Planner: Use a planner to schedule and track your self-care activities. A planner helps make self-care a priority and ensures you're regularly taking time for yourself, even amid a busy schedule.
- Relaxation Tools: Invest in tools like aromatherapy diffusers, bath salts, or massage rollers to create a calming environment. The right tools make it easier to relax and unwind, turning self-care into a rejuvenating experience.
- Mindfulness Practices: Incorporate mindfulness practices, such as meditation or yoga, into your self-care routine. Mindfulness helps you stay present, reduce stress, and connect more deeply with yourself, enhancing your self-care.

## 3. Techniques and Tips

- Listen to Your Body: Pay attention to your body's signals and take action when you need rest, nourishment, or relaxation. By listening to its cues, you ensure you're taking care of yourself in the best way possible.
- Set Boundaries: Set boundaries to protect your time and energy, ensuring space for self-care. Whether it's saying no to extra commitments, turning off your phone, or creating a dedicated space for relaxation, boundaries are essential for your well-being.
- Make It a Habit: Make self-care a regular habit, integrating it into your daily routine rather than treating it as an occasional indulgence. Consistent self-care helps prevent burnout, maintain your health, and enjoy a greater sense of balance and fulfillment.

# *August 26: Time Management*

## 1. The Efficiency of Time Management

Time management is the process of planning and controlling how you spend your time to achieve goals more effectively. It's about maximizing productivity, reducing stress, and finding balance in your life. Good time management allows you to accomplish more in less time, freeing up space for what matters most. Effective time management isn't just about working faster; it's about working smarter, prioritizing tasks, and making the most of your time. Whether managing a busy schedule, balancing responsibilities, or making time for hobbies, good time management skills help you stay organized, focused, and in control of your day.

## 2. Tools and Materials

- Time Management Apps: Use apps like Todoist or Trello to organize tasks, set priorities, and track deadlines. These tools help you stay on top of tasks, avoid procrastination, and ensure progress toward your goals each day.
- Daily Planner: Maintain a daily planner to schedule activities, appointments, and goals. A well-organized planner helps you visualize your day, stay focused on priorities, and avoid overcommitting your time.
- Pomodoro Timer: Use a Pomodoro timer to work in focused intervals with regular breaks, improving concentration and efficiency. The Pomodoro technique, involving 25 minutes of work followed by a 5-minute break, helps you stay productive without burning out.

## 3. Techniques and Tips

- Prioritize Tasks: Prioritize tasks based on importance and urgency, focusing on high-impact activities first. By tackling important tasks early, you can make significant progress, reduce stress, and increase your sense of accomplishment.
- Break Down Projects: Break larger projects into smaller, manageable tasks to make progress feel achievable. By focusing on one step at a time, you can avoid feeling overwhelmed and stay motivated to complete even the most challenging projects.
- Avoid Procrastination: Tackle tasks promptly to avoid the stress of last-minute work. Procrastination leads to unnecessary stress and lower-quality work; developing the habit of taking action right away reduces anxiety and improves productivity.

# *August 27: Understanding Body Language*

## 1. The Insight of Understanding Body Language

Understanding body language means interpreting non-verbal cues like facial expressions, gestures, and posture to gain insight into emotions, intentions, and communication styles. It's a valuable skill for personal and professional interactions, helping build rapport, read situations accurately, and enhance communication. Body language often conveys more than words. Attuning to it helps you connect better with others, navigate social situations, and detect underlying emotions. Whether in a meeting, gathering, or conversation, understanding body language improves communication and strengthens relationships.

## 2. Tools and Materials

- Body Language Books: Read books to deepen your understanding of non-verbal communication. These resources provide insights into subtle cues people use to convey thoughts and feelings, making you more perceptive in interactions.
- Observation Practice: Observe people in various settings to sharpen your ability to read body language. Paying attention to how people move, gesture, and express themselves builds a more intuitive understanding of non-verbal cues and improves social awareness.
- Feedback Tools: Seek feedback on your body language and work on areas where you may send unintended signals. Awareness ensures your body language aligns with your words and enhances your message.

## 3. Techniques and Tips

- Observe Consistency: Look for consistency between verbal and non-verbal cues to accurately interpret a person's true feelings. When words and body language sync, they're likely honest; inconsistencies may indicate discomfort, dishonesty, or hidden emotions.
- Focus on the Eyes: Pay attention to eye contact, as it reveals confidence, interest, or discomfort. Eyes are often called the "windows to the soul," and observing eye movements provides insights into feelings and intentions.
- Mirror Body Language: Subtly mirroring another person's body language helps build rapport and create a connection. Mirroring their posture, gestures, and expressions makes them feel more comfortable and understood.

# *August 28: Visualization*

## 1. The Power of Visualization

Visualization is a mental technique that involves creating a vivid image or scenario in your mind to achieve a specific goal. It's a powerful tool for motivation, confidence-building, and manifesting desires. Visualization can be applied in various areas, from personal development to professional success. By visualizing your goals, you create a mental blueprint that guides your actions and decisions, helping you stay focused and motivated. Visualization is not just daydreaming; it's about using the power of your mind to create the reality you want. Regular practice can build the confidence and clarity needed to achieve your goals and overcome obstacles.

## 2. Tools and Materials

- Vision Board: Create a vision board that visually represents your goals and dreams, serving as a daily reminder of what you're working towards. A vision board keeps your objectives clear, reinforces intentions, and keeps your goals top of mind.
- Guided Visualization: Use guided visualization recordings or apps to help you practice this technique effectively. These resources provide structure, making it easier to develop a consistent and effective practice.
- Meditation Space: Set up a quiet, comfortable space for visualization, free from distractions. A dedicated space helps you focus deeply and creates a sense of ritual around the practice.

## 3. Techniques and Tips

- Detailed Imagery: Visualize your goals in detail, including the sights, sounds, and emotions of achieving them. The more vivid and realistic your visualization, the more powerful it will be in motivating and guiding your actions.
- Positive Focus: Focus on positive outcomes and the steps to reach your goals, reinforcing your belief in success. Visualizing success builds confidence and determination to overcome challenges.
- Consistency: Practice visualization regularly, ideally as part of your morning or evening routine, to build a strong mental image of your desired future. Consistency makes visualization a powerful tool for staying focused on your goals and aligned with your vision.

# *August 29: Writing Affirmations*

## 1. The Practice of Writing Affirmations

Writing affirmations involves crafting positive, empowering statements that you repeat daily. This practice reprograms your subconscious mind, replacing negative thoughts with positive beliefs. Writing affirmations allows you to control your mindset and create a more optimistic outlook. They are powerful tools for shaping your reality and transforming your inner dialogue. By writing and repeating affirmations regularly, you can change thought patterns, boost self-esteem, and manifest the life you desire. Whether improving self-confidence, achieving goals, or cultivating a positive mindset, affirmations can be tailored to your needs and aspirations.

## 2. Tools and Materials

- Affirmation Journal: Use a journal to write your affirmations daily, focusing on areas where you want growth or change. A journal provides space for reflection and tracks your progress over time, reinforcing your commitment.
- Sticky Notes: Write affirmations on sticky notes and place them around your home or workspace as daily reminders. These visual cues help you stay focused on positive intentions throughout the day.
- Calligraphy Pens: Use calligraphy pens to write affirmations beautifully, adding a personal touch to the practice. Writing affirmations creatively can enhance their impact and make the practice more enjoyable.

## 3. Techniques and Tips

- Present Tense: Write affirmations in the present tense, as if the desired outcome is already happening, to reinforce a positive mindset. This sends a message to your subconscious that you already possess the qualities or circumstances you're affirming.
- Positive Language: Use positive language, focusing on what you want to achieve rather than what you want to avoid. Positive language fosters an optimistic mindset, making it easier to manifest your goals.
- Daily Practice: Make writing affirmations a daily habit, ideally in the morning or before bed, to start and end your day positively. Consistency is key to making affirmations a powerful tool for personal growth, helping you maintain a positive mindset and focus on your goals.

# *August 30: Yoga*

## 1. The Practice of Yoga

Yoga is a physical, mental, and spiritual practice involving breath control, meditation, and specific postures. It's a holistic approach to health and well-being, offering benefits like improved flexibility, strength, mental clarity, and stress reduction. Yoga is versatile and accessible for all ages and fitness levels. It's not just about postures; it connects the mind, body, and spirit through mindful movement and breath. Regular practice enhances physical health, reduces stress, and cultivates inner peace and balance. Whether you're a beginner or experienced, yoga supports overall well-being and helps you lead a more balanced, fulfilling life.

## 2. Tools and Materials

- Yoga Mat: Use a non-slip mat for comfort and stability. A good mat provides the support and cushioning needed to perform poses safely, whether at home or in a studio.
- Yoga Blocks: Incorporate blocks to assist with balance and support in various poses. Blocks help modify poses to suit your flexibility and strength levels, making yoga more accessible and comfortable.
- Yoga Strap: Use a strap to deepen stretches and improve flexibility. A strap helps achieve proper alignment and supports your body in poses requiring greater flexibility or reach.

## 3. Techniques and Tips

- Breath Awareness: Focus on your breath throughout your practice, using it to guide movements and maintain mindfulness. Breath awareness is key in yoga, helping you stay present, calm, and centered.
- Start Slow: Begin with beginner poses and gradually progress to advanced sequences as your flexibility and strength improve. Starting slow builds a strong foundation and helps avoid injury, making your practice more sustainable and enjoyable.
- Consistency: Practice yoga regularly, even for a few minutes daily, to experience the full benefits. Consistency makes yoga transformative, helping you build strength, flexibility, and inner peace over time.

# *August 31: Zen Habits*

## 1. The Philosophy of Zen Habits

Zen habits are simple, mindful practices focused on living in the present and finding peace in simplicity. Inspired by Zen philosophy, these habits encourage slowing down, decluttering your mind and surroundings, and approaching life with calm and centeredness. Incorporating Zen habits into daily life can lead to greater mindfulness, reduced stress, and more fulfillment. Zen habits aren't about perfection but embracing simplicity, letting go of distractions, and cultivating peace in everyday life. By adopting Zen habits, you create a more intentional way of living, allowing you to focus on what truly matters and experience life with clarity and purpose.

## 2. Tools and Materials

- Meditation Space: Create a quiet, serene space for meditation and reflection, free from distractions. A dedicated space helps cultivate calm and focus, making it easier to practice mindfulness and Zen habits daily.
- Mindfulness Books: Read books on Zen philosophy and mindfulness to deepen your understanding of Zen habits. These resources offer insights and practical guidance for incorporating Zen principles into everyday life.
- Simple Living Tools: Use tools that promote simplicity, like a minimal wardrobe, decluttered environment, and mindful practices. Simplifying your physical space creates a peaceful environment, supporting your Zen habits and well-being.

## 3. Techniques and Tips

- Mindful Breathing: Practice mindful breathing throughout the day, bringing focus back to the present moment. Mindful breathing is a simple yet powerful way to cultivate awareness and calm, keeping you centered in daily activities.
- Simplify: Simplify your life by decluttering your space, reducing commitments, and focusing on what truly matters. Letting go of excess creates space for what brings joy, peace, and fulfillment.
- Let Go: Practice letting go of attachments to material possessions, outcomes, and expectations, finding peace in acceptance and simplicity. Letting go is a central Zen principle, encouraging you to embrace the present with an open heart.

## *Conclusion for August*

August has been a transformative month dedicated to personal development, offering tools and techniques to enhance your mind, body, and spirit. From affirmations and anxiety management to leadership skills and Zen habits, these activities have guided you on a journey of self-improvement and growth. Each day's practice has provided valuable insights and skills that will continue to benefit you long after the month is over. As you move forward, remember that personal development is an ongoing process—one that requires commitment, self-awareness, and a willingness to embrace change. Keep nurturing your mind, body, and spirit, and let the lessons of August inspire you to live a more balanced, fulfilling, and intentional life.

# September: Science and Technology

*September is dedicated to the wonders of science and technology, inviting you to delve into fields that push the boundaries of human understanding and innovation. This month's activities are designed to ignite your curiosity, expand your knowledge, and explore both the theoretical and practical aspects of these disciplines. From artificial intelligence to zoology, each day offers an opportunity to learn something new, engage with cutting-edge technology, or appreciate the natural world through a scientific lens.*

# *September 1: Artificial Intelligence*

## 1. The Rise of Artificial Intelligence

Artificial Intelligence (AI) involves developing computer systems capable of tasks that typically require human intelligence, such as visual perception, speech recognition, decision-making, and language translation. AI is revolutionizing industries like healthcare, finance, entertainment, and transportation. It has the potential to improve efficiency, drive innovation, and solve complex problems previously thought unsolvable. AI systems learn from data, adapt to new inputs, and perform tasks with increasing accuracy over time. As AI evolves, it raises ethical questions about privacy, job displacement, and the potential for AI to surpass human intelligence. Understanding AI and its implications is crucial for navigating the future of technology.

## 2. Tools and Materials

- Machine Learning Algorithms: Machine learning, a subset of AI, involves training algorithms to recognize patterns in data. Familiarize yourself with algorithms like decision trees, neural networks, and support vector machines to understand how AI systems learn and make decisions.
- Programming Languages: Learn programming languages commonly used in AI development, such as Python, R, and Java. These languages are essential for writing AI algorithms and developing applications.
- AI Frameworks: Use AI frameworks like TensorFlow, PyTorch, and Keras to build and deploy AI models. These frameworks provide tools and libraries that simplify AI development.

## 3. Techniques and Tips

- Data Preprocessing: Clean and preprocess data before feeding it into AI models. This step is crucial for improving the accuracy and reliability of AI predictions.
- Model Training and Evaluation: Train AI models on large datasets and evaluate their performance using metrics like accuracy, precision, and recall. Fine-tune the models to optimize performance.
- Ethical Considerations: Consider the ethical implications of AI development, such as bias in algorithms, privacy concerns, and the impact of AI on society. Strive to create AI systems that are fair, transparent, and beneficial to all.

# *September 2: Biology*

## 1. The Study of Life

Biology is the scientific study of life and living organisms, encompassing a wide range of topics from genetics and evolution to ecology and anatomy. It explores the structure, function, growth, origin, evolution, and distribution of living organisms. Understanding biology is fundamental to comprehending the natural world and addressing challenges such as disease, environmental conservation, and biotechnology. Biology is divided into various subfields, including botany, zoology, microbiology, and molecular biology, each focusing on different aspects of life. Advances in biology have led to breakthroughs in medicine, agriculture, and environmental science, making it a critical field of study for the future of humanity.

## 2. Tools and Materials

- Microscopes: Use microscopes to observe cells, tissues, and microorganisms. Microscopes are essential tools for studying the structure and function of living organisms at a microscopic level.
- Laboratory Equipment: Familiarize yourself with basic laboratory equipment such as petri dishes, pipettes, and centrifuges. These tools are commonly used in biological research and experiments.
- Biology Textbooks: Study biology textbooks to gain a deeper understanding of biological concepts, theories, and discoveries. Textbooks provide a comprehensive overview of the field and serve as valuable reference materials.

## 3. Techniques and Tips

- Observation and Experimentation: Practice observation and experimentation to explore biological phenomena. Conduct experiments, collect data, and analyze results to gain insights into the workings of living organisms.
- Fieldwork: Engage in fieldwork to study organisms in their natural habitats. Fieldwork provides opportunities to observe ecological interactions, species behavior, and environmental factors that influence life.
- Stay Updated: Stay updated on the latest developments in biology by reading scientific journals, attending conferences, and participating in online courses. Biology is a rapidly evolving field with new discoveries being made regularly.

# September 3: Blockchain Technology

## 1. The Innovation of Blockchain Technology

Blockchain technology is a decentralized, distributed ledger that records transactions across multiple computers. It underpins cryptocurrencies like Bitcoin, but its applications extend far beyond digital currency. Blockchain offers a secure, transparent, and tamper-proof way to store data and verify transactions, with the potential to revolutionize industries like finance, supply chain management, healthcare, and real estate by providing a more efficient and trustworthy way to conduct transactions. Operating on principles of decentralization, cryptography, and consensus, blockchain is resistant to fraud and cyberattacks. As blockchain technology evolves, it holds promise for creating a more transparent and equitable digital economy.

## 2. Tools and Materials

- Cryptographic Algorithms: Understand cryptographic algorithms like SHA-256 and elliptic curve cryptography, essential for securing blockchain transactions and ensuring data integrity.
- Blockchain Platforms: Explore platforms like Ethereum, Hyperledger, and Ripple, which provide the infrastructure for building decentralized applications (DApps) and smart contracts.
- Wallets and Exchanges: Learn to use cryptocurrency wallets and exchanges to store, send, and receive digital assets. Wallets secure private keys, while exchanges facilitate buying and selling cryptocurrencies.

## 3. Techniques and Tips

- Smart Contracts: Develop smart contracts, self-executing contracts with terms directly written into code, automating and enforcing agreements without intermediaries.
- Consensus Mechanisms: Familiarize yourself with consensus mechanisms like Proof of Work (PoW) and Proof of Stake (PoS), used to validate transactions and maintain blockchain integrity.
- Security Best Practices: Follow best practices to protect digital assets and secure blockchain networks, including strong passwords, two-factor authentication, and regular software updates.

# September 4: Chemistry

## 1. The Science of Matter

Chemistry is the branch of science that studies the composition, structure, properties, and changes of matter. It explores the elements and compounds that make up the universe and the reactions that transform substances. Chemistry is fundamental to understanding the physical world and is essential to various industries, including medicine, agriculture, energy, and manufacturing. The study of chemistry involves analyzing chemical reactions, understanding the periodic table, and exploring principles like thermodynamics and quantum mechanics. Advances in chemistry have led to new materials, medicines, and technologies, making it vital for scientific progress.

## 2. Tools and Materials

- Periodic Table: The periodic table is a key tool in chemistry, organizing elements by atomic number, electron configurations, and chemical properties. Understanding the periodic table is essential for predicting chemical behavior and reactions.
- Laboratory Glassware: Familiarize yourself with laboratory glassware such as beakers, flasks, and test tubes. These tools are commonly used in chemical experiments to mix, heat, and store substances.
- Chemical Reagents: Use chemical reagents to perform experiments and analyze reactions. Reagents are substances or compounds added to a system to cause a chemical reaction or test for the presence of other chemicals.

## 3. Techniques and Tips

- Chemical Safety: Always follow safety guidelines when handling chemicals and conducting experiments. This includes wearing protective equipment, working in a well-ventilated area, and properly disposing of hazardous materials.
- Balancing Equations: Practice balancing chemical equations to understand the stoichiometry of reactions. Balancing equations ensures the law of conservation of mass is upheld, with the same number of atoms on both sides.
- Titration: Learn titration techniques to determine the concentration of a solution. Titration involves adding a solution of known concentration to one of unknown concentration until the reaction reaches its endpoint.

# *September 5: Cryptography*

## 1. The Art of Cryptography

Cryptography is the science of securing communication and information by transforming it into an unreadable form for unauthorized users. It uses mathematical algorithms and keys to encrypt and decrypt data, ensuring confidentiality, integrity, and authenticity. Cryptography is vital in today's digital world, where protecting sensitive information like financial transactions, personal data, and confidential communications is paramount. It underpins security protocols like SSL/TLS for secure web browsing and is used in applications ranging from digital signatures to blockchain technology. Understanding cryptography is crucial for safeguarding digital assets and maintaining privacy in an increasingly interconnected world.

## 2. Tools and Materials

- Encryption Algorithms: Familiarize yourself with encryption algorithms like AES (Advanced Encryption Standard) and RSA (Rivest–Shamir–Adleman). These are widely used to secure data and communications.
- Cryptographic Keys: Learn about cryptographic keys, used to encrypt and decrypt data. Keys can be symmetric (same key for encryption and decryption) or asymmetric (public key for encryption and private key for decryption).
- Cryptographic Software: Use cryptographic software like OpenSSL or GnuPG to encrypt and decrypt data, create digital signatures, and manage cryptographic keys.

## 3. Techniques and Tips

- Key Management: Implement effective key management practices to protect cryptographic keys from unauthorized access. This includes securely storing keys, rotating them regularly, and using hardware security modules (HSMs) for added protection.
- Hash Functions: Understand the role of hash functions in cryptography, which generate a fixed-size output (hash) from any input size. Hash functions are used in digital signatures, data integrity checks, and password storage.
- Public Key Infrastructure (PKI): Learn about PKI, a framework for managing digital certificates and public-key encryption. PKI is essential for establishing trust in online communications and transactions.

# September 6: Data Science

## 1. The Power of Data Science

Data science is the field of study that uses scientific methods, algorithms, and systems to extract knowledge and insights from structured and unstructured data. It combines elements of statistics, computer science, and domain expertise to analyze large datasets, identify patterns, and make data-driven decisions. Data science is at the heart of modern technology, powering innovations in artificial intelligence, machine learning, and big data analytics. It has applications in various industries, including finance, healthcare, marketing, and social media, where data is used to optimize operations, predict trends, and enhance customer experiences. Mastering data science skills can open doors to a wide range of career opportunities in the digital age.

## 2. Tools and Materials

- Programming Languages: Learn programming languages commonly used in data science, such as Python, R, and SQL. These languages are essential for data manipulation, analysis, and visualization.
- Data Visualization Tools: Use data visualization tools like Tableau, Matplotlib, and Seaborn to create compelling visual representations of your data. Visualization helps to communicate insights and trends effectively.
- Machine Learning Libraries: Familiarize yourself with machine learning libraries such as Scikit-learn, TensorFlow, and PyTorch, which provide tools for building and deploying predictive models.

## 3. Techniques and Tips

- Data Cleaning: Practice data cleaning techniques to prepare your data for analysis. This involves handling missing values, removing duplicates, and correcting inconsistencies in the dataset.
- Exploratory Data Analysis (EDA): Conduct EDA to explore the data, identify patterns, and generate hypotheses. EDA is a critical step in understanding the structure and characteristics of the data before applying advanced analytics.
- Model Evaluation: Evaluate the performance of machine learning models using metrics like accuracy, precision, recall, and F1 score. Model evaluation helps to ensure that your models are reliable and effective in making predictions.

# *September 7: Drone Flying*

## 1. The Thrill of Drone Flying

Drone flying is a rapidly growing hobby and profession that involves piloting unmanned aerial vehicles (UAVs) for recreational, commercial, or scientific purposes. Drones are equipped with cameras, sensors, and other technology that allow them to capture aerial footage, conduct surveys, and even deliver packages. The accessibility and versatility of drones have made them popular tools for photography, videography, agriculture, environmental monitoring, and search and rescue operations. However, drone flying requires skill, knowledge of aviation regulations, and an understanding of the technology involved. Whether you're flying for fun or work, mastering drone piloting opens up new perspectives and opportunities.

## 2. Tools and Materials

- Drone: Choose a drone that suits your needs, whether it's for aerial photography, racing, or surveying. Drones vary in size, capabilities, and price, so select one that aligns with your goals and budget.
- Flight Controller: Use a flight controller to operate your drone, controlling its movements, speed, and altitude. Flight controllers often come with advanced features like GPS, obstacle avoidance, and automated flight modes.
- Camera and Gimbal: Equip your drone with a camera and gimbal for stable, high-quality aerial footage. Gimbals help to keep the camera steady, even in windy conditions or during fast maneuvers.

## 3. Techniques and Tips

- Learn the Rules: Familiarize yourself with local and national regulations governing drone flight. This includes restrictions on where and how high you can fly, as well as requirements for registration and licensing.
- Practice Maneuvers: Practice basic maneuvers such as takeoff, landing, hovering, and turning to build your piloting skills. Start in an open, obstacle-free area before attempting more complex flights.
- Maintenance: Regularly maintain your drone by checking the propellers, batteries, and sensors. Proper maintenance ensures safe and reliable flights, reducing the risk of crashes or malfunctions.

# *September 8: Electronics*

## 1. The World of Electronics

Electronics is the branch of science and technology focused on the design, development, and application of electronic circuits, devices, and systems. It powers modern technology, from smartphones and computers to medical devices and industrial machinery. Understanding electronics involves learning about components like resistors, capacitors, transistors, and microcontrollers, and how they work together to perform specific functions. Electronics is a hands-on field requiring experimentation, problem-solving, and creativity. Whether building your own gadgets or pursuing a career in engineering, electronics offers endless possibilities for innovation and discovery.

## 2. Tools and Materials

- Multimeter: A multimeter is essential for measuring voltage, current, and resistance in electronic circuits. It's used to diagnose problems and ensure circuits function correctly.
- Breadboard and Jumper Wires: Use a breadboard and jumper wires to prototype and test electronic circuits without soldering. Breadboards allow easy connection and disconnection of components as you experiment.
- Soldering Kit: A soldering kit is necessary for building permanent electronic circuits. It includes a soldering iron, solder, and other tools for securely connecting components on a circuit board.

## 3. Techniques and Tips

- Circuit Design: Learn the basics of circuit design, including how to create schematics and diagrams representing the flow of electricity through a circuit. Understanding circuit design is crucial for building functional electronic devices.
- Component Selection: Select the right components for your circuit based on specifications like resistance, capacitance, and power rating. Choosing the correct components ensures your circuit performs as intended.
- Troubleshooting: Develop troubleshooting skills to identify and fix issues in your circuits. This involves using tools like a multimeter to test connections, checking for short circuits, and replacing faulty components.

# September 9: *Forensics*

## 1. The Science of Forensics

Forensics is the application of scientific methods and techniques to investigate crimes and solve legal disputes. It involves the analysis of physical evidence, such as fingerprints, DNA, bloodstains, and digital data, to identify suspects, reconstruct events, and support legal proceedings. Forensic science is a multidisciplinary field that combines biology, chemistry, physics, and computer science to uncover the truth and ensure justice. Advances in forensic technology have revolutionized the way crimes are investigated, leading to more accurate and reliable results. Understanding forensics is essential for careers in law enforcement, criminal justice, and forensic science, as well as for anyone interested in the intersection of science and law.

## 2. Tools and Materials

- DNA Analysis Kits: DNA analysis is a cornerstone of forensic science, used to identify individuals based on their genetic makeup. DNA kits are used to extract, amplify, and analyze DNA samples from crime scenes.
- Fingerprinting Equipment: Fingerprinting is a classic forensic technique for identifying individuals. Equipment includes ink pads, fingerprint powder, and lifting tape for collecting and analyzing fingerprints.
- Digital Forensics Software: Digital forensics involves the recovery and analysis of data from electronic devices. Software tools are used to extract and examine data from computers, smartphones, and other digital media.

## 3. Techniques and Tips

- Evidence Collection: Learn the proper techniques for collecting and preserving evidence to avoid contamination or degradation. This includes using gloves, sealing evidence in bags, and documenting the collection process.
- Chain of Custody: Maintain a clear chain of custody for all evidence, documenting who handled it and when. This ensures that evidence is admissible in court and has not been tampered with.
- Data Recovery: Develop skills in data recovery, including retrieving deleted files, analyzing digital footprints, and uncovering hidden data. Digital forensics plays a crucial role in solving cybercrimes and other technology-related cases.

# *September 10: Geology*

## 1. The Study of the Earth

Geology is the scientific study of the Earth, its structure, materials, processes, and history. It involves the examination of rocks, minerals, fossils, and the forces that shape the planet, such as plate tectonics, erosion, and volcanic activity. Geology provides insights into the Earth's past, including the formation of continents, the evolution of life, and the impact of natural disasters. It also plays a critical role in resource exploration, environmental protection, and natural hazard assessment. Understanding geology is essential for careers in environmental science, mining, oil and gas exploration, and academia. It also enhances our appreciation of the Earth's dynamic and ever-changing nature.

## 2. Tools and Materials

- Rock Hammer: A rock hammer is a key tool for geologists, used to break rocks, collect samples, and examine rock formations in the field.
- Field Notebook: Keep a field notebook to record observations, sketches, and data collected during geological fieldwork. Accurate field notes are essential for interpreting geological features and processes.
- Geological Maps: Use geological maps to understand the distribution of different rock types, fault lines, and other geological features. These maps are crucial for exploring and studying specific areas.

## 3. Techniques and Tips

- Rock Identification: Learn how to identify different types of rocks, such as igneous, sedimentary, and metamorphic, based on their physical characteristics and formation processes.
- Stratigraphy: Study stratigraphy, the analysis of rock layers (strata), to understand the sequence of geological events and the relative ages of rock formations.
- Fieldwork Preparation: Prepare for geological fieldwork by researching the area, packing the necessary tools, and ensuring safety protocols are in place. Fieldwork often involves exploring remote and rugged terrain, so preparation is key.

# September 11: Hacking

## 1. The World of Hacking

Hacking refers to the practice of exploiting weaknesses in computer systems, networks, or software to gain unauthorized access or cause disruption. While hacking is often associated with illegal activities, ethical hacking (or white-hat hacking) involves using the same techniques to identify and fix security vulnerabilities, helping to protect systems from malicious attacks. Hacking requires a deep understanding of computer systems, programming, and cybersecurity principles. It plays a critical role in defending against cyber threats, ensuring the integrity and confidentiality of data, and maintaining the security of digital infrastructure. Whether pursued as a career in cybersecurity or as a hobby, hacking involves constant learning and adaptation to stay ahead of evolving threats.

## 2. Tools and Materials

- Penetration Testing Tools: Penetration testing tools like Metasploit, Nmap, and Burp Suite are used to test the security of systems by simulating attacks. These tools help identify vulnerabilities and assess the effectiveness of security measures.
- Virtual Machines: Use virtual machines to create isolated environments for testing and experimentation. Virtual machines allow you to run different operating systems and software without affecting your main system.
- Coding Skills: Learn programming languages commonly used in hacking, such as Python, C, and JavaScript. Coding skills are essential for writing scripts, automating tasks, and developing exploits.

## 3. Techniques and Tips

- Reconnaissance: Practice reconnaissance techniques to gather information about a target system, such as scanning for open ports, analyzing network traffic, and identifying software versions.
- Exploit Development: Develop and test exploits to target specific vulnerabilities in software or systems. Exploit development requires a deep understanding of programming, reverse engineering, and system internals.
- Ethical Considerations: Always adhere to ethical guidelines when hacking. Obtain proper authorization before testing systems, respect privacy, and report vulnerabilities responsibly to prevent misuse.

# *September 12: Internet of Things (IoT)*

## 1. The Connectivity of the Internet of Things (IoT)

The Internet of Things (IoT) refers to the network of interconnected devices that communicate and share data with each other over the internet. These devices range from everyday household items like smart thermostats and wearables to industrial machinery and autonomous vehicles. IoT has the potential to transform how we live and work by enabling automation, improving efficiency, and providing real-time insights through data collection and analysis. However, the widespread adoption of IoT also raises concerns about security, privacy, and the management of vast amounts of data. Understanding IoT is essential for navigating the future of smart technology and harnessing its potential to improve our lives.

## 2. Tools and Materials

- Microcontrollers: Microcontrollers like Arduino and Raspberry Pi are popular platforms for developing IoT projects. These small, programmable devices can control sensors, actuators, and other hardware components.
- Sensors and Actuators: Use sensors to collect data from the environment, such as temperature, humidity, or motion, and actuators to respond to that data by controlling devices like motors or lights.
- IoT Platforms: Explore IoT platforms like AWS IoT, Google Cloud IoT, and Azure IoT Hub, which provide the infrastructure for managing, analyzing, and visualizing data from IoT devices.

## 3. Techniques and Tips

- Device Integration: Learn how to integrate different IoT devices and sensors into a cohesive system, enabling them to communicate and work together seamlessly.
- Data Management: Develop skills in managing and analyzing the vast amounts of data generated by IoT devices. This includes using cloud services, databases, and data analytics tools to gain insights from the data.
- Security Best Practices: Implement security best practices to protect IoT devices from cyber threats. This includes using encryption, regularly updating firmware, and securing communication channels.

# *September 13: Java Programming*

## 1. The Versatility of Java Programming

Java is a high-level, object-oriented programming language widely used for developing various applications, from web and mobile apps to large-scale enterprise systems. Java's platform independence, security features, and robust performance have made it a popular choice among developers. Known for its "write once, run anywhere" capability, Java code can run on any device with a Java Virtual Machine (JVM). Understanding Java programming is essential for building scalable, reliable, and secure applications in today's software-driven world. Java's extensive libraries and frameworks also make it a versatile language for a wide range of development tasks.

## 2. Tools and Materials

- Integrated Development Environment (IDE): Use an IDE like Eclipse, IntelliJ IDEA, or NetBeans to write, debug, and manage your Java code. IDEs provide powerful tools and features that enhance productivity and streamline development.
- Java Libraries and Frameworks: Familiarize yourself with popular Java libraries and frameworks such as Spring, Hibernate, and Apache Commons. These tools offer pre-built functionality that saves time and effort in development.
- Build Tools: Use build tools like Maven or Gradle to automate compiling, packaging, and deploying Java applications. Build tools help manage dependencies and ensure that your projects are consistent and repeatable.

## 3. Techniques and Tips

- Object-Oriented Design: Master object-oriented design principles, including encapsulation, inheritance, and polymorphism. These concepts are fundamental to writing clean, maintainable Java code.
- Concurrency: Learn to manage concurrency in Java, allowing multiple threads to run simultaneously without conflicts or performance issues. Concurrency is critical for building responsive and efficient applications.
- Testing and Debugging: Develop strong testing and debugging skills to identify and fix issues in your Java code. Use testing frameworks like JUnit and debugging tools in your IDE to ensure your code is reliable and error-free.

# *September 14: Kinematics*

## 1. The Study of Motion: Kinematics

Kinematics is a branch of mechanics that focuses on the motion of objects without considering the forces that cause the motion. It involves analyzing the position, velocity, and acceleration of objects as they move through space and time. Kinematics is fundamental to understanding the behavior of physical systems, from the motion of planets to the dynamics of machines and vehicles. By studying kinematics, you can predict and describe the motion of objects, solve problems related to motion, and apply these principles to fields such as engineering, robotics, and physics.

## 2. Tools and Materials

- Motion Sensors: Use motion sensors to measure the position, velocity, and acceleration of objects in real-time. Motion sensors are commonly used in experiments to collect data on moving objects.
- Graphing Software: Use graphing software to plot position, velocity, and acceleration data over time. Visualizing motion helps to better understand the relationships between these variables.
- Kinematic Equations: Familiarize yourself with the kinematic equations, which describe the motion of objects in one or more dimensions. These equations are essential for solving problems related to linear and rotational motion.

## 3. Techniques and Tips

- Vector Analysis: Use vector analysis to describe motion in multiple dimensions. Vectors represent quantities like displacement, velocity, and acceleration, and are crucial for understanding motion in 2D and 3D space.
- Graph Interpretation: Practice interpreting position-time, velocity-time, and acceleration-time graphs to analyze the motion of objects. Graphs provide valuable insights into how motion changes over time.
- Problem Solving: Develop problem-solving skills by working through kinematics problems, applying the kinematic equations, and using diagrams to visualize motion scenarios.

# *September 15: Laser Engraving*

## 1. The Precision of Laser Engraving

Laser engraving is a process that uses a laser beam to etch designs, patterns, or text onto a variety of materials, including wood, metal, glass, and plastic. The laser precisely removes material from the surface, creating detailed and permanent engravings. Laser engraving is widely used in industries such as manufacturing, jewelry, and signage, as well as for personal projects like custom gifts and artwork. The precision and versatility of laser engraving make it an ideal method for creating intricate designs and professional-quality products. Understanding the principles of laser engraving allows you to explore its creative and practical applications, whether for business or hobby.

## 2. Tools and Materials

- Laser Engraving Machine: Choose a laser engraving machine that suits your needs, whether for hobbyist projects or commercial production. Machines vary in power, size, and capabilities, so select one based on the materials you plan to engrave.
- Design Software: Use design software like Adobe Illustrator, CorelDRAW, or AutoCAD to create digital designs for laser engraving. These programs allow you to draw and edit vector graphics that the laser machine will follow.
- Material Selection: Select materials that are compatible with your laser engraving machine. Common materials include wood, acrylic, leather, and coated metals. Each material reacts differently to laser engraving, affecting the quality and appearance of the final product.

## 3. Techniques and Tips

- Focus Adjustment: Adjust the focus of the laser to achieve optimal engraving results. Proper focus ensures that the laser beam is concentrated on the material's surface, resulting in clean, sharp engravings.
- Speed and Power Settings: Experiment with different speed and power settings on your laser engraving machine to achieve the desired depth and detail in your engravings. Higher power and slower speeds typically produce deeper engravings, while lower power and faster speeds create lighter marks.
- Safety Precautions: Follow safety precautions when operating a laser engraving machine, including wearing protective eyewear, ensuring proper ventilation, and never leaving the machine unattended while in use.

# *September 16: Microbiology*

## 1. The Study of Microorganisms: Microbiology

Microbiology is the branch of biology that focuses on the study of microorganisms, including bacteria, viruses, fungi, and protozoa. These tiny organisms play crucial roles in ecosystems, human health, and biotechnology. Microbiology explores the structure, function, genetics, and behavior of microorganisms, as well as their interactions with other living organisms and their environments. Understanding microbiology is essential for fields such as medicine, agriculture, environmental science, and pharmaceuticals. Advances in microbiology have led to the development of antibiotics, vaccines, and biotechnological applications that have transformed modern life.

## 2. Tools and Materials

- Microscopes: Use microscopes to observe microorganisms, as they are too small to be seen with the naked eye. Microscopes are essential tools in microbiology for studying the morphology and behavior of microbes.
- Culture Media: Use culture media to grow and isolate microorganisms in a laboratory setting. Different types of media support the growth of specific microbes, allowing for their identification and study.
- Staining Kits: Use staining techniques, such as Gram staining, to differentiate and visualize microorganisms under the microscope. Staining enhances the contrast of microbial cells, making them easier to observe and identify.

## 3. Techniques and Tips

- Aseptic Technique: Practice aseptic techniques to prevent contamination of microbial cultures. This includes sterilizing equipment, using proper hand hygiene, and working in a clean environment.
- Microbial Identification: Learn how to identify microorganisms based on their morphology, biochemical properties, and genetic characteristics. Accurate identification is essential for diagnosing infections and developing treatments.
- Antibiotic Sensitivity Testing: Conduct antibiotic sensitivity testing to determine the effectiveness of antibiotics against specific bacterial strains. This technique is critical for guiding the treatment of bacterial infections and combating antibiotic resistance.

# *September 17: Nanotechnology*

## 1. The World of Nanotechnology

Nanotechnology involves manipulating matter at the nanoscale, typically between 1 and 100 nanometers. At this scale, materials exhibit unique properties, enabling new technologies and applications. Nanotechnology is revolutionizing fields like medicine, electronics, energy, and materials science with innovative solutions. From drug delivery systems targeting cancer cells to ultra-efficient solar panels, nanotechnology can transform industries and improve quality of life. Understanding nanotechnology involves exploring nanoscale materials' principles, fabrication, and applications.

## 2. Tools and Materials

- Scanning Electron Microscope (SEM): Use an SEM to visualize and analyze materials at the nanoscale. SEMs provide high-resolution images of nanomaterials' surface structure and composition.
- Nanofabrication Techniques: Familiarize yourself with nanofabrication techniques like lithography, self-assembly, and chemical vapor deposition. These methods create nanoscale structures and devices with precision.
- Nanomaterials: Explore types of nanomaterials like carbon nanotubes, quantum dots, and nanoparticles. Each has unique properties suitable for applications in electronics, medicine, or catalysis.

## 3. Techniques and Tips

- Surface Functionalization: Learn to modify the surface of nanomaterials to enhance their properties or tailor them for specific uses. Surface functionalization can improve the biocompatibility, stability, or reactivity of nanomaterials.
- Characterization Methods: Use methods like X-ray diffraction (XRD) and atomic force microscopy (AFM) to analyze the structure and properties of nanomaterials. These techniques provide detailed information about composition, morphology, and behavior at the nanoscale.
- Safety Considerations: Follow safety guidelines when working with nanomaterials, as their small size can pose unique health risks. Proper ventilation, protective equipment, and safe handling practices are essential to minimize exposure.

# *September 18: Optics*

## 1. The Science of Light: Optics
Optics is the branch of physics that studies the behavior and properties of light, including its interactions with matter and the construction of instruments that use or detect light. Optics is a fundamental field of study with applications in various industries, including telecommunications, medicine, and manufacturing. It covers topics such as reflection, refraction, diffraction, and polarization of light, as well as the development of optical devices like lenses, mirrors, and lasers. Understanding optics is crucial for designing and improving technologies like cameras, eyeglasses, microscopes, and fiber optic communication systems.

## 2. Tools and Materials
- Lenses and Mirrors: Use lenses and mirrors to manipulate light in various optical experiments. These components are essential for focusing, reflecting, and redirecting light in optical systems.
- Laser: Employ lasers in experiments to study the properties of light, such as coherence, wavelength, and intensity. Lasers are widely used in optics for their ability to produce highly focused and monochromatic beams of light.
- Optical Bench: An optical bench provides a stable platform for setting up and aligning optical experiments. It allows precise positioning of lenses, mirrors, and other components to study the behavior of light.

## 3. Techniques and Tips
- Ray Tracing: Practice ray tracing techniques to analyze and predict the behavior of light as it passes through different optical components. Ray tracing is essential for designing optical systems like cameras and telescopes.
- Interference and Diffraction: Explore the phenomena of interference and diffraction by conducting experiments with double-slit setups and diffraction gratings. These phenomena demonstrate the wave nature of light and are fundamental concepts in optics.
- Optical Alignment: Learn to align optical components with precision to achieve the desired optical effects. Proper alignment is crucial for ensuring the accuracy and efficiency of optical systems.

# September 19: Physics

## 1. The Foundation of Natural Science: Physics

Physics is the natural science that studies matter, energy, and the fundamental forces of the universe. It seeks to understand the laws that govern the behavior of everything from subatomic particles to galaxies. Physics is divided into several branches, including classical mechanics, electromagnetism, thermodynamics, quantum mechanics, and relativity. The principles of physics are applied in various fields, from engineering and technology to medicine and environmental science. Understanding physics is essential for explaining natural phenomena, developing new technologies, and solving complex problems in science and industry.

## 2. Tools and Materials

- Physics Textbooks: Study foundational physics textbooks to gain a comprehensive understanding of key concepts, theories, and equations in physics. Textbooks provide essential knowledge for exploring advanced topics in the field.
- Laboratory Equipment: Use laboratory equipment like pendulums, inclined planes, and oscilloscopes to conduct physics experiments. Hands-on experimentation is crucial for testing theories and observing physical principles in action.
- Simulation Software: Utilize simulation software to model physical systems and phenomena. Simulations allow you to explore complex scenarios and visualize the behavior of systems that may be difficult to study experimentally.

## 3. Techniques and Tips

- Problem Solving: Develop strong problem-solving skills by practicing physics problems regularly. Work on problems that require the application of multiple concepts and equations to deepen your understanding of the material.
- Experimental Design: Learn to design experiments that test specific hypotheses or explore physical principles. Carefully controlled experiments are essential for validating theories and discovering new phenomena.
- Mathematical Rigor: Strengthen your mathematical skills, as physics relies heavily on mathematics to describe and predict the behavior of physical systems. Focus on calculus, linear algebra, and differential equations, which are commonly used in physics.

# *September 20: Quantum Computing*

## 1. The Frontier of Technology: Quantum Computing

Quantum computing is an emerging field that harnesses quantum mechanics to perform calculations far more efficiently than classical computers. Unlike classical computers, which use bits, quantum computers use qubits that can exist in multiple states simultaneously due to superposition. Quantum computing could revolutionize fields like cryptography, materials science, and artificial intelligence by solving problems currently intractable for classical computers. Understanding quantum computing involves exploring quantum entanglement, quantum gates, and quantum algorithms, along with the challenges of building and scaling quantum hardware.

## 2. Tools and Materials

- Quantum Programming Languages: Learn quantum programming languages like Qiskit (Python-based) and Microsoft's Q# to write quantum algorithms and run simulations. These languages provide tools to explore and develop quantum software.
- Quantum Simulators: Use quantum simulators to model quantum systems and test algorithms. Simulators let you experiment with quantum principles without needing physical quantum hardware.
- Quantum Research Papers: Read research papers to stay informed about the latest advancements and challenges in quantum computing, gaining deep insights into cutting-edge technologies and theories.

## 3. Techniques and Tips

- Understanding Superposition and Entanglement: Master the concepts of superposition and entanglement, fundamental to quantum computing. These differentiate quantum computing from classical computing and are key to understanding quantum algorithms.
- Quantum Algorithms: Study algorithms like Shor's and Grover's, which show quantum computing's potential to outperform classical algorithms in specific tasks.
- Stay Updated: Quantum computing is rapidly evolving, so stay updated with the latest developments by following research journals, attending conferences, and participating in online courses and forums.

# *September 21: Robotics*

## 1. The Integration of Mechanics and Intelligence: Robotics

Robotics is the interdisciplinary field that combines mechanical engineering, electronics, computer science, and artificial intelligence to design, build, and operate robots. Robots are machines capable of carrying out complex tasks autonomously or semi-autonomously, often in environments that are dangerous, repetitive, or inaccessible to humans. Robotics has applications in industries such as manufacturing, healthcare, agriculture, and space exploration. The study of robotics involves understanding sensors, actuators, control systems, and programming, as well as the ethical and societal implications of increasingly intelligent and autonomous machines.

## 2. Tools and Materials

- Microcontrollers and Sensors: Use microcontrollers like Arduino or Raspberry Pi to control robots and interface with sensors that detect light, sound, motion, and other environmental factors.
- Robotics Kits: Explore robotics kits that include motors, gears, wheels, and structural components for building and programming robots. These kits are ideal for hands-on learning and experimentation.
- CAD Software: Use Computer-Aided Design (CAD) software to design and simulate robotic systems before building them. CAD software allows for precise modeling and testing of mechanical components.

## 3. Techniques and Tips

- Programming for Robotics: Learn programming languages like Python, C++, or Robot Operating System (ROS) for developing software that controls robotic systems. Programming is essential for defining the behavior and responses of robots.
- Sensor Integration: Practice integrating sensors with your robots to enable them to perceive their environment and make decisions based on sensor data. Sensor integration is key to creating responsive and intelligent robots.
- Control Systems: Study control systems and algorithms that govern the movement and actions of robots. Control systems ensure that robots operate smoothly and accurately, even in dynamic environments.

# September 22: Space Exploration

## 1. The Final Frontier: Space Exploration

Space exploration is the scientific investigation and exploration of outer space, using both crewed and uncrewed spacecraft. It involves the study of celestial bodies such as planets, moons, asteroids, and stars, as well as the development of technologies for traveling beyond Earth's atmosphere. Space exploration has led to significant advancements in science, technology, and our understanding of the universe. It has also inspired generations of scientists, engineers, and enthusiasts to push the boundaries of what is possible. The study of space exploration covers topics like rocket science, orbital mechanics, space missions, and the challenges of human spaceflight.

## 2. Tools and Materials

- Telescopes: Use telescopes to observe celestial objects and phenomena from Earth. Telescopes are essential tools for amateur and professional astronomers alike, allowing detailed observations of the night sky.
- Simulation Software: Utilize space mission simulation software to model and plan space missions, including trajectory calculations, fuel requirements, and mission timelines. This software helps in understanding the complexities of space travel.
- Astronomy Books: Read books on astronomy and space exploration to deepen your knowledge of the cosmos and the history of space missions. These resources provide valuable insights into past, present, and future space endeavors.

## 3. Techniques and Tips

- Orbital Mechanics: Study orbital mechanics to understand how spacecraft navigate the gravitational fields of planets and moons. This knowledge is crucial for planning space missions and achieving successful trajectories.
- Rocket Design: Learn the basics of rocket design, including propulsion systems, aerodynamics, and materials science. Understanding how rockets work is key to developing and launching spacecraft.
- Astronaut Training: Explore the rigorous training that astronauts undergo to prepare for space missions, including physical fitness, survival training, and simulations of space environments. This training ensures that astronauts are ready for the challenges of spaceflight.

# *September 23: Tinkering*

## 1. The Art of Tinkering

Tinkering involves experimenting with materials, tools, and ideas to create, modify, or repair devices and systems. It is a hands-on approach to learning and problem-solving that encourages creativity, curiosity, and innovation. Tinkering can range from simple DIY projects to complex engineering tasks, making it a valuable skill for hobbyists, inventors, and engineers alike. The process of tinkering often leads to unexpected discoveries and improvements, as well as a deeper understanding of how things work. Whether you're fixing a broken appliance, building a custom gadget, or prototyping a new invention, tinkering allows you to explore and apply scientific and technical concepts in practical ways.

## 2. Tools and Materials

- Basic Hand Tools: Equip yourself with basic hand tools such as screwdrivers, pliers, wrenches, and hammers for disassembling and reassembling devices. These tools are essential for any tinkering project.
- Soldering Iron: Use a soldering iron to join electrical components and repair circuit boards. Soldering is a fundamental skill for working with electronics and creating custom circuits.
- 3D Printer: Consider using a 3D printer to create custom parts, prototypes, and models. 3D printing allows you to bring your ideas to life with precision and creativity.

## 3. Techniques and Tips

- Reverse Engineering: Practice reverse engineering by taking apart devices to understand how they work. This approach helps you learn about the design and function of various components and systems.
- Prototyping: Develop your prototyping skills to quickly create and test new ideas. Prototyping allows you to experiment with different designs and concepts before committing to a final product.
- Documentation: Keep detailed notes and diagrams of your tinkering projects, including challenges encountered and solutions discovered. Documentation helps you refine your ideas and share your knowledge with others.

# *September 24: Underwater Robotics*

## 1. The Exploration of the Ocean Depths: Underwater Robotics

Underwater robotics involves the design, development, and operation of robots that can explore and work in underwater environments. These robots, known as remotely operated vehicles (ROVs) or autonomous underwater vehicles (AUVs), are used for tasks such as ocean exploration, underwater archaeology, marine research, and offshore industry operations. Underwater robots are equipped with sensors, cameras, and manipulator arms to perform a variety of tasks in challenging and often hazardous underwater conditions. The study of underwater robotics requires knowledge of marine engineering, control systems, hydrodynamics, and environmental sensors. It is a field that combines cutting-edge technology with the adventure of exploring the unknown.

## 2. Tools and Materials

- ROV Kits: Use ROV kits to build and customize your own underwater robot. These kits provide the components and instructions needed to assemble and operate an ROV, including thrusters, cameras, and control systems.
- Waterproof Cameras: Equip your underwater robot with waterproof cameras to capture video and images from beneath the surface. Cameras are essential for navigation, exploration, and documentation of underwater environments.
- Sonar Sensors: Integrate sonar sensors into your underwater robot to detect objects and navigate in low-visibility conditions. Sonar technology is widely used in underwater robotics for mapping and obstacle avoidance.

## 3. Techniques and Tips

- Buoyancy Control: Learn how to control the buoyancy of your underwater robot to ensure it can maintain a stable position in the water column. Proper buoyancy control is crucial for maneuverability and precise operations.
- Remote Operation: Practice remote operation skills to effectively control your underwater robot from the surface. This involves using a control console or software interface to navigate, manipulate objects, and collect data.
- Environmental Considerations: Consider the environmental challenges of underwater robotics, such as pressure, temperature, and corrosion. Designing robots to withstand these conditions is essential for successful underwater missions.

# September 25: Virtual Reality

## 1. The Immersive World of Virtual Reality

Virtual Reality (VR) is a technology that creates immersive, computer-generated environments that users can interact with in a seemingly real way. VR is used in a variety of applications, including gaming, education, training, and simulation. It allows users to experience and interact with 3D environments, objects, and scenarios that would be impossible or impractical in the real world. VR systems typically consist of a headset that displays the virtual environment, motion tracking sensors, and controllers for interacting with the virtual world. The study of VR involves understanding computer graphics, human-computer interaction, and the design of immersive experiences.

## 2. Tools and Materials

- VR Headset: Choose a VR headset that suits your needs, whether for gaming, development, or educational purposes. Popular options include the Oculus Rift, HTC Vive, and PlayStation VR.
- Development Platforms: Use development platforms like Unity or Unreal Engine to create and program VR experiences. These platforms provide the tools and resources needed to build 3D environments and interactive elements.
- Motion Controllers: Utilize motion controllers to interact with the virtual environment. These devices track your hand movements and translate them into actions within the VR world.

## 3. Techniques and Tips

- Design for Immersion: Focus on creating immersive experiences that engage the user's senses and attention. This includes designing realistic environments, intuitive controls, and responsive interactions.
- User Comfort: Consider user comfort when designing VR experiences, including minimizing motion sickness by optimizing frame rates and reducing latency.
- Iterative Development: Use an iterative development process to test and refine your VR applications. Gather feedback from users and make adjustments to improve the experience and usability.

# *September 26: Weather Science*

## 1. The Dynamics of Weather Science

Weather science, also known as meteorology, is the study of the atmosphere and the processes that govern weather patterns and climate. Meteorologists use a combination of observational data, computer models, and theoretical principles to understand and predict weather phenomena such as storms, hurricanes, and temperature changes. Weather science is essential for forecasting weather, understanding climate change, and preparing for natural disasters. It involves the study of atmospheric physics, fluid dynamics, and the interactions between the Earth's surface and the atmosphere. Advances in weather science have significantly improved the accuracy of weather forecasts and our ability to respond to extreme weather events.

## 2. Tools and Materials

- Weather Stations: Use weather stations to collect real-time data on temperature, humidity, wind speed, and atmospheric pressure. These instruments provide the essential data needed for weather analysis and forecasting.
- Satellite Imagery: Analyze satellite imagery to observe weather patterns on a global scale. Satellites provide valuable information about cloud cover, storm development, and the movement of weather systems.
- Weather Models: Utilize weather models to simulate and predict weather conditions. These models use mathematical equations to represent the behavior of the atmosphere and can provide short-term and long-term forecasts.

## 3. Techniques and Tips

- Data Interpretation: Develop skills in interpreting weather data, including reading weather maps, charts, and radar images. Understanding how to analyze this data is key to making accurate weather predictions.
- Climate Study: Explore the study of climate science to understand long-term weather patterns and trends. Climate study involves analyzing historical data and modeling future climate scenarios.
- Weather Safety: Learn about weather safety protocols for different types of weather events, such as tornadoes, hurricanes, and blizzards. Being prepared for severe weather is crucial for minimizing risk and protecting lives and property.

# *September 27: X-ray Imaging*

## 1. The Technology of X-ray Imaging

X-ray imaging is a technique that uses X-rays, a form of electromagnetic radiation, to create images of the inside of an object or body. It is widely used in medicine, security, and industrial applications to visualize structures that are otherwise invisible. In medicine, X-ray imaging is essential for diagnosing fractures, infections, and tumors. In security, it is used to scan luggage and cargo for hidden items. In industry, X-rays are used for non-destructive testing to inspect materials and structures. The study of X-ray imaging involves understanding the principles of radiation, image formation, and the safe use of X-ray technology.

## 2. Tools and Materials

- X-ray Machine: Use an X-ray machine to produce X-ray images by passing X-rays through an object and capturing the resulting image on a detector. X-ray machines vary in size and capability, depending on their intended use.
- Radiation Detectors: Employ radiation detectors to measure and monitor exposure levels when working with X-ray equipment. These detectors are crucial for ensuring the safety of operators and patients.
- Image Processing Software: Use image processing software to enhance and analyze X-ray images. This software allows you to adjust contrast, zoom in on specific areas, and detect anomalies in the images.

## 3. Techniques and Tips

- Image Interpretation: Develop skills in interpreting X-ray images, recognizing the different shades of gray that represent various materials or tissues. Accurate interpretation is essential for diagnosing medical conditions or identifying structural issues.
- Radiation Safety: Follow strict radiation safety protocols to minimize exposure to X-rays. This includes using lead shielding, maintaining a safe distance from the X-ray source, and monitoring radiation levels with dosimeters.
- Quality Control: Implement quality control measures to ensure that X-ray equipment is functioning correctly and producing high-quality images. Regular calibration and maintenance of X-ray machines are essential for accurate and reliable imaging.

# *September 28: Y2K Bug History*

## 1. The Story of the Y2K Bug

The Y2K bug, also known as the Millennium Bug, was a computer flaw that was expected to cause significant problems when the date changed from December 31, 1999, to January 1, 2000. The bug stemmed from the practice of representing years with two digits (e.g., "99" for 1999), which could cause computers to misinterpret the year 2000 as 1900. This was anticipated to lead to widespread failures in computer systems, affecting industries such as banking, transportation, and utilities. The Y2K bug prompted a massive global effort to update software and hardware systems to prevent disruptions. While the transition to the year 2000 passed with relatively few issues, the Y2K bug remains a significant event in the history of computing, highlighting the importance of robust software design and testing.

## 2. Tools and Materials

- Historical Documentation: Study historical documentation and reports on the Y2K bug, including government and industry assessments, to understand the scope of the problem and the actions taken to address it.
- Legacy Systems: Explore legacy computer systems from the 1990s to see how date representation was handled and how the Y2K issue was mitigated.
- Interviews and Testimonials: Read interviews and testimonials from IT professionals who worked on Y2K remediation projects to gain insights into the challenges and solutions of the time.

## 3. Techniques and Tips

- Software Testing: Learn about the software testing techniques used to identify and fix Y2K-related bugs. This includes regression testing, date simulation, and system integration testing.
- Risk Management: Study the risk management strategies employed by organizations to prepare for Y2K, including contingency planning, backup systems, and crisis management protocols.
- Legacy Code Analysis: Practice analyzing and updating legacy code to address date-related issues. Understanding how to work with older codebases is a valuable skill for maintaining and upgrading long-running software systems.

# *September 29: Zoological Illustration*

## 1. The Art of Zoological Illustration

Zoological illustration involves creating detailed, accurate drawings or paintings of animals for scientific and educational purposes. These illustrations are used in field guides, textbooks, research papers, and museums to aid in identifying and studying species. Zoological illustration demands a deep understanding of animal anatomy, behavior, and habitats, along with artistic skill in rendering textures, colors, and proportions. The goal is to convey an animal's appearance and characteristics in a way that is both scientifically accurate and visually appealing. This field merges art and science, making it vital for biologists, naturalists, and educators.

## 2. Tools and Materials

- Drawing Supplies: Use high-quality pencils, pens, and brushes to create detailed illustrations. Different tools are suited for textures like fur, scales, or feathers.
- Reference Materials: Gather reference materials such as photos, field notes, and anatomical studies to ensure accuracy. Observing live animals, when possible, is valuable for capturing natural poses and behaviors.
- Digital Illustration Software: Consider digital tools like Adobe Illustrator or Procreate for creating and editing zoological illustrations. Digital software offers flexibility and precision in adding color, shading, and details.

## 3. Techniques and Tips

- Anatomical Accuracy: Prioritize anatomical accuracy by studying the skeletal and muscular structures of animals. Understanding anatomy is crucial for realistic and informative illustrations.
- Textural Detail: Focus on the textures of different animal parts, such as the smoothness of scales or the softness of fur. Use shading, cross-hatching, and stippling to render these textures convincingly.
- Composition and Layout: Consider composition and layout, especially when creating plates with multiple views or stages of an animal's life cycle. Effective composition enhances the clarity and impact of your work.

# *September 30: Zoology*

## 1. The Study of Animals: Zoology

Zoology is the branch of biology that studies animals, focusing on their behavior, physiology, classification, and distribution. It covers topics from the anatomy and genetics of species to the ecosystems and evolutionary relationships of animal groups. Zoologists study animals in natural habitats, captivity, and laboratories to understand their biology and environmental interactions. Zoology is foundational for understanding biodiversity, conservation, and the impact of human activities on wildlife, playing a critical role in advancing medicine, agriculture, and environmental management.

## 2. Tools and Materials

- Field Equipment: Use tools like binoculars, GPS devices, and traps to observe animals in their natural habitats. Fieldwork is vital for zoological research, providing firsthand data on animal behavior and ecology.
- Laboratory Instruments: Employ tools like microscopes, DNA sequencers, and dissection kits to study animal anatomy, genetics, and physiology. Laboratory work complements field studies by enabling detailed specimen analysis.
- Zoological Databases: Access databases and journals to stay updated on the latest zoological research and discoveries, offering valuable information on species distribution, taxonomy, and conservation status.

## 3. Techniques and Tips

- Species Identification: Build skills in species identification by studying field guides, taxonomic keys, and observing morphological traits. Accurate identification is crucial for zoological research and biodiversity records.
- Behavioral Observation: Practice behavioral observation techniques like ethograms and time-budget studies to document and analyze animal behavior in the wild or captivity. Understanding behavior is key to studying social structures, communication, and adaptation.
- Conservation Biology: Study conservation biology principles to understand challenges and strategies for protecting endangered species and preserving biodiversity, which is increasingly vital as human activities threaten wildlife.

## *Conclusion for September*

September has taken you on a journey through the fascinating worlds of science and technology, offering insights into fields that shape our understanding of the universe and drive innovation. From the theoretical principles of physics and quantum computing to the practical applications of robotics and nanotechnology, this month has expanded your knowledge and skills in profound ways. As you continue to explore these disciplines, remember that science and technology are ever-evolving, offering endless opportunities for discovery, creativity, and problem-solving. Let the lessons of September inspire you to keep questioning, experimenting, and pushing the boundaries of what is possible.

# October: Sports and Fitness

*October is a month dedicated to physical well-being, focusing on sports and fitness activities that improve your health, endurance, strength, and mental clarity. Whether you're looking to start a new exercise routine, challenge yourself with a competitive sport, or simply stay active, this month offers a wide range of activities to keep you motivated and moving. From traditional sports to modern fitness trends, each day introduces you to a new way to stay fit and healthy.*

# October 1: *Aerobics*

## 1. The Benefits of Aerobics

Aerobics is a form of physical exercise that combines rhythmic aerobic movements with stretching and strength training routines. It is designed to improve cardiovascular health, increase stamina, and enhance overall fitness. Aerobics can be performed in a group setting, such as in a fitness class, or individually, making it accessible to people of all fitness levels. The high-energy movements, often set to music, make aerobics a fun and effective way to stay active and healthy. Consistent practice of aerobics can lead to weight loss, improved heart health, and increased endurance.

## 2. Tools and Materials

- Exercise Mat: Use an exercise mat to provide cushioning and support during floor exercises, reducing the impact on your joints.
- Step Platform: Incorporate a step platform into your aerobics routine to add intensity and variety to your workout.
- Comfortable Footwear: Wear supportive, cushioned shoes designed for aerobic activities to protect your feet and prevent injuries.

## 3. Techniques and Tips

- Warm-Up and Cool-Down: Always begin with a warm-up to prepare your body for exercise and end with a cool-down to gradually reduce your heart rate.
- High-Intensity Intervals: Mix high-intensity intervals with lower-intensity periods to maximize calorie burn and improve cardiovascular fitness.
- Listen to Your Body: Adjust the intensity of your workout based on your fitness level and listen to your body to avoid overexertion.

# *October 2: Archery*

## 1. The Precision of Archery

Archery is a skill that requires focus, control, and physical strength. Historically used for hunting and warfare, it is now a popular recreational and competitive sport. Archery involves shooting arrows with a bow at a target, and success depends on accuracy, consistency, and concentration. Practicing archery can improve your hand-eye coordination, mental focus, and upper body strength. Whether you're aiming for a bullseye or simply enjoying the meditative aspect of drawing a bow, archery is a rewarding activity that challenges both mind and body.

## 2. Tools and Materials

- Bow: Choose between a recurve bow, compound bow, or longbow based on your skill level and interest.
- Arrows: Use arrows made from wood, carbon, or aluminum, ensuring they match the draw weight and length of your bow.
- Target: Practice with a durable target, such as a foam block or straw bale, to improve your accuracy and consistency.

## 3. Techniques and Tips

- Proper Stance: Maintain a steady stance with your feet shoulder-width apart, facing perpendicular to the target for stability and control.
- Focus on Breathing: Control your breathing to help steady your aim, exhaling slowly as you release the arrow.
- Consistent Release: Practice a smooth and consistent release of the bowstring to improve accuracy and reduce arrow deviation.

# *October 3: Badminton*

## 1. The Agility of Badminton

Badminton is a fast-paced racquet sport that requires quick reflexes, agility, and strategic thinking. Played with a shuttlecock instead of a ball, badminton can be enjoyed as a casual backyard game or as a competitive sport. The game involves hitting the shuttlecock over a net and scoring points by landing it in the opponent's court. Badminton improves cardiovascular health, coordination, and hand-eye coordination. Its combination of speed, agility, and tactical play makes it an engaging and challenging sport for players of all ages.

## 2. Tools and Materials

- Racquet: Choose a lightweight, balanced racquet that suits your playing style, whether you prefer power or control.
- Shuttlecocks: Use feathered or synthetic shuttlecocks, with feathered ones offering better flight characteristics for advanced play.
- Net and Court: Set up a standard badminton net on a flat, non-slip surface for official play or adjust the height for casual games.

## 3. Techniques and Tips

- Footwork: Practice quick and efficient footwork to reach the shuttlecock and maintain balance during fast exchanges.
- Smashes and Drops: Master the smash for powerful, attacking shots and the drop shot for delicate, tactical plays close to the net.
- Game Strategy: Develop a game strategy that leverages your strengths, whether it's aggressive attacks or consistent defense, to outmaneuver your opponent.

# October 4: Biking

## 1. The Freedom of Biking

Biking is a versatile activity that can be enjoyed for recreation, fitness, or transportation. It's an excellent way to explore the outdoors, stay active, and improve cardiovascular health. Biking strengthens the lower body, enhances balance and coordination, and provides a low-impact workout that is easy on the joints. Whether you're cycling on roads, trails, or in urban environments, biking offers a sense of freedom and adventure. It's also an eco-friendly mode of transport that contributes to reducing your carbon footprint.

## 2. Tools and Materials

- Bike: Choose a bike that suits your riding style, whether it's a road bike for speed, a mountain bike for rugged trails, or a hybrid for versatility.
- Helmet: Wear a properly fitted helmet to protect your head in case of falls or accidents.
- Bike Lights: Use front and rear bike lights to increase visibility and safety, especially when riding in low-light conditions.

## 3. Techniques and Tips

- Proper Gear Shifting: Learn to shift gears smoothly to maintain a consistent cadence and manage different terrains efficiently.
- Bike Maintenance: Regularly check your bike's tire pressure, brakes, and chain to ensure it's in good working condition.
- Route Planning: Plan your routes based on your fitness level and goals, whether you're looking for a leisurely ride or a challenging workout.

# *October 5: Canoeing*

## 1. The Serenity of Canoeing

Canoeing is a water-based activity that involves paddling a canoe through lakes, rivers, or streams. It offers a peaceful way to explore waterways, connect with nature, and engage in physical activity. Canoeing can be enjoyed solo or with others, making it a versatile and social outdoor activity. The rhythmic motion of paddling works the upper body and core, while the serene surroundings provide a mental escape from the stresses of daily life. Canoeing is accessible to people of all skill levels, from beginners to experienced paddlers.

## 2. Tools and Materials

- Canoe: Choose a canoe based on your intended use, whether for calm waters or whitewater adventures.
- Paddle: Use a lightweight paddle that is the correct length for your height and paddling style.
- Life Jacket: Always wear a life jacket to ensure safety while on the water.

## 3. Techniques and Tips

- Paddling Strokes: Learn different paddling strokes, such as the forward stroke, J-stroke, and draw stroke, to maneuver your canoe effectively.
- Balance and Posture: Maintain balance by sitting low in the canoe and distributing weight evenly. Proper posture helps with control and reduces fatigue.
- Water Safety: Be aware of weather conditions and water currents, and always let someone know your route and expected return time.

# *October 6: CrossFit*

## 1. The Intensity of CrossFit

CrossFit is a high-intensity fitness program that combines elements of weightlifting, aerobic exercise, and bodyweight movements. It's designed to improve overall fitness by building strength, endurance, agility, and flexibility. CrossFit workouts, often referred to as WODs (Workouts of the Day), vary daily and challenge participants with different exercises and intensity levels. The community aspect of CrossFit, where participants encourage and support each other, adds to its appeal. CrossFit is known for its effectiveness in pushing physical limits and achieving rapid fitness gains.

## 2. Tools and Materials

- Kettlebells and Dumbbells: Use kettlebells and dumbbells for strength training exercises that target multiple muscle groups.
- Barbell and Plates: Incorporate a barbell with weight plates for Olympic lifts like the clean and jerk or snatch.
- Jump Rope: Include a jump rope in your workouts for cardiovascular conditioning and agility training.

## 3. Techniques and Tips

- Form and Technique: Prioritize proper form and technique to prevent injuries, especially when performing complex lifts or high-intensity movements.
- Scaling Workouts: Scale workouts to match your fitness level, gradually increasing intensity as you build strength and endurance.
- Recovery: Allow time for recovery between workouts to let your muscles heal and adapt to the increased demands.

# *October 7: Dance Fitness*

## 1. The Joy of Dance Fitness

Dance fitness combines the fun of dancing with the benefits of a cardiovascular workout. It includes popular programs like Zumba, hip-hop dance classes, and Latin dance workouts. Dance fitness routines are set to upbeat music and are designed to improve cardiovascular health, coordination, and flexibility while burning calories. The energetic and rhythmic movements make dance fitness an enjoyable way to stay active. Whether you're a seasoned dancer or a beginner, dance fitness offers a fun and social way to work out while learning new dance styles.

## 2. Tools and Materials

- Dance Sneakers: Wear supportive dance sneakers that allow for easy movement and protect your feet during high-impact routines.
- Water Bottle: Stay hydrated during your dance fitness sessions by keeping a water bottle nearby.
- Stretch Bands: Use stretch bands for warm-up and cool-down stretches to increase flexibility and prevent injury.

## 3. Techniques and Tips

- Follow the Beat: Stay in sync with the music by focusing on the rhythm and letting it guide your movements.
- Modify Moves: Modify dance moves to match your fitness level, making adjustments to reduce impact or increase intensity as needed.
- Enjoy the Process: Focus on having fun and expressing yourself through movement rather than perfecting every step. The joy of dancing is at the heart of dance fitness.

# *October 8: Disc Golf*

## 1. The Fun of Disc Golf

Disc golf is a sport that combines elements of golf and frisbee. Players throw a disc (similar to a frisbee) from a tee area towards a target, typically a metal basket, trying to complete each hole in the fewest throws possible. Disc golf is played on outdoor courses with varying terrain and obstacles, making each game unique and challenging. It's a low-cost, low-impact sport that provides exercise, fresh air, and the opportunity to enjoy nature. Disc golf can be played individually or in groups, making it a social activity that's accessible to people of all ages and skill levels.

## 2. Tools and Materials

- Discs: Use different types of discs for various shots, including drivers for long throws, mid-range discs for accuracy, and putters for short, controlled shots.
- Disc Golf Bag: Carry your discs and other gear in a disc golf bag designed to hold multiple discs and accessories.
- Scorecard: Keep track of your scores with a scorecard or a disc golf app that records your performance and helps you analyze your game.

## 3. Techniques and Tips

- Proper Grip: Master the proper grip for each type of disc to improve your accuracy and control.
- Disc Selection: Choose the right disc for each shot, considering factors like distance, wind, and obstacles.
- Course Strategy: Develop a strategy for each course, planning your throws to avoid obstacles and maximize your chances of landing close to the basket.

# October 9: Endurance Running

## 1. The Discipline of Endurance Running

Endurance running is a long-distance running discipline that tests your stamina, mental toughness, and physical conditioning. It includes activities like marathons, half-marathons, and ultra-marathons. Endurance running is not just about speed; it's about maintaining a steady pace over long distances, managing energy levels, and pushing through physical and mental barriers. This type of running builds cardiovascular endurance, strengthens muscles, and enhances mental resilience. Training for endurance running involves structured plans, including long runs, interval training, and recovery periods.

## 2. Tools and Materials

- Running Shoes: Invest in high-quality running shoes that provide support, cushioning, and comfort for long-distance running.
- Hydration Gear: Use hydration belts or backpacks to carry water and electrolytes during long runs.
- Running Watch: Track your distance, pace, and heart rate with a running watch to monitor your progress and optimize your training.

## 3. Techniques and Tips

- Pacing Strategy: Develop a pacing strategy that allows you to conserve energy for the later stages of the run, avoiding burnout early on.
- Fueling: Learn about proper fueling techniques, including when and what to eat before, during, and after long runs to maintain energy levels.
- Mental Toughness: Build mental toughness by practicing visualization, setting small milestones during runs, and staying positive even when the run gets challenging.

# *October 10: Exercise Routines*

## 1. The Structure of Exercise Routines

Exercise routines are structured plans that include a variety of exercises designed to achieve specific fitness goals, such as building strength, increasing flexibility, or improving cardiovascular health. A well-rounded exercise routine balances different types of exercises, including aerobic, strength training, and flexibility work. Whether you're a beginner or an experienced athlete, having a consistent exercise routine helps you stay motivated, track progress, and achieve your fitness objectives. Tailoring your exercise routine to your individual needs, preferences, and schedule is key to maintaining long-term fitness habits.

## 2. Tools and Materials

- Resistance Bands: Use resistance bands for strength training exercises that target different muscle groups with varying levels of resistance.
- Workout Journal: Keep a workout journal to record your exercises, sets, reps, and progress over time.
- Exercise Videos: Access exercise videos or apps that offer guided workouts to provide variety and instruction for your routine.

## 3. Techniques and Tips

- Goal Setting: Set clear, achievable goals for your exercise routine, whether it's increasing strength, losing weight, or improving endurance.
- Variety: Incorporate a variety of exercises into your routine to target different muscle groups and prevent boredom.
- Consistency: Stay consistent with your routine, gradually increasing intensity and duration as you progress.

# *October 11: Fencing*

## 1. The Precision of Fencing

Fencing is a competitive sport that involves swordplay between two opponents, using weapons like the foil, epee, or saber. It's a fast-paced and strategic sport that requires agility, precision, and quick reflexes. Fencing combines physical and mental challenges, as fencers must anticipate their opponent's moves, respond swiftly, and execute their own attacks with accuracy. The sport is deeply rooted in tradition, with a rich history of technique and etiquette. Practicing fencing improves coordination, speed, and tactical thinking, making it a unique and engaging form of exercise.

## 2. Tools and Materials

- Fencing Sword: Choose the appropriate sword for your style—foil, epee, or saber—each with its own rules and techniques.
- Protective Gear: Wear protective gear, including a mask, jacket, gloves, and chest protector, to ensure safety during matches.
- Fencing Shoes: Use specialized fencing shoes that provide grip, support, and flexibility for quick footwork.

## 3. Techniques and Tips

- Footwork Drills: Practice footwork drills to improve your agility and positioning, allowing you to move quickly and efficiently in the fencing piste.
- Blade Control: Focus on blade control, learning how to parry, riposte, and execute precise thrusts with your sword.
- Strategic Thinking: Develop strategic thinking by studying your opponents' habits and tendencies, planning your attacks and defenses accordingly.

# *October 12: Gymnastics*

## 1. The Art of Gymnastics

Gymnastics is a sport that combines strength, flexibility, balance, and coordination to perform a variety of exercises on apparatuses such as the balance beam, pommel horse, rings, and uneven bars. It's a highly disciplined sport that requires years of training to master the complex movements and routines. Gymnastics enhances overall physical fitness, including core strength, agility, and body awareness. It also fosters mental discipline and perseverance. Whether practiced competitively or recreationally, gymnastics offers a challenging and rewarding way to stay fit and agile.

## 2. Tools and Materials

- Gymnastics Mat: Use a thick, cushioned mat to practice floor exercises and landings safely.
- Balance Beam: Incorporate a balance beam into your training to develop balance, poise, and precision in your movements.
- Gymnastics Grips: Wear grips on your hands to protect your palms and enhance your grip on the bars during routines.

## 3. Techniques and Tips

- Flexibility Training: Incorporate daily stretching and flexibility exercises to improve your range of motion and prevent injuries.
- Strength Conditioning: Focus on strength conditioning exercises that build the muscle groups needed for specific gymnastics skills, such as push-ups, pull-ups, and core work.
- Practice Drills: Break down complex routines into smaller drills, mastering each element before combining them into full routines.

# October 13: Handball

## 1. The Speed of Handball

Handball is a fast-paced team sport that combines elements of soccer and basketball. It's played on a court where players pass, dribble, and shoot a ball into the opponent's goal. Handball requires speed, agility, teamwork, and quick reflexes, making it an exciting and physically demanding game. The sport is played professionally in many countries and is also a popular recreational activity. Handball is a great way to improve cardiovascular fitness, coordination, and teamwork skills. The game's dynamic nature makes it both challenging and fun, appealing to players of all ages.

## 2. Tools and Materials

- Handball: Use a regulation handball that is designed for the specific playing surface, whether indoors or outdoors.
- Goalkeeper Gloves: Wear goalkeeper gloves if you're playing as a goalie to protect your hands and improve your grip on the ball.
- Court Shoes: Use non-slip court shoes that provide traction, support, and cushioning for the quick movements required in handball.

## 3. Techniques and Tips

- Passing and Dribbling: Practice passing and dribbling drills to improve ball control and coordination with your teammates.
- Shooting Accuracy: Focus on shooting drills that enhance your accuracy and power when aiming for the goal.
- Defensive Strategies: Develop defensive strategies that involve anticipating the opponent's moves, positioning yourself effectively, and working as a team to block shots.

# *October 14: Ice Hockey*

## 1. The Intensity of Ice Hockey

Ice hockey is a high-speed, full-contact team sport played on an ice rink. Players use sticks to hit a puck into the opponent's goal, with the team scoring the most goals winning the game. Ice hockey requires a combination of speed, strength, agility, and teamwork. It's a physically demanding sport that improves cardiovascular fitness, muscle strength, and coordination. Ice hockey is also known for its fast pace and physicality, making it an exhilarating game to play and watch. The sport's unique challenges, such as skating on ice and handling the puck, add to its appeal.

## 2. Tools and Materials

- Hockey Stick: Choose a hockey stick that matches your playing style, with the right length, flex, and blade curve.
- Protective Gear: Wear protective gear, including a helmet, shoulder pads, elbow pads, shin guards, and gloves, to stay safe on the ice.
- Skates: Use ice skates that provide support, comfort, and agility, allowing you to maneuver quickly and effectively on the rink.

## 3. Techniques and Tips

- Skating Skills: Focus on improving your skating skills, including speed, agility, and balance, as they are fundamental to playing ice hockey.
- Puck Handling: Practice puck handling drills to enhance your control and precision when passing, shooting, or maneuvering around opponents.
- Team Coordination: Work on team coordination by developing strategies, communicating effectively, and understanding your role within the team.

# *October 15: Jogging*

## 1. The Simplicity of Jogging

Jogging is a form of running at a slower, more relaxed pace. It's a popular exercise that offers numerous health benefits, including improved cardiovascular fitness, weight management, and mental well-being. Jogging is accessible to people of all fitness levels and can be done almost anywhere, making it a convenient and low-cost way to stay active. The rhythmic motion of jogging helps to reduce stress, boost mood, and increase energy levels. Whether you're jogging in a park, on a treadmill, or along city streets, it's an effective way to maintain overall health and fitness.

## 2. Tools and Materials

- Running Shoes: Invest in a good pair of running shoes that provide cushioning, support, and comfort for your feet during jogs.
- Fitness Tracker: Use a fitness tracker to monitor your distance, pace, and heart rate, helping you track your progress and set goals.
- Reflective Gear: Wear reflective gear if you're jogging early in the morning or late in the evening to increase visibility and safety.

## 3. Techniques and Tips

- Warm-Up and Cool-Down: Always start with a warm-up to prepare your muscles and joints for jogging, and end with a cool-down to gradually reduce your heart rate.
- Pacing: Maintain a steady, comfortable pace that allows you to jog for extended periods without fatigue.
- Breathing Techniques: Practice rhythmic breathing techniques to optimize oxygen intake and reduce the risk of side stitches during your jog.

# October 16: Kickboxing

## 1. The Power of Kickboxing

Kickboxing is a high-intensity combat sport that combines elements of boxing and martial arts. It involves punching, kicking, and footwork, making it a full-body workout that improves cardiovascular fitness, strength, and agility. Kickboxing is also an effective self-defense practice, teaching you how to strike with power and precision. The sport is known for its intensity, providing a challenging workout that burns calories and builds muscle. Whether practiced in a gym, in a class, or at home, kickboxing offers a dynamic and empowering way to stay fit and strong.

## 2. Tools and Materials

- Boxing Gloves: Use boxing gloves to protect your hands and wrists during punches and strikes.
- Hand Wraps: Wear hand wraps under your gloves for additional support and protection of your knuckles and wrists.
- Punching Bag: Incorporate a punching bag into your training to practice strikes, build strength, and improve accuracy.

## 3. Techniques and Tips

- Proper Technique: Focus on mastering proper technique for punches and kicks to maximize power and prevent injuries.
- Combination Drills: Practice combination drills that involve sequences of punches and kicks, improving your coordination and speed.
- Conditioning: Include conditioning exercises such as jump rope, sprints, and bodyweight circuits to enhance your endurance and overall fitness for kickboxing.

# *October 17: Lacrosse*

## 1. The Speed of Lacrosse

Lacrosse is a fast-paced team sport that involves using a long-handled stick, known as a crosse, to catch, carry, and pass a small rubber ball with the goal of scoring in the opponent's net. It's a game that requires agility, speed, teamwork, and strategic thinking. Lacrosse is played both indoors and outdoors, with variations in rules and field size. The sport's combination of physical contact, quick transitions, and precise ball handling makes it exciting and challenging. Lacrosse improves cardiovascular fitness, hand-eye coordination, and teamwork skills, making it a popular choice for athletes of all ages.

## 2. Tools and Materials

- Lacrosse Stick: Choose a lacrosse stick that matches your position, with different lengths and designs for attackers, midfielders, and defenders.
- Protective Gear: Wear protective gear, including a helmet, gloves, shoulder pads, and mouthguard, to stay safe during play.
- Lacrosse Ball: Use a regulation lacrosse ball for practice and games, designed for optimal grip and control.

## 3. Techniques and Tips

- Catching and Passing: Practice catching and passing drills to improve your accuracy and speed in moving the ball up the field.
- Shooting: Focus on shooting techniques that enhance your power and precision when aiming for the goal.
- Team Strategy: Develop team strategies that involve quick transitions, effective communication, and understanding each player's role on the field.

# October 18: Marathon Training

## 1. The Commitment of Marathon Training

Marathon training involves preparing your body and mind to run a 26.2-mile race. It's a demanding and rewarding process that requires months of consistent training, discipline, and determination. Marathon training not only builds physical endurance but also mental toughness, as you push through long distances and challenging workouts. The training process includes a combination of long runs, speed work, strength training, and rest days. Completing a marathon is a significant achievement that reflects dedication and perseverance, making it a goal for runners of all levels.

## 2. Tools and Materials

- Running Shoes: Invest in high-quality running shoes that provide support, cushioning, and durability for long-distance running.
- Hydration System: Use a hydration belt or pack to carry water and electrolytes during long training runs.
- Training Plan: Follow a marathon training plan that outlines your workouts, mileage, and rest days over several months.

## 3. Techniques and Tips

- Pacing Strategy: Develop a pacing strategy that allows you to conserve energy and maintain a steady pace throughout the marathon.
- Fueling and Nutrition: Focus on proper fueling and nutrition, including pre-run meals, mid-run energy gels, and post-run recovery foods.
- Mental Preparation: Prepare mentally for the marathon by visualizing the race, setting small milestones, and staying positive through the training process.

# October 19: Netball

## 1. The Teamwork of Netball

Netball is a team sport similar to basketball but with distinct rules and no dribbling. It's played on a rectangular court with seven players on each team, aiming to score by shooting the ball through the opponent's goal ring. Netball requires agility, coordination, teamwork, and strategic play. It's a popular sport in many countries, particularly among women. Netball enhances cardiovascular fitness, improves hand-eye coordination, and promotes teamwork. The sport's fast-paced nature and emphasis on passing and positioning make it both challenging and enjoyable.

## 2. Tools and Materials

- Netball: Use a regulation netball that is designed for optimal grip and control during play.
- Netball Shoes: Wear shoes specifically designed for netball, offering support, cushioning, and traction for quick movements.
- Goal Post: Practice shooting with a netball goal post, ensuring it's the correct height for regulation play.

## 3. Techniques and Tips

- Passing Drills: Practice passing drills to improve accuracy, speed, and teamwork on the court.
- Shooting Technique: Focus on shooting technique, including hand positioning and follow-through, to increase your scoring accuracy.
- Court Awareness: Develop court awareness by understanding your positioning, anticipating the opponent's moves, and communicating effectively with teammates.

# *October 20: Obstacle Course Racing*

## 1. The Challenge of Obstacle Course Racing

Obstacle course racing (OCR) is a physical challenge that involves running a course filled with various obstacles, such as walls, ropes, mud pits, and climbing structures. OCR events, like Tough Mudder and Spartan Race, test participants' strength, endurance, agility, and mental grit. Training for OCR includes a combination of running, strength training, and obstacle-specific skills. OCR is not just about speed; it's about overcoming physical and mental challenges, working as a team, and pushing your limits. Completing an obstacle course race is a rewarding experience that showcases determination and resilience.

## 2. Tools and Materials

- Trail Running Shoes: Use trail running shoes with good grip and durability to handle the varied terrain and obstacles.
- Gloves: Wear gloves to protect your hands during rope climbs, walls, and other obstacles that require grip and strength.
- Hydration Pack: Carry a hydration pack to stay hydrated during long races, especially in hot or challenging conditions.

## 3. Techniques and Tips

- Strength Training: Incorporate strength training exercises that target the upper body, core, and legs to prepare for obstacles like walls and ropes.
- Obstacle Practice: Practice specific obstacles, such as monkey bars, rope climbs, and balance beams, to improve your technique and confidence.
- Pacing and Energy Management: Manage your energy by pacing yourself, taking short breaks when needed, and staying focused on the next obstacle.

# *October 21: Pilates*

## 1. The Core Strength of Pilates

Pilates is a low-impact exercise method that focuses on core strength, flexibility, and body alignment. It involves controlled movements and breathing techniques that engage the deep muscles of the abdomen, back, and pelvis. Pilates is suitable for people of all fitness levels and is often used for rehabilitation, posture improvement, and overall fitness. The exercises can be performed on a mat or using specialized equipment like the Reformer. Pilates improves muscle tone, balance, and coordination while reducing the risk of injury. It's a mindful practice that promotes a strong, flexible, and balanced body.

## 2. Tools and Materials

- Yoga Mat: Use a yoga mat to provide cushioning and support during mat-based Pilates exercises.
- Pilates Ring: Incorporate a Pilates ring into your workouts to add resistance and target specific muscle groups.
- Resistance Bands: Use resistance bands for added resistance and variety in your Pilates routine.

## 3. Techniques and Tips

- Breath Control: Focus on breath control, using your breath to support and enhance each movement.
- Precision and Alignment: Perform each exercise with precision, paying attention to proper alignment and form to maximize effectiveness and prevent injury.
- Consistent Practice: Practice Pilates consistently to build strength, improve flexibility, and achieve a balanced, well-aligned body.

# *October 22: Quidditch*

## 1. The Magic of Quidditch

Quidditch, inspired by the fictional sport from the Harry Potter series, is a real-world, mixed-gender sport that combines elements of rugby, dodgeball, and tag. It's played on a rectangular field with three hoops at each end, where players on brooms attempt to score points by throwing a ball (the Quaffle) through the opponent's hoops. Quidditch is a fast-paced and physically demanding game that requires speed, teamwork, and strategy. The sport has grown in popularity, with leagues and tournaments held around the world. Quidditch is a unique and inclusive sport that promotes physical fitness, teamwork, and a sense of community.

## 2. Tools and Materials

- Broomstick: Use a broomstick as part of the game's equipment, holding it between your legs while running, passing, and scoring.
- Quaffle: Play with a Quaffle, a slightly deflated volleyball used to score points by throwing it through the hoops.
- Hoops: Set up three hoops of varying heights at each end of the field for scoring.

## 3. Techniques and Tips

- Team Coordination: Focus on team coordination and communication to effectively pass the Quaffle, defend the hoops, and execute plays.
- Speed and Agility: Develop speed and agility through sprint drills and footwork exercises, as Quidditch requires quick movements and fast reflexes.
- Strategic Play: Plan strategic plays that involve the whole team, using decoys, feints, and coordinated attacks to outmaneuver the opponents.

# *October 23: Rock Climbing*

## 1. The Thrill of Rock Climbing

Rock climbing is a sport that involves ascending natural rock formations or artificial climbing walls using hands, feet, and specialized equipment. It's a physically demanding and mentally challenging activity that requires strength, endurance, and problem-solving skills. Rock climbing can be done indoors at climbing gyms or outdoors on cliffs and mountains. The sport offers a unique combination of physical exertion, mental focus, and the exhilaration of reaching new heights. Climbing improves muscle strength, flexibility, and balance while also fostering mental resilience and determination.

## 2. Tools and Materials

- Climbing Shoes: Wear climbing shoes with a snug fit and sticky rubber soles for better grip and control on the rock.
- Harness and Rope: Use a climbing harness and rope for safety, especially when climbing higher or more challenging routes.
- Chalk Bag: Carry a chalk bag to keep your hands dry and improve your grip on the rock.

## 3. Techniques and Tips

- Body Positioning: Focus on body positioning and balance, using your legs to push up rather than relying solely on your arms.
- Route Planning: Study the climbing route before you start, identifying key holds and sequences.
- Safety First: Always check your gear and climbing partner's setup before starting, and never climb without proper safety measures in place.

# *October 24: Soccer*

## 1. The Global Game of Soccer

Soccer, also known as football in many countries, is the world's most popular sport. It's played on a rectangular field with two teams of eleven players each, who aim to score by getting a ball into the opponent's goal. Soccer is a fast-paced game that requires teamwork, agility, endurance, and strategic thinking. The sport is played at all levels, from casual pickup games to professional leagues and international tournaments like the World Cup. Soccer improves cardiovascular fitness, coordination, and teamwork skills. Its universal appeal and accessibility make it a beloved sport around the world.

## 2. Tools and Materials

- Soccer Ball: Use a regulation soccer ball for practice and games, designed for optimal grip and control.
- Cleats: Wear soccer cleats that provide traction, support, and comfort on the field.
- Goal Nets: Set up goal nets for shooting practice, ensuring they are the correct size for the level of play.

## 3. Techniques and Tips

- Dribbling Skills: Practice dribbling drills to improve your control and ability to maneuver the ball past opponents.
- Passing and Shooting: Focus on passing and shooting techniques that enhance your accuracy and power when moving the ball or aiming for the goal.
- Game Strategy: Develop game strategies that involve effective communication, positioning, and understanding your role within the team.

# *October 25: Tennis*

## 1. The Elegance of Tennis

Tennis is a racquet sport played on a rectangular court with a net dividing the two sides. Players use racquets to hit a ball over the net, aiming to land it in the opponent's court in a way that prevents them from returning it. Tennis is played in singles (one-on-one) or doubles (two-on-two) formats. The sport requires agility, precision, endurance, and strategic thinking. Tennis improves cardiovascular fitness, hand-eye coordination, and mental focus. It's a versatile sport that can be enjoyed recreationally or competitively, offering a lifetime of physical and mental benefits.

## 2. Tools and Materials

- Tennis Racquet: Choose a tennis racquet that suits your playing style, with the right weight, grip size, and string tension.
- Tennis Balls: Use regulation tennis balls that provide consistent bounce and performance on the court.
- Tennis Shoes: Wear tennis shoes that offer support, cushioning, and traction for quick movements on the court.

## 3. Techniques and Tips

- Serve Practice: Focus on serving techniques that enhance your power, accuracy, and consistency when starting a point.
- Footwork: Practice footwork drills to improve your agility, balance, and ability to reach the ball quickly.
- Strategy and Tactics: Develop strategies and tactics that involve mixing up shots, exploiting your opponent's weaknesses, and maintaining control of the court.

# October 26: Ultimate Frisbee

## 1. The Spirit of Ultimate Frisbee

Ultimate Frisbee, often referred to as Ultimate, is a fast-paced, non-contact team sport played with a flying disc (Frisbee). The game combines elements of soccer, football, and basketball, with the objective of scoring points by catching the disc in the opponent's end zone. Ultimate is known for its emphasis on sportsmanship, self-officiating, and the "Spirit of the Game," which encourages respect, fair play, and camaraderie. The sport requires agility, speed, endurance, and teamwork. Ultimate Frisbee is popular in schools, colleges, and recreational leagues, offering a fun and inclusive way to stay active and build community.

## 2. Tools and Materials

- Flying Disc: Use a regulation Ultimate Frisbee disc designed for accurate flight and control.
- Cleats: Wear cleats that provide traction and support on grass or turf fields, allowing for quick movements and cuts.
- Cones: Set up cones to mark the boundaries of the field and the end zones for scoring.

## 3. Techniques and Tips

- Throwing Skills: Practice different throwing techniques, such as the forehand, backhand, and hammer throw, to improve your accuracy and versatility in the game.
- Catching Techniques: Focus on catching techniques, including the two-handed catch and the "clap catch," to secure the disc reliably during play.
- Field Awareness: Develop field awareness by understanding your positioning, anticipating the disc's flight path, and communicating effectively with your teammates.

# *October 27: Volleyball*

## 1. The Teamwork of Volleyball

Volleyball is a team sport played on a rectangular court divided by a net. The objective is to score points by sending the ball over the net and landing it in the opponent's court, with teams allowed up to three touches to return the ball. Volleyball requires coordination, agility, teamwork, and strategic play. The sport is played both indoors and on the beach, with variations in rules and court size. Volleyball improves cardiovascular fitness, hand-eye coordination, and communication skills. Its fast-paced nature and emphasis on teamwork make it a popular and exciting sport worldwide.

## 2. Tools and Materials

- Volleyball: Use a regulation volleyball designed for indoor or beach play, depending on your setting.
- Knee Pads: Wear knee pads to protect your knees during dives and quick movements on the court.
- Volleyball Net: Set up a volleyball net at the correct height for men's or women's play, ensuring it's secure and taut.

## 3. Techniques and Tips

- Serving Practice: Focus on serving techniques that enhance your accuracy, power, and consistency, whether you're performing an overhand or underhand serve.
- Blocking and Spiking: Practice blocking and spiking drills to improve your timing, reach, and effectiveness at the net.
- Team Communication: Develop team communication strategies that involve calling the ball, positioning yourself effectively, and supporting your teammates during play.

# *October 28: Weightlifting*

## 1. The Strength of Weightlifting

Weightlifting is a strength-based sport that involves lifting barbells loaded with weights in specific movements, such as the snatch and the clean and jerk. It's a competitive sport as well as a foundational exercise for building muscle strength, power, and endurance. Weightlifting requires proper technique, concentration, and mental discipline. The sport is not only about lifting heavy weights but also about improving form, balance, and coordination. Weightlifting is a key component of many fitness routines, helping to build muscle mass, increase metabolism, and improve overall physical performance.

## 2. Tools and Materials

- Barbell and Plates: Use a barbell with weight plates that can be adjusted to match your strength level and training goals.
- Weightlifting Belt: Wear a weightlifting belt to support your lower back and core during heavy lifts.
- Lifting Shoes: Use weightlifting shoes with a solid, non-compressible sole to provide stability and support during lifts.

## 3. Techniques and Tips

- Proper Form: Focus on maintaining proper form and technique for each lift, including keeping your back straight and using your legs to drive the weight.
- Progressive Overload: Apply the principle of progressive overload by gradually increasing the weight lifted over time to build strength and muscle.
- Recovery: Incorporate rest days and proper nutrition into your routine to allow your muscles to recover and grow after intense weightlifting sessions.

# *October 29: Xtreme Sports*

## 1. The Adrenaline of Xtreme Sports

Xtreme sports, also known as action sports, are high-risk, high-adrenaline activities that often involve speed, height, and a significant level of physical exertion. Examples include skateboarding, BMX, snowboarding, and base jumping. Xtreme sports attract thrill-seekers who enjoy pushing their physical and mental limits. These sports require a combination of strength, agility, balance, and fearlessness. Safety is paramount in Xtreme sports, with participants often wearing protective gear and undergoing rigorous training. The appeal of Xtreme sports lies in the challenge, the rush of adrenaline, and the sense of accomplishment that comes from mastering difficult and daring feats.

## 2. Tools and Materials

- Protective Gear: Wear helmets, pads, and other protective gear specific to the Xtreme sport you're participating in to minimize the risk of injury.
- Specialized Equipment: Use specialized equipment, such as skateboards, BMX bikes, or snowboards, that are designed for high-performance and durability.
- Action Camera: Capture your Xtreme sports experiences with an action camera mounted on your gear, allowing you to relive and share your adventures.

## 3. Techniques and Tips

- Skill Development: Focus on skill development and mastering the basics before attempting more advanced tricks or stunts.
- Safety First: Always prioritize safety by checking your equipment, practicing in controlled environments, and knowing your limits.
- Mental Preparation: Develop mental toughness and confidence by visualizing successful performances and staying calm under pressure.

# *October 30: Yoga*

## 1. The Harmony of Yoga

Yoga is a holistic practice that combines physical postures (asanas), breath control (pranayama), and meditation to promote physical, mental, and spiritual well-being. It's a versatile practice that can be tailored to meet individual needs, whether for relaxation, flexibility, strength, or inner peace. Yoga has been practiced for thousands of years and offers numerous benefits, including improved flexibility, strength, balance, and stress reduction. Yoga can be practiced in various styles, from the gentle and restorative to the vigorous and dynamic, making it accessible to people of all ages and fitness levels.

## 2. Tools and Materials

- Yoga Mat: Use a non-slip yoga mat to provide stability and comfort during your practice.
- Yoga Blocks: Incorporate yoga blocks into your practice to assist with balance and alignment in various poses.
- Yoga Strap: Use a yoga strap to deepen stretches and improve flexibility in your practice.

## 3. Techniques and Tips

- Breath Awareness: Focus on your breath throughout your yoga practice, using it to guide your movements and maintain mindfulness.
- Start Slow: Begin with beginner-friendly poses and gradually work your way up to more advanced sequences as your flexibility and strength improve.
- Consistency: Practice yoga regularly, even if it's just for a few minutes each day, to experience the full benefits of this holistic practice.

## *October 31: Zumba*

### 1. The Energy of Zumba

Zumba is a dance-based fitness program that combines Latin and international music with dance moves to create a fun and energetic workout. Zumba routines incorporate interval training—alternating between fast and slow rhythms—to improve cardiovascular fitness, burn calories, and tone muscles. The high-energy, party-like atmosphere of Zumba classes makes it a popular choice for those looking to enjoy exercise in a social and motivating environment. Zumba is accessible to people of all fitness levels, offering a full-body workout that's as enjoyable as it is effective.

### 2. Tools and Materials

- Dance Sneakers: Wear supportive dance sneakers that allow for easy movement and protect your feet during high-impact routines.
- Water Bottle: Stay hydrated during your Zumba sessions by keeping a water bottle nearby.
- Stretch Bands: Use stretch bands for warm-up and cool-down stretches to increase flexibility and prevent injury.

### 3. Techniques and Tips

- Follow the Beat: Stay in sync with the music by focusing on the rhythm and letting it guide your movements.
- Modify Moves: Modify dance moves to match your fitness level, making adjustments to reduce impact or increase intensity as needed.
- Enjoy the Process: Focus on having fun and expressing yourself through movement rather than perfecting every step. The joy of dancing is at the heart of Zumba fitness.

## *Conclusion for October*

October has been a month dedicated to elevating both your physical and mental health through a diverse range of sports and fitness activities. From the adrenaline of Xtreme sports to the calm focus of yoga, you've explored how movement and exercise can enhance your overall well-being. Whether you've found a new passion in a particular sport or simply enjoyed staying active, these activities are all about improving your strength, endurance, and mental clarity. As you move forward, continue incorporating these practices into your routine to maintain a healthy and balanced lifestyle, staying motivated and challenged along the way.

# November: Travel and Exploration

*November is a month dedicated to travel and exploration, encouraging you to step out of your comfort zone and discover the beauty, culture, and adventure the world has to offer. Whether you're traversing through rugged landscapes, immersing yourself in different cultures, or seeking thrilling experiences, this month's activities are designed to inspire wanderlust and provide unforgettable memories. Each day introduces you to a new way to explore, whether it's through physically challenging adventures or serene, reflective journeys.*

# *November 1: Adventure Travel*

## 1. The Thrill of Adventure Travel

Adventure travel is about pushing boundaries, both physically and mentally. It's not just about the destination but the journey, filled with unexpected challenges and exhilarating experiences. Whether it's white-water rafting in the Amazon, trekking through the Himalayas, or exploring the Sahara by camel, adventure travel immerses you in the environment and culture of a place. It offers a unique perspective that typical tourism often misses, giving you stories to tell for a lifetime. Adventure travel is more than just an activity; it's a way to break out of the routine, challenge yourself, and discover new strengths and passions.

## 2. Tools and Materials

- Versatile Backpack: Invest in a high-quality backpack that can handle different terrains and weather conditions, offering both comfort and durability.
- Portable Charger: A portable charger is essential for keeping your devices powered up in remote areas where electricity is scarce.
- Travel Insurance: Ensure you have comprehensive travel insurance that covers adventure activities, providing peace of mind in case of accidents.

## 3. Techniques and Tips

- Research Extensively: Before embarking on an adventure trip, research the local customs, climate, and terrain to be well-prepared.
- Physical Preparation: Train for the physical demands of your trip. Whether it's hiking, climbing, or diving, ensure you're fit enough to handle the challenges.
- Pack Smart: Pack light but efficiently, focusing on multi-purpose gear that can be used in various situations. For example, a waterproof jacket that doubles as a windbreaker can be invaluable.

# *November 2: Backpacking*

## 1. The Freedom of Backpacking

Backpacking is a journey of exploration and self-discovery. With just a pack on your back, you can traverse the world, experiencing cultures and landscapes on a deeply personal level. Backpacking is not just about seeing the sights; it's about immersing yourself in the experience, from staying in hostels and sharing stories with fellow travelers to navigating foreign cities on your own. This form of travel encourages independence, resilience, and a deep appreciation for simplicity. The freedom to move at your own pace and the thrill of the unknown make backpacking a unique and rewarding way to explore the world.

## 2. Tools and Materials

- Lightweight Gear: Invest in ultralight gear to reduce strain on your back, including a lightweight tent, sleeping bag, and cooking stove.
- Water Filtration System: A portable water filter is crucial for staying hydrated, especially in areas where clean water is not readily available.
- Travel Journal: Keep a travel journal to document your experiences, thoughts, and the people you meet along the way.

## 3. Techniques and Tips

- Learn Basic Language Skills: Knowing a few phrases in the local language can make a big difference in your interactions and ease of travel.
- Budget Wisely: Stretch your budget by choosing affordable accommodations, cooking your meals, and using public transportation.
- Stay Safe: Always be aware of your surroundings, keep copies of important documents, and inform someone of your travel plans, especially when venturing into remote areas.

# November 3: Camping

## 1. The Simplicity of Camping

Camping allows you to escape the distractions of modern life and reconnect with nature. Whether in a remote forest, by a serene lake, or in a well-equipped campsite, camping offers the chance to enjoy the natural world in its purest form. It's an opportunity to slow down, breathe fresh air, and enjoy the simple pleasures of life, like cooking over a campfire, stargazing, or waking up to the sounds of birds. Camping fosters a sense of self-reliance and adventure, whether you're solo or with family and friends. It's a versatile activity that can be as rugged or as comfortable as you choose.

## 2. Tools and Materials

- All-Season Tent: Choose an all-season tent that can withstand various weather conditions, ensuring a safe and comfortable shelter.
- Camp Kitchen Gear: Invest in compact, durable cooking equipment, including a portable stove, pots, and utensils, to prepare meals in the wilderness.
- Sleeping System: A quality sleeping bag paired with a sleeping pad or air mattress can make a huge difference in comfort during overnight stays.

## 3. Techniques and Tips

- Practice Fire Safety: Learn how to build, manage, and extinguish a campfire safely, and always follow local regulations regarding open fires.
- Leave No Trace: Follow the principles of Leave No Trace to minimize your environmental impact, including proper waste disposal and respecting wildlife.
- Stay Organized: Keep your campsite organized to make your camping experience more enjoyable and to ensure that all your gear is easily accessible.

# *November 4: Cave Exploring*

## 1. The Mystery of Cave Exploring

Cave exploring, or spelunking, offers a unique glimpse into the earth's hidden chambers and underground worlds. It's an activity that combines adventure, geology, and a sense of discovery. Caves can be mysterious and beautiful, with stalactites, stalagmites, and underground rivers creating surreal landscapes. Exploring these natural wonders requires physical stamina, technical skills, and a respect for the delicate ecosystems found within. Cave exploring can range from easy, guided tours in well-lit caverns to challenging expeditions that involve crawling through narrow passages and rappelling into deep chambers.

## 2. Tools and Materials

- Climbing Harness: For more technical caves, a climbing harness with ropes and carabiners is essential for safety and maneuverability.
- Headlamps and Backup Lights: A reliable headlamp with backup lights and extra batteries is crucial for navigating the dark, often damp, cave environments.
- Protective Clothing: Wear durable, moisture-wicking clothing and gloves to protect against sharp rocks, cold temperatures, and potential scrapes.

## 3. Techniques and Tips

- Always Explore in Groups: Never explore caves alone. Always go with a group and ensure everyone is aware of the plan and has the necessary skills.
- Respect the Environment: Avoid touching or damaging formations, and follow the cave's rules to preserve its natural beauty.
- Stay Calm: If you encounter tight spaces or unexpected challenges, stay calm and think through the situation carefully. Panic can make difficult situations worse.

# *November 5: Cultural Tours*

## 1. The Enrichment of Cultural Tours

Cultural tours provide an immersive experience into the history, traditions, and lifestyle of a place. Unlike typical sightseeing, cultural tours focus on deep, meaningful interactions with local communities and environments. They often include visits to historical sites, museums, and traditional villages, where you can learn about the customs, languages, and beliefs that shape a culture. These tours are not only educational but also transformative, offering a new perspective on the world. They encourage respect, understanding, and appreciation for the diversity of human life and provide opportunities to connect with people in ways that go beyond superficial tourism.

## 2. Tools and Materials

- Translation Guide or App: A translation guide or app can help bridge language barriers, allowing you to communicate more effectively with locals.
- Cultural Etiquette Guide: Familiarize yourself with the cultural norms and etiquette of the region to show respect and avoid unintentional offense.
- Camera with High Zoom: A camera with a high zoom capability allows you to capture detailed images of cultural artifacts and distant landmarks.

## 3. Techniques and Tips

- Be a Respectful Observer: When visiting sacred sites or cultural events, observe respectfully without imposing or disrupting the atmosphere.
- Engage with Locals: Take the time to engage with locals, asking questions and showing genuine interest in their stories and way of life.
- Learn Before You Go: Research the history, customs, and challenges of the region before your trip to gain a deeper understanding and appreciation during your tour.

# *November 6: Desert Camping*

## 1. The Solitude of Desert Camping

Desert camping offers an experience of unparalleled solitude and stark beauty. Unlike forest or mountain camping, desert camping brings you into a landscape of vast horizons, towering sand dunes, and brilliant night skies. The silence and space of the desert provide a serene environment, perfect for reflection and stargazing. However, the desert's harsh conditions—extreme temperatures, limited water, and fragile ecosystems—require careful planning and respect. Desert camping is about embracing simplicity and the rawness of nature, away from the comforts of modern life. It's an opportunity to experience the wilderness in one of its most extreme forms.

## 2. Tools and Materials

- Desert-Ready Tent: Choose a tent with good ventilation and protection against sand and wind, essential for a comfortable night's sleep in the desert.
- Water Storage: Carry an ample supply of water in durable, collapsible containers, as water sources are scarce in desert environments.
- Sunshade or Tarp: A sunshade or tarp can provide much-needed relief from the intense desert sun during the day.

## 3. Techniques and Tips

- Plan for Temperature Swings: The desert can be scorching hot during the day and freezing cold at night. Pack clothing that can handle these temperature extremes.
- Navigational Tools: Use GPS, maps, and a compass to navigate, as landmarks can be difficult to identify in the desert, and getting lost is a serious risk.
- Respect Wildlife: Be cautious of desert wildlife such as snakes and scorpions. Learn how to identify them and avoid disturbing their habitats.

# November 7: Eco-Tourism

## 1. The Responsibility of Eco-Tourism

Eco-tourism is more than just a travel trend; it's a commitment to sustainable travel that respects both the environment and local communities. Eco-tourism involves visiting natural areas that are often remote and pristine, with the goal of conserving the environment and improving the well-being of local people. It encourages a low-impact, environmentally conscious approach to travel, where visitors engage in activities that promote conservation, education, and sustainable development. Eco-tourism offers a way to see the world without harming it, fostering a deeper connection to nature and a greater understanding of the challenges facing our planet.

## 2. Tools and Materials

- Reusable Utensils and Containers: Reduce your environmental impact by bringing reusable utensils, water bottles, and containers, minimizing the need for disposable products.
- Eco-Friendly Toiletries: Use biodegradable soaps, shampoos, and sunscreens that don't harm the local ecosystems, particularly in sensitive areas like coral reefs.
- Solar-Powered Gadgets: Opt for solar-powered chargers and lights to reduce your carbon footprint during your travels.

## 3. Techniques and Tips

- Support Local Economies: Choose locally-owned accommodations, tour operators, and restaurants to ensure your money supports the local economy.
- Minimize Waste: Practice waste reduction by avoiding single-use plastics, recycling whenever possible, and leaving no trace in natural areas.
- Educate Yourself: Take the time to learn about the environmental issues affecting the regions you visit, and consider how you can contribute positively to conservation efforts.

# *November 8: Fishing*

## 1. The Patience of Fishing

Fishing is an age-old practice that combines skill, patience, and a deep connection to nature. Whether you're casting a line into a tranquil lake, a fast-moving river, or the open sea, fishing offers a unique way to engage with the natural world. It's a contemplative activity, where the rhythm of casting and reeling becomes almost meditative. Fishing teaches patience, as waiting for a bite can take hours, but the reward of landing a fish—whether you keep it or release it—brings a sense of accomplishment. Fishing can be a solitary pursuit or a social activity, offering opportunities to bond with others in a shared love for the outdoors.

## 2. Tools and Materials

- Rod and Reel: Choose a fishing rod and reel suited to the type of fishing you plan to do, whether freshwater, saltwater, or fly fishing.
- Tackle Box: A well-organized tackle box with a variety of hooks, lures, lines, and sinkers is essential for a successful fishing trip.
- Bait: Depending on your target species, bring the appropriate bait, such as live worms, minnows, or artificial lures.

## 3. Techniques and Tips

- Learn the Local Rules: Familiarize yourself with local fishing regulations, including licensing requirements, catch limits, and seasonal restrictions.
- Master Basic Knots: Learn a few essential fishing knots, such as the improved clinch knot and the loop knot, to secure your lines and lures effectively.
- Respect the Waterways: Always leave the fishing area cleaner than you found it, and practice catch and release whenever possible to preserve fish populations.

# *November 9: Glamping*

## 1. The Comfort of Glamping

Glamping, or glamorous camping, offers the best of both worlds—the beauty of nature with the comforts of luxury. Unlike traditional camping, which involves roughing it in the wilderness, glamping provides amenities such as comfortable beds, electricity, and even gourmet meals, all set in stunning natural locations. Whether staying in a safari tent, a yurt, or a treehouse, glamping allows you to experience the great outdoors without sacrificing comfort. It's perfect for those who want to connect with nature but prefer to do so in style. Glamping can be as adventurous or as relaxing as you choose, offering a unique way to unwind and enjoy the environment.

## 2. Tools and Materials

- Luxury Tent or Yurt: Stay in a spacious, well-equipped tent or yurt that includes comfortable bedding, heating or cooling, and stylish furnishings.
- Outdoor Cooking Gear: Glamping often involves gourmet cooking outdoors, so bring high-quality cooking equipment or take advantage of provided amenities.
- Decorative Touches: Enhance the ambiance with fairy lights, lanterns, and comfortable outdoor furniture, making your glamping site both cozy and inviting.

## 3. Techniques and Tips

- Choose the Right Location: Select a glamping site that offers the activities and natural surroundings you enjoy, whether it's near a beach, in a forest, or by a river.
- Embrace the Luxury: Take full advantage of the amenities, whether it's soaking in a hot tub under the stars or enjoying a gourmet breakfast in bed.
- Disconnect to Reconnect: Use your glamping experience as an opportunity to disconnect from technology and reconnect with nature and loved ones.

# *November 10: Hiking*

## 1. The Adventure of Hiking

Hiking is one of the most accessible ways to explore the natural world, offering a physical challenge coupled with the rewards of breathtaking scenery and a sense of accomplishment. Whether you're traversing forest trails, climbing mountain paths, or walking along coastal cliffs, hiking provides a unique opportunity to experience nature up close. It's an activity that can be tailored to any fitness level, from leisurely walks on flat trails to challenging ascents that test your endurance. Hiking allows you to disconnect from the hustle of everyday life, immerse yourself in the beauty of the landscape, and find peace in the rhythm of your footsteps.

## 2. Tools and Materials

- Trail-Ready Footwear: Invest in high-quality hiking boots or shoes that provide support, grip, and comfort for various terrains.
- Hydration System: A hydration pack or water bottles are essential for staying hydrated on the trail, especially on longer hikes.
- First Aid Kit: A compact first aid kit should always be in your pack, equipped with bandages, antiseptic wipes, and pain relievers for minor injuries.

## 3. Techniques and Tips

- Know Your Route: Study maps and trail guides before heading out, and make sure to inform someone of your planned route and expected return time.
- Pace Yourself: Start your hike at a comfortable pace, allowing time for breaks, especially on steep or challenging sections.
- Stay Safe: Carry a whistle, flashlight, and emergency shelter in case you encounter difficulties or need to spend the night on the trail unexpectedly.

# *November 11: Island Hopping*

## 1. The Freedom of Island Hopping

Island hopping offers the thrill of exploring multiple islands within a single trip, each with its own unique landscape, culture, and attractions. Whether in the Mediterranean, the Caribbean, or Southeast Asia, island hopping allows you to experience the diversity of each island, from pristine beaches and coral reefs to historic towns and local markets. It's a travel style that combines adventure with relaxation, offering the freedom to move at your own pace and the opportunity to discover hidden gems. Island hopping is perfect for those who love the sea, as it often involves boat trips, snorkeling, and beachcombing, all while enjoying the changing scenery and cultures.

## 2. Tools and Materials

- Waterproof Bag: A waterproof bag or dry sack is essential for protecting your belongings during boat transfers and water activities.
- Snorkeling Gear: Bring your own snorkeling gear to explore underwater life at your leisure, as not all islands provide rentals.
- Island Guidebook: A guidebook specifically about the islands you're visiting can help you discover lesser-known spots and local experiences.

## 3. Techniques and Tips

- Plan Flexibly: While it's good to have a general plan, leave room for flexibility as ferry schedules can change and you might discover new places you want to spend more time.
- Travel Light: Pack light, as you'll be moving frequently and often by boat, where space can be limited.
- Embrace Local Culture: Take the time to learn about the local customs and try regional foods, as each island can offer a different cultural experience.

# *November 12: Jungle Trekking*

## 1. The Adventure of Jungle Trekking

Jungle trekking is a thrilling and immersive way to experience the world's most diverse ecosystems. Whether in the Amazon, Borneo, or the Congo, trekking through the jungle brings you face-to-face with unique wildlife, towering trees, and hidden waterfalls. It's a physically demanding activity that requires stamina, navigation skills, and a respect for the natural world. The jungle's dense foliage and rugged terrain can be challenging, but the rewards are immense: seeing animals in their natural habitats, discovering rare plants, and experiencing the raw beauty of the rainforest. Jungle trekking is not just a hike; it's an exploration of some of the most remote and untouched places on earth.

## 2. Tools and Materials

- Machete: In some jungles, a machete is necessary for cutting through dense vegetation, creating a path, and ensuring safe passage.
- Insect Protection: Strong insect repellent and protective clothing are essential to protect against mosquitoes and other biting insects common in jungle environments.
- Water Purification System: A water purification system, such as a filter or tablets, is crucial for ensuring safe drinking water in areas where clean sources are scarce.

## 3. Techniques and Tips

- Hire a Local Guide: A knowledgeable local guide can enhance your trekking experience by identifying wildlife, explaining local customs, and ensuring your safety.
- Stay Hydrated and Nourished: The jungle's heat and humidity can quickly lead to dehydration and fatigue, so carry plenty of water and high-energy snacks.
- Move Carefully: The jungle floor can be slippery and uneven, so move carefully to avoid falls and injuries, and always watch where you step.

# *November 13: Kayaking*

## 1. The Serenity of Kayaking

Kayaking offers a unique perspective on the world, allowing you to glide silently through water, whether on tranquil lakes, meandering rivers, or the open sea. It's an activity that combines physical fitness with a deep connection to nature. From the seat of a kayak, you can explore remote coastlines, paddle through mangrove forests, or navigate white-water rapids. Kayaking is versatile, offering both the thrill of adventure and the peace of solitude, depending on the water you choose. It's an activity that can be enjoyed by beginners and experienced paddlers alike, providing an intimate way to experience the beauty of water landscapes.

## 2. Tools and Materials

- Sit-On-Top Kayak: Ideal for beginners, a sit-on-top kayak is stable and easy to use, making it perfect for calm waters and casual paddling.
- Sea Kayak: For those interested in ocean kayaking, a sea kayak offers greater speed and stability, designed to handle waves and open water.
- Dry Bag: Keep your essentials dry by using a dry bag, especially important when kayaking in rougher waters or on extended trips.

## 3. Techniques and Tips

- Learn Basic Paddling Strokes: Master the forward stroke, sweep stroke, and draw stroke to navigate your kayak effectively and efficiently.
- Safety First: Always wear a life jacket, even if you're a strong swimmer, and be aware of weather and water conditions before heading out.
- Respect Wildlife: Maintain a respectful distance from wildlife, especially nesting birds or marine animals, to avoid disturbing their natural behaviors.

# *November 14: Luxury Travel*

## 1. The Indulgence of Luxury Travel

Luxury travel is about experiencing the world in the most comfortable and exclusive way possible. It's not just about high-end hotels and fine dining, but about personalized service, unique experiences, and attention to detail. Whether it's a private island retreat, a five-star safari, or a first-class cruise, luxury travel offers unparalleled comfort, privacy, and style. It's an opportunity to relax and rejuvenate in beautiful surroundings, with every need anticipated and met. Luxury travel allows you to experience destinations in a way that is both immersive and indulgent, creating unforgettable memories.

## 2. Tools and Materials

- Designer Luggage: High-quality, stylish luggage that combines form and function is essential for luxury travel.
- Travel Concierge Service: Utilize a concierge service to arrange exclusive experiences, from private tours to bespoke dining experiences.
- Luxury Travel Apps: Use apps that cater to luxury travelers, offering insider access, VIP experiences, and seamless booking services.

## 3. Techniques and Tips

- Plan Ahead for Exclusivity: Luxury travel often involves exclusive experiences that require advance booking, so plan ahead to secure the best options.
- Personalize Your Trip: Tailor your travel experiences to your interests, whether it's a private cooking class with a renowned chef or a guided art tour with a local expert.
- Relax and Indulge: Allow yourself to fully enjoy the luxury experience, from the plush accommodations to the gourmet meals, and take advantage of all the amenities offered.

# *November 15: Mountain Climbing*

## 1. The Challenge of Mountain Climbing

Mountain climbing is the ultimate test of physical and mental endurance. It involves scaling steep, often rugged terrains to reach summits that offer breathtaking views and a profound sense of achievement. Whether you're climbing a high-altitude peak or a challenging rock face, mountain climbing requires careful planning, physical fitness, and the ability to navigate difficult and sometimes dangerous conditions. It's an activity that demands respect for nature, as weather conditions can change rapidly, and the terrain can be unforgiving. The rewards, however, are immense—standing on a summit, looking out over the world, and knowing you've conquered both the mountain and your own limits.

## 2. Tools and Materials

- Technical Climbing Gear: Ropes, harnesses, carabiners, and belay devices are essential for safe ascents, especially on technical routes.
- Mountaineering Boots: High-quality boots designed for mountain terrain provide the necessary grip, insulation, and ankle support.
- Crampons and Ice Axes: For climbing on ice or snow-covered peaks, crampons and ice axes are crucial for maintaining traction and safety.

## 3. Techniques and Tips

- Acclimate Properly: To avoid altitude sickness, take the time to acclimatize by ascending slowly and spending time at intermediate elevations.
- Plan for All Conditions: Weather in the mountains can change quickly; always be prepared for cold, wind, and storms, even on short climbs.
- Respect the Mountain: Climbing requires humility and respect for nature. Know your limits, and don't take unnecessary risks—sometimes turning back is the wisest choice.

# *November 16: National Park Tours*

## 1. The Beauty of National Park Tours

National parks are the crown jewels of natural conservation, preserving some of the world's most stunning landscapes and diverse ecosystems. Touring these parks offers the chance to see breathtaking scenery, from towering mountains and vast deserts to lush forests and serene lakes. National park tours can be as leisurely or as adventurous as you like, with opportunities for hiking, wildlife viewing, camping, and photography. These tours provide a deeper appreciation for nature, highlighting the importance of conservation and the need to protect these wild places for future generations. National parks are a refuge for both wildlife and people, offering a space to reconnect with the natural world.

## 2. Tools and Materials

- National Park Pass: An annual pass grants access to multiple parks, making it a cost-effective choice for frequent visitors.
- Field Guides: Bring field guides for the local flora and fauna, enhancing your understanding and appreciation of the park's natural inhabitants.
- Binoculars and Camera: Binoculars for wildlife viewing and a camera for capturing the stunning landscapes are essential for any national park tour.

## 3. Techniques and Tips

- Respect Park Regulations: Follow all park rules, including staying on marked trails, respecting wildlife, and adhering to camping regulations, to protect the park's natural resources.
- Plan Ahead for Popular Parks: Some national parks, like Yellowstone or Yosemite, can be very crowded during peak seasons. Plan ahead by booking accommodations and permits well in advance.
- Take Your Time: Don't rush through the parks. Take the time to explore lesser-known areas, observe wildlife, and enjoy the tranquility of nature.

# November 17: Off-Roading

## 1. The Excitement of Off-Roading

Off-roading is a high-adrenaline activity that involves driving specialized vehicles over rugged, unpaved terrain. It's about pushing the limits of what vehicles can do, navigating through mud, rocks, sand, and steep inclines. Off-roading offers a unique way to explore remote and wild landscapes, from deserts and forests to mountains and riverbeds. It's a sport that requires skill, control, and a good understanding of your vehicle's capabilities. Off-roading can be a solo adventure or a group activity, with clubs and events bringing enthusiasts together to share their passion. The thrill of conquering challenging terrain and the freedom to explore off-the-beaten-path destinations make off-roading an exciting and rewarding pursuit.

## 2. Tools and Materials

- 4x4 Off-Road Vehicle: A four-wheel-drive vehicle with high ground clearance, all-terrain tires, and a robust suspension system is essential for tackling rough terrain.
- Recovery Gear: Always carry recovery gear, including a winch, tow straps, and a shovel, to handle potential challenges like getting stuck in mud or sand.
- Navigation Tools: A GPS unit and detailed maps are crucial for navigating remote areas where roads may be unmarked or non-existent.

## 3. Techniques and Tips

- Know Your Vehicle: Understand your vehicle's capabilities and limitations, including how to engage four-wheel drive, use low gears, and adjust tire pressure for different terrains.
- Respect the Environment: Stick to designated trails to avoid damaging fragile ecosystems and always follow the principle of Tread Lightly to minimize your environmental impact.
- Safety in Numbers: Off-roading can be risky, especially in remote areas, so it's wise to travel with another vehicle or group for added safety and assistance if needed.

# *November 18: Photography Tours*

## 1. The Art of Photography Tours

Photography tours combine the joy of travel with the art of capturing stunning images. These tours are designed for photographers of all levels, offering guided experiences in breathtaking locations, from vibrant cities to remote wildernesses. Photography tours allow you to focus on your craft while exploring new environments, with expert guides providing tips and insights to help you improve your skills. Whether you're interested in wildlife, landscapes, architecture, or street photography, these tours offer the opportunity to create a portfolio of images that reflect your personal style and the beauty of the world around you. It's an immersive experience that hones your technical skills while inspiring your creativity.

## 2. Tools and Materials

- DSLR or Mirrorless Camera: A high-quality camera with interchangeable lenses offers the versatility needed to capture a wide range of subjects, from landscapes to wildlife.
- Tripod: A sturdy tripod is essential for sharp, stable shots, especially in low light or when using long exposures.
- Lens Kit: Bring a variety of lenses, such as a wide-angle lens for landscapes, a telephoto lens for wildlife, and a prime lens for portraits or street photography.

## 3. Techniques and Tips

- Golden Hour Shooting: The soft, warm light during the golden hours of sunrise and sunset is ideal for photography, enhancing colors and creating beautiful shadows.
- Composition Techniques: Focus on composition by using techniques like the rule of thirds, leading lines, and framing to create visually compelling images.
- Patience and Persistence: Great photography often requires patience, especially when waiting for the perfect light, wildlife behavior, or a scene to unfold naturally.

# *November 19: Quadcopter Flying*

## 1. The Innovation of Quadcopter Flying

Quadcopter flying, or drone flying, is a modern hobby that combines technology with creativity and exploration. Quadcopters, or drones, offer a bird's-eye view of the world, allowing you to capture stunning aerial shots and videos. They are used for various purposes, from professional photography and videography to surveying and recreational flying. Quadcopter flying offers a unique perspective, enabling you to explore hard-to-reach areas, monitor wildlife, and even race against other drones. It's a hobby that requires skill, precision, and an understanding of the technology, offering endless possibilities for innovation and creativity.

## 2. Tools and Materials

- Quadcopter with Camera: Choose a quadcopter equipped with a high-resolution camera if your focus is on aerial photography or videography.
- Remote Controller: Use a remote controller with advanced features like GPS, altitude hold, and camera gimbal control for smooth and stable flying.
- Extra Batteries: Drones often have limited flight time, so bring extra batteries to extend your flying sessions and capture more footage.

## 3. Techniques and Tips

- Practice Basic Maneuvers: Start by practicing basic maneuvers such as takeoff, landing, hovering, and directional flying to build your confidence and control.
- Follow Regulations: Familiarize yourself with local drone regulations, including altitude limits, no-fly zones, and privacy laws, to avoid legal issues.
- Respect Privacy: Be mindful of privacy concerns when flying your quadcopter, avoiding flying over private property or people without permission.

# *November 20: Road Tripping*

## 1. The Freedom of Road Tripping

Road tripping is a classic form of travel that offers the freedom to explore new places at your own pace. It's about the journey as much as the destination, with the open road providing endless opportunities for discovery and adventure. Road trips can take you through scenic landscapes, charming small towns, and iconic landmarks, all on your own schedule. Whether it's a cross-country expedition or a weekend getaway, road tripping allows you to experience the world in a way that is flexible, spontaneous, and deeply personal. It's an opportunity to create your own adventure, with the freedom to stop wherever and whenever you choose.

## 2. Tools and Materials

- Reliable Vehicle: Ensure your vehicle is in good condition for the journey, with regular maintenance and checks before hitting the road.
- Navigation Tools: Use GPS, maps, and a navigation app to plan your route, with room for detours and spontaneous stops.
- Camping Gear: If you plan to camp along the way, bring camping gear including a tent, sleeping bag, and portable stove for cooking meals.

## 3. Techniques and Tips

- Plan Your Route: While spontaneity is part of the fun, having a general route and knowing your key destinations can help ensure you don't miss important sights.
- Stay Flexible: Be open to changes in your itinerary, whether it's taking a detour to see an unexpected attraction or extending your stay in a place you love.
- Budget Wisely: Road trips can be as budget-friendly or as luxurious as you like. Plan your budget to include fuel, food, accommodations, and any activities you want to do along the way.

# November 21: Sailing

## 1. The Adventure of Sailing

Sailing is a timeless and exhilarating way to explore the world's waterways, whether on a peaceful lake, along a rugged coastline, or across the open ocean. It combines the thrill of adventure with the tranquility of nature, as you navigate your vessel using wind power alone. Sailing offers a deep connection to the elements, with the wind, water, and sky as your companions. It's a skill that requires knowledge, precision, and a respect for the sea, offering a unique perspective on travel. Whether you're racing, cruising, or simply enjoying a day on the water, sailing provides a sense of freedom and self-reliance that is unmatched by other forms of travel.

## 2. Tools and Materials

- Sailboat: Whether you're sailing a small dinghy or a large yacht, ensure your sailboat is well-maintained and equipped for your journey.
- Navigation Tools: Use nautical charts, a compass, and GPS to navigate, especially when sailing in unfamiliar waters.
- Safety Gear: Life jackets, flares, and a first aid kit are essential safety gear that should always be on board.

## 3. Techniques and Tips

- Learn the Basics: Before heading out, learn the basic sailing skills, including how to tack, jibe, and read the wind and water conditions.
- Check the Weather: Always check the weather forecast before setting sail, as conditions can change rapidly, especially at sea.
- Respect the Ocean: Sailing requires a deep respect for the ocean and its power. Always sail within your limits and be prepared for emergencies.

# *November 22: Train Travel*

## 1. The Romance of Train Travel

Train travel offers a nostalgic and scenic way to see the world, with the journey itself becoming an integral part of the experience. Unlike flying or driving, trains allow you to relax and enjoy the passing landscapes, whether you're traveling through the Swiss Alps, along the coasts of Italy, or across the vast plains of Canada. Train travel is comfortable and often luxurious, with amenities like dining cars, sleeper cabins, and observation lounges. It's a way to travel that harks back to a slower, more elegant era, offering a unique perspective on the world. Train travel is perfect for those who want to take their time and savor the journey, making the most of every moment on the rails.

## 2. Tools and Materials

- Comfortable Luggage: Choose luggage that's easy to store in train compartments, such as a rolling suitcase or a large backpack.
- Travel Pillow and Blanket: For longer journeys, a travel pillow and blanket can make your trip more comfortable, especially if you're sleeping on the train.
- Guidebooks and Maps: Bring guidebooks and maps to learn about the regions you're passing through and plan stops along the way.

## 3. Techniques and Tips

- Book in Advance: For popular routes, book your tickets well in advance to secure the best seats and accommodations.
- Pack Snacks: While most trains offer dining options, packing your own snacks can be a good idea, especially for long journeys or when traveling on a budget.
- Engage with Fellow Travelers: Train travel often attracts a diverse group of people, making it a great opportunity to meet and engage with fellow travelers.

# November 23: Urban Exploration

## 1. The Intrigue of Urban Exploration

Urban exploration, or urbex, involves exploring abandoned or hidden areas within cities, such as old factories, tunnels, or historic buildings. It's a hobby that combines history, adventure, and a touch of mystery, as you uncover the stories behind these forgotten spaces. Urban explorers seek out places that are often off-limits to the public, capturing the beauty of decay and the passage of time. It's an activity that requires a sense of curiosity, a respect for the sites being explored, and an understanding of the risks involved. Urban exploration offers a unique perspective on cities, revealing layers of history and culture that are often overlooked.

## 2. Tools and Materials

- Flashlight and Extra Batteries: A powerful flashlight is essential for navigating dark, abandoned spaces, and extra batteries ensure you're never left in the dark.
- Protective Gear: Wear sturdy, protective clothing, including gloves, boots, and a hard hat, to protect against hazards like broken glass, rusted metal, and unstable structures.
- Camera: A camera is essential for documenting your explorations and capturing the eerie beauty of abandoned places.

## 3. Techniques and Tips

- Research Your Sites: Before you go, research the history and current status of the site you plan to explore, including potential risks and legal considerations.
- Go with a Group: Urban exploration can be dangerous, so it's safer to explore with a group, ensuring you have help if needed.
- Respect the Space: Take only pictures and leave only footprints. Avoid vandalizing or taking items from the sites you explore, preserving them for future explorers.

# *November 24: Volcano Hiking*

## 1. The Thrill of Volcano Hiking

Volcano hiking is a unique and exhilarating way to explore the Earth's most powerful and dynamic landscapes. Hiking up an active or dormant volcano offers breathtaking views, a sense of adventure, and a close encounter with the forces that shape our planet. Whether you're trekking across lava fields, climbing to the crater's edge, or watching molten lava flow, volcano hiking provides a profound connection to the natural world. It's a physically demanding activity that requires preparation, respect for the environment, and an understanding of the risks involved. Volcano hiking is not just about reaching the summit; it's about experiencing the raw power and beauty of the Earth in a way few other activities can offer.

## 2. Tools and Materials

- Sturdy Hiking Boots: Wear durable, ankle-supporting boots designed for rough, rocky terrain, essential for navigating volcanic landscapes.
- Protective Clothing: Wear protective clothing, including long sleeves and pants, to shield against sharp rocks, ash, and potential heat.
- Gas Mask or Respirator: In areas with volcanic gases or ash, a gas mask or respirator may be necessary to protect your lungs.

## 3. Techniques and Tips

- Check Volcanic Activity: Always check the current volcanic activity and weather conditions before your hike, as conditions can change rapidly and become dangerous.
- Hire a Guide: Consider hiring a local guide who knows the area and can help you navigate safely, especially on active volcanoes.
- Respect the Environment: Volcanoes are fragile ecosystems. Stick to designated trails, avoid disturbing wildlife, and take care not to damage the landscape.

# *November 25: Wildlife Safaris*

## 1. The Adventure of Wildlife Safaris

Wildlife safaris offer the chance to see some of the world's most iconic animals in their natural habitats, from the big five in Africa to the tigers of India and the kangaroos of Australia. Safaris provide an immersive experience of the natural world, where you can observe wildlife behaviors up close, often in stunning and remote locations. Whether it's a traditional game drive, a walking safari, or a river cruise, these experiences are about more than just seeing animals—they're about understanding ecosystems, conservation efforts, and the delicate balance of nature. Safaris are both educational and exhilarating, offering unforgettable encounters with nature's most majestic creatures.

## 2. Tools and Materials

- Binoculars: A good pair of binoculars is essential for spotting wildlife at a distance, allowing you to observe animals without disturbing them.
- Camera with Telephoto Lens: Capture close-up shots of wildlife with a camera equipped with a telephoto lens, ideal for safaris.
- Field Guide: Bring a field guide to help identify the animals and birds you encounter, enriching your safari experience.

## 3. Techniques and Tips

- Follow the Guide's Instructions: Your guide knows the area and the animals, so always follow their instructions to ensure your safety and the safety of the wildlife.
- Be Patient and Quiet: Wildlife safaris often require patience, as animals move on their own schedule. Stay quiet and still to increase your chances of seeing them up close.
- Respect the Wildlife: Maintain a respectful distance from animals, never feed them, and avoid making sudden movements or loud noises that could startle them.

# November 26: X-Country Skiing

## 1. The Joy of X-Country Skiing

Cross-country skiing, or Nordic skiing, is a winter sport that combines the beauty of the snowy landscape with a full-body workout. Unlike downhill skiing, cross-country skiing involves gliding across flat or gently rolling terrain, allowing you to explore wintery forests, frozen lakes, and open fields. It's a sport that offers both solitude and serenity, as well as physical challenge and endurance. Cross-country skiing is accessible to people of all ages and skill levels, making it a perfect activity for families, fitness enthusiasts, and outdoor lovers alike. It's a way to enjoy the winter season while staying active and connected to nature.

## 2. Tools and Materials

- Cross-Country Skis: Choose the right skis for your experience level and the type of terrain you'll be skiing on, whether groomed trails or backcountry paths.
- Layered Clothing: Dress in layers to stay warm and dry, with moisture-wicking base layers, insulating mid-layers, and a waterproof outer layer.
- Poles and Boots: Use poles and boots designed for cross-country skiing to provide the necessary support and balance.

## 3. Techniques and Tips

- Learn the Basics: Before hitting the trails, learn the basic techniques of cross-country skiing, including how to glide, turn, and stop.
- Pace Yourself: Cross-country skiing can be physically demanding, so pace yourself, take breaks, and stay hydrated to avoid exhaustion.
- Stay on Marked Trails: For safety, especially in unfamiliar areas, stick to marked trails and avoid skiing alone in remote or backcountry areas.

# *November 27: Yacht Cruising*

## 1. The Luxury of Yacht Cruising

Yacht cruising offers a luxurious and leisurely way to explore the world's coastlines, islands, and open seas. It's a form of travel that combines adventure with comfort, as you sail on a private yacht equipped with all the amenities of a high-end resort. Yacht cruising allows you to visit remote beaches, hidden coves, and vibrant seaside towns, all while enjoying the privacy and exclusivity of your own vessel. Whether it's a day trip along the coast or an extended voyage across the ocean, yacht cruising is about indulgence, relaxation, and the freedom to explore at your own pace. It's a unique way to experience the beauty of the sea, with the added benefit of personalized service and luxury.

## 2. Tools and Materials

- Luxury Yacht: Choose a yacht that suits your needs, whether it's a small, sleek vessel for coastal cruising or a larger, fully-crewed yacht for extended voyages.
- Navigation Equipment: Ensure your yacht is equipped with the latest navigation tools, including GPS, radar, and nautical charts, for safe and accurate sailing.
- Water Sports Gear: Enhance your cruising experience with water sports gear such as snorkeling equipment, kayaks, and paddleboards.

## 3. Techniques and Tips

- Plan Your Route: Whether you're cruising the Mediterranean, the Caribbean, or another destination, plan your route carefully, including stops at ports and anchorages.
- Hire a Crew: For a truly relaxing experience, consider hiring a professional crew to handle the sailing, cooking, and cleaning, allowing you to fully enjoy your time on the water.
- Enjoy the Amenities: Take full advantage of your yacht's amenities, from sunbathing on the deck to dining al fresco under the stars.

# *November 28: Zip Lining*

## 1. The Excitement of Zip Lining

Zip lining is an adrenaline-pumping activity that involves gliding along a cable from one point to another, often high above the ground. It's a thrilling way to experience the natural world, whether you're soaring over a forest canopy, across a river, or between mountains. Zip lining offers a unique perspective on the landscape, allowing you to see it from above while enjoying the sensation of flight. It's an activity that combines adventure with safety, as modern zip lines are designed with high-quality equipment and expert guides to ensure a fun and secure experience. Zip lining is perfect for thrill-seekers and nature lovers alike, offering an unforgettable way to explore the outdoors.

## 2. Tools and Materials

- Harness and Helmet: Wear a secure harness and helmet provided by the zip line operator to ensure your safety during the ride.
- Gloves: Gloves are often provided or recommended to help you grip the cable and protect your hands during the ride.
- Closed-Toe Shoes: Wear sturdy, closed-toe shoes that provide good grip and protection for your feet while zip lining.

## 3. Techniques and Tips

- Follow the Guide's Instructions: Pay close attention to the safety briefing and instructions provided by your guides to ensure a smooth and safe ride.
- Relax and Enjoy the View: Once you're on the line, relax, lean back, and enjoy the ride, taking in the breathtaking views around you.
- Capture the Moment: If allowed, bring a small action camera to capture your zip lining experience, but make sure it's securely attached to avoid losing it.

# November 29: Zoo Tours

## 1. The Wonder of Zoo Tours

Zoo tours offer a unique and educational way to learn about wildlife from around the world. Unlike a typical zoo visit, guided tours provide in-depth information about the animals, their habitats, and conservation efforts. These tours can include behind-the-scenes access, allowing you to see how animals are cared for, meet the keepers, and even participate in feeding sessions or enrichment activities. Zoo tours are designed to inspire a deeper understanding and appreciation of wildlife, highlighting the importance of conservation and the challenges faced by many species. They're perfect for animal lovers, families, and anyone interested in learning more about the natural world.

## 2. Tools and Materials

- Comfortable Walking Shoes: Zoos often cover large areas, so wear comfortable shoes suitable for walking long distances.
- Binoculars: Bring binoculars to get a closer look at animals in large enclosures or those that may be resting far from the viewing areas.
- Notebook or Journal: Use a notebook to jot down interesting facts, observations, and the names of animals you learn about during the tour.

## 3. Techniques and Tips

- Book in Advance: Popular zoos and special tours often require advance booking, so plan ahead to secure your spot.
- Engage with the Guides: Ask questions and engage with the tour guides to gain more insight and make the most of your zoo experience.
- Respect the Animals: Always follow the zoo's rules, including not feeding or disturbing the animals, and stay within designated areas to ensure the safety of both visitors and wildlife.

# *November 30: Zorbing*

## 1. The Fun of Zorbing

Zorbing is a unique and thrilling activity that involves rolling down a hill inside a large, inflatable ball. It's a fun and exhilarating experience that combines the sensation of speed with the safety of a cushioned environment. Zorbing can be done on a gentle slope for a leisurely ride or on steeper terrain for a more intense experience. It's a great activity for groups, offering lots of laughs and a chance to try something completely different. Zorbing is all about embracing the excitement of the ride, feeling the adrenaline rush, and enjoying the pure, childlike fun of rolling down a hill in a giant ball.

## 2. Tools and Materials

- Zorb Ball: The Zorb ball is a large, transparent inflatable sphere that you ride inside. It's designed to be durable and provide a cushioned environment for the rider.
- Helmet and Pads: Some zorbing courses provide helmets and pads for extra safety, especially on more intense courses.
- Comfortable Clothing: Wear comfortable, athletic clothing that allows you to move freely inside the Zorb ball.

## 3. Techniques and Tips

- Choose Your Course: Zorbing courses vary in intensity, so choose one that matches your comfort level and desired thrill factor.
- Stay Relaxed: Inside the Zorb ball, stay relaxed and let the ball carry you down the hill. There's no need to try and control the roll; just go with the flow.
- Have Fun: Zorbing is all about fun, so embrace the silliness of the activity, laugh, and enjoy the unique experience of rolling downhill in a giant inflatable ball.

## *Conclusion for November*

November has been a month of exploration and discovery, offering you the chance to immerse yourself in new environments, cultures, and adventures. Whether you've traversed the peaks of mountains, sailed serene waters, or delved into the mysteries of urban landscapes, each day has provided a unique opportunity to see the world from a different perspective. As you reflect on these experiences, consider how travel and exploration enrich your life, broadening your horizons and deepening your understanding of the world. Continue to seek out new adventures, embracing the spirit of exploration in all that you do.

# December: Writing and Literature

*December, the final month of the year, invites you to explore the vast and creative world of writing and literature. Whether you're looking to pen your autobiography, start a blog, or delve into the intricacies of novel writing, this month is dedicated to the craft of storytelling, self-expression, and the art of the written word. Each day offers a new way to engage with writing, whether for personal reflection, creative exploration, or professional development.*

# *December 1: Anthology Editing*

## 1. The Craft of Anthology Editing

Anthology editing is the art of curating a collection of works—whether they be stories, poems, or essays—around a central theme or topic. It requires a keen eye for quality, a deep understanding of the subject matter, and the ability to balance diverse voices while maintaining a cohesive collection. An anthology editor must select contributions that resonate with the theme, ensuring that each piece contributes to the overall narrative and provides variety in tone, style, and perspective. Editing an anthology is both a creative and logistical challenge, demanding strong organizational skills and a passion for literature.

## 2. Tools and Materials

- Submission Management Software: Use software like Submittable to manage submissions, track progress, and communicate with contributors.
- Editing Tools: Utilize editing software such as Microsoft Word or Google Docs with track changes to collaborate with writers on revisions.
- Reference Books: Keep reference materials handy, such as style guides (like the Chicago Manual of Style) and anthologies of similar themes, to maintain consistency and draw inspiration.

## 3. Techniques and Tips

- Theme Selection: Choose a compelling and specific theme that will attract high-quality submissions and provide a strong foundation for the anthology.
- Contributor Guidelines: Provide clear guidelines to contributors, outlining the submission requirements, including word count, format, and deadline.
- Balancing Voices: Strive to include a diverse range of voices and perspectives while ensuring that each piece aligns with the anthology's theme and tone.
- Editing and Sequencing: Carefully edit each piece for quality and coherence, and sequence the contributions to create a natural flow that enhances the reader's experience.

# *December 2: Autobiography Writing*

## 1. The Journey of Autobiography Writing

Writing an autobiography is a deeply personal endeavor, offering the opportunity to reflect on one's life, share experiences, and leave a legacy. It involves more than just recounting events; it's about finding meaning in those events and conveying that significance to readers. An autobiography allows the writer to explore their identity, values, and the lessons learned throughout their life. This process requires introspection, honesty, and the ability to connect with readers on an emotional level.

## 2. Tools and Materials

- Writing Software: Use software like Scrivener or Microsoft Word to organize and draft your autobiography, keeping track of chapters, notes, and revisions.
- Memory Aids: Gather photographs, journals, letters, and other personal artifacts to help trigger memories and provide details for your writing.
- Interview Tools: If you're collaborating with others to recount certain events, use a voice recorder or interview software to capture their perspectives accurately.

## 3. Techniques and Tips

- Chronological Structure: Consider structuring your autobiography chronologically, but don't be afraid to use thematic or flashback techniques to highlight significant moments.
- Honesty and Vulnerability: Be honest and vulnerable in your writing, sharing not just successes but also challenges and failures, which can make your story more relatable and impactful.
- Focus on Themes: Identify key themes in your life, such as resilience, love, or career, and weave these into your narrative to give your autobiography depth and cohesion.
- Revision and Feedback: Revise your work multiple times and seek feedback from trusted individuals to ensure that your autobiography resonates with readers and accurately reflects your life story.

# *December 3: Blogging*

## 1. The World of Blogging

Blogging is a dynamic and versatile form of writing that allows individuals to share their thoughts, expertise, and stories with a global audience. It's an excellent platform for building a personal brand, connecting with like-minded individuals, and even generating income. A successful blog requires consistent content creation, an understanding of your audience, and the ability to engage readers through compelling and relevant posts. Whether you're blogging for business, pleasure, or both, it's an effective way to communicate your ideas and establish your voice online.

## 2. Tools and Materials

- Blogging Platforms: Use platforms like WordPress, Blogger, or Medium to create and manage your blog. These platforms offer various themes, plugins, and customization options to suit your style and needs.
- SEO Tools: Incorporate SEO tools like Yoast or Ahrefs to optimize your blog posts for search engines, helping you reach a broader audience.
- Content Calendar: Use a content calendar to plan your blog posts in advance, ensuring consistency and allowing time for research and writing.

## 3. Techniques and Tips

- Know Your Audience: Understand your target audience's interests, needs, and preferences, and tailor your content to meet those expectations.
- Engaging Headlines: Craft attention-grabbing headlines that entice readers to click and read your posts, using action words and addressing reader pain points or curiosities.
- Visual Content: Enhance your blog posts with images, infographics, or videos to break up text and add visual interest.
- Consistency: Publish regularly to build and maintain your audience, whether it's weekly, bi-weekly, or monthly, and interact with your readers through comments and social media to foster a community around your blog.

# *December 4: Book Reviewing*

## 1. The Skill of Book Reviewing

Book reviewing involves critically analyzing and evaluating a book's content, style, and impact, and then sharing your insights with potential readers. It's a way to engage with literature on a deeper level, offering both praise and constructive criticism to guide others in their reading choices. Book reviewing can be a rewarding hobby for avid readers, as it allows you to express your opinions, participate in literary discussions, and contribute to the literary community. A well-crafted review goes beyond a simple summary, providing thoughtful analysis that considers the book's strengths, weaknesses, and its overall contribution to the genre or field.

## 2. Tools and Materials

- Reading Journal: Keep a reading journal to jot down your thoughts, favorite quotes, and key points as you read, making it easier to write your review later.
- Review Guidelines: Familiarize yourself with any review guidelines provided by platforms where you plan to publish your review, such as Goodreads, Amazon, or literary magazines.
- Reference Books: Use reference books on literary criticism to help you develop your analytical skills and provide deeper insights in your reviews.

## 3. Techniques and Tips

- Balanced Perspective: Offer a balanced perspective by discussing both what you liked and what didn't work for you in the book, providing examples to support your views.
- Contextual Analysis: Consider the book's context—its genre, the author's previous works, and its place in current literary trends—to enrich your review.
- Audience Consideration: Tailor your review to your intended audience, whether they're casual readers or literary enthusiasts, by adjusting your tone and level of detail accordingly.
- Conciseness: Keep your review concise and focused, highlighting the most important aspects of the book without overloading the reader with information.

# December 5: Copywriting

## 1. The Art of Copywriting

Copywriting is the craft of creating persuasive and compelling text for marketing and advertising purposes. It's about using words to drive action, whether that's making a purchase, signing up for a newsletter, or following a brand on social media. Effective copywriting requires an understanding of your target audience, a strong command of language, and the ability to convey a clear and compelling message. It's a critical skill in the business world, as well-written copy can significantly impact a brand's success and customer engagement.

## 2. Tools and Materials

- Grammar and Style Checkers: Use tools like Grammarly or Hemingway to ensure your copy is clear, concise, and free of errors.
- Thesaurus and Synonym Tools: Keep a thesaurus handy or use online tools to find the best words to convey your message and avoid repetition.
- Marketing Books: Read books on marketing and psychology to deepen your understanding of consumer behavior and how to craft copy that resonates with your audience.

## 3. Techniques and Tips

- Know Your Audience: Research your target audience's needs, preferences, and pain points to tailor your copy effectively.
- Clear Calls to Action: Always include a clear call to action (CTA) that tells your audience exactly what you want them to do next, whether it's clicking a link, making a purchase, or signing up for something.
- Benefit-Driven Language: Focus on the benefits your product or service offers, rather than just its features, to appeal to your audience's desires and motivations.
- A/B Testing: Use A/B testing to experiment with different versions of your copy to see which performs best, helping you refine your approach and maximize effectiveness.

# *December 6: Creative Writing*

## 1. The Freedom of Creative Writing

Creative writing is a form of artistic expression that allows you to explore your imagination and create original works of fiction, poetry, or non-fiction. It's a way to tell stories, convey emotions, and connect with readers on a deeper level. Unlike more structured forms of writing, creative writing offers the freedom to experiment with language, narrative techniques, and genres. Whether you're writing a novel, short story, poem, or memoir, creative writing is a rewarding pursuit that nurtures your creativity and enhances your ability to communicate complex ideas and emotions.

## 2. Tools and Materials

- Writing Prompts: Use writing prompts to spark your creativity and get your ideas flowing, especially when you're feeling stuck.
- Writing Software: Utilize writing software like Scrivener or Google Docs to organize your work, track progress, and collaborate with others if needed.
- Creative Writing Books: Read books on creative writing techniques to improve your craft, explore different styles, and gain inspiration from successful authors.

## 3. Techniques and Tips

- Show, Don't Tell: Use vivid descriptions and sensory details to show what's happening in your story, rather than simply telling the reader, to create a more immersive experience.
- Character Development: Spend time developing your characters, giving them depth, flaws, and motivations that drive the story forward.
- Experiment with Structure: Don't be afraid to experiment with non-linear narratives, multiple perspectives, or different forms of storytelling to create unique and engaging works.
- Revise Relentlessly: Embrace the revision process as an opportunity to refine your work, polish your prose, and strengthen the overall impact of your writing.

# December 7: Diary Keeping

## 1. The Practice of Diary Keeping

Diary keeping is the personal practice of recording daily events, thoughts, and feelings in a private journal. It's a way to reflect on your experiences, track your growth, and preserve memories. Keeping a diary can be therapeutic, providing an outlet for emotions and a space to explore your innermost thoughts without judgment. It also serves as a historical record, allowing you to look back and see how you've evolved over time. Whether you write daily or occasionally, diary keeping is a valuable habit that fosters self-awareness and personal development.

## 2. Tools and Materials

- Diary or Journal: Choose a diary or journal that suits your style, whether it's a simple notebook, a leather-bound journal, or a digital diary app.
- Pens and Markers: Use pens, markers, or colored pencils to add creativity and personal touches to your diary entries.
- Prompts and Stickers: Incorporate prompts or stickers to make your diary keeping more engaging and visually appealing.

## 3. Techniques and Tips

- Consistency: Try to write regularly, whether daily, weekly, or whenever you feel the need, to build a consistent habit.
- Honesty: Be honest with yourself in your entries, expressing your true thoughts and feelings without filtering or self-censorship.
- Reflect and Learn: Use your diary as a tool for self-reflection, revisiting past entries to see patterns in your thoughts and behaviors and learn from your experiences.
- Personalize Your Entries: Personalize your diary by including drawings, photos, or mementos that capture the essence of your experiences and make your entries more meaningful.

# *December 8: Digital Publishing*

## 1. The Future of Digital Publishing

Digital publishing is the process of publishing books, articles, and other written content in digital formats, such as e-books, blogs, and online magazines. It has revolutionized the way content is created, distributed, and consumed, making it accessible to a global audience at the click of a button. Digital publishing offers opportunities for writers to reach readers directly, bypassing traditional gatekeepers like publishers and editors. It also allows for greater flexibility in terms of format, interactivity, and multimedia integration. As the digital landscape continues to evolve, digital publishing remains at the forefront of the writing industry.

## 2. Tools and Materials

- Publishing Platforms: Use platforms like Amazon Kindle Direct Publishing (KDP), Smashwords, or Wattpad to publish your digital content.
- Formatting Tools: Utilize formatting tools like Vellum or Scrivener to prepare your manuscript for digital publication, ensuring it looks professional on all devices.
- Marketing Resources: Invest in digital marketing tools and resources, such as social media schedulers and email marketing software, to promote your published works and reach your target audience.

## 3. Techniques and Tips

- Understand Your Audience: Know your target audience and tailor your content to meet their preferences and expectations, whether you're publishing fiction, non-fiction, or academic work.
- Optimize for Search Engines: Incorporate SEO strategies into your digital content, using relevant keywords and metadata to increase visibility and attract readers.
- Leverage Social Media: Use social media platforms to build an online presence, engage with readers, and drive traffic to your digital publications.
- Embrace Multimedia: Experiment with multimedia elements, such as videos, interactive graphics, and hyperlinks, to enhance your digital content and offer readers a more engaging experience.

# *December 9: Editing*

## 1. The Precision of Editing

Editing is the process of reviewing and refining a written work to improve its clarity, coherence, and overall quality. It involves correcting grammar, punctuation, and spelling errors, as well as restructuring sentences, paragraphs, and sections to enhance the flow of the text. Editing is a critical step in the writing process, as it transforms a rough draft into a polished, professional piece of work. Whether you're editing your own writing or someone else's, attention to detail and a thorough understanding of language are essential.

## 2. Tools and Materials

- Editing Software: Use editing software like Grammarly, ProWritingAid, or the Hemingway App to catch errors and suggest improvements.
- Style Guides: Keep a style guide, such as the Chicago Manual of Style or the AP Stylebook, on hand to ensure consistency in formatting, citation, and usage.
- Thesaurus and Dictionary: Refer to a thesaurus and dictionary to find the best words and clarify meanings, helping to eliminate redundancy and ambiguity in your writing.

## 3. Techniques and Tips

- Take Breaks: Step away from the manuscript for a while before editing, allowing you to approach the text with fresh eyes and a clear mind.
- Read Aloud: Read the text aloud to catch awkward phrasing, rhythm issues, and other subtleties that might be missed when reading silently.
- Focus on One Task at a Time: Break the editing process into stages, focusing on one task at a time, such as grammar, structure, or style, to avoid feeling overwhelmed.
- Seek Feedback: Don't hesitate to seek feedback from others, whether through peer review, beta readers, or professional editing services, to gain new perspectives and improve the quality of the work.

# *December 10: Essay Writing*

## 1. The Discipline of Essay Writing

Essay writing is a structured form of writing that involves presenting an argument, analysis, or exploration of a topic in a clear and concise manner. It's a common academic exercise, but also a valuable skill in professional and personal contexts. Essays require critical thinking, research, and the ability to articulate ideas logically and persuasively. Whether writing a persuasive essay, an analytical essay, or a reflective essay, the key is to maintain focus, support your points with evidence, and communicate your thoughts effectively.

## 2. Tools and Materials

- Research Tools: Use online databases, libraries, and academic journals to gather reliable sources and evidence for your essay.
- Essay Planner: Create an essay planner to organize your thesis statement, main points, and supporting evidence before you start writing.
- Citation Tools: Use citation tools like EasyBib or Zotero to manage your references and format citations correctly according to the required style.

## 3. Techniques and Tips

- Thesis Statement: Develop a strong thesis statement that clearly presents your main argument or perspective, serving as the foundation for your essay.
- Structured Outline: Create a structured outline that breaks down your essay into introduction, body paragraphs, and conclusion, ensuring each section flows logically into the next.
- Evidence and Analysis: Support your points with evidence from credible sources, and provide analysis to explain how the evidence supports your thesis.
- Revise for Clarity: After writing your essay, revise it for clarity, coherence, and conciseness, eliminating unnecessary words and refining your arguments.

# *December 11: Flash Fiction*

## 1. The Art of Flash Fiction
Flash fiction is a genre of writing that tells a complete story in a very limited word count, typically under 1,000 words. It's a challenging but rewarding form of storytelling that requires precision, economy of language, and a deep understanding of narrative structure. In flash fiction, every word counts, and writers must convey character, setting, and plot in a succinct and impactful way. Despite its brevity, flash fiction can be just as powerful and memorable as longer works, making it an excellent exercise in creativity and discipline.

## 2. Tools and Materials
- Word Count Tools: Use word count tools to track your progress and ensure you stay within the strict word limit of flash fiction.
- Writing Prompts: Start with writing prompts that are designed for flash fiction, encouraging you to develop concise and compelling stories.
- Editing Software: Utilize editing software to polish your flash fiction, ensuring every word contributes to the story's impact.

## 3. Techniques and Tips
- Start In Media Res: Begin your story in the middle of the action, immediately engaging the reader and making the most of the limited word count.
- Focus on a Moment: Concentrate on a single moment, emotion, or event, using it as the focal point of your story to create depth without the need for extensive exposition.
- Imply More Than You Say: Use implication and suggestion to convey more than what is explicitly stated, allowing readers to fill in the gaps with their imagination.
- End with Impact: Craft a strong, resonant ending that leaves a lasting impression on the reader, often with a twist or revelation that recontextualizes the entire story.

# *December 12: Ghostwriting*

## 1. The Profession of Ghostwriting

Ghostwriting is the practice of writing on behalf of someone else, where the credited author is not the person who actually wrote the content. It's a common practice in publishing, particularly for autobiographies, memoirs, and thought leadership books. Ghostwriters must be skilled at capturing the voice, tone, and style of their clients while delivering high-quality content that meets the client's objectives. It's a unique career that requires discretion, adaptability, and the ability to write across a variety of genres and subjects.

## 2. Tools and Materials

- Voice Recording Tools: Use voice recording tools to capture interviews and conversations with your client, ensuring you accurately convey their voice and message.
- Contract Templates: Have contract templates ready that outline the terms of your ghostwriting services, including confidentiality clauses and payment structures.
- Research Tools: Utilize research tools to gather background information, statistics, and context for the content you're ghostwriting.

## 3. Techniques and Tips

- Understand the Client's Voice: Spend time with your client to understand their voice, tone, and style, ensuring that the final product feels authentic to them.
- Maintain Confidentiality: Respect the confidentiality of your ghostwriting work, keeping client details and content private unless otherwise agreed upon.
- Set Clear Expectations: Establish clear expectations with your client regarding deadlines, revisions, and the scope of the project to avoid misunderstandings.
- Adaptability: Be prepared to adapt your writing style to suit different clients and genres, demonstrating versatility and professionalism in your ghostwriting career.

# December 13: Historical Fiction Writing

## 1. The Craft of Historical Fiction Writing

Historical fiction is a genre that combines real historical events, settings, and figures with fictional characters and narratives. Writing historical fiction requires extensive research to accurately portray the time period, along with creative storytelling to weave a compelling narrative that resonates with modern readers. It's a genre that allows writers to explore the past, bringing history to life while offering insights into human nature, societal changes, and cultural evolution.

## 2. Tools and Materials

- Historical Research Books: Use books, academic journals, and primary sources to research the historical period you're writing about, ensuring accuracy and authenticity.
- Timeline Tools: Create timelines to keep track of historical events, dates, and the chronological order of your story.
- Character Profiles: Develop detailed character profiles that reflect the historical context, including their social status, occupation, and cultural norms of the time.

## 3. Techniques and Tips

- Blend Fact and Fiction: Skillfully blend historical facts with fictional elements, creating a narrative that is both educational and entertaining.
- Authentic Dialogue: Write dialogue that reflects the language, slang, and cultural nuances of the historical period, adding authenticity to your characters and setting.
- Avoid Anachronisms: Be mindful of anachronisms—elements that are out of place in the time period—and avoid them to maintain the credibility of your historical fiction.
- Explore Universal Themes: Use your historical setting to explore universal themes, such as love, war, or justice, that resonate with readers across time periods.

# *December 14: Inspirational Writing*

## 1. The Power of Inspirational Writing

Inspirational writing is a genre that seeks to uplift, motivate, and encourage readers, often drawing on personal experiences, wisdom, and positive messages. It's a genre that resonates with people looking for hope, guidance, and a sense of connection. Inspirational writing can take many forms, including essays, memoirs, speeches, and self-help books. The key to success in this genre is authenticity, empathy, and the ability to connect with readers on an emotional level.

## 2. Tools and Materials

- Writing Journal: Keep a journal to capture moments of inspiration, personal reflections, and ideas for your writing.
- Books on Inspirational Writing: Read books by successful inspirational writers to understand the techniques and styles that resonate with readers.
- Motivational Quotes: Collect motivational quotes and anecdotes that can be woven into your writing to reinforce your message and connect with readers.

## 3. Techniques and Tips

- Write from the Heart: Authenticity is key in inspirational writing; share your true thoughts, experiences, and feelings to create a genuine connection with your readers.
- Empathy and Understanding: Demonstrate empathy by acknowledging your readers' struggles and offering encouragement, understanding, and practical advice.
- Positive Messaging: Focus on positive messaging, emphasizing hope, resilience, and the possibility of change, even in difficult circumstances.
- Call to Action: End your piece with a call to action, encouraging readers to take steps toward improving their lives or embracing a positive mindset.

# *December 15: Journaling*

## 1. The Therapeutic Practice of Journaling

Journaling is the practice of writing down your thoughts, feelings, and experiences regularly. It's a powerful tool for self-reflection, emotional processing, and personal growth. Journaling allows you to explore your inner world, gain clarity on your emotions, and track your personal development over time. Whether you journal daily or on occasion, it's a therapeutic practice that can reduce stress, improve mental health, and enhance your overall well-being.

## 2. Tools and Materials

- Journal or Notebook: Choose a journal or notebook that you feel comfortable writing in, whether it's a simple spiral-bound book or a beautifully designed journal.
- Pens and Markers: Use pens, markers, or colored pencils to express your thoughts creatively and add visual interest to your journal entries.
- Journaling Prompts: Use journaling prompts to inspire your writing and explore topics you might not have considered on your own.

## 3. Techniques and Tips

- Free Writing: Practice free writing, where you write continuously for a set period without worrying about grammar, spelling, or structure, allowing your thoughts to flow freely.
- Reflect on Your Day: Use your journal to reflect on your day, noting significant events, emotions, and lessons learned.
- Goal Setting: Incorporate goal setting into your journaling, writing down your aspirations and tracking your progress over time.
- Express Gratitude: End each journal entry with a note of gratitude, acknowledging the positive aspects of your life and fostering a sense of appreciation.

# December 16: Kinetic Poetry

## 1. The Creativity of Kinetic Poetry
Kinetic poetry is a form of visual poetry that incorporates motion and interactivity, often using digital media to create a dynamic reading experience. It's a blend of traditional poetry and modern technology, where the words and their arrangement move, change, or respond to the reader's actions. Kinetic poetry challenges conventional notions of poetry by adding a visual and interactive dimension, making it a unique and engaging form of expression.

## 2. Tools and Materials
- Digital Software: Use digital software like Adobe After Effects, HTML5, or JavaScript to create kinetic poetry that moves or changes over time.
- Interactive Platforms: Publish your kinetic poetry on platforms that support interactivity, such as digital poetry websites or multimedia e-books.
- Visual Design Tools: Utilize visual design tools to create the graphical elements of your kinetic poetry, enhancing the overall aesthetic and impact.

## 3. Techniques and Tips
- Integrate Movement and Meaning: Ensure that the motion or interactivity of your poetry enhances its meaning, rather than serving as a mere gimmick. The movement should complement the themes and emotions of the poem.
- Experiment with Form: Don't be afraid to experiment with different forms and structures, using technology to push the boundaries of traditional poetry.
- Test Interactivity: Test your kinetic poetry on different devices and platforms to ensure it works smoothly and provides a seamless experience for the reader.
- Engage the Senses: Consider how you can engage multiple senses, incorporating sound, visuals, and motion to create a more immersive poetic experience.

# *December 17: Letter Writing*

## 1. The Tradition of Letter Writing

Letter writing is a timeless form of communication that allows you to connect with others on a personal and intimate level. Whether handwritten or typed, letters convey thoughts, feelings, and news in a way that is often more meaningful than modern digital communication. Writing letters encourages thoughtfulness and reflection, making it a cherished practice in both personal and professional contexts. In an age of instant messaging and emails, letter writing stands out as a deliberate and heartfelt way to maintain relationships, express gratitude, or share important life updates.

## 2. Tools and Materials

- Stationery: Invest in quality stationery that reflects your personal style, whether it's classic parchment, colorful letterhead, or custom-designed paper.
- Pens and Ink: Choose a pen that you enjoy writing with, and consider using colored or fountain pen ink to add a special touch to your letters.
- Stamps and Seals: Use decorative stamps, seals, or wax to add a traditional and elegant finish to your letters, making them feel even more special to the recipient.

## 3. Techniques and Tips

- Personal Touch: Add a personal touch by including details that show you've taken the time to think about the recipient, such as mentioning shared memories or addressing specific interests.
- Express Gratitude: Use letters as an opportunity to express gratitude and appreciation, whether you're thanking someone for a gift, a favor, or simply their friendship.
- Structure and Tone: Pay attention to the structure and tone of your letter, ensuring it matches the occasion and your relationship with the recipient—whether formal, casual, or affectionate.
- Take Your Time: Don't rush your letter; take the time to craft your words carefully, ensuring your message is clear, thoughtful, and well-articulated.

# *December 18: Memoir Writing*

## 1. The Journey of Memoir Writing

Memoir writing is the art of telling your own story, focusing on specific experiences, themes, or periods of your life. Unlike a full autobiography, which covers an entire life, a memoir zeroes in on particular events or insights that have shaped you as a person. Writing a memoir allows you to explore your identity, reflect on your past, and share your personal journey with others. It's a deeply introspective process that requires honesty, vulnerability, and a willingness to examine both the highs and lows of your life.

## 2. Tools and Materials

- Memory Aids: Gather photographs, journals, letters, and other mementos to help trigger memories and provide rich details for your memoir.
- Writing Software: Use writing software like Scrivener or Microsoft Word to organize your memoir, keeping track of chapters, themes, and revisions.
- Memoir Workshops: Consider joining a memoir writing workshop or group to receive feedback, support, and encouragement from fellow writers.

## 3. Techniques and Tips

- Focus on a Theme: Identify a central theme or lesson that your memoir will explore, such as resilience, love, or self-discovery, and let it guide your narrative.
- Use Vivid Detail: Bring your experiences to life by using vivid, sensory details that immerse the reader in your story, making it more engaging and relatable.
- Balance Honesty with Discretion: While honesty is crucial in memoir writing, consider the impact of your words on others involved in your story, balancing transparency with discretion.
- Revise and Reflect: After completing your memoir, take time to revise and reflect, ensuring that your story is not only well-written but also true to your voice and experiences.

# *December 19: Novel Writing*

## 1. The Challenge of Novel Writing

Novel writing is a long-form creative endeavor that involves crafting a complex, multi-layered story with fully developed characters, settings, and plotlines. It's a journey that requires dedication, discipline, and a deep love for storytelling. Writing a novel allows you to explore vast worlds, delve into the human psyche, and create a narrative that resonates with readers. The process is challenging, but it's also immensely rewarding, offering the satisfaction of seeing your ideas come to life on the page.

## 2. Tools and Materials

- Story Planning Tools: Use story planning tools like mind maps, outlines, or plot grids to organize your novel's structure, plot arcs, and character development.
- Character Sheets: Create detailed character sheets to track your characters' backgrounds, motivations, and relationships, ensuring consistency throughout the novel.
- Writing Routine: Establish a writing routine that fits your lifestyle, whether it's daily writing sessions or weekly marathons, to maintain momentum and progress.

## 3. Techniques and Tips

- Strong Opening: Craft a strong opening that grabs the reader's attention, introduces the main characters, and sets the tone for the rest of the novel.
- Show, Don't Tell: Use the "show, don't tell" technique to reveal character traits, emotions, and conflicts through actions, dialogue, and descriptions, rather than exposition.
- Pacing and Structure: Pay attention to pacing, balancing scenes of action and tension with quieter moments of reflection or character development.
- Persistence and Patience: Writing a novel is a marathon, not a sprint; be patient with the process, and stay persistent, even when faced with writer's block or self-doubt.

# *December 20: Opinion Pieces*

## 1. The Influence of Opinion Pieces

Opinion pieces are a form of journalism or essay writing where the author expresses their personal views on a particular issue, event, or topic. These pieces are meant to persuade, inform, or provoke thought, often reflecting the writer's stance on current events, societal issues, or cultural debates. Writing opinion pieces allows you to share your perspective with a wider audience, contributing to public discourse and potentially influencing opinions. It's a powerful way to engage with the world around you and articulate your beliefs.

## 2. Tools and Materials

- Research Sources: Gather reliable sources and evidence to support your argument, ensuring your opinion piece is well-informed and credible.
- Editorial Guidelines: Familiarize yourself with the editorial guidelines of the publication or platform where you plan to submit your opinion piece, adjusting your style and length accordingly.
- Writing Software: Use writing software to draft and revise your opinion piece, focusing on clarity, logic, and persuasive language.

## 3. Techniques and Tips

- Clear Thesis Statement: Start with a clear thesis statement that outlines your main argument or viewpoint, setting the stage for the rest of the piece.
- Support with Evidence: Back up your opinions with factual evidence, statistics, or expert quotes to strengthen your argument and lend credibility to your writing.
- Engage the Reader: Write in a way that engages the reader, using rhetorical questions, anecdotes, or relatable examples to draw them into your argument.
- Be Concise: Opinion pieces are typically brief, so make every word count, avoiding unnecessary details or tangents that could dilute your message.

# December 21: *Playwriting*

## 1. The Dynamics of Playwriting

Playwriting is the craft of writing scripts for theatrical performances, involving dialogue, stage directions, and character development. It's a unique form of storytelling that relies on live performance to convey emotion, conflict, and narrative. Playwriting allows writers to explore the intricacies of human relationships, social issues, and moral dilemmas in a dramatic, often intense, format. The process requires a deep understanding of character dynamics, pacing, and the visual aspects of storytelling, making it both challenging and rewarding.

## 2. Tools and Materials

- Scriptwriting Software: Use scriptwriting software like Final Draft or Celtx to format your play according to industry standards, making it easier to share with directors and actors.
- Character Outlines: Develop character outlines to understand each character's background, motivations, and relationships, ensuring they are well-rounded and integral to the plot.
- Stage Diagrams: Create stage diagrams or sketches to visualize the setting and block scenes, helping you plan the physical movement and interaction of characters on stage.

## 3. Techniques and Tips

- Natural Dialogue: Write dialogue that feels natural and authentic to each character, reflecting their personality, background, and current situation.
- Show, Don't Tell: Use action and dialogue to reveal character traits and advance the plot, rather than relying on exposition or monologues.
- Pacing and Tension: Maintain pacing and tension by balancing moments of conflict with quieter, introspective scenes, keeping the audience engaged throughout the performance.
- Collaboration: Be open to collaboration with directors, actors, and other creatives, as playwriting is often a collaborative art form where input from others can enhance the final production.

# *December 22: Quoting*

## 1. The Precision of Quoting

Quoting is the practice of using someone else's words in your writing, whether to support an argument, illustrate a point, or add authority to your work. It's a critical skill in academic, journalistic, and creative writing, requiring accuracy, proper attribution, and the ability to integrate quotes seamlessly into your own narrative. Quoting effectively involves selecting relevant passages, understanding the context, and ensuring that the quote enhances rather than overshadows your writing.

## 2. Tools and Materials

- Citation Tools: Use citation tools like EasyBib or Zotero to format your quotes according to the required style (APA, MLA, Chicago, etc.) and avoid plagiarism.
- Quotation Resources: Keep a collection of quotations from literature, speeches, and other sources that you can reference and incorporate into your writing.
- Style Guides: Refer to style guides for the correct formatting of quotes, especially for block quotes, in-text citations, and punctuation.

## 3. Techniques and Tips

- Relevance: Choose quotes that are directly relevant to your topic and add value to your argument or narrative, rather than including them for the sake of it.
- Contextualization: Always provide context for the quote, explaining its significance and how it relates to your own writing or argument.
- Attribution: Ensure that all quotes are properly attributed to their original source, including the author's name, title of the work, and publication details.
- Integration: Integrate quotes smoothly into your writing by using lead-in phrases, avoiding abrupt insertions that can disrupt the flow of your text.

# *December 23: Research Writing*

## 1. The Rigor of Research Writing

Research writing is a formal, structured form of writing that involves investigating a topic, analyzing information, and presenting findings in a clear, logical manner. It's a fundamental aspect of academic work but is also crucial in various professional fields, such as science, journalism, and business. Research writing requires a thorough understanding of the subject, critical thinking skills, and the ability to synthesize complex information into a coherent narrative. The goal is to contribute new knowledge or insights to a field while maintaining accuracy, objectivity, and scholarly integrity.

## 2. Tools and Materials

- Academic Databases: Use academic databases like JSTOR, PubMed, or Google Scholar to access peer-reviewed articles, journals, and papers relevant to your research topic.
- Citation Management Software: Employ citation management software like EndNote or Mendeley to organize your references and ensure proper citation throughout your paper.
- Research Notebooks: Keep a research notebook to record observations, hypotheses, and key findings as you gather and analyze data.

## 3. Techniques and Tips

- Thorough Literature Review: Conduct a thorough literature review to understand the current state of research on your topic and identify gaps or areas for further investigation.
- Clear Thesis Statement: Develop a clear and concise thesis statement that guides your research and provides a focal point for your writing.
- Data Analysis: Use appropriate data analysis methods, whether qualitative or quantitative, to interpret your findings and support your conclusions.
- Draft and Revise: Write multiple drafts of your research paper, revising for clarity, coherence, and depth, and seek feedback from peers or mentors to refine your work.

# December 24: Scriptwriting

## 1. The Craft of Scriptwriting

Scriptwriting is the process of writing scripts for film, television, or radio, involving dialogue, action, and scene direction. It's a specialized form of writing that requires an understanding of visual storytelling, character development, and the technical aspects of production. Scriptwriting allows writers to create immersive worlds, compelling narratives, and dynamic characters, all while working within the constraints of time, budget, and medium. It's a highly collaborative process, often involving input from directors, producers, and actors, making it essential for scriptwriters to be flexible and open to revisions.

## 2. Tools and Materials

- Scriptwriting Software: Use scriptwriting software like Final Draft, Celtx, or WriterDuet to format your script according to industry standards and streamline the writing process.
- Storyboard Tools: Incorporate storyboard tools to visualize scenes, plan camera angles, and map out the flow of the narrative, helping you see how your script will translate to the screen.
- Script Analysis Books: Read books on script analysis and structure, such as "Save the Cat!" by Blake Snyder, to learn the principles of successful screenwriting and enhance your craft.

## 3. Techniques and Tips

- Visual Storytelling: Focus on visual storytelling, using action, setting, and imagery to convey emotion and plot, rather than relying solely on dialogue.
- Character Arcs: Develop strong character arcs that show growth, change, or conflict over the course of the script, adding depth and complexity to your characters.
- Scene Structure: Pay attention to scene structure, ensuring that each scene has a clear purpose, whether it's advancing the plot, revealing character, or building tension.
- Collaborate and Revise: Be prepared to collaborate with others in the production process and revise your script multiple times to meet the needs of the project and enhance the final product.

# *December 25: Travel Writing*

## 1. The Adventure of Travel Writing

Travel writing is a genre that combines storytelling with vivid descriptions of places, cultures, and experiences. It's about capturing the essence of a destination and sharing it with readers, transporting them to new and exciting locations through the power of words. Travel writing can take many forms, from guidebooks and travel blogs to personal essays and feature articles. The key to successful travel writing is the ability to observe and articulate the unique aspects of a place, offering readers insights, inspiration, and a sense of adventure.

## 2. Tools and Materials

- Travel Journal: Keep a travel journal to document your experiences, observations, and impressions while on the road, serving as a valuable resource when writing.
- Camera: Use a camera or smartphone to capture images of the places you visit, providing visual references for your writing and enhancing your articles or blogs.
- Research Materials: Gather research materials about your destination, including history, culture, and local customs, to add depth and context to your writing.

## 3. Techniques and Tips

- Engage the Senses: Use sensory details—sights, sounds, smells, tastes, and textures—to create a vivid and immersive experience for your readers.
- Tell a Story: Frame your travel writing as a story, with a clear beginning, middle, and end, focusing on a particular experience, challenge, or discovery that made the trip memorable.
- Cultural Sensitivity: Approach travel writing with cultural sensitivity, respecting local customs, traditions, and perspectives, and avoiding stereotypes or clichés.
- Inspire Action: Encourage your readers to explore new destinations and experiences by highlighting the unique and rewarding aspects of travel, offering practical tips and advice.

# *December 26: Urban Fantasy Writing*

## 1. The World of Urban Fantasy Writing

Urban fantasy is a genre that blends the magical or supernatural with a modern, urban setting. It's a genre that allows writers to explore the coexistence of the ordinary and the extraordinary, often involving hidden worlds, magical beings, and contemporary challenges. Writing urban fantasy requires a balance between building a believable urban environment and introducing fantastical elements that seamlessly integrate into the setting. It's a genre that appeals to readers who enjoy the intersection of reality and fantasy, with themes that often explore power, identity, and the unknown.

## 2. Tools and Materials

- World-Building Tools: Use world-building tools or software to create a detailed setting where the urban and the fantastical coexist, including maps, city layouts, and magical systems.
- Character Profiles: Develop character profiles that reflect both their ordinary lives and their connections to the supernatural, exploring how these aspects interact and conflict.
- Genre Research: Read other urban fantasy novels to understand genre conventions, tropes, and reader expectations, while finding ways to bring originality to your work.

## 3. Techniques and Tips

- Blend Genres: Successfully blend the urban and fantasy elements, ensuring that the magical aspects feel natural within the contemporary setting and contribute to the overall narrative.
- Establish Rules: Set clear rules for how magic or the supernatural works in your world, maintaining consistency to avoid plot holes or confusion.
- Character Dynamics: Explore the dynamics between ordinary humans and supernatural beings, focusing on how they interact, collaborate, or conflict within the urban environment.
- Pacing and Suspense: Maintain pacing and suspense by gradually revealing the fantastical elements, keeping readers engaged as they uncover the hidden layers of your urban fantasy world.

# December 27: Verse Writing

## 1. The Art of Verse Writing

Verse writing, or poetry, is the craft of expressing emotions, ideas, and narratives through rhythmic, often rhymed, lines of text. It's a highly creative and versatile form of writing that can convey deep meaning and evoke powerful emotions in a concise format. Writing verse requires an understanding of poetic forms, meter, and literary devices, as well as the ability to play with language and sound. Whether you're writing free verse, sonnets, or haikus, the goal is to distill complex thoughts into beautifully crafted lines that resonate with readers.

## 2. Tools and Materials

- Poetry Collections: Read collections of poetry from various genres and time periods to expose yourself to different styles, forms, and themes, inspiring your own verse writing.
- Rhyme and Meter Tools: Use rhyme dictionaries or online tools to find rhymes, assonance, and consonance that fit your verse, and to help maintain a consistent meter.
- Poetry Journals: Keep a poetry journal to jot down ideas, images, and fragments of verse as they come to you, providing a reservoir of inspiration for future poems.

## 3. Techniques and Tips

- Experiment with Form: Experiment with different poetic forms, from traditional sonnets and villanelles to free verse, to find the structure that best suits your content and style.
- Play with Sound: Focus on the sound of your verse, using techniques like alliteration, onomatopoeia, and internal rhyme to create a musical quality that enhances the poem's impact.
- Economy of Language: Embrace the economy of language, choosing each word carefully for its meaning, sound, and emotional weight, ensuring that every line carries significance.
- Revise Relentlessly: Don't be afraid to revise your verse multiple times, refining the rhythm, imagery, and wording until the poem achieves its desired effect.

# *December 28: Wordplay*

## 1. The Joy of Wordplay

Wordplay is the playful and creative use of language, where writers manipulate words, sounds, and meanings to entertain, amuse, or provoke thought. It's a linguistic game that can take many forms, including puns, anagrams, palindromes, and more. Wordplay adds humor, wit, and a sense of fun to writing, making it an enjoyable and engaging way to connect with readers. Whether used in poetry, prose, or dialogue, wordplay showcases a writer's creativity and command of language.

## 2. Tools and Materials

- Thesaurus and Dictionary: Keep a thesaurus and dictionary handy to explore synonyms, homophones, and other word relationships that can be used for wordplay.
- Word Games: Engage in word games like Scrabble, Boggle, or crossword puzzles to sharpen your linguistic skills and inspire new forms of wordplay.
- Language Books: Read books on linguistics, word origins, and etymology to deepen your understanding of language and discover new ways to play with words.

## 3. Techniques and Tips

- Puns and Double Entendres: Create puns and double entendres by playing with the multiple meanings of words or phrases, adding layers of humor and wit to your writing.
- Anagrams and Palindromes: Experiment with anagrams (rearranging letters to form new words) and palindromes (words or phrases that read the same backward and forward) to challenge yourself and delight readers.
- Sound Play: Use alliteration, assonance, and consonance to play with the sounds of words, creating rhythm and enhancing the musicality of your writing.
- Surprise and Delight: Use wordplay to surprise and delight your readers, catching them off guard with clever twists of language that make them think or smile.

# *December 29: Xerox Art*

## 1. The Innovation of Xerox Art

Xerox art, also known as copy art or electrostatic art, is a form of visual art that involves creating images using photocopiers or similar machines. It's a medium that emerged in the 1960s and 1970s as artists began experimenting with the possibilities of copying technology to produce unique, often abstract works. Xerox art challenges traditional notions of originality and reproduction, offering a platform for creativity that combines elements of printmaking, photography, and collage. The process allows artists to manipulate images, distort reality, and explore themes of duplication and variation.

## 2. Tools and Materials

- Photocopier or Scanner: Use a photocopier or scanner to create your Xerox art, experimenting with different settings, exposures, and movements to achieve various effects.
- Paper and Ink: Select different types of paper and ink to explore the textures, contrasts, and tonal ranges that can be achieved in your Xerox art.
- Found Objects: Incorporate found objects, such as leaves, fabric, or other textures, into the copying process to add depth and dimension to your work.

## 3. Techniques and Tips

- Experiment with Distortion: Manipulate the photocopier's settings, or move objects while copying, to create distortions, overlaps, and abstract patterns that add complexity to your art.
- Layering and Collage: Combine multiple copies, layers, and cutouts to create collage effects, building up the image in a way that challenges traditional two-dimensional art forms.
- Monochrome and Color: Play with both monochrome (black and white) and color copying to explore different aesthetic possibilities, contrasting stark, high-contrast images with more vibrant, colorful compositions.
- Conceptual Themes: Use Xerox art to explore conceptual themes, such as the nature of reproduction, the role of technology in art, or the relationship between original and copy.

# *December 30: Year-End Reflection Writing*

## 1. The Practice of Year-End Reflection Writing

Year-end reflection writing is a practice of looking back on the past year, evaluating your experiences, accomplishments, and challenges, and setting intentions for the year ahead. It's a valuable exercise in self-awareness and personal growth, offering an opportunity to celebrate successes, learn from failures, and plan for the future. Whether written in a journal, a letter to yourself, or a public blog post, year-end reflections help you gain perspective on your life journey and clarify your goals for the coming year.

## 2. Tools and Materials

- Reflection Prompts: Use reflection prompts to guide your writing, such as "What were my biggest achievements this year?" or "What challenges did I overcome?"
- Journal or Digital Platform: Choose a medium that suits your style, whether it's a physical journal, a digital diary, or an online blog, to record your reflections and plans.
- Goal-Setting Tools: Incorporate goal-setting tools, such as vision boards, planners, or SMART goal frameworks, to translate your reflections into actionable steps for the new year.

## 3. Techniques and Tips

- Honest Reflection: Be honest with yourself in your reflections, acknowledging both your strengths and areas for improvement, without judgment or self-criticism.
- Celebrate Successes: Take time to celebrate your successes and milestones, recognizing the progress you've made and the effort it took to get there.
- Learn from Challenges: Reflect on the challenges and setbacks you faced, considering what you learned from them and how they contributed to your personal growth.
- Set Intentions: Use your reflections to set clear intentions or resolutions for the new year, focusing on areas where you want to grow, change, or continue your journey.

# December 31: Zine Creation

## 1. The DIY World of Zine Creation

Zine creation is a DIY, grassroots form of self-publishing that allows creators to produce small, often handmade magazines or booklets on a wide range of topics. Zines are a form of alternative media, embracing creative freedom, personal expression, and subversive ideas. They have a rich history in countercultural movements, from punk rock to feminist activism, and continue to be a popular medium for sharing unique perspectives, art, and writing. Creating a zine involves everything from writing and editing to design, illustration, and distribution, making it a comprehensive creative project.

## 2. Tools and Materials

- Paper and Printing Supplies: Choose your paper, whether standard copy paper, cardstock, or recycled materials, and have access to a printer or photocopier for reproducing your zine.
- Cutting and Binding Tools: Use scissors, glue, staples, or thread to cut, assemble, and bind your zine, creating a physical object that reflects your aesthetic and message.
- Art Supplies: Incorporate art supplies like markers, pens, stickers, and collage materials to add visual elements and personalize your zine, making each copy unique.

## 3. Techniques and Tips

- Choose a Theme: Start by choosing a theme or central topic for your zine, whether it's personal stories, political commentary, poetry, or art, to give your zine focus and coherence.
- DIY Aesthetic: Embrace the DIY aesthetic of zine-making, where imperfections and handmade qualities add to the charm and authenticity of your work.
- Collaboration: Consider collaborating with other writers, artists, or activists to bring diverse voices and perspectives to your zine, enhancing its content and reach.
- Distribute Creatively: Distribute your zine creatively, whether through local bookstores, zine fairs, or online platforms, connecting with a community of readers and fellow creators who appreciate the zine culture.

# *Conclusion for December*

December has been a month of creative exploration and introspection, offering you the chance to dive deep into the art and craft of writing and literature. Whether you've penned a memoir, crafted poetry, or experimented with zine creation, each day has provided an opportunity to express yourself, reflect on your experiences, and share your voice with the world. As the year comes to a close, take pride in the creative journey you've embarked on and look forward to continuing your writing practice in the year ahead. Let the skills and insights gained this month fuel your passion for the written word, inspiring new projects, stories, and ideas for the future.

# Conclusion: Reflecting on Your Year of Hobbies

As we conclude HowExpert Guide to 365 Hobbies: The Ultimate A to Z Handbook to Discover, Learn, and Explore a New Hobby Every Day of the Year, it's time to reflect on the incredible journey you've embarked upon. Over the past year, you've delved into a wide array of hobbies—each offering its own unique set of challenges, rewards, and opportunities for personal growth. Whether you've discovered new passions, honed existing skills, or simply enjoyed the pleasure of trying something different, this journey has been a celebration of creativity, curiosity, and the joy of learning.

## 1. Reflecting on Your Year of Hobbies

Reflecting on your experiences throughout this year, consider the following:
- **Personal Growth:** How have these hobbies contributed to your personal development? Have you gained new skills, increased your confidence, or found new ways to express yourself?
- **New Discoveries:** Which hobbies surprised you the most? Perhaps there were activities you initially overlooked but later found to be incredibly fulfilling.
- **Challenges and Triumphs:** Every hobby comes with its own set of challenges. Reflect on the obstacles you overcame and the triumphs you achieved. These moments are a testament to your perseverance and willingness to step out of your comfort zone.
- **Favorite Moments:** What were your favorite moments from this year of exploration? Whether it was the thrill of mastering a difficult skill or the simple joy of creating something with your own hands, these memories are worth cherishing.

## 2. How to Continue Exploring New Hobbies

Your year-long journey through 365 hobbies has only scratched the surface of what's possible. To continue exploring new hobbies, consider these steps:
- **Set New Goals:** As you move forward, set new goals for your hobby exploration. Perhaps you want to dive deeper into a specific hobby or try a new one each month. Setting goals keeps your hobby journey purposeful and engaging.

- **Stay Curious:** Curiosity is the driving force behind hobby exploration. Keep asking questions, seeking out new activities, and challenging yourself to try things you've never considered before.
- **Join Communities:** Many hobbies have vibrant communities, both online and in person. Joining a community can provide support, inspiration, and opportunities to share your experiences with like-minded individuals.
- **Balance Depth and Breadth:** While it's exciting to try a wide variety of hobbies, don't hesitate to dive deeper into the ones that truly resonate with you. Balancing depth with breadth allows you to develop expertise in certain areas while still enjoying the thrill of new discoveries.

## 3. Encouragement for Lifelong Learning and Creativity

Hobbies are not just pastimes; they are powerful tools for lifelong learning and creativity. As you continue your journey, keep these principles in mind:
- **Embrace Lifelong Learning:** The pursuit of hobbies is a lifelong journey. Embrace the mindset of a learner—always open to new experiences, knowledge, and growth. Whether you're learning a new skill or deepening your understanding of a favorite hobby, the process of learning itself is invaluable.
- **Cultivate Creativity:** Creativity is at the heart of many hobbies. Whether you're crafting, cooking, writing, or playing music, these activities offer endless opportunities to express yourself and think outside the box. Let your hobbies be a playground for your imagination.
- **Stay Passionate:** Passion is the fuel that drives hobby exploration. Keep your passion alive by continuously seeking out new challenges, setting ambitious goals, and celebrating your progress along the way.
- **Inspire Others:** Your journey can serve as inspiration for others. Share your experiences, encourage friends and family to explore their own hobbies, and be a source of motivation for those around you.

## Final Thoughts

The HowExpert Guide to 365 Hobbies has taken you on an incredible journey of discovery, creativity, and personal growth. As you reflect on this past year, take pride in all that you've accomplished. Remember that the world of hobbies is vast and ever-expanding, with endless opportunities to learn, create, and explore. Keep your curiosity alive, embrace the spirit of lifelong learning, and continue to let your hobbies enrich your life in meaningful ways.

# Appendices

The Appendices in *HowExpert Guide to 365 Hobbies* are designed to provide you with additional resources, tools, and connections to enhance your hobby exploration. Whether you're looking for further reading, a way to track your progress, or a community to share your interests with, these sections offer valuable support as you continue your journey through the diverse world of hobbies. Dive into the resources, templates, and communities outlined here to deepen your engagement, refine your skills, and connect with others who share your passions.

## *Appendix A: Resources for Hobbies*

In this appendix, you'll discover a range of carefully selected resources that can help you expand your knowledge, skills, and enjoyment of your hobbies. Whether you're delving deeper into a particular interest or exploring new ones, these resources offer expert guidance, inspiration, and practical tips to support your journey.

**1. Books**

Books offer a wealth of information and insights, often providing more in-depth exploration of hobbies than you might find online. Here are some essential reads for hobby enthusiasts:
- **The Complete Book of Hobbies by Paul Mann:** This comprehensive guide covers a wide spectrum of hobbies, from traditional crafts to modern-day activities. It's an excellent resource for anyone looking to explore multiple interests or deepen their understanding of a particular hobby.
- **The Creative's Guide to DIY by Meg Allan Cole:** For those who enjoy hands-on projects, this book is a must-read. It provides step-by-step instructions for a variety of DIY projects, along with tips on sourcing materials and tools, making it perfect for both beginners and seasoned crafters.
- **Mastering the Art of Photography by Bruce Barnbaum:** Photography enthusiasts will appreciate the depth of knowledge in this book, which covers both the technical aspects of photography and the creative process. It's ideal for those looking to take their photography skills to the next level.
- **The Gardener's Year by Karel Čapek:** A classic read for gardening hobbyists, this book combines practical advice with philosophical reflections

on the joys of gardening. It's a delightful and informative guide for anyone with a passion for cultivating plants.

## 2. Websites

The internet is a vast resource for hobbyists, offering tutorials, community forums, and endless inspiration. Here are some top websites to explore:
- **Instructables.com:** This website is a haven for DIY enthusiasts, offering thousands of user-generated tutorials on a wide range of topics, from electronics and robotics to crafts and cooking. It's a great place to find project ideas, step-by-step guides, and tips from fellow hobbyists.
- **Craftsy.com:** Craftsy is an online learning platform that offers video courses taught by expert instructors in various creative fields, including knitting, quilting, painting, and more. The courses are designed for all skill levels, allowing you to learn at your own pace and revisit lessons as needed.
- **Ravelry.com:** For knitting and crochet enthusiasts, Ravelry is the ultimate online community. It provides a platform to share projects, find patterns, and connect with other crafters. The site also features an extensive database of yarns, tools, and techniques, making it an invaluable resource for textile hobbyists.
- **Reddit:** Specific subreddits such as r/DIY, r/Cooking, and r/Photography are excellent online communities where you can ask questions, share your work, and receive feedback from others who share your interests. The collaborative nature of Reddit makes it a dynamic and interactive resource for hobbyists.

## 3. Tools and Apps

The right tools and apps can significantly enhance your hobby experience by offering convenience, organization, and new ways to engage with your interests. Here are some recommendations:
- **Pinterest:** Pinterest is a visual discovery platform that allows you to search for and save ideas related to your hobbies. Whether you're looking for DIY project inspiration, recipes, or craft techniques, Pinterest provides a visually engaging way to explore new ideas and organize your favorite finds.
- **Trello:** Trello is a project management tool that can be adapted for personal use, particularly for organizing and tracking hobby projects. You can create boards for different hobbies, set deadlines for specific tasks, and keep all your ideas and resources in one place. It's particularly useful for hobbyists who juggle multiple projects at once.

- **Evernote:** Evernote is an app designed for note-taking and organization. It's perfect for hobbyists who like to keep detailed records of their projects, ideas, and progress. You can use Evernote to clip web pages, store photos, and create checklists, all synced across your devices.
- **Adobe Creative Suite:** For digital artists, designers, and photographers, Adobe Creative Suite offers a comprehensive set of tools, including Photoshop, Illustrator, and Lightroom. These professional-grade applications provide everything you need to create and refine digital artwork, edit photos, and design graphics.
- **Gardenate:** An app specifically for gardening enthusiasts, Gardenate helps you plan your planting schedule based on your location and climate. It offers reminders for when to plant, water, and harvest, making it a practical tool for both novice and experienced gardeners.

By leveraging these books, websites, and tools, you can continue to explore and deepen your engagement with your hobbies, ensuring that your journey remains dynamic, rewarding, and fulfilling.

# *Appendix B: Hobby Journals and Logs*

Keeping a hobby journal or log is an excellent way to track your progress, reflect on your experiences, and stay motivated as you explore new activities. Whether you're mastering a craft, learning a new skill, or simply documenting your journey, these templates provide a structured approach to recording your hobby adventures.

### 1. Daily Hobby Log

A daily hobby log is perfect for those who want to capture their day-to-day experiences and insights. This log helps you document each session, track your progress, and reflect on what you've learned.

**Template:**
- Date: [Record the date of your activity]
- Hobby: [Specify the hobby you engaged in]
- Goals for the Session: [List the objectives you aimed to achieve]
- Materials Used: [Detail the tools, materials, or resources you used]
- Challenges Encountered: [Note any difficulties or obstacles you faced]
- Achievements: [Highlight what you accomplished during the session]
- Reflections: [Reflect on what you learned or how you felt during the activity]
- Next Steps: [Outline your plans or goals for the next session]

## 2. Project Tracker

For more complex hobbies that involve long-term projects, such as woodworking, quilting, or model building, a project tracker helps you stay organized and focused. This template allows you to break down your project into manageable steps and keep track of your progress from start to finish.

**Template:**
- Project Title: [Name your project]
- Start Date: [Record when you began the project]
- End Date (if applicable): [Set a target completion date]
- Materials and Tools Needed: [List everything required for the project]
- Steps: [Break down the project into individual steps or phases]
  - Step 1: [Description of the first step]
  - Step 2: [Description of the second step]
  - ...
- Progress Notes: [Regularly update with notes on your progress, adjustments made, or insights gained]
- Completion Date: [Record when you finish the project]
- Final Reflections: [Reflect on the overall experience and what you learned]

## 3. Creative Ideas Journal

A creative ideas journal is ideal for hobbyists who want to capture inspiration and brainstorm new projects. This freeform journal allows you to jot down ideas, sketch designs, or compile resources that can fuel future projects.

**Template:**
- Date: [Record the date of your entry]
- Inspiration Source: [Note where the idea came from, e.g., a book, a walk in nature, a conversation]
- Idea Description: [Describe your idea or inspiration in detail]
- Sketches/Designs: [Include any sketches, diagrams, or design elements related to your idea]
- Potential Materials/Tools: [List any materials or tools you might need to bring the idea to life]
- Next Steps: [Outline the actions you plan to take to develop this idea further]
- Reflection: [Reflect on how this idea fits into your broader hobby journey or how it might evolve]

## 4. Monthly Reflection Log

This log is designed to help you reflect on your hobby experiences at the end of each month. It encourages you to think about your achievements, challenges, and growth, providing a broader perspective on your hobby journey.

**Template:**
- Month: [Record the month of your reflection]
- Hobbies Explored: [List the hobbies you engaged in during the month]
- Highlights: [Detail your biggest achievements or most enjoyable experiences]
- Challenges: [Note any significant challenges or obstacles you encountered]
- Skills Learned: [List any new skills or techniques you acquired]
- Favorite Moments: [Describe the moments that brought you the most joy or satisfaction]
- Goals for Next Month: [Set new goals or intentions for the coming month]
- Overall Reflection: [Summarize your thoughts on the month's hobby experiences, including what you've learned and how you've grown]

By using these templates, you can effectively track your progress, stay organized, and gain deeper insights into your hobby experiences. Keeping a journal or log not only helps you document your journey but also enhances your engagement and enjoyment of the activities you love.

# *Appendix C: Community and Clubs*

One of the most enriching aspects of pursuing hobbies is the opportunity to connect with others who share your interests. Whether you're looking for local groups to meet in person or online communities to engage with enthusiasts from around the world, finding the right community can greatly enhance your hobby experience. This appendix provides guidance on how to find and join these communities, helping you to build connections, share experiences, and learn from others.

### 1. Finding Local Hobby Communities

Engaging with local hobby communities can provide valuable face-to-face interactions, opportunities for hands-on learning, and the chance to build lasting friendships. Here's how to find local groups and clubs:

- **Community Centers and Libraries:** Start by checking your local community centers, libraries, and recreational facilities. Many of these places offer hobby-related classes, workshops, and clubs. You can find everything from knitting circles to photography clubs to DIY workshops. Ask for event calendars or bulletin boards where local groups post their meetings.
- **Specialty Stores:** Hobby shops, bookstores, craft stores, and other specialty retailers often host events or know of local clubs. For example, a local yarn shop might organize knitting nights, or a game store might host weekly board game sessions. Don't hesitate to ask the staff for recommendations or join in-store events to meet like-minded hobbyists.
- **Meetup.com:** Meetup is a fantastic platform for finding and joining local groups based on your interests. Whether you're into hiking, crafting, coding, or cooking, Meetup has thousands of groups worldwide. Simply search for your hobby, browse through local meetups, and join the ones that interest you. The platform also allows you to start your own group if you can't find one that matches your interests.
- **Local Universities and Colleges:** Many universities and colleges offer community education programs or have clubs open to the public. These can range from art classes to environmental clubs. Check with the continuing education department or student union for information on public events and groups.

## 2. Engaging with Online Communities

Online communities offer the convenience of connecting with fellow hobbyists from the comfort of your home. They're great for finding support, sharing your projects, and learning new techniques. Here's where to look:
- **Reddit:** Reddit hosts a wide variety of hobby-specific subreddits where users share tips, ask questions, and post their work. Some popular subreddits include r/DIY, r/knitting, r/cooking, and r/woodworking. Joining these communities allows you to tap into a vast pool of collective knowledge and connect with hobbyists from around the world.
- **Facebook Groups:** Facebook has numerous groups dedicated to virtually every hobby imaginable. Simply search for your hobby in the Facebook search bar, and you'll find groups ranging from beginner-friendly spaces to niche expert communities. Many of these groups are highly interactive, offering a platform to ask questions, share progress, and even participate in challenges or group projects.

- **Discord:** Originally popular among gamers, Discord has expanded to include a wide range of communities, including those centered around hobbies. Servers on Discord offer real-time chat, voice channels, and often a sense of close-knit community. You can find Discord servers dedicated to everything from book clubs to creative writing to gardening. Some servers may be private, but many are open to new members through invites shared on forums or social media.
- **Forums and Specialty Websites:** There are countless forums and websites dedicated to specific hobbies. For example, Ravelry is a go-to site for knitters and crocheters, providing a space to share patterns, projects, and ideas. Stack Exchange has numerous Q&A forums for hobbies like photography, gardening, and DIY electronics. These platforms offer more in-depth discussions and are great for finding detailed advice and tutorials.

## 3. Creating Your Own Community

If you can't find a community that suits your needs, consider starting your own. This can be as simple as gathering a few friends with similar interests or as ambitious as launching a public group online or in your local area.
- **Start Small:** Begin with a small, manageable group. You might invite friends, family, or coworkers who share your hobby to meet regularly. Once the group is established, consider expanding by inviting others or promoting your group locally or online.
- **Use Social Media and Online Platforms:** Create a Facebook group, Instagram page, or Meetup event to attract members. Use relevant hashtags and tags to reach a wider audience. Consistent posting and engagement will help build your group's presence.
- **Host Events:** Organize events, either online or in-person, to bring your community together. This could be a regular meetup, a workshop, or a themed event related to your hobby. Events are a great way to foster interaction and keep the group active.
- **Collaborate with Existing Groups:** If you're launching a new group, consider collaborating with existing groups or businesses. For example, partnering with a local bookstore for a book club or a craft store for a DIY night can help you reach a broader audience.

By finding and joining communities, or even creating your own, you can enrich your hobby experience with the support, knowledge, and camaraderie that comes from connecting with others. Whether you prefer the personal interaction of local groups or the global reach of online communities, there's a place for every hobbyist to belong.

# About the Author

HowExpert publishes how to guides on all topics from A to Z. Visit HowExpert.com to learn more.

# About the Publisher

Byungjoon "BJ" Min is an author, publisher, entrepreneur, and the founder of HowExpert. He started off as a once broke convenience store clerk to eventually becoming a fulltime internet marketer and finding his niche in publishing. He is the founder and publisher of HowExpert where the mission is to discover, empower, and maximize everyday people's talents to ultimately make a positive impact in the world for all topics from A to Z. Visit BJMin.com and HowExpert.com to learn more. John 14:6

# Recommended Resources

- HowExpert.com – How To Guides on All Topics from A to Z by Everyday Experts.
- HowExpert.com/free – Free HowExpert Email Newsletter.
- HowExpert.com/books – HowExpert Books
- HowExpert.com/courses – HowExpert Courses
- HowExpert.com/clothing – HowExpert Clothing
- HowExpert.com/membership – HowExpert Membership Site
- HowExpert.com/affiliates – HowExpert Affiliate Program
- HowExpert.com/jobs – HowExpert Jobs
- HowExpert.com/writers – Write About Your #1 Passion/Knowledge/Expertise & Become a HowExpert Author.
- HowExpert.com/resources – Additional HowExpert Recommended Resources
- YouTube.com/HowExpert – Subscribe to HowExpert YouTube.
- Instagram.com/HowExpert – Follow HowExpert on Instagram.
- Facebook.com/HowExpert – Follow HowExpert on Facebook.
- TikTok.com/@HowExpert – Follow HowExpert on TikTok.

Printed in Dunstable, United Kingdom